DATABASES AND INFORMATION SYSTEMS V

Frontiers in Artificial Intelligence and Applications

FAIA covers all aspects of theoretical and applied artificial intelligence research in the form of monographs, doctoral dissertations, textbooks, handbooks and proceedings volumes. The FAIA series contains several sub-series, including "Information Modelling and Knowledge Bases" and "Knowledge-Based Intelligent Engineering Systems". It also includes the biennial ECAI, the European Conference on Artificial Intelligence, proceedings volumes, and other ECCAI – the European Coordinating Committee on Artificial Intelligence – sponsored publications. An editorial panel of internationally well-known scholars is appointed to provide a high quality selection.

Volume 187

Recently published in this series

Vol. 186. G. Lambert-Torres, J.M. Abe, J.I. da Silva Filho and H.G. Martins (Eds.), Advances in Technological Applications of Logical and Intelligent Systems – Selected Papers from the Sixth Congress on Logic Applied to Technology
Vol. 185. A. Biere, M. Heule, H. van Maaren and T. Walsh (Eds.), Handbook of Satisfiability
Vol. 184. T. Alsinet, J. Puyol-Gruart and C. Torras (Eds.), Artificial Intelligence Research and Development – Proceedings of the 11th International Conference of the Catalan Association for Artificial Intelligence
Vol. 183. C. Eschenbach and M. Grüninger (Eds.), Formal Ontology in Information Systems – Proceedings of the Fifth International Conference (FOIS 2008)
Vol. 182. H. Fujita and I. Zualkernan (Eds.), New Trends in Software Methodologies, Tools and Techniques – Proceedings of the seventh SoMeT_08
Vol. 181. A. Zgrzywa, K. Choroś and A. Siemiński (Eds.), New Trends in Multimedia and Network Information Systems
Vol. 180. M. Virvou and T. Nakamura (Eds.), Knowledge-Based Software Engineering – Proceedings of the Eighth Joint Conference on Knowledge-Based Software Engineering
Vol. 179. A. Cesta and N. Fakotakis (Eds.), STAIRS 2008 – Proceedings of the Fourth Starting AI Researchers' Symposium
Vol. 178. M. Ghallab et al. (Eds.), ECAI 2008 – 18th European Conference on Artificial Intelligence
Vol. 177. C. Soares et al. (Eds.), Applications of Data Mining in E-Business and Finance
Vol. 176. P. Zaraté et al. (Eds.), Collaborative Decision Making: Perspectives and Challenges
Vol. 175. A. Briggle, K. Waelbers and P.A.E. Brey (Eds.), Current Issues in Computing and Philosophy

ISSN 0922-6389

Databases and Information Systems V

Selected Papers from the Eighth International Baltic Conference, DB&IS 2008

Edited by

Hele-Mai Haav

Institute of Cybernetics at Tallinn University of Technology, Estonia

and

Ahto Kalja

Department of Computer Engineering of Tallinn University of Technology, Estonia

IOS Press

Amsterdam • Berlin • Oxford • Tokyo • Washington, DC

ISBN 978-1-58603-939-4
Library of Congress Control Number: 2008939113

Publisher
IOS Press
Nieuwe Hemweg 6B
1013 BG Amsterdam
Netherlands
fax: +31 20 687 0019
e-mail: order@iospress.nl

Distributor in the UK and Ireland
Gazelle Books Services Ltd.
White Cross Mills
Hightown
Lancaster LA1 4XS
United Kingdom
fax: +44 1524 63232
e-mail: sales@gazellebooks.co.uk

Distributor in the USA and Canada
IOS Press, Inc.
4502 Rachael Manor Drive
Fairfax, VA 22032
USA
fax: +1 703 323 3668
e-mail: iosbooks@iospress.com

PRINTED IN THE NETHERLANDS

Databases and Information Systems V
H.-M. Haav and A. Kalja (Eds.)
IOS Press, 2009

Preface

The Eighth International Baltic Conference on Databases and Information Systems (Baltic DB&IS'2008) took place on June 2–5 2008 in Tallinn. This conference is continuing a series of successful bi-annual Baltic conferences on databases and information systems, which have been held in Trakai (1994), Tallinn (1996, 2002), Riga (1998, 2004), and Vilnius (2000, 2006).

The conference was organised by the Institute of Cybernetics at Tallinn University of Technology and the Department of Computer Engineering of Tallinn University of Technology in co-operation with the Estonian Informatics Centre (Ministry of Economic Affairs and Communications of Estonia).

The aim of the Baltic DB&IS series of conferences is to provide a wide international forum for academics and practitioners in the field of databases and modern information systems for exchanging their achievements in this area. The objective of the conference is to bring together researchers as well as practitioners and PhD students to present their work and exchange ideas, and trigger co-operation.

The International Programme Committee had representatives from 22 countries all over the world. They received 43 submissions from 12 countries. Each conference paper was reviewed by three referees from different countries. As a result, 29 regular papers were accepted for presentation at the conference. From the presented papers, 22 best papers were selected and are included in this volume.

The original research results presented in the conference papers mostly belong to novel fields of IS and database research such as database technology and semantic web, ontology-based IS, IS and AI technologies, IS integration. The invited talk by Dr. Jari Palomäki showed how different ontological commitments affect the way we are modeling the world when creating an information system.

As semantic technologies have been gaining more attention recently, then special session on semantic interoperability of IS was organised. The invited talks from each Baltic State gave a good insight how semantic interoperability initiatives are developing in each of the Baltic States and how they relate to the European semantic interoperability framework. Two of these papers are included in this book.

Finally, we would like to thank the authors for their contributions and the invited speakers for sharing with us their views. We are very grateful to members of the Programme Committee and the additional referees for carefully reviewing the submissions.

We wish to thank all the organising team and our sponsors, who have made this conference and proceedings possible. We express our special thanks to Mr. T. Robal for technical editing of the proceedings. Last, but not least, we thank all the participants, who really made the conference.

September 2008

Hele-Mai Haav
Ahto Kalja

Conference Committee

Organising Co-Chairs:

Andres Keevallik, Tallinn University of Technology, Estonia
Margus Kruus, Department of Computer Engineering of Tallinn University of Technology, Estonia

Co-ordinators

Saulius Maskeliunas, Institute of Mathematics and Informatics, Lithuania
Juris Borzovs, Riga Institute of Information Technology, Latvia
Janis Barzdins, University of Latvia, Latvia
Hannu Jaakkola, Tampere University of Technology, Pori, Finland

Advisory Committee

Janis Bubenko, Royal Institute of Technology, Sweden
Arne Solvberg, Norwegian University of Science and Technology, Norway

Programme Co-Chairs

Hele-Mai Haav, Institute of Cybernetics at Tallinn University of Technology, Estonia
Ahto Kalja, Department of Computer Engineering of Tallinn University of Technology, Estonia

Programme Committee

Witold Abramowicz, Poland
Irina Astrova, Estonia
Janis Barzdins, Latvia
Andras Benzcur, Hungary
Juris Borzovs, Latvia
Sjaak Brinkkemper, The Netherlands
Albertas Caplinskas, Lithuania
Dale Dzemydiene, Lithuania
Johann Eder, Austria
Hans-Dieter Ehrich, Germany
Jorgen Fischer Nilsson, Denmark
Janis Grundspenkis, Latvia
Jozef M. Zurada, USA
Hui Ma, New Zealand
Rainer Manthey, Germany
Saulius Maskeliunas, Lithuania
Mihhail Matskin, Sweden
Boris Novikov, Russia
Monika Oit, Estonia
Algirdas Pakstas, UK
Jaan Penjam, Estonia
Jaroslav Pokorny, Czech Republic
Gunter Saake, Germany
Kuldar Taveter, Australia

Remigijus Gustas, Sweden
Hyoil Han, USA
Mirjana Ivanovic, Serbia
Leonid Kalinichenko, Russia
Peep Küngas, Estonia
Rein Kuusik, Estonia
Marion Lepmets, Estonia
Audrone Lupeikene, Lithuania
Kalle Lyytinen, USA
Jaak Tepandi, Estonia
Bernhard Thalheim, Germany
Enn Tyugu, Estonia
Olegas Vasilecas, Lithuania
Tatjana Welzer, Slovenia
Robert Wrembel, Poland
Stanislaw Wrycza, Poland
Naoki Yonezaki, Japan

Additional Referees

Nasreddine Aoumeur, Germany
Guntis Barzdins, Latvia
Janis Eiduks, Latvia
Sven Hartmann, New Zealand
Akira Imada, Belarus
Marijke Janssen, Netherlands
Vahur Kotkas, Estonia
Algirdas Laukaitis, Lithuania
Mario Pukall, Germany
Eike Schallehn, Germany
Peggy Schmidt, Germany
Wai Shiang Cheah, Australia
Rebekah Velicescu, Australia
Marek Wiśniewski, Poland

Doctoral Consortium Co-Chairs:

Jaan Penjam, Institute of Cybernetics at Tallinn University of Technology, Estonia
Vahur Kotkas, Institute of Cybernetics at Tallinn University of Technology, Estonia

Organising Committee

Kristiina Kindel, Institute of Cybernetics at Tallinn University of Technology, Estonia
Sulev Kuiv, Institute of Cybernetics at Tallinn University of Technology, Estonia
Rein Lõugas, Institute of Cybernetics at Tallinn University of Technology, Estonia
Monika Perkmann, Institute of Cybernetics at Tallinn University of Technology, Estonia
Tarmo Robal, Department of Computer Engineering of Tallinn University of Technology, Estonia
Marje Tamm, Institute of Cybernetics at Tallinn University of Technology, Estonia
Kristi Uustalu, Institute of Cybernetics at Tallinn University of Technology, Estonia

Contents

Invited Talk

Databases and Information Systems V
H.-M. Haav and A. Kalja (Eds.)
IOS Press, 2009

doi:10.3233/978-1-58603-939-4-3

Ontology Revisited: Concepts, Languages, and the World(s)

Jari PALOMÄKI[1]
Tampere University of Technology/Pori
Department of Information Technology

Abstract. In this paper the role of ontology is considered in the context of information systems and conceptual modelling. Firstly we describe information systems and conceptual modelling *without* using the word "ontology". Then two senses of ontology are presented: philosophical and knowledge representation views. In this connection both Gruber's and Guarino's definitions of "ontology" are scrutinized. It is proposed that the kind of terminological shifts concerning the word "ontology", and practiced e.g. by Gruber and Guarino, have caused more confusion than clarification in the field of information systems and conceptual modelling. Instead of given a new or a better definition of our own, our view is that the word "ontology" should be used in its traditional philosophical sense only, whereas our aim in the field of information systems and conceptual modelling is to reach conceptual clarity.

Keywords. ontology, conceptual modelling, information systems, knowledge representation

Introduction

In the field of information system the word "ontology" has nowadays at least three different meanings. Firstly it may mean a conceptual model, or a conceptualized knowledge representation. Secondly it may mean a vocabulary or a dictionary containing the basic terms used in conceptualization, i.e., a language. Finally, and in its original philosophical meaning, ontology is a part of metaphysics concerning the universe of discourse and the ultimate building blocks of the world.

A definition of ontology, which has gained some agreement among the information system community, is the following one: "An ontology is a formal explicit specification of a shared conceptualization for a domain of interest", [1]. In this definition the word "ontology" means a formal language, although the two other possible meanings for ontology are presented as well. This definition has been criticized by Guarino and Giaretta in [2], and elaborated by Guarino in [3], in which he gives the definition of his own: "An ontology is a logical theory accounting for the *intended meaning* of a formal vocabulary, i.e. its *ontological commitment* to a particular *conceptualization* of the world". We shall scrutinize both of these definitions.

[1] Corresponding Author: Jari Palomäki, Tampere University of Technology/Pori, Department of Information Technology, Pohjoisranta, P.O.Box 300, FI-28101 Pori, Finland ; E-mail : jari.palomaki@tut.fi

This paper is composed as follows. Firstly we define the basic modelling situation consisting of objects to be modelled, a modeller, i.e. a person who is modelling, a model, and the relationships between these. We continue this process by describing an information system as an instance of a basic modelling situation. Having described information systems we consider a conceptual modelling process, the goal of which is to develop a conceptual schema of the domain of an application. In this context also the nature of concepts and concept theory are considered. The above account of information systems and conceptual modelling are described *without* using the word "ontology". Then two senses of ontology are presented: philosophical and knowledge representation views. In this connection both Gruber's and Guarino's definitions of "ontology" are scrutinized. Then some reasons are given why we should avoid using the word "ontology" in the area of information systems and conceptual modelling.

1. Basic Modelling Situation

Modelling starts when for some special purposes something is to be modelled. This creates a basic modelling situation, which consists of 1) objects to be modelled, 2) a modeller, who is doing the modelling, 3) a model, which is to be a result of the modelling, and 4) different relationships between these. The basic modelling situation is then a three-place relation: M(object(x), modeller(y), model(z)), which is to be read: "an object x is modelled by y as z." From this definition it follows that modelling is always an intentional activity.

The objects to be modelled form the *object domain*, i.e. the universe of discourse. The objects in the object domain do not have necessarily to be concrete things in space and time of which we are to have immediate sense perception, but can as well be abstract objects consisting e.g. expert's knowledge. Moreover, the objects to be modelled do not have to exist before the model of it is created. This situation happens, for example, when designing or planning something.

A *modeller* is the subject of a modelling situation. In most cases a modeller consists of the group of persons having different expertises. The most important task for a modeller is to consider those features of the objects to be modelled which are relevant for the purpose of modelling.

A *model* is a result of an abstraction that is used to represent the objects in the object domain. Abstraction is an epistemological process, where some relevant aspect of the objects in the object domain is separated. There are also other epistemological processes connected with creating a model, for example, *classification*, i.e. grouping the objects into classes on the basis of some of common properties; *generalization*, i.e. arriving at some general notion from the instances; *axiomatization*, i.e. by giving the basic propositions (truths) from which we can deduce other propositions (truths) the result of which is called an axiom system; etc.

Finally, *modelling relations* consist of logical and epistemological relationships between the modeller, model, and an object domain. Depending on the order of modelling relations, we can talk about the descriptive and the "normative" use of the model. The model is *descriptive*, when we start from the object domain, and via the modeller we will end to the model, whereas the model is "*normative*", when we start from the modeller, and via the model we will end to the object domain.

2. Information System

Having defined the basic modelling situation, we shall proceed to an information system. Firstly, any *system* may be characterized as a set of interrelated components that interact with each others to form a whole, and work together toward a common goal. The four major components of a system are (1) inputs, (2) processes, (3) outputs, and (4) feedback control. An i*nput* is anything that enters the system. A system may have one or many inputs. An o*utput* is anything leaving the system. Outputs are the goal of the system, the purpose for which the system exists. The outputs of one system can become the inputs of another system. A *process* performs the work: it transforms an input into an output. The system exchanges inputs and outputs with its environment. Changes in the environment affect the system. To adopt itself to changing conditions the system have a *feedback*. A feedback reintroduces a portion of the output of a system as an input into the same system, and thus, a feedback is actually a special kind of input. It is used as a control mechanism within the system to indicate the difference between the goals and actual performance of a system, see e.g. [4], [5].

In *information system* inputs are of two kinds: firstly, they are result of gathering and capturing data to be stored in databases and, secondly, they consist of queries concerning the data stored in databases. Information processing involves converting or transforming queries into valuable information, and it can be done manually or with the assistance of a computer. Processing performed by a computer is actually performed by the computer's Central Processing Unit (CPU) which, in doing that, interplays with databases and a conceptual schema, sometimes also called the logical schema in relational data models. Resulting information, as an answer to a query, may be used as a feedback to make changes to input or processing activities.

An information system is not isolated from its environment, and so it has also a larger sense. An *information system* is a set of people, data, and processes that work together to achieve the common goal of information management. A *computer-based information system* includes also hardware, which consists of everything in the physical layer, and software, which consists of systems programs that control the hardware and application programs used to produce the required information.

3. Conceptual Modelling and Conceptual Schema

A *conceptual modelling* consists of analysing and synthesising concepts which are "drawn" from a given object domain, and constructing a conceptual model of it by means of those concepts, [6], [7], [8]. The result of this process is presented in a form of *conceptual schema*, which provides a conceptual description of the data under inspection. Accordingly, databases are used to store data representing a certain section of the reality, and the classification and organization of that data is described by means of a conceptual schema. A conceptual schema of the object domain, in turn, is used as an input to a support system, e.g. CASE tool, which generates a database of it. The database implementation includes update and query functionalities as well.

In the construction of the conceptual schema at least the following four principles would serve as guidelines, [9], [10], [11]:

1. *The conceptualization principle*, according to which only conceptual aspects should be taken into account when constructing the conceptual schema.

2. *100% -principle*, according to which all the relevant aspects of the domain should be described in the conceptual schema.
3. *The formalization* principle, according to which conceptual schemata should be formalisable in order to be implementable.
4. *The semiotic* principle according to which conceptual schemata should be easily interpretable and understandable.

From the principles 1. and 2. it follows that all the relevant aspects of the domain appearing in the conceptual schema are to be conceptual. The principle 3. is essentially a restrictive principle, and it is partly opposite to the principle 4. The motivation for the principle 4. is that the language for representing conceptual schemata should be common for everyone taking part in the modelling process, and be appropriate for fulfilling the task of modelling. A reason why the principle 4. may sometimes be opposite to the principle 3. is that not everyone is familiar with the formalisms used in this area.

In order to express the result of conceptual modelling as a conceptual schema, we need a modelling language. The three most popular notations for information modelling are Object-Role Modelling (ORM), Entity-Relationship (ER) diagrams, and Unified Modelling Language (UML), see e.g. [12]. However, many accounts of conceptual modelling emphasize an intensional aspect concept as opposed to real world things in the domain of objects, which belong to the extensions of those concepts. This means that intensionality should be visible in the modelling language as well, [7], [8].

Let us note that there are two different inquires each having a right to the name "conceptual modelling". The first one is when we are actually doing conceptual modelling, and the second one is when we are describing the process of conceptual modelling. The first one is more basic, since in the second one conceptual modelling is conceptually modelled, and hence, it has different status than the first one. In any given discussion, it is easy to fall into confusion through failure to determine to which of the two inquiries the discussion is intended to belong. In this paper we are interested in the second one from which the first one follows.

4. Concepts and Concept Theory

A conceptual model is composed of particular concepts and particular relations between them. A *concept theory*, in turn, is studying concepts and the relations and operations between them in general. There are numerous theories of concepts, for example, concepts can be thought of as any of the following: *supersensible entities* as universals, meanings, abstract objects, definitions, or predicates and relations; *mental entities* or *states* as composite images, ideas, thoughts, conceptions, or innate ideas; *neutral entities* joining e.g. words, thoughts, and things; human or animal *skills* or *abilities,* etc., see e.g. [13]. In order to condense this great number of theories without sacrificing too many of their indispensable properties, the following more abstract classifications can be made:

1. *The entity theories of concepts*, according to which concepts are entities such as ideas, images, thought, abstract objects, etc.
2. *The dispositional theories of concepts*, according to which concepts are understood to be the abilities or skills to do something, especially the ability to use language correctly.

We may go even further. One of the major doctrines of both the entity and the dispositional theories of concepts is that a concept, in order to be a concept, must be characterized by a definite set of necessary and sufficient criteria. This is called a *closed* concept, and the requirement that all concepts are to be closed is called the *closure principle of concepts*, [14]. Thus we have abstracted the particular conceptions of concepts to the point where there are just concepts, and whatever form these take, they must satisfy the closure principle of concepts. The advantage of this approach is that developing a concept theory it does not confine us to any particular theory of concepts with its specific accompanying restrictions and special characteristics.

Relations between concepts enable us to establish conceptual structures. The most essential relation between concepts is the intentional containment relation, which is based on the intensions of concepts, see [7], [8], [14], [15]. Another important relation between concepts is the conceptual containment relation between concepts, which is based on the conceptual constituents of concepts, and is thus a different relation than the intentional containment, [16], [17].

The idea of the concept of a concept and the relations between concepts serves as the basis for all conceptual modelling, and all conceptual structures are ultimately reducible to concept theory, which is to be understood in the similar way as "all mathematics is ultimately reducible to set theory", [18].

5. Ontology: Philosophical and Knowledge Representational Views

The above account of forming an information systems and doing conceptual modelling is written *without* using the word "ontology". Nowadays there are two sense of the definition of that word: the traditional one used in *philosophy* and the more modern one used in the area of *information systems*, [19]. We will consider firstly the philosophical view and then turn to the area of information systems, where the view is called a knowledge representational view.

5.1. Ontology: A Philosophical View

In philosophy ontology is a part of metaphysics, which aims to answer at least the following three questions:

1. What is there?
2. What is it, that there is?
3. How is that, that there is?

The first is (1) is perhaps the most difficult one, as it asks what elements the world is made up of, or rather, what are the building blocks from which the world is composed. A traditional answer to this question is that the world consists of things and properties (and relations). An alternative answer can be found in Wittgenstein's *Tractatus* 1.1: "The world is the totality of facts, not of things" [20], that is to say, the world consists of facts. Still another answer can be a process ontology proposed by Alfred North Whitehead in [21] and presented e.g. in [22].

The second question (2) concerns the basic stuff from which the world is made. The world could be made out of one kind of stuff only, for example, water, as Thales suggested, or the world may be made out of two or more different kinds of stuff, for example, mind and matter.

The third question (3) concerns the mode of existence. Answers to this question could be the following ones, according to which something exists in the sense that:

a) it has some kind of concrete space-time existence,
b) it has some kind of abstract (mental) existence,
c) it has some kind of transcendental existence, in the sense that it extends beyond the space-time existence.

In conceptual modelling the most crucial ontological question is: "What modes of existence may concepts have?" This question is related to the third question (3) above. The traditional answers to it are that

(i) concepts are merely predicate expressions of some *language*, i.e. they exist concretely, (nominalism);
(ii) concepts exist in the sense that we have the socio-biological *cognitive capacity* to identify, classify, and characterize or perceive relationships between things in various ways, i.e. they exist abstractly, (conceptualism);
(iii) concepts exist independently of both language and human cognition, i.e. *transcendentally*, (realism).

If the concepts exist only concretely as linguistic terms, then there are only extensional relationships between them. If the concepts exist abstractly as a cognitive capacity, then conceptualization is a private activity done by human mind. If the concepts exist transcendentally independently of both language and human cognition, then we have a problem of knowledge acquisition of them. Thus, the ontological question of the mode of existence of concepts is such a deep philosophical issue, and part of a reason to adopt the *closure principle of concepts* is to be more neutral on these questions.

However, if we take an ontological commitment to a certain view of the mode of the existence of concepts, consequently we are making other ontological commitments as well. For example, realism on concepts is usually connected with realism of world as well. In conceptualism we are more or less creating our world(s) by conceptualization, and in nominalism there are neither intensionality nor abstract (not to say transcendental) entities like numbers.

5.2. Ontology: A Knowledge Representative View

The second sense of the word "ontology" is used in research on information systems, artificial intelligence and knowledge representation. One of the best known definitions is Tom Gruber's:

> "An ontology is a formal explicit specification of a shared conceptualization for a domain of interest" [1].

In this definition the word "ontology" means a formal language, or more exactly, by using the language of the Section 4, a conceptual schema, cf. [6]. Although Gruber's definition has been criticized by Guarino and Giaretta in [2], it has gained some agreement among the information system community, see Preface in [23] and [24].

According to Gruber [1], the reason to use the word "ontology" to refer to a language is that for knowledge-based systems only those items "exist" which can be represented in a language which comes with a formal semantics. Using this formal approach to ontology provides the machine interpretable meaning of concepts and relations between them. When knowledge of a domain is represented in a language, the set of objects so represented form the universe of discourse.

This language dominated view to the world has a strong resemblance with Rudolf Carnap's empirical approach to semantics and (philosophical) ontology, cf. [25]. He distinguishes between *internal* and *external* linguistic frameworks. Meaningful questions are empirical questions about the world, which can be asked only within the linguistic framework, i.e. they are internal questions, whereas the external questions concerning the existence or reality of the systems of entities as a whole are pseudo-questions. That is, the above mentioned ontological questions presented in philosophy are more or less meaningless.

From this, in turn, it follows that if our knowledge of the universe of discourse can only be thought in connection with a language and a conceptual schema, and not as independent of them, then the truth of the world can only be defined internally – and hence, there does not need to be one, but many worlds. Moreover, as far as a "conceptualization" is a private mental process done by a human being, and which aim is to form a concept of something, there cannot be a "shared conceptualization" either. Hence, it seems that from the philosophical point of view Gruber's definition of "ontology" in [1] as well as in [25] is simply incoherent.

Nicola Guarino, on the other hand, in [3] recognizes the two readings of "ontology": AI reading and the philosophical reading. He says firstly that he will adopt the AI reading, i.e. the knowledge representation view, and will use the word "conceptualization" to refer to the philosophical one. However, instead of the philosophical view of ontology represented in the Section 5 above, Guarino refers by the philosophical readings to "an ontology as a particular system of categories accounting for a certain vision of the world".

Now, Guarino's definition of "ontology" in the context of information systems is the following:

> "An ontology is a logical theory accounting for the *intended meaning* of a formal vocabulary, i.e. its *ontological commitment* to a particular *conceptualization* of the world" [3].

In the first reading of this definition we may think that by using the language of the Section 4, the "intended meaning" refers to a conceptual model, in which a conceptual model is a product of conceptualization of the world, and the conceptual model is a mental "vision of the world" with a certain formal structure, (a formal ontology). However, when Guarino starts to formalize his account of "ontology" by using the possible world semantics,[2] we will learn that the "ontology" for him is a set of axioms (a language) **O** such that its models approximate as well as possible the intended models of a language **L** according to an ontological commitment to a particular conceptualization ***C*** of the world. He also emphasizes that "it is important to stress that an ontology is *language-dependent*, while a conceptualization is *language-independent*" [3]. Here, however, the word "conceptualization" means "a set of conceptual relations defined on a domain space", whereas by "the ontological

[2] Although Guarino emphasizes intensional aspect of modelling it is to be noted that possible world semantics reduces to an extensional view by using possibly partial, but indeed extensional set-theoretic functions from the possible worlds to extensions of those worlds.

commitments" Guarino means the relation between the language and the conceptualization.

Thus, in [3] Guorino is using the word "conceptualization" to mean two different things: on one hand the philosophical readings of "ontology", and, on the other hand, a formal structure ***C*** = <D,W,*R*>, where D is a domain, W is a set of possible worlds, and *R* is a set of conceptual relations on the domain space <D,W>. A conceptual relation, in turn, is a total (extensional) function from the set of possible worlds W to a power set of domain D. Still, the standard meaning of the word "conceptualization" is "to form a concept" of something.

To illustrate the above definition of the word "ontology", (i.e. making it more confusing), Guarino gives a picture, in which this time the word "ontology" refers not to a language **O**, but to an intended model of the language **L**, see Figure 1.

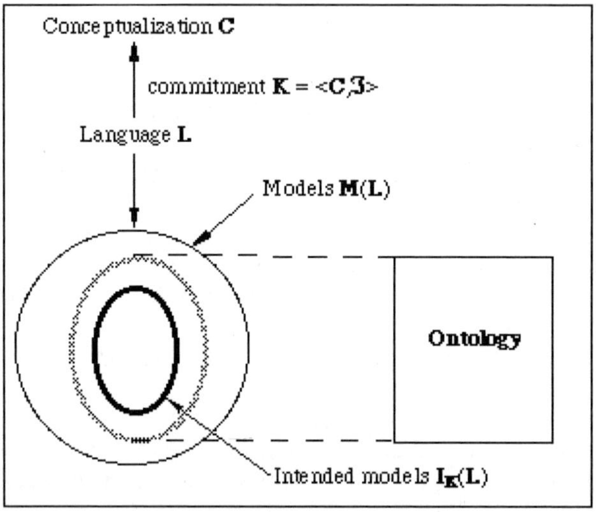

Figure 1. The intended models of a logical language reflect its commitment to a conceptualization, [3]

No doubt the Figure 1 is misleading. It does not describe the situation as Guarino actually writes about it in [3]. So, instead we will propose the following illustration, see Figure 2.

In Figure 2 "ontology" O_{L}_ is a language associated with the language L, and its model M(O_L) includes the intended model IM(L), and which is also included into the all of possible models of L, i.e. M(L). Provided that the Figure 2 is more correct illustration of Guarino's idea, we can make the following observations concerning ontology O_L. Firstly, O_L is a language, which is only indirectly connected with a "conceptualization" ***C*** as well as an "ontological commitment" *K*, which connects the language L with the "conceptualization" ***C***. Secondly, the interpretation function of O_L is missing and no formal structure, i.e. a "conceptualization", of it is given. Thirdly, in order the model M(O_L) of O_L to approximate and include the intended model IM(L) of L, O_L should be a kind of a meta-language of L restricting the interpretation of the language L to the intended model of it, i.e. IM(L). Fourthly, both languages O_L and L

are making (in a philosophical sense) ontological commitments to possible worlds, and to the basic domain D consisting of things, properties, and relations.

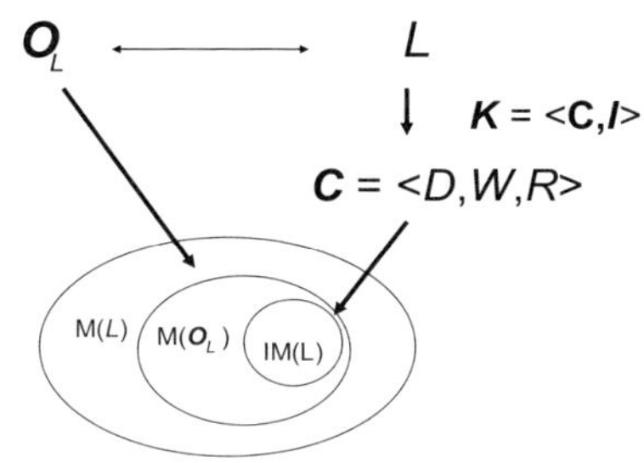

Figure 2. Ontology O_L as a language connected with the language L and its model $M(O_L)$ approaching and including the intended model $IM(L)$ of the language L

5.3. So, Why Should We Worry?

There is a wide variety of possible interpretations of the word "ontology", see [2]:

1. A philosophical discipline
2. A conceptual system
3. A representation of a conceptual system
4. A formal semantic
5. A specification of a "conceptualization"
6. A specification of a logical theory
7. The vocabulary used by a logical theory

The interpretation 1. is a traditional philosophical use of the word "ontology", whereas all the other interpretations 2.-7. belong to the knowledge representation view and appear in the literature of information systems. Now, for example, an "ontology" for Guarino as well as for Gruber was seen to be a language-dependent, which takes in account of its explication both concepts and the world(s).[3] Since it is possible to describe the process of information systems and conceptual modelling *without* using the word "ontology" as was shown in the Sections 1.-5. above, it should be possible to replace the word "ontology" used in knowledge representation view by using more common words such as a "concept", a "language", and a "world", or possible "worlds". Usually, when we want to give an explication of some particular concept, we replace of a vague concept (the *explicandum*) by a more precise one (the *explicatum*), i.e. we are searching out new definitions for old concept. The new definitions should be superior to the old in clarity, exactness, and it should fit into systematic structure of concepts. Now, in this case, a 'sect' of information systems community is doing *exactly opposite*.

Moreover, if we are not going to follow the logical positivist view of ontology by simply rejecting all the ontological problems appearing in philosophy, cf. [25], a deviation from the standard philosophical use of the word "ontology" used by other scientists and in other disciplines creates communication problems and will estrange and isolate that 'sect' of information systems community. Also, a language-dependent

---

[3] The same hold also for The OWL Web Ontology Language, [26], as well as The Protégé Ontology Editor, [27].

"ontology" is constrained with the ontological commitment inherent in the structure of the used language, i.e. as Wittgenstein says it in *Tractatus* 5.6: "The limits of my language mean the limits of my world" [20].

6. Conclusion

In this paper the role and the proper place of ontology was considered in the context of information systems and conceptual modelling. Firstly, an information systems and a conceptual modelling were described *without* using the word "ontology". Then two senses of ontology are presented: philosophical and knowledge representation views. In this connection both Gruber's and Guarino's definitions of "ontology" were scrutinized. An "ontology" for Guarino as well as for Gruber was seen to be a language-dependent, which takes in account of its explication both concepts and the world(s).

Unfortunately, the kind of terminological shifts concerning the word "ontology", and practiced e.g. by Gruber and Guarino, have caused more confusion than clarification in the field of information systems and conceptual modelling. Accordingly, it should be better to use the word "ontology" in its traditional philosophical sense only, whereas our aim in the field of information systems and conceptual modelling is to reach a conceptual clarity.

References:

[1] Gruber, T. R. (1993) A Translation Approach to Portable Ontology Specifications, In Knowledge Acquisition 5(2), 199-220

[2] Guarino, N. and Giaretta, P. (1995) Ontologies and Knowledge Bases: Towards a Terminological Clarification. Towards Very Large Knowledge Bases: Knowledge Building and Knowledge Sharing. Ed. By N. Mars. Amsterdam, Washington, Tokyo: IOS Press, pp. 25-32.

[3] Guarino, N. (1998) Formal Ontology in Information Systems. In Formal Ontology in Information Systems. In Guarino, N. (eds) Proceedings of FOIS'98, 6-8 June, Trento, Italy, Amsterdam, Washington, Tokyo: IOS Press, pp. 3-15.

[4] Whitten, J., Bentley, L., & Dittman, K. (2001) Systems Analysis and Design Methods, Boston, etc.: McGraw-Hill/ Irwin.

[5] Zwass, V. (1998) Foundations of Information Systems. Boston, etc.: McGraw-Hill/Irwin.

[6] Kangassalo, H. (1990) Foundations of Conceptual Modelling: A Theory Construction View. In Information Modelling and Knowledge Bases. Eds. H. Kangassalo, S. Ohsuga, & H. Jaakkola. Amsterdam, Washington, Tokyo: ISO Press, pp. 19-35.

[7] Kangassalo, H. (1992/93) COMIC: A system and methodology for conceptual modelling and information construction, In Data and Knowledge Engineering 9 (1992/93), 287-319

[8] Kangassalo, H. (2007) Approaches to the Active Conceptual Modelling of Learning. In Active Conceptual Modeling of Learning: Next Generation Learning-Base System Development, LNCS 4512, Eds. P.P. Chen and L.Y. Wong., Berlin, Heidelberg: Springer-Verlag, pp. 168–193.

[9] van Griethuysen, J. J., ed. (1982) Concepts and Terminology of the Conceptual Schema and the Information Base. A Report ISO/TC97/SC5-N695.

[10] Kangassalo, H. (1983) Structuring Principles of Conceptual Schemas and Conceptual Models. In Bubenko, J. A. (eds) Information Modeling, Lind: Studentlitteratur, pp. 223-307.

[11] Marjomaa, E. (1997) Aspects of Relevance in Information Modelling: Methodological Principles and Conceptual Problems. Filosofisia tutkimuksia Tampereen yliopistosta, Vol. 63, Tampere: Tampereen yliopisto

[12] Halpin, T. (2001) Information Modelling and Relational Databases – From Conceptual Analysis to Logical Design. San Fransisco: Morgan Kaufmann Publishers

[13] Weitz, M. (1988) Theories of Concepts: A History of the Major Philosophical Tradition. London and New York: Routledge

[14] Palomäki, J. (1994) From Concepts to Concept Theory. Acta Universitatis Tamperensis. A(416), Tampere: University of Tampere
[15] Kauppi, R. (1967) Einführung in die Theorie der Begriffssysteme. Acta Universitatis Tamperensis. A(15), Tampere: Tampereen yliopisto
[16] Palomäki, J. (1997) Three Kinds of Containment Relations of Concepts. In Kangassalo, H., Nilsson, J.F., Jaakkola, H. & Ohsuga, S. (eds) Information Modelling and Knowledge Bases VIII, Amsterdam, Berlin, Oxford, Tokyo, Washington, DC.: IOS Press, pp. 261-277.
[17] Palomäki, J. (2003) Intensional vs. Conceptual Content of Concepts. In Jaakkola, H., Kangassalo, H., Kawaguchi, E. & Thalheim, B. (eds) Information Modelling and Knowledge Bases XIV. Amsterdam, Berlin, Oxford, Tokyo, Washington, DC.: IOS Press, 2003, pp. 128-134.
[18] Palomäki, J. & Radiĉević, M. (2006) Concept Theory in the Context of Information System. In Y. Kioki, J. Henno, H. Jaakkola, & H. Kangassalo (eds) Information Modelling and Knowledge Bases XVII. Amsterdam, Berlin, Oxford, Tokyo, Washington, DC.: IOS Press, pp. 321-328.
[19] Corazzon, R. (2008) Ontology. A Resource Guide for Philosophers, (available at http://www.formalontology.it/index.htm)
[20] Wittgenstein, L. (1921) Tractatus Logico-Philosophicus. Trans. by D. F. Pears and B.F. McGuinness. Routledge and Kegan Paul: London, 1961.
[21] Whitehead, A. N. (1929) Process and Reality: An Essay in Cosmology, New York: The Macmillan Co.
[22] Palomäki, J. & Keto, H. (2006) A Process-Ontological Model for Software Engineering. In Latour, T. & Petit, M (eds) CAiSE'06, The 18th International Conference on Advanced Information Systems Engineering – Trusted Information Systems. Proceedings of the Workshops and Doctoral Consortium. Namur: Namur University Press, 2006, pp. 720-726, (available at www.kybele.etsii.urjc.es/phise06/papers/sesionI/PalomakiKeto.pdf)
[23] Staab, S., & Studer. R., Eds. (2004) Handbook on Ontologies. Berlin, etc.: Springer.
[24] Gruber, T. R. (2007) Ontology. In Tamer, Ö. M. & Ling, L. (eds) Encyclopedia of Database Systems Springer-Verlag, 2009 (To appear), (available at http://tomgruber.org/writing/ontology-definition-2007.htm)
[25] Carnap, R. (1983) Empiricism, Semantics, and Ontology. In Philosophy of Mathematics – Selected Readings. Eds. P. Benacerraf & H. Putnam. 2nd edition. Cambridge: Cambridge University Press, pp. 241-257.
[26] The OWL Web Ontology Language Reference (2004) (available at http://www.w3.org/TR/owl-ref/)
[27] The Protégé Ontology Editor and Knowledge Acquisiton Systems, (available at http://protege.stanford.edu/)

Database Technology and Semantic Web

Databases and Information Systems V
H.-M. Haav and A. Kalja (Eds.)
IOS Press, 2009

doi:10.3233/978-1-58603-939-4-17

The Label Based Concurrency Control in XML Databases

Andrzej SIKORSKI[1]
Technical University Poznań

Abstract. We propose a label based technique for an effective management of structural locks in XML databases. In particular we consider two types of such locks, acquired by transactions on sets of nodes. These are path locks and range locks – the latter understood as some subset of document's nodes defined by a pair of labels, with the sub-tree lock being a special case of range lock. We put forward algorithms for consolidation of shared locks that define a continuous covering, a way of initial processing simplifying and accelerating the lock manager. Two algorithms for the lock manager are framed with the use of XML labels for both the 2PL protocol and the cooperative one. We also point to some interesting ties between the lock management and the shortest path problem. Our motivation is given in the context of the SEDNA native XML DB isolation rules, however, our technique is useful for most of the fine-granular lock protocols.

Keywords. concurrency, XML, combinatorial algorithms

Introduction

The problem of concurrency control in XML documents has been an area of current interest in many papers such as [1], [2], [3] to name but a few. These articles coherently and completely tackle the question of serializability pertaining to concurrency control in XML documents. These works tackle various strategies of lock management in the context of serializability. Our work focuses on lock management, performance and the feasibility of locking strategies. We aim to propose some general form of architecture for locks manager putting to work node labels as an indexing apparatus. The original idea of using labels for the purpose of concurrency control was suggested in [3]. Apparently, the authors did not pursue this line of thought in practice (i.e. within their SEDNA database system) and gave it up in favor of DataGuide technique (cf. [2]). Although DataGuide and label based lock management viewed as classes of methods are alike they differ when it comes to defining sets of nodes. DataGuide does this by means of its nodes, which embrace sets of document nodes sharing the same type and having the same parent, and our method makes use of predicates on labels. We claim that our technique is a noteworthy option, especially for the fine-granular lock management, enabling efficient operations on sets of nodes.

The main drawback of fine-granular lock management is that an oversized manager state is liable to incur excessive time and memory costs. We claim that the use of labels for indexing entries of the locks manager state gives a chance to operate on

---

[1] Corresponding Author: Andrzej Sikorski, Technical University Poznań, IAiI, pl. Marii Skłodowskiej-Curie 5, 60-965 Poznań, Poland; E-mail:andrzejs@et.put.poznan.pl

sets of nodes such as path, sub-tree or range. In consequence, this method improves greatly the manager's performance. As if by a lucky coincidence our technique preserves the most characteristic advantage of the fine-granular locking i.e. high level of concurrency. The main reason for this is that the manager handles all the types of locks in the same uniform way – doing indexing by the labels. Note that locks acquired on sets are a special case of predicate locking with labels values as arguments of predicates. Since labels identify the position of nodes relative to each other in the data structure (e.g. XML document), we will use this beneficial feature and refer to these particular label locks as predicate structure locking. We will also take advantage of special properties of label bounded node ranges, allowing efficient processing.

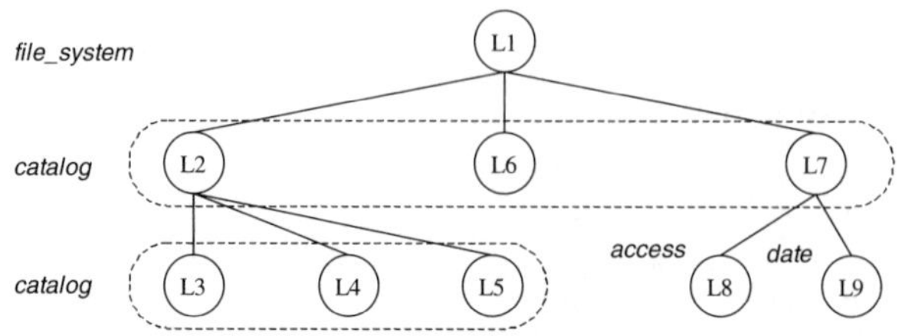

Figure 1. An XML document referred to in examples

We will motivate our ideas in the context of two examples from [2] (namely example 2 and example 3). These examples operate on an instance of XML document given in Figure 1, which is a model of a file system with hierarchical directories (catalogs), each catalog can include recursively catalog elements, each optionally annotated with date element or access element. The nodes are labeled with preorder values. These values need not be integers, as we only compare them and never do any explicit arithmetic. We will use the same concurrency rules as [2], however, unlike the original, our lock manager will operate on node labels. The general idea is that labels can define XML node sets equally well, making the successful implementation of fully fledged concurrency rules (as those in [2]) independent of the DataGuide availability. We also claim that the label approach may offer sometimes better granularity, as it is defining node sets in a flexible way.

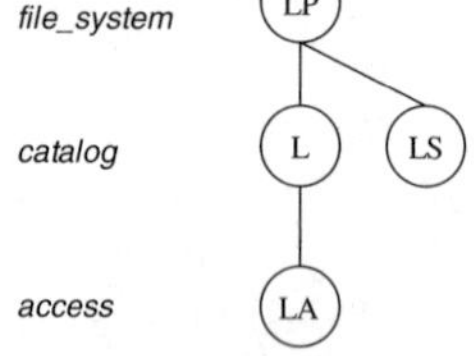

Figure 2. Labeling *L* a catalog element and *LS* is next sibling

See example 2 to start with. A transaction inserts an <access/> element into a <catalog> node, acquiring the suitable lock. While the first transaction is still active, another transaction attempts to insert a <date/> element into the same parent; the parent is labeled with *L*, its next sibling with *LS* (Figure 2). These are two conflicting operations. Now, to enforce the respective concurrency rule it suffices for the lock manager to add a single entry when the first transaction inserts a node. Such an entry would be:

(L,LS,*lock-type*,*trans-id*),

where *L,LS* are node labels, *trans-id* refers to the transaction which holds the lock and *lock-type* denotes the kind of acquired lock, possibly annotated with a condition predicate. When another transaction performs an insert within the *L,LS* range, the data manager generates a new node label first, and then the lock manager retrieves the relevant entry or entries thus enabling the application of the concurrency rules. Note, that with all relevant entries at hand the lock manager is able to apply isolation rules directly, deciding whether the requested lock can be acquired. Evidently, this particular lock could be handled in a more straightforward way, however we will see further, that our labeling scheme integrates nicely with other locking rules enabling their effective implementation.

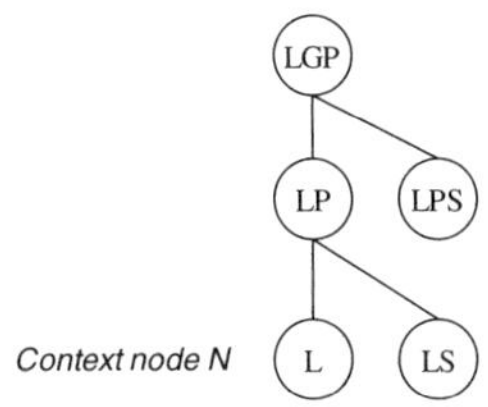

Figure 3. Using current context node *N* labeled *L* for further search steps on alternative axes

More generally we can consider search axes: *child::*, *following-sibling::* and *preceding-sibling::* and see how lock manager could obtain locks required for the corresponding search steps. Let us assume that an XPath expression established a current context node *N,* labeled *L* (Figure 3) and that the transaction operates on the most restrictive isolation level. Now, the next search step is to be performed. For the search on the child axis lock manager adds a (L,LS,*lock-type,trans-id*) entry, enforcing the verification of the argument predicate for any relevant future operation within the range between *L,LS* . The *lock-type* field may include parameters (e.g. a predicate that can determine whether the lock was acquired on all nodes within the range or only on the direct descendants of *L*). For searches on the two other axes the respective entries would be (L,LPS,*lock-type,trans-id*) and (LP,L,*lock-type,trans-id*).

The next example (example 3 from [2]) refers to a file search in a subdirectory. We are going to enhance this example somewhat, by locating the target search subdirectory deeper in the file system. Suppose the query is:
/file_system/catalog[@name='usr']/catalog[@name='bin']//file[@name='apache']
When a transaction executes on the serialization isolation level (i.e. equivalent to the SQL level 3), it expects that no phantoms appear. With the labeling based method, this lock type is easy to implement, as the lock manager merely adds a single entry into its state:

(L1,L2, ,*L("<file name='apache'/>"), T*),.

no matter how big the directory is. Where L1 is the label of */usr/bin* directory and L2 labels its next sibling. Any subsequent operation, which attempts to insert an element into any of */usr/bin* subdirectories triggers an action of the lock manager. When a node is to be inserted, the data manager generates a label, say *LX*. Now, the lock manager searches its state and retrieves an entry such that $L1<LX<L2$, enabling the manager to decide whether a node can be inserted and the suitable lock can be acquired. Note, that in this case, the lock is not restricted to the direct descendants of *L1*, however, the cost of the manager operation remains the same.

The indexing of the manager entries with node labels enables effective processing of arbitrarily large sets of nodes without compromising the fine-granularity as both the node sets and the individual document nodes are handled uniformly. The only trouble with arbitrary labels bounded node ranges is that they cannot be ordered linearly, which makes impossible a direct use of a B-Tree like search index. We can consider a set of ranges as a set of segments on the line, where each segment corresponds to a node range, bounded by its start and ending labels. In the general case segments can overlap when respective locks are compatible, nevertheless the lock manager should be able to verify efficiently whether a given node is located in some range. We will see later (Section 5), that the special case of exclusive locks is much simpler as ranges do not intersect and in the general case some initial processing would be necessary. Note, that the efficient processing of data objects indexed by two linearly orderable keys (i.e. two dimensional indexing) is one of the most fundamental problems of computational geometry, as rightly pointed in [4]. Although, unlike [4] we do not restrict ourselves to the lattices (i.e. in lattices segments can only either include each other or are disjoint), a more careful analysis will show, that the range lock case is special enough and some contrived techniques can be used to handle it efficiently.

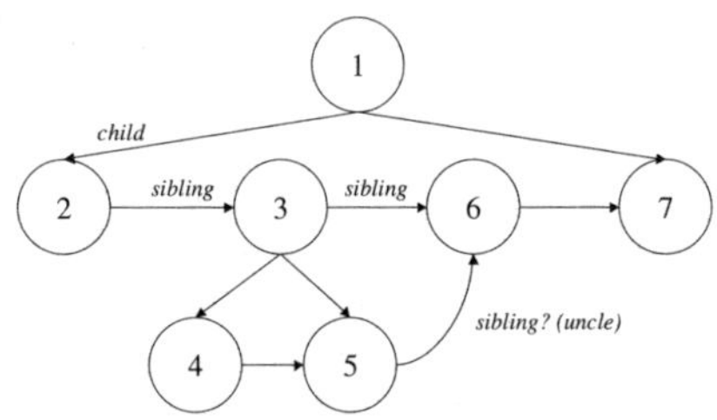

Figure 4. The extended model of an XML document

1. The Model of an XML Document, Labels

Although, the presented results were obtained in the context of concurrent processing of XML documents they pertain in general to hierarchical data structures. Figure 4 shows the model of the hierarchical data structure we adopted. It consists of nodes represented as rings connected with lines that denote a hierarchy: *parent-child* and *sibling*. The relation defined as *sibling* is a bit extended (with respect to DOM), i.e. in the case the node is the youngest of siblings, *sibling* points to the younger sibling of the closest ancestor, which has such a sibling. If there is no such ancestor then the *sibling* is an empty pointer. Empty pointers always appear in the rightmost path of the tree.

In the assumed model nodes have already been labeled. Figure 4 shows labels as numbers sequenced in *preorder*. This labeling turns out to be sufficient for our purposes. However, let us keep in mind that in a general case the data object being a label must verify a number of following requirements [5]:

1. The relative position in hierarchy between vertices can be determined by inspecting how labels values compare,
2. A change of the sub-tree structure brought about by a modification, removing or adding vertices should not entail any re-labeling,
3. Labels should have limited memory requirements,

4. Labels should nicely cooperate with XPath and XQuery.

For the purpose of this paper the first condition is most relevant. The requirement that any change of structure (for instance insertion of a new node) would not entail re-labeling remains unfulfilled. If we use integers the *preorder* enumeration has not this property. There are now two labeling methods that satisfy more or less the conditions set for the contents modifications: ORDPATHs of Microsoft make [6] (US Patent 6889226) and Prime [5]. The only assumption we make is that labels should be data objects that can be linearly ordered.

2. Structural Locks

Path, sub-tree or labels defined range can be specified in a hierarchical data structure. They are natural items subject to processing in a database of XML documents. There arises the need to effectively manage locks acquired for these structures. There are two reasons why structural locks are meaningful. First, processing of the data structure is likely to ignore the hierarchical order, i.e. access to a child node can be obtained leaving out parents' nodes (c.f. [1], [8]). In this case we need to acquire a lock for the entire path from root to the node being processed. The simplest solution is a walk down this path with setting of locks for consecutive nodes. Such a solution is ineffective with regard both to the time complexity (depending on the root's depth) and memory. This follows from the need to acquire and maintain a number of extensional locks. It should also be noted that if we deal with a server architecture using an external implementation DOM (e.g. a single threaded, run to completion server on asynchronous sockets) with embedded XPath interpreter then any access to the resulting nodes is going on leaving out paths leading to these nodes.

Acquiring a lock for sub-trees, the second characteristic component next to paths, is fairly simple, provided access to nodes always goes through their roots. However, an XPath interpreter can severely restrict this assumption and reasons for this are not only the jumps that turn a tree into a general graph. The data manager architecture is likely to prefer other sequences of processing, retrieval or modification. In this situation it would be beneficial to have an effective check whether the given node was locked or not. If it was, we would need to verify the mode, without necessarily traversing first all the way on the path leading from root to the node.

Locking of ranges bounded by labels values might also be interesting as a support for escalation of locks. Unlike in relational databases, where some strictly hierarchical set of data objects is assumed, a locked range in an XML document can be defined arbitrarily following a statistical analysis of the density of extensional locks acquired by transactions. When a threshold given in the configuration is exceeded then the manager proceeds to an *escalation* by removing multiple extensional locks and replacing them with a single range. Let us note that "granules" in the relational model follow from concepts of this model and implementations techniques (row, page of a data manager, table, cluster etc.). In an XML document the number of available levels of granularity corresponds to the tree's height. However, it is also possible to consider a strictly statistical approach where a lock manager pays no attention to the document's structure (i.e. ranges need not be sub-trees).

3. A Path Lock

The lock manager records a path lock by storing a single entry keyed by the label of the node at the path end. If the manager is to resolve whether a node is on the locked path the following predicate is verified:

$$is\_path\_locked(N) \equiv \exists_{X} is\_locked(X) \wedge label(N) < label(X) < label(sibling(N)) \tag{1}$$

where *label(N)* denotes a label assigned to the node N, whereas *sibling(N)* denotes the sibling described in Section 1. Moreover, it is assumed *label(null)* takes up the maximum value, out of use for labeling nodes in the tree.

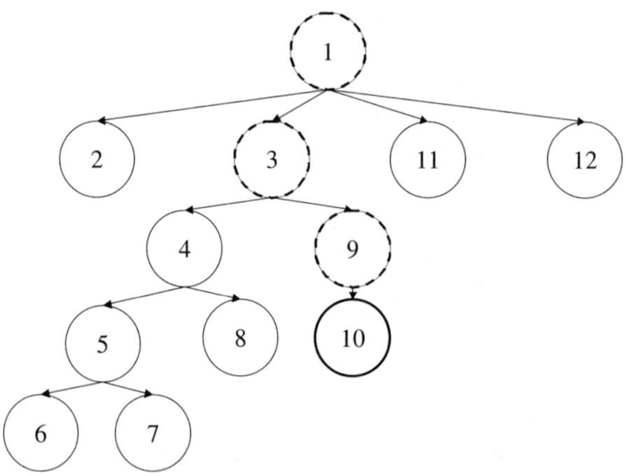

Figure 5. An example path lock

Consider an example. If a lock manager gets a request to lock a node labeled 10 and a path leading to it then it is sufficient it records this label and puts in the appropriate tag about the type of lock. A verification of the predicate is preceding an attempt to get access to any node on the path. For 3 it is going to turn out that there exists such an x that 3<x<11 (x=10). The cost of verification by means of an ordering index costs at most *log(n)*, where *n* is the number of acquired locks.

4. A Range Lock

Similarly to locking a path the manager stores only values of labels. This time the information about an acquired lock is keyed by two labels that identify the start and ending of the locked range. The appropriate predicate by means of which the manager verifies whether the node *N* belongs to the locked range is of the form:

$$is\_range\_locked(N) \equiv \exists_{X,Y} label(X) < label(N) < label(Y) \wedge is\_locked(X,Y) \tag{2}$$

Thus, the manager must verify whether there exists an entry that identifies a range lock with two labels that includes the current node. In particular, $Y = sibling(X)$ can hold, if the range refers to a sub-tree. The detailed discussion of an effective decidability of this predicate is given in the next section. We are going to see that the special cases of exclusive, 2PL shared, cooperative shared (which is most complex) must be studied separately. As the set of lock entries can be searched with respect to one key only we are going to discuss the issue of effective decidability of this predicate in more detail. Let us give a simple example, without referring to the operational complexities.

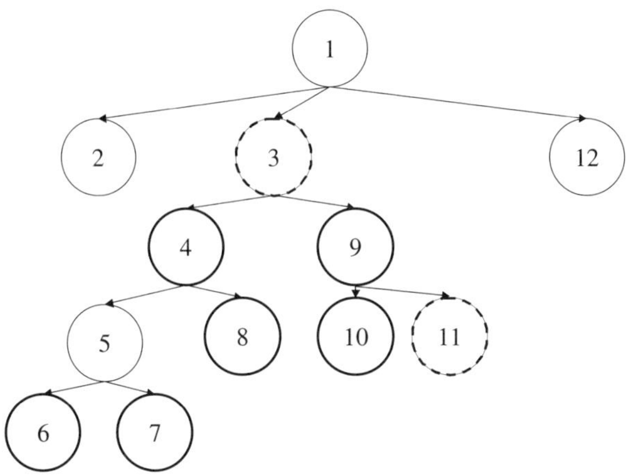

Figure 6. An example range lock replacing a set of extensional locks

Figure 6 shows a case when a lock is acquired on the range defined by nodes labeled 3 and 11. For instance, for the node 10 the manager can find out there is a lock with labels 3 and 11, so 3<10<11. The range lock comes as a result of a lock escalation and replaces extensional locks on 4,6,7,8,9,10 nodes, at the cost of an overhead lock on 5.

5. An Exclusive Range Lock

As range locks are identified with two labels they cannot be indexed so as to settle conclusively in a general case the appropriate predicate in the time *log(n)*. However, it is fairly straightforward to check whether a node is placed in a range locked in exclusive mode. It is sufficient to find for a given node the value of its greatest predecessor that identifies the start of a locked range. Next, it suffices to verify whether the label identifying the ending of the locked range is bigger then the label of node being verified. It is easily seen that if there is no such lock the node is not locked. Now, we are going to give an equivalent form of the predicate that makes use of the previous remark and can be verified in time *log(n)*. First, introduce an auxiliary predicate:

$$left\_range(N) \equiv \max\{label(X) : is\_locked(X,Y) \wedge label(X) < label(N)\} \quad (3)$$

For a given node *N* the predicate determines the label of the node that is starting a locked range such that it is located to the left from the argument node and such that its label defining the start has maximum value. The modified predicate takes the form:

$$is\_locked\_excl(N) \equiv is\_locked(left\_range(N), Y) \wedge label(Y) > label(N) \tag{4}$$

To check it effectively it is sufficient for the lock manager to maintain an ascending index ordering locks with respect to labels defining range's start. Let us note that maintaining such an index is not going to put an extra load on the manager. This follows from the fact that extensional locks are stored mostly in the index ordered by objects keys as it is.

```
public static List<XmlNodeRangeLock>
    CoverSet(List<XmlNodeRangeLock> rangeLocks)
    {
      List<XmlNodeRangeLock> set = new List<XmlNodeRangeLock>();

      List<XmlNodeRangeLock> sortedRangeLocks = SortByLeftAsc(rangeLocks);
      XmlNodeRangeLock last = new XmlNodeRangeLock(NegInfinity, NegInfinity);

      foreach (XmlNodeRangeLock xnrl in sortedRangeLocks)
        if (xnrl.left.value > last.right.value)
        {
          last = new XmlNodeRangeLock(xnrl); set.Add(last);
        }
        else if (xnrl.right.value > last.right.value)
                last.right.value = xnrl.right.value;
      return set;}
```

Figure 7. The procedure determining covering set of continuous ranges

6. A Shared Range Lock

The case of a shared lock is more complex because ranges can overlap. In this case the solution would be to maintain by the manager an additional data structure containing continuous ranges covered by shared locks. Let us now present a mechanism for a preprocessing of shared locks that is going to determine such ranges bounded by labels. Let us note that maintaining a data structure that stores information about continuous ranges (and not only about acquired locks) is going to enable us to resolve a lock in *log(n)* time, where *n* denotes now the number of continuous ranges. Nevertheless, the time/space required to create and maintain this additional structure depends on the manager's mode. There are two different ways to proceed: one when we have to do with 2PL (locks can be released only at the moment transaction commits or aborts), second when the manager supports a version of the cooperative protocol that handles the locks in a more casual way.

6.1. Managing Shared Range Locks for the 2PL Protocol

One can assume for the 2PL protocol that releasing the locks (including the range locks) occurs less frequently as compared to frequency of incoming requests for acquiring a lock. Releasing can really happen when a transaction is done. For this reason it is acceptable that the manager at the moment a transaction completes updates the state of its auxiliary data structure by means of regenerating it for every XML document kept locked by this transaction. Let us note that when a new lock appears the procedure is simple. It can easily be integrated with the resolution of the respective predicate because in both cases the appropriate index needs to be searched.

Every time a transaction completes and locks it acquired are released, the manager calls the procedure *CoverSet* (Figure 7). The greedy algorithm is quite simple. As the result we are getting a sequence of continuous ranges covered by shared locks acquired by transactions that are still active. Now, for continuous ranges we can apply the same modified predicate we gave for the case of exclusive locks.

6.2. Managing Shared Range Locks for Cooperative Protocols

Unlike 2PL protocol cooperative transactions are able to acquire locks and release them any time. In the preceding section we have shown that releasing a shared lock from a range makes it necessary to generate a set of covering ranges anew. Thus, advantages gained by making use of a less restrictive protocol are liable to be lost because of the additional load on the lock manager. A straightforward solution could be delaying the release of the locks. Such a plain technical solution reduces advantages of cooperative locking because released objects would be still kept locked.

```
public static List<List<XmlNodeRangeLock>>
        MinCover1Pass(List<XmlNodeRangeLock> rangeLocks)
  { List<List<XmlNodeRangeLock>> set = new List<List<XmlNodeRangeLock>>();
    List<XmlNodeRangeLock> range=null;
    XmlNodeRangeLock last=null;
    XmlNodeLabel l=MinLabel();
    foreach (XmlNodeRangeLock xnrl in SortByLeftAsc(rangeLocks))
      if (xnrl.left.value > l.value) //←{1}
      { last = xnrl;
        range = new List<XmlNodeRangeLock>();
        set.Add(range);
        range.Add(last); l = last.right; }
      else if (xnrl.right.value > l.value)
        { if (range.Count > 1 &&
              range[range.Count - 2].right.value > xnrl.left.value)
             range[range.Count - 1] = xnrl;//←{2}
          else range.Add(xnrl);// ←{3}
          last = xnrl; l = last.right; }
    return set;
    }
```

Figure 8. The optimal algorithm determining minimal list of covering locks

Cooperative applications support data consistency at their own expense as it is so, this contingency would be undesirable [9]. In consequence, the solution we present here is to find the minimum subset of range locks constituting the current range covering. It is easily seen that if the lock manager held an additional minimal list of locks (i.e. list of minimum length) covering a continuous range then this list could be used for the optimized processing. This is so because only the release of the range lock included in this list can trigger the update. As the list has the minimum number of members it follows that the likelihood the released range lock belongs to it is minimal.

For this reason the lock manager will have to update ranges the least frequently possible.

The algorithm that determines the smallest covering is finding a list of continuous ranges locked in the shared mode and more – it is also finding a minimal list of locks covering each of these ranges. Two versions of this algorithm are going to be given - optimal and extended. The first features a short time of execution, the second is able to find all versions of the smallest covering. We are going to account later for the reason why this opportunity to consider more candidate coverings can be advantageous in case of a lock manager operating in the cooperative mode.

A C# implementation of the optimal algorithm is given in Figure 8. The complexity is linear, which proves its optimality because every single range lock must be processed at least once. The function *MinCover1Pass* finds sequences of locks for individual continuous ranges reviewing manager state by means of the ordering index(←{1}). Note, that at the moment of executing the instruction marked with comment (←{2}) it can be asserted, that the range's length cannot be shorter than the current one (i.e. equals *range.Count*). Moreover, the range becoming the predecessor of the new range being inserted must belong to the minimum covering. Both properties can be easily shown. As for the complexity order it is linear, provided we disregard the sorting.

```
public static List<List<XmlNodeRangeLock>>
            MinCover(List<XmlNodeRangeLock> rangeLocks)
    {
    List<XmlNodeRangeLock> sortedRangeLocks = SortByLeftAsc(rangeLocks);
    foreach (XmlNodeRangeLock xnrl in sortedRangeLocks) //←{1}
    {
    if (xnrl.pred==int.MaxValue) xnrl.pred = 0;
        foreach (XmlNodeRangeLock xnrl1 in GetSuccessors(xnrl, sortedRangeLocks))
           xnrl1.pred =min( xnrl.pred + 1,xnrl1.pred);
    }
    sortedRangeLocks = SortByRightDesc(rangeLocks);    //←{2}
    List<List<XmlNodeRangeLock>> set = new List<List<XmlNodeRangeLock>>();
    List<XmlNodeRangeLock> range = null;
    int pred = 0;
    foreach (XmlNodeRangeLock xnrl in sortedRangeLocks)
    {
     if (pred == 0)
     { range = new List<XmlNodeRangeLock>();set.Add(range); range.Add(xnrl);}
      else
         if (pred == xnrl.pred + 1)// ←{3}
         range.Add(xnrl);
         pred = xnrl.pred;}
      return set;
    }
```

Figure 9. The extended algorithm determining minimal list of covering locks

It can be easily shown that the optimal algorithm determines only some particular, greedy minimum covering because at any moment it has the maximum range (in terms of labels ordering). However, cooperative transactions are likely to provide the lock manager with some additional information related to planned interactions with the database it works with. For instance, a manager could be in a position to estimate the remaining time a cooperative transaction would be still active. This can improve the performance greatly as cooperative transactions are known to be lengthy. If there existed a possibility to review multiple variants of the minimum covering, the manager could take into consideration additional criteria while finding the optimal one. One could recommend to include in such a covering locks known to be kept by their transactions in the future.

The extended algorithm determining the smallest list of locks we frame here is of the two-pass type. It returns a list consisting of lists. At the same time, it defines the smallest subset of range locks covering a continuous range. The code in Figure 9 shows the implementation. The first pass (labeled with ←{1}) processes locks in ascending order with respect to start labels. It also makes a review of the resulting list after sorting in order to determine the minimum lengths of the range sequences covering a continuous range. These lengths are stored in an auxiliary field *pred*. The range marking the start of a continuous range has 0 in this field. The second pass (←{2}) is making a review in descending order, this time with respect to endings. Each time either a predecessor on the minimal list or the beginning of a continuous range is found. The instruction labeled (←{3}), is the key because the condition can be verified positively many times. Thus, we can apply additional choice criteria based on information transactions provided for the manager. The possibility to replace the last range in the minimum covering requires a tiny modification of the code. This modification is left to the reader as an exercise.

Correctness of the extended algorithm follows from the fact that it is a particular case of the Dijkstra scheme for determining shortest paths in graphs. The problem of finding the smallest range covering can be thought of as a problem of finding the shortest path in a graph with equal edge weights (lengths). In this case individual ranges correspond to vertices. Edges connect these vertices whose corresponding coverings overlap. However, let us note that both problems of finding the smallest covering and finding the path of minimal length are not isomorphic (the problem is *monomorphic* as algebra puts it [10]).

As far as the computational complexity is concerned we note that the characteristics of the Dijkstra algorithm applies (cf. [11]). The complexity is *nlog(n)*, where *n* denotes the number of vertices (in our case range locks). The locks sorting appears twice only in the experimental implementation because the actual lock manager (as frequently stressed) would hold an auxiliary index containing identifiers of locked objects as it is. This index is available for generating the minimal list as well. However, even for the case of an experimental manager or the one that is managing sets of locks in any other way the computational complexity remains the same because the sorting complexity is still *nlog(n)*.

7. Conclusions

The idea to make use of nodes labels has been thoroughly tested in the setup of an implementation of our experimental XML server. The architecture of the experimental system has been based on an idea which puts forward using the MSXML2 as a query processor and data manager. The isolation level has been adopted as the basic working mode, where modified nodes are locked in the exclusive mode whereas paths leading to them in the shared one. It can be easily seen that the cost of locking a node along with its path equals the one of inserting a single object into the ordered index. Future work will include implementation of more comprehensive isolation levels as those given in [2], in an attempt to make its implementation independent of *DataGuide*.

We have taken the ingredients of the nodes labeling for the experimental implementation from Tarjan's and Willard's papers of the 80-ties [12], [13], [14]. These authors obtained interesting results pertaining to indexing data with labels that allow insertion of new objects without any need to re-label or with re-labeling at a cost bounded by a constant. We do not discuss these topics because the explanation of our idea required only that labels could be linearly ordered.

Further studies of an experimental system deal with support for MGL and applicability of initial processing on the level of individual transactions. The covering determined for locks acquired for one transaction can be used by the locks escalation method. This is so because a set of range locks that comprises a continuous one can be replaced by a single lock. This consolidation can then be carried out on-line. Then, the lock manager checks whether acquiring a new lock relates to a range that has already been locked or they partly overlap. In the first case the request is already satisfied. In the second one the manager verifies whether an extension of the lock is possible and if so, it is appropriately updating its state.

References

[1] Fomichev A., Grinev M., & Kuznetsov S.D. (2006) Sedna: A Native XML DBMS. In Wiedermann J., Tel G., Pokorný J., Bieliková M., & Stuller J. (eds) Theory and Practice of Computer Science, 32nd Conference on Current Trends in Theory and Practice of Computer Science, SOFSEM 2006, January 21-27, Merín, Czech Republic, Berlin: Springer, (LNCS), pp. 272-281

[2] Pleshachkov P., Chardin P., Kuznetsov S.D. (2005) A DataGuide-Based Concurrency Control Protocol for Cooperation on XML Data. In Eder J., Haav H.-M., Kalja A., & Penjam J. (eds) Advances in Databases and Information Systems, 9th East European Conference, ADBIS 2005, September 12-15, Tallinn, Estonia, Berlin: Springer, (LNCS), pp. 268-282

[3] Pleshachkov P., & Novak L. (2004) Transaction Isolation in the Sedna Native XML DBMS, SYRCoDIS, St. Petersburg 2004, (available at http://syrcodis.citforum.ru/2004/pleshachkov.pdf)

[4] Tropashko V. (2005) Nested Intervals for Tree Encoding in SQL, ACM SIGMOD Record, 34(2): 47-52

[5] Wu X., Lee M.L., & Hsu W. (2004) A Prime Number Labeling Scheme for Dynamic Ordered XML Trees. Proceedings of the 20th International Conference on Data Engineering, ICDE 2004, 30 March - 2 April, Boston, MA, USA. IEEE Computer Society, pp.66-78

[6] O'Neil P., O'Neil E., Shankar P., Cseri I., Schaller G., & Westbury N. (2004) ORDPATHs: Insert-Friendly XML Node Labels, SIGMOD, Paris, pp. 903-908

[7] Al-Khalifa S., Jagadish H.V., Koudas N., Patel J., Srivastava D., & Wu Y. (2002) Structural Joins: A Primitive for Efficient XML Query Pattern Matching. Proceedings of the 18th International Conference on Data Engineering, ICDE 2002, 26 February - 1 March, San Jose, CA. IEEE Computer Society, pp. 141-152

[8] Jagadish H.V., Al-Khalifa S., Chapman A., Lakshmanan L.V.S, Nierman A., Paparizos S., Patel J.M., Srivastava D., Wiwatwattana N., & Wu Y. (2002) A Native XML Database, VLDB Journal 11(4): 274-291

[9] Rusinkiewicz M., Klas W., Tesch T., Wäsch J., & Muth P. (1995) Towards a Cooperative Transaction Model – The Cooperative Activity Model. In Dayal U., Gray P.M.D., & Nishio S. (eds) VLDB'95, Proceedings of 21th International Conference on Very Large Data Bases, September 11-15, Zurich, Switzerland. Morgan Kaufmann, pp. 194-205

[10] Lidl R. (1975) Algebra für Naturwissenschaftler und Ingenieure. Walter de Gruyter, Berlin, 329 p.

[11] Dijkstra E. (1959) Two Problems in Connection with Graphs, Num. Math, 1: 269-271

[12] Sleator D.D., & Tarjan R.E. (1985) Amortized Efficiency of List Updates and Paging Rules, CACM, 28(2): 202-208

[13] Tarjan R.E. (1983) Data Structures and Network Algorithms. Society for Industrial and Applied Mathematics. Philadelphia, PA, 140 p.

[14] Willard. D.E. (1982) Maintaining dense sequential files in a dynamic environment. Proceedings of the 14th Annual ACM Symposium on Theory of Computing, May 5-7, San Francisco, California, USA, pp. 114-121

Databases and Information Systems V
H.-M. Haav and A. Kalja (Eds.)
IOS Press, 2009

doi:10.3233/978-1-58603-939-4-29

Accurate XML Summarization – A Comparison of Differing Approaches

José de Aguiar MORAES FILHO [a,1] and Theo HÄRDER [a]
[a] *Department of Computer Science, AGDBIS, University of Kaiserslautern*

Abstract. We explore existing methods to summarize XML data based on document levels, document paths, and element distribution. Using empirical data, we cross-compare them according to size and time needed for summary representation and estimate computation and, most important, the estimation accuracy achieved.

Keywords. XML summarization, histograms, XML query optimization

Motivation

The structure of XML documents brings new challenges when building a structural summary. What is the best way to shrink the stored document representations to be representative enough for the original document to enable cardinality estimations and, hence, to support a cost-based XML query optimizer. One difficulty in designing suitable XML summaries is due to the XML document structure itself, which often exhibits a "fuzzy degree" of variability. XML documents may, in practice, be irregular with some parts of shallow or skinny subtrees whereas other parts may have deep or broad ones. Furthermore, some subtrees may exist having no text values at all and, at the same time, other subtrees having a plethora of text values which present varying distributions. Another issue is the presence of recursive structures in the document. In such cases, summarization of statistical values and, in turn, estimation of path steps becomes more complex. The situation is even worse when recursion also appears in the query expression.

XQuery and XPath queries contain up to 8 different axis relationships in their path expressions. In typical query workloads, the child (/) and descendant (//) axes are absolutely dominant and, therefore, prime candidates requiring cardinality estimation to support query optimization. Compared to them, other axes such as parent and ancestor are second-class citizens for which support is less urgently needed. Following (sibling) and preceding (sibling) axes are only of minor importance in practical applications.

The variability of path expressions and predicates involved may be so rich that a single auxiliary structure (as complex as conceivable) for an XML summary would not solve all query optimization problems. Moreover, the more sophisticated a summary is, the more maintenance overhead would be needed. Hence, a practical XML summary is necessarily confined in its scope, but should be expressive enough to capture the most

[1]Corresponding Author: José de Aguiar Moraes Filho. University of Kaiserslautern, AG DBIS, P.O. Box 3049, D-67653 Kaiserslautern, Germany; E-mail:aguiar@cs.uni-kl.de.

important structural properties of XML data and flexible enough to deliver, as accurate as possible, the most frequently requested cardinality estimates for cost-based XQuery/XPath query optimization.

Numerous competing methods [1,2,3,4,5] exist primarily supporting child (/) and descendant (//) axes of path expressions. Including our own proposals, we compare three differing kinds to build summaries based on document levels, document paths, and element distribution, for which impressive results are known regarding accuracy, storage needs, and/or estimation/building time. After having introduced the basic concepts in Section 1, we sketch in sections 2–4 the three ways of proceeding called Level-wide Element Summarization (LWES) [6], XSeed [5], and Element-wise XML Summarization (EXsum) [7]. While LWES leverages the use of histograms [8] to capture element distributions in each level of an XML tree, XSeed applies a directed graph to represent parent-child relationships and to enable path-based cardinality estimates; it is specifically designed to support highly recursive XML documents. Compared to these level- or path-based methods, EXsum uses an entirely novel approach by turning the summarization problem upside down and collecting statistics per element name. By doing that, EXsum gains much more expressiveness for axes support and other statistical information, and yet captures the structural characteristics of an XML document. We have implemented the different approaches in XTC [9] and proven their validity by comparative experiments described in Section 5. Finally, Section 6 concludes the paper.

1. Basic Concepts and Definitions

XML documents usually exhibit a high degree of redundancy in their structural part, i.e., they contain many paths having identical sequences of element/attribute names. For example see Figure 1a, where many path instances in the document only differ in the leaf values and the order they occur in the document. Therefore, the structure part of them can be represented by a single unique path, called *path class* (see Figure 1b). Taking advantage of this observation, DataGuides [10] was the first approach to XML summarization aimed at providing a structural overview for the user and a data structure for storing statistical document information, thus, enabling query optimization. Later proposals, called path synopses, are similar to DataGuides, but are used as a query (document) guide and a compact structure view in the first place. In the context of XTC, the primary use of the path synopsis is for document structure virtualization, concurrency control, and supporting indexing and query processing [11] and has to be complemented by a summarization structure for statistical information concerning elements and axis relationships [6].

A cyclic-free XML schema captures all information needed for the path synopsis; otherwise, this data structure can be constructed while the document–sent by a client–is stored in the database. Typical path synopses have only a limited number of element names and path classes and can, therefore, be represented in a small memory-resident data structure (see Table 1). As shown in the following, such a concise description of the document structure is a prerequisite for effective query optimization. Element names that occur more than once in the path synopsis are called *homonyms*. A *unique* element name such as *a*, *c*, or *u* in the path synopsis results in an unambiguous summarization, which makes path expression estimation very simple in some cases. In turn, a homonym-free document has only unique element names in its path synopsis, is non-recursive by

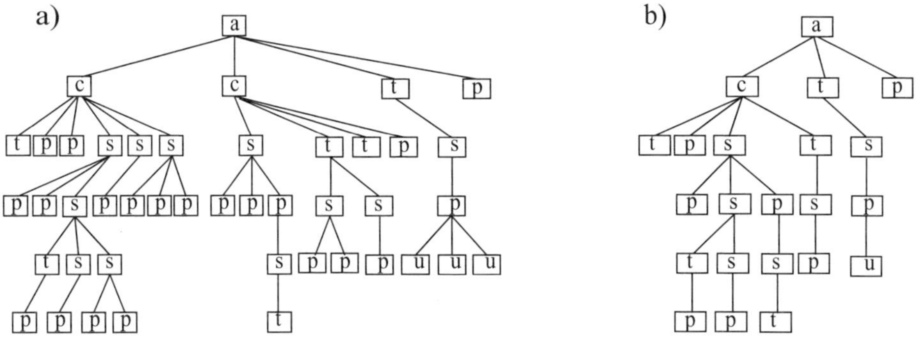

Figure 1. a) XML document structure (without leaf values) and b) path synopsis

definition, but may be an exception. In the typical case, a document contains a varying degree of homonyms, but most of its paths are recursion-free, i.e., homonyms do not occur in the same path class. In contrast, we have to deal with *recursion* in a document as soon as an element name occurs more than once in a single path class, e.g., in paths */a/c/s/s/s/p* or */a/c/s/p/s/t*.

Highly recursive XML documents such as *treebank* (see Table 1) are exotic outliers and not frequent in practice; therefore, they do not deserve first-class citizenship. However, some degree of recursion may be anticipated in (a small class of) documents. Thus, we analyze recursiveness for reasons of generality and evaluate summarization structures that support documents exhibiting a (limited) kind of structural recursion, too.

The concept of recursion level (RL) was introduced in [12] and explained for the case where only a single element name could recur in a path. Recursion levels were defined as: *Given a rooted path in the XML tree, the maximum number of occurrences of any label (element name) minus 1 is the path recursion level (PRL). The recursion level of a node in the XML tree is defined to be the PRL of the path from root to this node.* Thus, given path */a/c/s/s/t*, the second *s* node has RL=1 and all other nodes have RL=0, whereas the PRL of this path is 1.

Recursion can also occur in query expressions making the estimation even more difficult (and, often, more imprecise). For recursive path expressions, we follow the definition in [12]: *A path expression is recursive with respect to an XML document if an element in the document could be matched by more than one node test in the expression.* Thus, it is easy to see that path expressions only consisting of /-axes (or parent axes) are not recursive. However, *//s//s* is a recursive path expression on the XML tree in Figure 1a, because a recursively occurring *s* node could be matched by both node tests. Hence, recursive path expressions always involve at least one //-axis (or ancestor axis) and are usually applied to recursive documents.

2. Level-Based Summarization

The first method [7] of our summarization comparison is based on the concept of Hierarchical Node Summarization (HNS, see Figure 2a) which closely follows the structure of the path synopsis. HNS embodies a structural summary of all (sub-) paths of the document. Each node in an HNS is related to an element/attribute name unique under the same parent. The HNS construction is recursive and records for each distinct element name—under the same (aggregated) parent in a document—the number of its instances (element nodes). Building an HNS proceeds top-down, where the same element/attribute names under the aggregated parent are counted. This information is depicted by a node labeled with *element:frequency*, where *element* is the element/attribute name and *frequency* is the number of occurrences counted. For example in Figure 1a, we have two elements c under parent a and 3 elements p under the two parents c. These elements are represented in the HNS of Figure 2a by an aggregated node c with frequency 2 (c:2) and by an aggregated node p with frequency 3 (p:3), respectively. It turns out that such an HNS precisely preserves the frequency information of all (sub-) paths of the original document. If we need the frequency of a path, we just traverse this path in the HNS from the root and the frequency kept in the final element addressed by the path delivers this information, e.g., */a/c/t/s* and */a/c/s/p* yield 2 and 9, respectively.

HNS has strong positive points. First, it delivers accurate cardinalities for all path expressions only containing child and descendant axes. For example, the path expression *//c//t* matches three nodes in the given HNS; hence, we can add the frequencies recorded in these nodes and immediately return 5 as the number of qualified document nodes (together with the fully specified paths). Recursive path expressions of the same kind can also be accurately computed using an HNS. After locating the qualified HNS nodes for a path expression, e.g., *//s//s*, their frequencies are accumulated and deliver the requested cardinality, which is 4 for the example. Second, all path classes in a document are preserved by an HNS, which prevents false positive errors. Third, HNS is memory efficient for documents exhibiting a certain degree of uniformity. However, HNS has also negative points. The number of HNS nodes may be high for deeply-structured documents. If the HNS tree has to be fully traversed (e.g., for descendant and ancestor axes), the number of nodes may negatively impact the estimation process. For deeply-structured and highly-recursive documents, HNS may consume enormous storage space which could impede cardinality estimation and, in turn, the entire query optimization.

2.1. Summary Compression

A way to compress an HNS tree is to capture the distribution of elements of a tree level by applying histograms. For example, Figure 2a shows two nodes s in level 3, one s:4 under c, and another s:1 under t; let us call them node occurrences of s. LWES [7] represents all such occurrences of s at the same level by using a single histogram. In a similar way, this rule is applied to all other HNS nodes, e.g., s and p (italicized in Figure 2b at level 4). LWES is a solution trying to deal with recursion in documents such as *treebank*, but it may also be beneficial for recursion-free documents, e.g., *dblp*.

A variety of histogram types [8] are applied in LWES, e.g., Biased, End-Biased (EB) and Equi-Height (EH) histograms. LWES uses them in a tailor-made fashion driven by several factors, where the query workload is especially important. If a specific workload is anticipated, one can choose the most suitable histogram type. For example, if most path expressions only include child (parent) and descendant (ancestor) axes, EB histograms could be applied, because they cause the least approximation error in such situations. Evaluation of predicates may benefit from other types, e.g., EH, of histograms.

When elements occur only once at an HNS level, LWES only records their frequency, as seen, e.g., at level 2. Moreover, for every node, LWES maintains a list of parent pointers (dashed lines in Figure 2b) which has a twofold goal: it properly captures the parent-child relationships of the document and it helps to distinguish the LWES node occurrences in the hierarchy. Both are exploited during cardinality estimation.

2.2. *Estimation of Path Expressions Using LWES*

LWES uses a function called $GetCard$ to determine the cardinality of a node. If a histogram is attached to a node, $GetCard$ obtains the estimated cardinality from it. Consider a simple rooted path expression containing only /-axes as */a/c/s*. The estimation process considers each step separately. First, *GetCard(/a)* delivers 1 in level 1. In the second step, the process probes for a child c in LWES which is found at the level below node a. In this case, *GetCard(a/c)* returns 2. In the final step, the process probes for an s under c at level 3. Here, *GetCard(c/s)* refers to a histogram to compute the estimated cardinality, e.g., 2.5. In general, when only (rooted) child axes are involved, the cardinality of the expression is exactly the *GetCard* value taken from the final step. Formally, *EstimCard(*$/v_1/\ldots/v_n$*)* = *GetCard(*v_n*)*.

A //-axis causes the estimation process to traverse several (potentially all) levels in LWES, to probe, in each level, for the specified element and to gather its cardinality using the $GetCard$ function. The estimated cardinality for //-axes is the sum of cardinalities of the probed nodes. Formally, we have *EstimCard(//v)* = Σ *GetCard(*v_i*)*, where v_i refers to the probed LWES nodes evaluated to *true* during the traversal. Because //-steps can gather LWES nodes at several levels, location steps following the //-step also have to probe at these levels. For example, consider *//s/p*. For the first step, LWES is traversed looking for s nodes, thereby identifying two s nodes at levels 3 and 4. Assume, the histograms deliver 2.5 and 2 which results in an estimated cardinality of 4.5. Then for all qualified s nodes, LWES is traversed probing for a child p. Hence, two nodes p are found at levels 4 with frequency 3 and level 5 with a histogram delivered an assumed value of 5. The expression cardinality is thus estimated as 8. Recursive queries are also supported. By traversing LWES and calling *GetCard*, the histogram of node s at level 5 returns for *//s/p/s* an assumed estimation of 1.5.

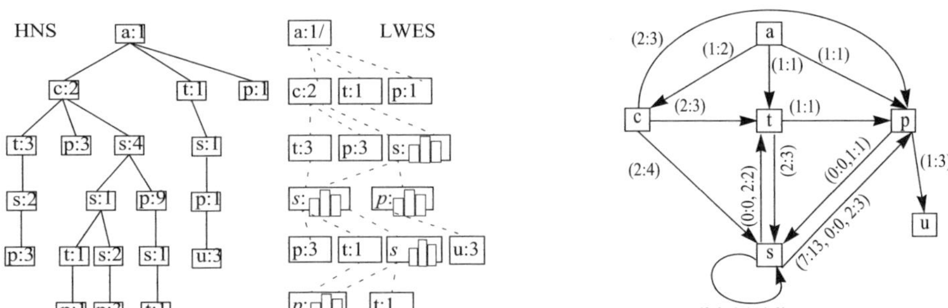

a) HNS and its compreesd LWES summary **b) XSeed summary**

Figure 2. Level-based(a) and Path-based(b) summaries

3. Path-Based Summarization

The XSeed [5] approach summarizes XML data using a directed graph (called XSeed kernel) in which each node represents an element/attribute name of the document. Each edge, in turn, represents a parent-child relationship and is labeled with a list of pairs of counters (p_i:c_i), i≥0. The p_i and c_i are called parent counter and child counter, respectively. Each pair indicates that, at recursion level (RL) i, there is a parent-child relationship between two nodes u and v, where p_i elements u and c_i elements v are involved. RL is thus applied in XSeed to capture parent-child relationships in recursive paths.

3.1. Building Algorithm

XSeed building is based on an event-driven XML parser (SAX parser) which scans the document and maintains a stack. When an opening-element event is detected, this element is pushed onto the stack. The kernel is then searched to possibly insert a new node together with its current list of out-edges. Each edge in the list contains, in turn, the RL information calculated from the rooted paths ending with this edge [12]. The calculation of recursion levels is made by an auxiliary data structure called "counter stacks" which is a list of stacks implemented as a hash table. The operations on counter stacks are similar to that of the main stack, i.e., in the opening (closing)-element event, an element is inserted into (removed from) the data structure. The path recursion level is indicated by the number of non-empty entries in the counter stacks minus 1. When a closing-element event is reached, then, for each out-edge in the list, RLs as well as parent and child counters are calculated and recorded in the corresponding edge in the graph. The element is then popped from the stack, its related entries in the counter stacks are also popped, and the process iterates over again when a new element comes from the parser. Processing all elements of Figure 1a results in an XSeed summary as shown in Figure 2b.

3.2. Estimating Path Expressions with XSeed

To estimate cardinalities of queries containing /- and //-axes and queries with predicates, XSeed applies the concept of forward selectivity (*fsel*) for the former and backward selectivity (*bsel*) for the latter. XSeed allows predicates only in the last step of a query.

Intuitively, given a path expression $/v_1/v_2/ \ldots /v_n/v_{n+1}$, *fsel* is a fraction of v_{n+1} nodes (obtained from the child counters) that are contributed by the path (v_1,v_2,...,v_n) (obtained from parent counters). In other words, the estimated cardinality of a path expression containing only child axes is the estimated cardinality of its last step. Given a path expression $/v_1/v_2/ \ldots /v_{n-1}/v_n[v_{n+1}]$, *bsel* captures the fraction of v_n nodes that: (1) are contributed by the path (v_1,v_2,...,v_{n-1}); and (2) have a child v_{n+1}. Note that, by the definition in [12], *fsel* (and *bsel*) make the independence assumption, i.e., the probability of v_i having a child v_{i+1} is independent of v_i's ancestors. Due to this assumption, *fsel* (*bsel*) can also be calculated for all sub-expressions. For example, for each step of the path expression */a/c/s/s/t*, cardinalities as well as *fsel* and *bsel* values are provided as follows: [/a:1,1,1], [a/c:2,1,1], [c/s:5,1,1], [s/s:2,1,0.4], [s/t:1,1,0.5]. For the fifth step (*s/t*), the counters with RL=1 are used to calculate *fsel* and *bsel*.

Another example illustrating the use of RL is *//s//s//p*. The estimated result for this query is (exactly) the sum of child counters in all RL>0 of the edge s→p. Thus, query steps with //-axes need to traverse the XSeed kernel and compute *fsel* (and *bsel*) at each node visited. Here, because of the graph structure of XSeed, false positive hits may worsen the estimation. In other words, some paths that can be derived from the summary may not exist in the document. Thus, path expressions as *//s/s/s/s* may be estimated in XSeed delivering a non-zero cardinality while the actual result is zero. To mitigate such situations, the traversal algorithm prunes the graph search based on a tuning parameter (called *card_threshold*). When the estimation process calculates a cardinality which is equal to *card_threshold*, the search stops and the cardinality of the step is set to the estimate calculated so far. This is clearly a time/accuracy trade-off. Lower values of *card_threshold* allow more accurate results at the expense of longer estimation times.

4. Element-Based Summarization

The EXsum [6] structure can be considered as a set of ASPE (axes summary per element) nodes where each of them, in turn, represents a distinct element/attribute name. An ASPE node is a compound of an element/attribute name, the number of related node occurrences (occ) in the document, and a varying number of "spokes"—an ASPE node resembles a "spoked wheel"—each primarily representing the related element distributions for a specific axis. In the following, we outline the methods used by EXsum for structural summarization of a document including the four main axes—child, descendant, parent, and ancestor—and, in turn, for the estimation of location step cardinalities.

4.1. Building Algorithm

The document is traversed in document order where, when visiting a node with element name x, all its axis relationships (as far as specified for EXsum) are recorded in ASPE(x). In that way, we derive step by step the exact number of occurrences per axis this element participates in. EXsum uses a stack mechanism to summarize axis relationships of an element name where stack S keeps, at any point in time, the path of the current node visited to the root. For our discussion, we refer to Figure 1a. Summarization proceeds node-by-node in document order. When a node is visited, its element name x is pushed onto S. Furthermore, it causes the allocation of ASPE(x) (if not already present) and the recording of all axes information that can be evaluated at that time. After allocating ASPE(a) in the initial step, a node with element name c is located and pushed onto S. Because ASPE(c) is not present, it is created and the related axes information is added to a and c. The general summarization principle is explained for the visit of the third node with element name t, resulting in $S = [a, c, t]$. From t's point of view, this path is recursion-free which means that $RL = 0$ for every axis relationship of t. After creation of ASPE(t), the axes information is incremented: *par(c:RL=0)* and *anc(a:RL=0)*. Further, *child(t:RL=0)* in ASPE(c) and *desc(t:RL=0)* in ASPE(a) are also incremented.

EXsum has to cope with recursion, too, here discussed for the visit of the 13th node with element name p and stack state $S = [a, c, s, s, s, p]$. To update EXsum with the axis relationships of p, the recursion levels of the elements in S are to be considered: *a:RL=0*; *c:RL=0*; *s:RL=0*; *s:RL=1*; *s:RL=2*, and *p:RL=0*. From p's point of view, (*s:RL=2*) is parent, whereas the other elements in S are ancestors. Hence, the value of ASPE(p) is increased by 1. Then in ASPE(p), the target elements of p's relationships—

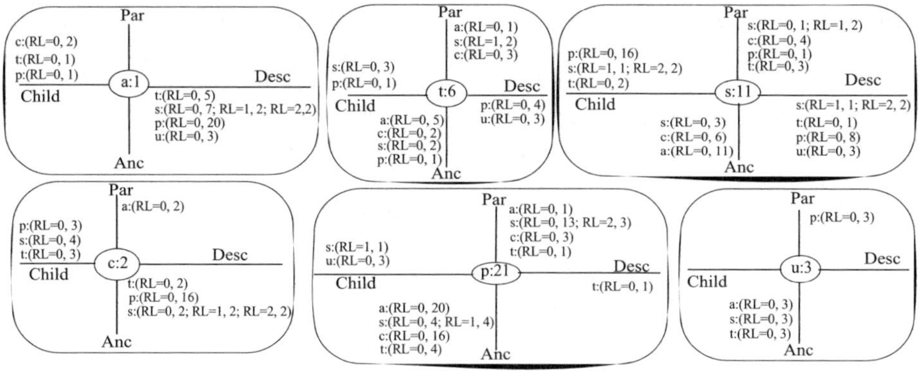

Figure 3. EXsum structure for our running example

par(s:RL=2), *anc(s: RL=1)*, *anc(s:RL=0)*, *anc(c:RL=0)*, and *anc(a:RL=0)*—are incremented by 1. Furthermore, the axis relationships of the remaining elements in S have to be maintained, because p with $RL = 0$ (as the target element of these relationships) becomes a new child resp. descendant of them. Therefore in ASPE(s), 1 is added to *child(p:RL=0)*, *desc(p:RL=0)*, and again *desc(p:RL=0)*. In ASPE(c) and ASPE(a), in turn, *desc(p:RL=0)* is incremented by 1.

Note that information for the child (parent) axis is kept separately from that of the descendant (ancestor) axis to enable higher flexibility for axis-wise estimation of location steps. In summary, when an element x is pushed onto S, the frequency counter of ASPE(x) is incremented. Furthermore, if S contains n elements, $n-1$ child/desc counters and $n-1$ par/anc counters have to be maintained. When a leaf node of a document D is encountered, the top-most entry (current element) of S is popped and the preorder traversal of D is continued with the next node not visited so far. When D is fully traversed, EXsum building is complete (shown in Figure 3). Note, if the estimation process refers to descendant or ancestor axes, the separated statistics for child and parent axes have to be considered, because child $\subseteq$ descendant or parent $\subseteq$ ancestor always hold.

4.2. EXsum-Based Cardinality Estimation

For path expressions with two location steps, the spoke referenced by the second step is followed in the ASPE node addressed by the first one. The construction principle of EXsum guarantees that such expressions on recursion-free documents (but only single location steps on recursive documents) deliver accurate cardinalities. When recursion and two location steps are involved, EXSum exhibits sometimes only approximate cardinalities [6]. Consider the estimation of *//s//s*, where estimation follows the child and descendant spokes in ASPE(s) and adds the values over all RLs of s, yielding an overestimation of occ(*//s//s*)=6, whereas occ(*//s/s*)=3 would deliver the accurate cardinality.

For n-step query expressions (n>2), however, EXsum cannot always guarantee accurate results, because ASPE nodes do not capture the complete root-to-leaf paths of a document. Instead, they keep axis relationships between pairs of element names and record their distribution on the basis of element names. For this reason, we decompose—if more than two location steps are involved—the expression, e.g., *//x/y//z*, in overlapping two-step fractions and need a kind of heuristics, e.g., interpolation, to combine their results. To evaluate the partial expressions *//x/y* and *y//z*, we access ASPE(x) and ASPE(y) (whose values is equivalent to occ(*//x*) and occ(*//y*), respectively). Because not all y nodes of *//y//z* find a matching partner in the y nodes of *//x/y*, we assume uniform element distribution for the z nodes to enable a straightforward combination of estimates for such partial expressions. Using the ratio *C1/C2*, we linearly interpolate the number of occurrences of the subsequent step *y//z* to estimate occ(*//x/y//z*). For that, *C1* is given by occ(*//x/y*) and *C2*—equivalent to occ(*//y*)—is recorded as value of ASPE(y); thus, $C1 \geq C2$ always holds. This interpolation could be applied step by step, such that we gain a heuristics for n-step path expressions. If more accurate information is present (e.g., by mining entire paths), it is used instead. As an example, the cardinality of *//s/s/p* is estimated by following the child spoke of ASPE(s) and summing the values over all recursion levels of s, yielding occ(*//s/s*)=3. Furthermore, occ(*s/p*) delivers 16. With the interpolation factor of ASPE(s)=11, the estimation is 3/11*16.

In summary, EXsum yields in non-recursive XML documents for arbitrary combinations of standard axes (child, descendant, parent, ancestor) accurate cardinalities when a unique element name is referenced in the final location step of an arbitrarily long path expression [6] or greatly improve its accuracy when it occurs somewhere in the middle of it. It obtains always accurate cardinalities for one and two location steps and for n location steps estimated cardinalities derived by interpolation of several EXsum results. For recursive documents, [6] describes the way how to derive estimates from them for non-recursive and recursive path expressions.

5. Empirical Evaluation

To compare the approaches outlined, we performed empirical experiments using a well-known set of XML documents listed in Table 1 and analyzed the results regarding timing, sizing and accuracy. Therefore, we assembled, for each document, a query workload and computed estimates for the path expressions. In Table 1, column *#nodes* shows the total number of nodes in a document according to the DOM specification. Column *#voc. names* indicates that, compared to nodes, only a few distinct element/attribute names exist. Hence, documents typically have a very repetitive structure. Columns *max. depth* and *avg. depth* give some hints on the variability of documents. For example, *swissprot* is quite a regular document, because its average depth is close to its maximum depth. In contrast, *treebank* is extremely irregular.

5.1. Query Workload

We have built a query workload as follows. For all documents except treebank, we have generated all possible queries encompassing only child axes. We have randomized the generation of queries whose path expressions contain the remaining axes, i.e., descendant, parent, and ancestor, and queries with predicates. For treebank, we have randomly generated queries having four axes and predicates. In total, we have experimented with approximately 3,000 queries.

Our empirical exploration is based on an EXsum structure with four spokes (see Figure 3) and LWES compressed by EB histograms. The reason for choosing such an histogram type is simple. End-Biased histograms typically exhibit the least approxima-

Table 1. Characteristics of documents considered.

Doc. name	Descr.	Size in MB	#nodes (inner / text)	#voc. names	max. depth	avg. depth
dblp	Comp. Sc. Index	330.0	9,070,558 / 8,345,289	41	7	3.39
nasa	Astron. data	25.8	532,96 / 359,993	70	9	6.08
swissprot	Protein data	109.5	5,166,890 / 2,013,844	100	6	4.07
uniprot	Protein data	1,820	81,983,492 / 53,502,972	89	7	4.53
treebank	Wall Street J.	86.1	2,437,667 / 1,391,845	251	37	8.44

tion error. We compare the results against those achieved by XSeed [5]. Because of its structure, XSeed is one of the most compact summaries known in the literature. All empirical experiments were run on a platform consisting of a 2GHz Pentium Centrino Duo processor with 1GB main memory, running under Windows XP SP2. For that purpose, we implemented and integrated all methods to be compared into our native XDBMS XTC [9], which is written in Java 6. The performance measurements used 512 MB of main memory for the Java Virtual Machine and 16 MB for the XTC buffer.

5.2. Sizing Analysis

All summaries compared need about 3–5 orders of magnitude less storage space than the full documents, except the treebank summaries, which reach only a reduction of 2–3 orders of magnitude. Hence, the summary sizes mostly vary between 0.001% and 0.2% of the document sizes (Figure 4a). Even for treebank, the summary structures only consume 0.1%, respectively 0.2% of the document size when XSeed and EXsum are used. XSeed exhibits the least space consumption for highly recursive documents, thus outperforming EXsum and LWES (0.8%) for such documents. Figure 4a shows that all summaries are compact enough to enable memory-resident use, although they may consume hundreds of kilobytes. Regarding the main-memory buffer to keep statistical data required for the estimates supporting the query optimization process, EXsum exhibits the lowest memory footprint. While competitor structures have to be entirely loaded into main memory, EXsum loads only the needed ASPE nodes. Consider *treebank* as a kind of bad case, for which EXsum requires 740 bytes on average per ASPE node. As ASPE nodes, loaded on demand to memory, are bounded by the number of query steps, the estimation of a query on treebank with ten path steps (covering, possibly, more than half of the treebank depth) would consume less than 8KB. Hence, according to our observations, EXsum needs 10 to 100 times less memory than that required for XSeed (70KB) and LWES (700KB) for the estimation process.

5.3. Estimation Time Analysis

A particular advantage of EXsum is that, in the worst case, the number of ASPE nodes to be accessed is equal to the number of query steps, even for recursive queries. Because we have implemented the ASPE nodes as hash tables, the time complexity for each access is in *O(1)*. As a consequence, our approach generally achieves low estimation times, as illustrated in Figure 4b. Contrary to EXsum, XSeed and LWES only provide low estimation times for non-recursive documents, which are typically not greater than 75 msec.

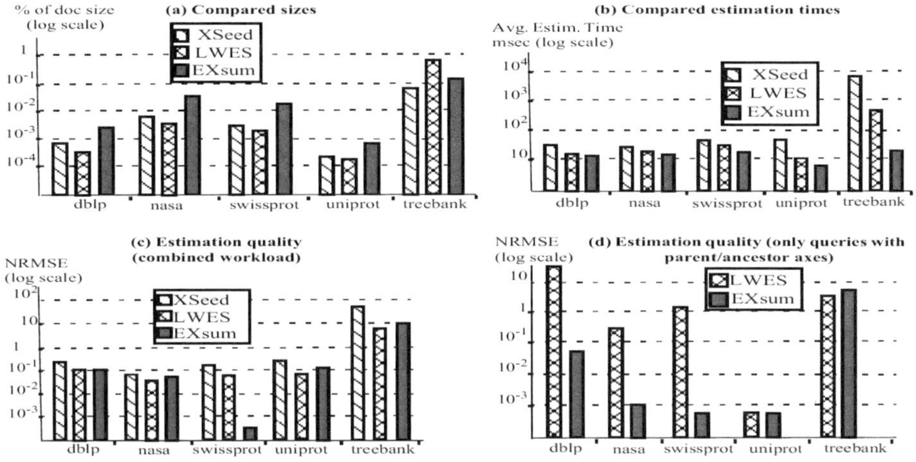

Figure 4. Analysis: a) Sizing, b) Estimation Time, c) Accuracy(combined) and d) Accuracy (only par/anc)

However, XSeed reaches up to 10 seconds for cardinality estimation concerning queries addressing *treebank*. For the same kind of estimation tasks, LWES only requires on the average 300 msec. EXsum, in contrast, consumes an average of 25 msec (including *treebank*) for documents. Indeed, it required not more than 56 msec for cardinality estimation in the worst case. This demonstrates that EXsum scales well for any type of XML document and provides the minimum impact on the query optimization process.

5.4. Estimation Accuracy

To evaluate the accuracy, we computed estimates for the path expressions of our workloads thereby contrasting actual values from the documents and estimated values. To determine accuracy and to facilitate cross-comparison of all approaches, we applied the metric Normalized Root Mean Square Error (NRMSE). NRMSE is defined by the formula: $\sqrt{\sum_{i=1}^{n}(e_i - a_i)^2}/(\sum_{i=1}^{n}(a_i)/n)$, where n is the number of queries in the query workload, e is the estimated result size and a is the actual result size. NRMSE measures the average error per unit of the accurate result. To analyze estimation accuracy (see Figure 4c), we have applied to each document a reference workload, involving different types of queries. With a smaller memory footprint than the competitors, EXsum reaches at least comparable and often more accurate estimation results. For example, EXsum has an estimation error near to zero for *swissprot* (a quite regular document). While comparable on the other documents, the estimation error on *treebank* was almost an order of magnitude less than that of XSeed. When we evaluate specific query types (e.g., queries with only parent and ancestor axes, see Figure 4d), EXsum exhibits even a better estimation quality in the majority of cases.

6. Conclusions

We have compared three different techniques for summarizing XML data. First, LWES leverages histograms to capture node distributions at entire document levels. XSeed, in turn, uses a graph structure for its path-based summarization. In contrast to both competitors, EXsum does not adhere to the document structure, but records all axis relationships per distinct element name. Our sizing analysis does not deliver a uniform result being consistently achieved. There is rather evidence that EXsum consumes slightly more storage space (consider the scale) in the recursion-free case than both counterparts compared. Only for highly recursive documents, XSeed considerably outperforms LWES and EXsum. As far as estimation time is concerned, we received a continuous impression that EXsum is clearly predominant, especially on recursive documents where XSeed obtained unacceptable results. The most important property of a summary is estimation quality for which our experiments revealed that EXsum is at least comparable and—in case of regularly structured documents—definitely superior to its competitors. In summary, it is safe to say that Exsum exhibits key benefits when all aspects are weighted at a time, not to mention its increased expressiveness concerning enhanced axis support (e.g., parent and ancestor). As EXsum has exhibited the best overall result, we plan to extend it in two directions. First, we want to explore the summarization of text values in XML documents (together with structural summarization). Second, we plan experiments with EXsum in real cost-based XML query optimization scenarios.

References

[1] Aboulnaga, A., Alameldeen, A. R., & Naughton, J. F. (2001) Estimating the Selectivity of XML Path Expressions for Internet Scale Applications. Proceedings of 27th Very Large Databases Conference (VLDB), September 11-14, Rome, Italy, pp. 591–600.

[2] Freire, J., Haritsa, Jayant R., Ramanath, M., Roy, P., & Simeon, J. (2002) StatiX: making XML count. In Proceedings of the 2002 ACM SIGMOD International Conference on Management of Data (SIGMOD), June 3-6, Madison, Winsconsin, USA, pp. 181–191.

[3] Lim, L., Wang, M., Padmanabahn, S., Vitter, Jeffrey S., & Parr, R. (2002) XPathLearner: An On-Line Self Tuning Markov Histogram for XML Path Selectivity Estimation. In Proceedings of 28th Very Large Databases Conference (VLDB), August 20-23, Hong-Kong, China, pp. 442–453.

[4] Polyzotis, N., & Garofalakis, M. (2002) Structure and Value Synopses for XML Data Graphs. In Proceedings of 28th Very Large Databases Conference (VLDB), August 20-23, Hong-Kong, China, pp. 466–477.

[5] Zhang, N., Özsu, M. T., Aboulnaga, A., & Ilyas, I. F. (2006) XSeed: Accurate and Fast Cardinality Estimation for XPath Queries. In Proceedings of the 22nd International Conference on Data Engineering (ICDE), April 3-8, Atlanta, USA, pp. 61–66.

[6] Aguiar Moraes Filho, J., & Härder T. (2008) EXsum – An XML Summarization Framework. In Proceedings of the 12th International Conference on Data Engineering and Application Systems (IDEAS), September 10-12, Coimbra, Portugal.

[7] Aguiar Moraes Filho, J., & Härder T. (2008) Tailor-made XML Synopses. In Haav, H-M and Kalja, A. (eds.) Proceedings of the 8th International Baltic Conference (DB& IS), June 3-5, Tallinn, Estonia, pp. 25–36.

[8] Ioannidis, Y. (2003) The History of Histograms (abridged). In Proceedings of 29th Very Large Databases Conference (VLDB), September 9-12, Berlin, Germany, pp. 19–30.

[9] Haustein, M. P., & Härder, T. (2007) An Efficient Infrastructure for Native Transactional XML Processing. Data& Knowledge Engineering 61(3): 500–523.

[10] Goldman, R. & Widom, J. (1997) DataGuides: Enabling Query Formulation and Optimization in Semistructured Databases. In Proceedings of 23rd Very Large Databases Conference (VLDB), August 25-29, Athens, Greece, pp. 436–445.

[11] Härder, T., Mathis, C., & Schmidt, K. (2007) Comparison of Complete and Elementless Native Storage of XML Documents. In Proceedings of the 11th International Conference on Data Engineering and Application Systems (IDEAS), September, 6-8, Banff, Canada, pp. 102–113.

[12] Zhang, N. (2006) Query Processing and Optimization in Native XML Databases, Ph. D. thesis, Technical Report CS-2006-29, University of Waterloo (Aug. 2006)

Databases and Information Systems V
H.-M. Haav and A. Kalja (Eds.)
IOS Press, 2009

doi:10.3233/978-1-58603-939-4-41

Web Systems Evaluation on Users' Behaviour Modelling

Tarmo ROBAL[1] and Ahto KALJA
Department of Computer Engineering, Tallinn University of Technology

Abstract. Websites employ different structures to provide information to visitors. Nevertheless, users are browsing the web according to their informational needs and comprehensions of the sites, based on the conceptual model in their mind. This delivers a good basis for evaluating web-based systems. Herein we propose a framework for web systems evaluation on the basis of users' actions. Exploiting a special log system and techniques of web usage mining, typical navigational patterns are recognized. As a result, measures for system evaluation are proposed with experimental data.

Keywords. web usage mining, web log, web system evaluation and improvement

Introduction

The Internet, consisting of websites in various forms, delivers an enormous source of information and has become an ordinary part of our life. While browsing, users follow certain patterns of behaviour, heavily dependent on their approach to the subject area rather than the conceptual model applied by the sites' authors. Factors as site attractiveness, visual experience, navigation organization, placement of objects, colour schema and page loading time [1-4] have also an effect on users' browsing behaviour. In real life it is quite easy for users to explicitly state what they are searching for and how they prefer to do it. However, for the web world the inability to do so remains a major drawback and calls for different methods for adapting web systems to the needs of users. Logging users' actions and analysing those afterwards can however reveal users intentions to some extent.

Commonly, web usage mining (WUM) for adaptive web, web personalization, and recommender systems are exploited on collected user and web system interaction data to provide users with customized views to web pages or dynamically discovered (personalized) recommendations assisting them to find needed information. This is accomplished via helping users to discover pages or page-sets they otherwise might not find during their site visit, e.g., by rising or highlighting certain navigation elements.

Still, little attention is paid to web sites usage and on the possibilities of improving it by studying users' behaviour. Typically, sites are developed according to the domain model established by the web development team. This model however may be different from the general conceptual model of the actual users, undetectable beforehand. Thus,

[1] Corresponding Author: Tarmo Robal, Tallinn University of Technology, Raja 15, 12618 Tallinn, Estonia; E-mail: tarmo@pld.ttu.ee.

there exists a gap between the conceptual model applied during development and the model employed by the actual users after system release.

We claim that logging users' actions and analysing their behaviour can be valuable in eliminating the aforementioned gap and deliver improvements to the web site and its structure. To detect the necessity for such an elimination process, the system needs to be evaluated based on users' behaviour efficiency. In this paper, we propose a framework to model users' behaviour for web systems evaluation along with needed measures and experimental results. The value of our research also relies in a fact that we have throughout the work compared initial and repeated visits made by the users.

The research is based on the interaction data collected on the website of the Department of Computer Engineering (DCE) at Tallinn University of Technology, run by the web kernel developed at our lab. The DCE web is aimed to deliver information to general public and serve as an environment for research and development.

The rest of the paper is organized as follows. Section 1 reviews related research by other authors and presents our previous work, connected to these studies. Section 2 discusses collecting and mining of web usage data. In section 3, we consider user behaviour modelling and measures for web systems evaluation with the results of our study performed at the DCE website. In section 4, we draw conclusions.

1. Related Works

The research in the field of WUM has mainly concentrated on analysing users' actions or trying to predict those by analysing web server logs, or using customized web browsers for that. Still, one has to consider that HTTP traffic logs are flawed [5] and issues of data incompleteness exist [6,7] with inability to identify visitor sessions [8].

The applied methods for data collection vary from implicit to explicit, where active participation of users is needed. Yet, researches have not yet come to a common understanding which method is the best to be exploited. Explicit data collection methods are useful in providing users' opinions and ideas; however users are usually not willing to actively participate in any evaluations, moreover to fill in forms. Sarwar et al. [9] concluded in their study that even though explicit rating provided by the users is precise, users are not willing to rate each page they visit, thus it cannot be as efficient as expected. Moreover, many authors [10,11] oppose to explicit rating, claiming it to disturb and greatly affect users' browsing activities and behaviour. Implicit techniques, usually involving data collection from server, proxy or client level using web server logs, modified browsers, or special log systems [6], help to overcome these disadvantages and provide a rather good accuracy. Al halabi et al. report in [12] an accuracy of more than 90% obtained by using implicit rating.

Users' interest towards web pages is another issue to be considered when talking about user behaviour on the web. Hofgesang outlines in [13] that the vast majority of WUM researchers usually apply a list of web pages visited and the order of these pages to express user interest, not paying any attention on time spent on pages (TSP). He argues that TSP is a clear and natural indicator of importance of a page in WUM - the more time users spend on a web page, the more important it is assumed to be. We consent to this, while the question of large TSP values remains unopened. In our research, we have found TSP to be a valuable part of interest indication, though we believe it should be used together with other measures, as has been done herein.

In our previous research we have studied the extraction of user profiles from the web usage data for providing recommendations for online user based on active profile discovery [14]. In [15] we proposed a new method for learning users' domain models in order to provide personalisation services, giving conceptual meaning to web usage mining results by using ontologies and automatic classification of concepts via ontology reasoning as a part of the system. As a result of our web mining studies, we have developed and put into operation a model for users' action prediction based on locality profiles [16]. Having gained the expertise in the field, we are able to analyse users' behaviour and propose the framework and measures for web systems evaluation.

2. Implicit Web System Usage Data Gathering

Automated and implicit data gathering methods enable to monitor pages users view, navigational paths they follow as well as to discover usage patterns. Using web mining techniques to model users' behaviour based on the collected log data, allows to evaluate web-based systems and their usage efficiency. Generally, web mining is divided into three categories: (1) web content mining, (2) structure mining and (3) usage mining [17]. However, some authors also highlight fourth category called user profile mining [18]. Herein, we have concentrated on the usage mining and characterization through extracting users' navigational paths and locality profiles.

Mainly for the reasons outlined in Section 1, we applied implicit data collection methods to capture web usage data. In particular, we employed a special log system [19] developed by our research team in 2003, which presently is an extension to our web systems kernel, enabling to capture data for analyses discussed in [19] and providing sufficient basis for studies proposed herein. From captured data in the log, we used the following in our studies: (1) requested page, (2) client identifier (session based ID), (3) operations performed during a session, (4) operation timestamp, (5) recurrent visit identifier.

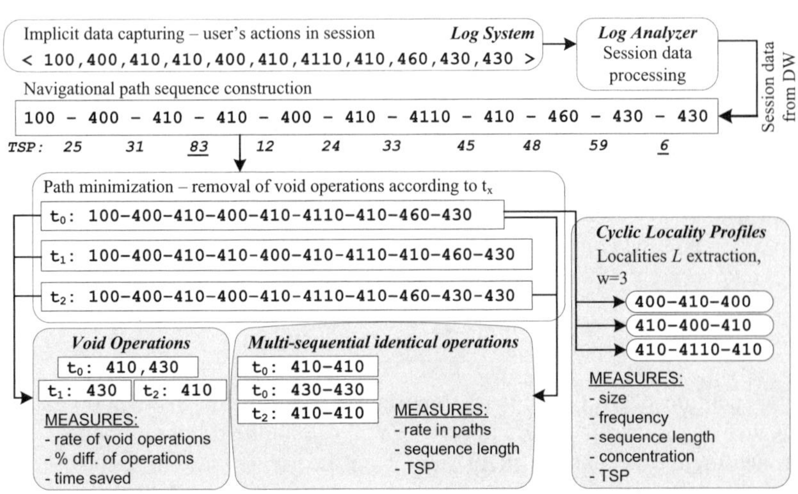

Figure 1. Implicit gathering of users' behaviour data and its processing into navigational paths for system evaluation. Process overview and an example

The collected usage log contains raw access data, which needs to be cleaned from noise and filtered before extracting users' navigational paths. Figure 1 describes the processing of usage data. Users' actions on the website are collected by the Log System and processed into session data using the Log Analyser tool. We derived 269 782 navigational paths as series of unique numerical identifiers set for each page in the web site management system in the order and occurrence of visited pages. Then, minimization procedures were applied on the paths according to the TSP thresholds. The majority of sessions (87.1%) were classified as non-recurrent, leaving 12.9% for sessions where returning users were identified. The produced paths describe users' behaviour while browsing the website and are basis for studies described here in further.

3. Measures for Web Systems Evaluation Based on Users Behaviour Modelling

Users are clicking items on websites while browsing and searching for information. With implicit data capturing techniques, these operations (clicks) can be stored in the log database along with timestamps, allowing to model users' behaviour afterwards and detect critical areas such as identical sequential operations and cyclic locality profiles in the followed navigational paths. Through this, web systems efficiency can be evaluated and a need for improvement detected. As discussed in [20], users are expecting websites to be easy to navigate, and contain accurate and up-to-date information amongst other features listed. The operations in the users' navigational paths with their attributes clearly describe the ease or difficulty of site navigability.

We claim that these navigational paths as users' behaviour patterns carry valuable information for evaluating web site usage accordance to its development model, indicating the gap existence between that model and the one users follow while browsing, and thus provide necessary basis for evaluation. Our framework for web systems evaluation contains the following models, which allow to identify some of the problematic areas and provide a basis for web system evaluation:

1. Void operations in navigational paths, with profit gained from minimization.
2. Multi-sequential identical operations in navigational paths.
3. Cyclic locality profiles in navigational paths.

In the models, sessions are classified into two categories: non-recurrent and recurrent. Non-recurrent sessions are initial web site visits, comprising also those visits, where the previous visit of that user could not be identified due to missing attributes, e.g. session cookie. For example, user has deleted the cookie or changed the computer or browser for accessing the website. Recurrent sessions are repeated site visits where a returning user is detected. A user session is defined as a sequence of accessed pages $s=\langle p_i, p_{i+1}, \ldots, p_n \rangle$, where $p_i \in P$ and P is the set of all the pages on the website. Figure 1 provides an overview of the evaluation models and related data processing.

3.1. Time Spent on Page

The time spent on pages (TSP) is an important indicator of user intention and interest towards web pages, and therefore plays a crucial role in the proposed models. The TSP can be measured either on the client side or on the server side. Srivastava et al. have found in their research [6] client- and server-side measure of TSP to be equal or in favour of server-side measuring because of the overhead on the client side. Ideally, the TSP is only the time user spent on particular page. Nevertheless, factors such as the time spent for page generation on the server, time spent on data transfer over the network and the effect of user distraction have to be also considered. From the aforementioned factors, user distraction as a set of activities unrelated to browsing (e.g. breaks, chatting, etc.) is the most troublesome as it cannot be measured. Therefore, in practice, an upper limit for TSP is usually applied. The formula for the ideal TSP is given by Eq. (1), where t_i is the timestamp of a given operation. For the DCE website the $t_{page\_generation}$ is averagely 0.07 seconds with a few higher peaks at high server load times, not exceeding the average of 0.1 seconds. Usually page sizes are a few hundred kilobytes making the transfer component in Eq. (1) small compared to other elements. Taking these facts into account, the TSP in our studies is given by Eq. (2).

$$t_{TSP} = t_{i+1} - t_i - t_{page\_generation} - t_{transfer} - t_{user\_distraction} \tag{1}$$

$$t_{TSP} = t_{i+1} - t_i - t_{page\_generation} \tag{2}$$

According to [21] users are unable to accurately assess interest towards a page in less than 5 second, evaluating the importance of the information found on the page during the first few seconds [22]. The averages for web page view times as a measure of interest rate however vary from 12 seconds [23] to 48 seconds [24]. For the DCE website the average TSP is 36 seconds for non-recurring visits and 29 seconds for repeated visits. This corresponds to the findings of other authors.

Weinreich et al. [23] have found that nearly in 50% of cases users were spending less than 12 seconds on visited pages, leading to a conclusion that they browsed for a next page before reading a substantial part of the page contents. Moreover, the experiments in [13] refer to a fact that the more users visit a page the less time they spend on it, evidently due to becoming familiar with the pages. Obviously, there exists a strong tendency for users to spend more time on pages they find interesting compared to those they find not so interesting, with a non-linear reference to page rank [12]. These aspects of TSP have also been considered in the proposed evaluation models.

3.2. Void Operations in Navigational Paths

The reconstructed user navigational paths as behaviour patterns may contain repeated sequential operations, meaning users have made for some reason more clicks than it would be necessary according to the planned flow through the site. These repeated operations form a set of void operations that could have been avoided. The level of void operations mirrors the site's usage efficiency, and thus is considered one of the measures in our framework. Evidently, a low or zero level of void operations depicts a clear website structure easily understandable by users. The evaluation herein is provided through the following measures:

- The difference between the actual navigational path and the minimized path (void operations removed), see Figure 1.
- Average number of void operations, and time-saving achieved.

In our research, we were looking at three possibilities for minimizing the navigational paths, while detecting redundant operations. Hence, we searched for such p_i in $s = \langle p_i, p_{i+1}, \ldots, p_n \rangle$ where $p_i = p_{i+1}$ and TSP(p_i) satisfied the threshold condition t_x according to Eq. (3), where t_{TSP} is time spent on p_i.

$$t_x = \begin{cases} x = 0, t_{TSP} \text{ not considered} \\ x = 1, t_{TSP} < T_{min} \,||\, t_{TSP} > T_{max} \\ x = 2, T_{min} \le t_{TSP} \le T_{max} \end{cases} \quad (3)$$

Applying t_0, results in a fully minimized navigational path, as all identical sequential operations are considered to be one. With t_1 and t_2 the classification of void operations depends on TSP as a measure of interest rate. We defined T_{min} as 5 seconds and T_{max} 60 seconds, except for t_0, considering the average TSP-s and the presumption that once visited, the user most probably will not access that page again in that timeframe. Pages visited after T_{max} are defined as intentional visits. Clicks made to force the page load faster and accidental (double-) clicks are excluded by condition t_1.

Table 1. Evaluation measures for void operations, calculations for the DCE website.

Measure of evaluation	**Non-recurrent sessions**			**Recurrent sessions**		
Threshold t_x	t_0	t_1	t_2	t_0	t_1	t_2
Average session length [sec]	374.9	837.9	493.1	308.1	482.7	317.9
Average session length for minimized path [sec]	231.4	830.8	194.5	240.4	477.1	235.2
Average time saved through minimization [sec]	143.5	7.1	298.5	67.7	5.7	82.7
Average void operations per session	1.4	0.3	1.1	0.8	0.3	0.5
Average % of void operations	38.0	6.5	31.8	17.9	4.5	13.7

The analysis of void operations in sessions (Table 1) revealed returning visitors to perform less such operations than those visiting it for the first time, as having become familiar with the site. The results show that there exist void operations, particularly with non-recurrent visits. Ideally, the level of such operations is at zero; however in reality we can be satisfied with averagely one void operation per session. Nevertheless, the most accessed patterns and their respective number of void operations have to be studied closely by a domain expert, taking into account the content of the page itself, to identify the nature of the problem and propose necessary acts for site improvement, if needed. Out of the studied sessions, only 10.7% contained void operations in the DCE case, which we consider to be good result, with a possibility for small improvement. The average amount of void operations is satisfactory low, although the almost three times higher rate for non-recurrent visits compared to recurrent visits is alarming and indicating possible problems of easily understanding the navigational structure at once. Thus, an in-depth study into the most frequent void operation patterns is needed.

3.3. Multi-Sequential Identical Operations in Navigational Paths

Multi-sequential identical operations, as the name implies, are a type of void operations with the exception that only the operations which are identical and made in the timeframe defined by threshold t_2 are counted. Thus, operations made during normal page view, when ideally there should not be any identical sequential operations, are of interest. If the time between two sequential identical operations is less than 5 seconds (T_{min}), the page was probably not accurately assessed by the user (as discussed in

Section 3.1), and if exceeds T_{max}, the page was probably reloaded or revisited. These operations belong to the domain of threshold t_1 and are not of interest herein.

We studied sessions where at least one of the operations was declared void, and constructed two models (for thresholds t_0 and t_2), performing calculations for the attributes shown in Table 2. Figure 1 shows an example of the process. Special attention needs to be paid to pages where users are usually going forth and back; for instance selecting news items from the list for full text reading etc. That kind of operations raise the number of identical sequential operations and interfere the interpretation of the results, as the target is on pages where such flow is not planned.

In our study, we extracted 33 158 such sequential paths for further analysis. The results (Table 2) once again confirm that returning users make less redundant operations also in the series of void operations. The majority of sequential operations (74%) were made after viewing a page more than 60 seconds. As seen, the percentage of sessions containing void operations is low (below 4% for non-recurrent visits and 1.3% for recurrent visits); yet the rate for first time visitors is a bit too high (3 times higher) compared to returning users, indicating that the structure might be too fuzzy for users to catch at once, causing the efficiency of information seek to suffer. Yet, the time between sequential operations refers to pages being viewed normally. The fact that the number of identical sequential operations is nearly 3 for t_2 is alarming, showing that there were sequences with more than two identical operations. Ideally, this number is 2.0 (the minimum required for a sequence to appear). Studying the results closer, we found a few sessions containing even 7 sequential identical operations. These sessions now need in-depth analysis of user behaviour and proper actions taken to minimize such identical operations in users browsing behaviour and are an interest of future studies. Sequential operations are inevitable and having no such operations over all the users' sessions is unreachable. The measure of efficiency is set on how many sequential operations users have in their sessions, evidently the less the better. Still, the results provide necessary measures for web systems evaluation at this point.

Table 2. Characterization of multi-sequential identical operations for sessions containing such operations.

Evaluation measures	Non-recurrent sessions	Recurrent sessions
% of sessions with multi-sequential identical operations (t_0) [%]	12.8	3.3
% of sessions with multi-sequential identical operations (t_2) [%]	3.9	1.3
Average number of identical sequential operations in sequence for t_0	3.3	2.8
Average number of identical sequential operations in sequence for t_2	2.8	2.7
Time between identical sequential operations for t_0 [sec]	607.6	458.9
Time between identical sequential operations for t_2 [sec]	24.4	21.0

3.4. Cyclic Operations in Users' Navigational Paths

The cycles in the users' navigational paths also render the efficiency of the web site usage. Short cycles refer to navigational fuzziness and rapid browsing. Therefore, they need to be carefully studied and possibilities for their elimination established.

To analyse the cyclic operations, we applied the locality model described and successfully employed in [14-16], as it is a convenient way to study user behaviour and is a continuation of our previous work. The locality model is based on the belief that if a large number of users frequently access a set of pages, then these pages must be related. The locality itself is defined by the users nearest activity history within the site, which is represented by the w latest operations. All the cyclic locality profiles $L=p_j, p_{j+1}, \ldots, p_m$ of size w are constructed based on fully minimized navigational paths such that $p_j = p_m$. The process is described on Figure 1. We were particularly keen on cyclic profiles of w=3 describing the nearest history of users operations. Also, previously we have found that the best suitable locality size for the DCE website is 3.

The efficiency is measured through the following:

- The size, frequency and concentration of cyclic locality profiles in sessions.
- TSP for cyclic profiles and number of operations needed for a cycle to occur.

3.4.1. The Size and Frequency of Cyclic Locality Profiles

The size and frequency of cyclic locality profiles allows to explore the round-connected page-sets, which are not usually planned into the normal flow of website browsing during the site development. Nevertheless, users browse the web differently, also making cycles in their browsing paths. The latter indicates either navigation fuzziness or a need for restructuring. We found cyclic profiles in 33 813 sessions out of 269 782 sessions, performing tests for locality sizes w=3 up to w=10. This was done in order to compare the results and observe the trends, although, in most of the cases, we should only be concerned about short cycles, e.g., w=3.

The distribution of cyclic profiles for different w is shown on Figure 2. As can be seen, the number of cyclic profiles in sessions occurred to be higher for non-recurrent visits; as expected returning users had fewer cycles in their navigational paths, due to already being familiar with the site. The frequency of cyclic profiles in sessions is clearly in inverse proportional relation to profile size. Evidently, the shorter the cycle is, the problematic it becomes, as this is not an efficient way of seeking information and the user is likely to be lost in the website structure. Nevertheless, without explicit studies the possibility of user returning to previously visited page to remind the content presented there cannot be ruled out.

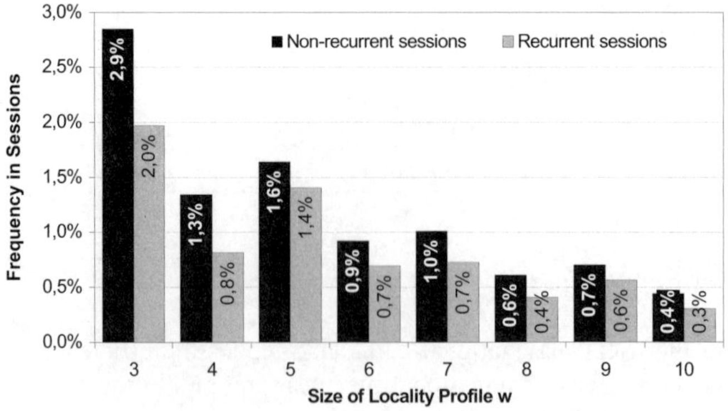

Figure 2. Concentration of cyclic profiles in sessions. Comparison for locality profiles sizes w=3..10

The concentration of cycles in navigational paths provides a measure of browsing efficiency. Each navigational path can contain zero or more cyclic profiles. The concentration rate shows the amount of cyclic profiles found in paths. Such cyclic profiles seem to occur more often on websites with problematic navigation structure. If the concentration is below 0.25, i.e. there occur cycles in less than quarter of the sessions, one can still consider it as a fairly good result.

As can be seen from Figure 2, cyclic profiles were found in less than 3% of non-recurrent sessions and less than 2% of recurrent sessions, showing a low rate of such profiles. Analysing the concentration of cyclic profiles, we found the average value to be 0.1, implying there are no major problems with cyclic operations on the DCE website. The small difference in the concentration rate between first-time and returning users is normal. Larger differences however refer to a need to consider revising the navigation, to mitigate the difference, thus bring the navigation closer to users.

3.4.2. TSP in Cyclic Profiles and Number of Operations Needed for Cycle to Occur

The number of operations needed for a cycle to appear shows in general how many operations are made before a cycle occurs in users navigational paths. Obviously, the higher this number is, the better is the performance. Our experiments (Figure 3) showed that this is most certainly bigger than the locality profile itself, to contain a fair amount of operations, including the cycle itself. In the worst case, the number of operations needed for cycle occurrence equals the cycle size. For sessions, which had at least one cyclic profile in it, the reference value was 9.2 operations needed for a cycle to occur. For all sessions this was 60.9 operations. For the shortest and most important cycle (w=3), the average was 23.2 operations per cycle occurrence, which is almost 8 times more than the cycle length itself, and can be considered a good result. We also analysed the cycle duration and discovered that interestingly the length of the cycle is in favour of recurring visits, due to longer page views ($TSP_{average}$ =20.4 seconds).

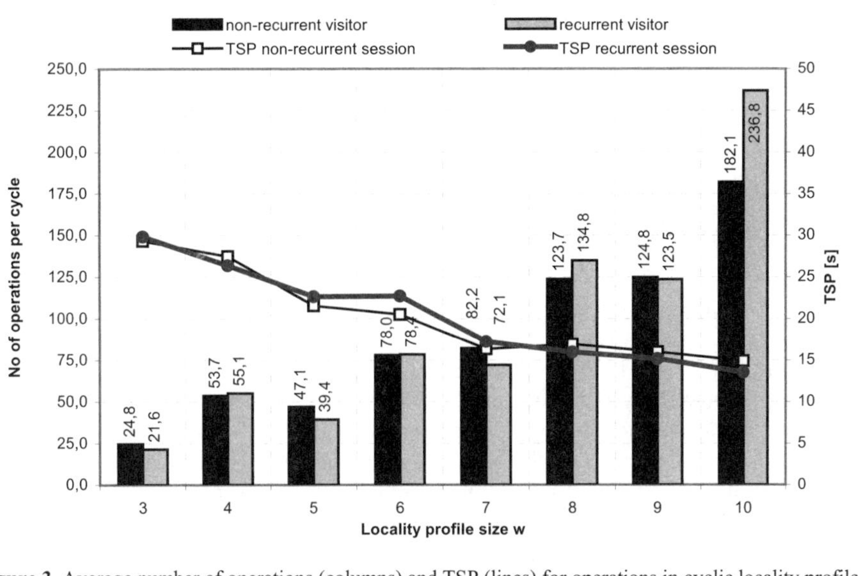

Figure 3. Average number of operations (columns) and TSP (lines) for operations in cyclic locality profiles

3.4.3. Evaluation and Elimination of Cyclic Profiles

Having discussed the measures for cyclic profiles evaluation, and showing that normally cycles occur despite of the success of the development, since users act differently employing various browsing patterns, let us turn to the aspects of evaluating the cycles in sense of their importance and possibilities of eliminating them.

As discussed, short cycle times refer to navigational fuzziness and rapid browsing. Here, we need to concentrate on those cyclic locality profiles, which occur the most in the results and have the shortest cycle durations. We define the short cycle time through the profile size w and TSP-s as provided by Eq. (4). Assuming that short time memory of humans lasts from 20 seconds to a few minutes, Eq. (4) provides classification sufficient enough to rule out cyclic profiles originated from user distraction, which are not a topic of our interest.

Of particular interest are cyclic locality profiles with high rank values, as these are the most commonly performed by users and therefore mirror the fuzziness in users navigation and thus the need to improve the navigation for those particular operations, for instance via highlighting something or restructuring some parts of the system. Using descending ordering of cyclic locality profiles based on the frequency is not considered the best solution for evaluating the profiles as the behaviour of users changes over time. Also, time spent on viewing pages, i.e., cycle duration has to be taken into account. Therefore, we propose to use ranking calculated of interest rate, inverse time, and TSP-s, given by Eq. (5). The frequency rate in the formula is the number of cyclic profile occurrences during Age(i) measured in days. TSP_C reflects the total time spent on pages in the cycle. This clearly gives more adequate results than just summing up the occurrences as a rank, which is traditionally done in WUM for page ranking, as referred in [13]. When we compared our results of Eq. (5) to the traditional WUM methods, the difference was obvious. For instance, a cyclic locality profile with occurrence rate of 428 gained rank 17.1, whereas profile with rate 241 gained rank of 40.2. As proven, the provided ranking algorithm enables better differentiation of cyclic profiles according to their usage and users' interest rate.

Thus, Eqs. (4) and (5) allow to filter out the most significant cyclic locality profiles for their further evaluation and actions of elimination. Before taking further actions, pre-planned cycles of that web system have to be identified to sort out the critical ones.

$$T_{short\_cycle\_time} < 2 * w * t_{TSP} \tag{4}$$

$$Rank_i = \sum_{i=1}^{n} \frac{\text{Frequency rate(i)} * TSP_C(i)}{\text{Age(i)}} \tag{5}$$

3.5. Discussion on Improving Web Systems

The proposed framework enables through its measures to indicate the possible need for improvement in web systems and provides a basis to minimize the gap between the conceptual model applied during development and the model employed by the actual users. In practice, this means that an expert of that web system must interpret the results, identifying the nature and criticalness of each of the problem. This leads into deeper research of the collected log data, and if needed, until the particular user session. For instance, reasons for void operations might rely in refreshing the page or in long response times (e.g. heavy server load, malfunctioning query, page overloaded with information), and users are usually sending another request for a page after a few seconds already. The emphasis is on the most accessed patterns with their respective number of void operations or cyclic profiles (also refer to Section 3.4.3).

Having identified the critical areas, conducting explicit studies with test user group (preferably unfamiliar with the web system) and a set of tasks on the previously identified critical areas, can provide valuable knowledge about the problems and possible improvement actions. Sometimes, simple restructuring or renaming of items can produce significant improvement through bringing the two conceptual models closer. Once modifications have been introduced, changes to measure results occur with a delay due to the applied algorithms and also the users, especially those revisiting the site, as they may find the site now unfamiliar for them.

As the scope of this paper was to provide a framework for evaluations indicating the need for improvement, we herein limit our discussion to the above.

4. Conclusions

The importance of the Internet and applications based on it has rapidly increased in our lives during the recent years. While browsing the enormous amount of information available on the Internet, users follow certain patterns of behaviour according to their view of the subject domain. This however may be different from the one set up for the site by its developers, introducing a gap between those two conceptual models. Taking advantage of implicit data collection and web usage mining, users' navigational paths for behavioural analyses can be constructed and methods applied to mitigate this gap.

In this paper we have developed a framework for web systems evaluation based on users' behaviour modelling. Fully automated log system was used for collecting data about users' actions on a website. These actions were modelled into navigational paths and processed to provide evaluation measures. The proposed framework provides necessary basis for evaluating web systems and allows to identify some of the problematic areas. It does not provide a 'silver-bullet' solution, and usually designers are competent enough to avoid large errors. Nevertheless, designers have no abilities to predict the sites' actual usage and its changing trends. Thus, evaluations based on users' behaviour modelling are needed to improve web based systems.

References

[1] Bernard, M. L. (2001) User Expectations for the Location of Web Objects. In Proceedings of CHI'01 Conference: Human Factors in Computing Systems, Seattle, USA, March 31 - April 5, pp. 171-172.

[2] Geissler, G., Zinkhan, G., & Watson, R. (2001) Web Home Page Complexity and Communication Effectiveness, Journal of the Association for Information Systems, 2(2): 1-48

[3] Bernard, M. L., & Chaparro, B. S. (2000) Searching within websites: A Comparison of Three Types of Sitemap Menu Structures. In Proc. of The Human Factors and Ergonomics Society 44th Annual Meeting in San Diego, pp. 441-444. (available at http://psychology.wichita.edu/hci/projects/sitemap.pdf)

[4] Lee, A.T. (1999) Web Usability: a Review of the Research, ACM SIGCHI Bulletin, 31(1): 38- 40

[5] Davison, B. (1999) Web Traffic Logs: An Imperfect Resource for Evaluation. In Proceedings of Ninth Annual Conference of the Internet Society (INET '99), June 22-25, San Jose, CA, (available at http://www.isoc.org/inet99/proceedings/4n/4n_1.htm)

[6] Srivastava, J. Cooley, R., Deshpande, M., & Tan, P-T. (2000) Web Usage Mining: Discovery and Applications of Usage Patterns from Web Data, SIGKDD Explorations, 1(2): 12-23

[7] Mobasher, B., Cooley, R., & Srivastava. J. (2000) Automatic Personalization Based on Web Usage Mining, Communications of the ACM, 43(8): 142-151

[8] Kimball, R., & Margy, R. (2002) The Data Warehouse Toolkit: The Complete Guide to Dimensional Modelling. John Wiley & Sons, 2002, 2nd ed., 464 p.

[9] Sarwar, B., Konstan, J., Borchers, A., Herlocker, J., Miller, B., & Reidl, J. (1998) Using Filtering Agents to Improve Prediction Quality in the GroupLens Research Collaborative Filtering System. In Proceedings of ACM Conference on Computer Supported Collaborative Work (CSCW), November 14-18, Seattle, Washington, USA, pp. 345-354.

[10] Middleton, S. E., Shadbolt, N. R., & De Roure, D. C. (2003). Capturing Interest through Inference and Visualization: Ontological User Profiling in Recommender Systems. In Proceedings of the 2nd International Conference on Knowledge Capture, October 23 - 25, Sanibel Is-land, FL, USA, pp. 62-69.

[11] Shapira, B., Taieb-Maimon, M., & Moskowitz, A. (2006) Study of Usefulness of Known and New Implicit Indicators and Their Optimal Combination for Accurate Inference of Users Interest. In Proceedings of the 2006 ACM Symposium on Applied Computing (SAC '06), April 23 -27, Dijon, France, pp. 1118-1119.

[12] Al halabi, W.S., Kubat, M., & Tapia, M. (2007) Time Spent on a Web Page is Sufficient to Infer a User's Interest, In Proceedings of the IASTED European Conference: internet and multimedia systems and applications, March 14-16, Chamonix, France, pp. 41-46

[13] Hofgesang, P.I. (2006) Relevance of Time Spent on Web Pages. WEBKDD'06: Knowledge Discovery on the Web, ACM SIGKDD Workshop on Web Mining and Web Usage Analysis, August 20-23, Philadelphia, Pennsylvania, USA, (available at http://webmining.spd.louisville.edu/webkdd06/papers/paper-13-Relevance-of-time-spent-Webpages-WM_1082%5B1%5D.pdf)

[14] Robal, T., & Kalja, A. (2007) Applying User Profile Ontology for Mining Web Site Adaptation Recommendations. In Ioannidis, Y., Novikov, B. & Rachev, B. (eds) 11th East-European Conference on Advances in Databases and Information Systems (ADBIS 2007), September 29 - October 03, Varna, Bulgaria., pp. 126-135.

[15] Robal, T., Haav, H-M., & Kalja, A. (2007) Making Web Users' Domain Models Explicit by Applying Ontologies. In Hainaut, J.-L., et. Al (eds) Advances in Conceptual Modeling - Foundations and Applications: ER 2007 Workshops CMLSA, FP-UML,ONISW, QoIS, RIGiM, SeCoGIS, November 5-9, Auckland, New Zealand, Berlin: Springer, (LNCS), pp.170 - 179.

[16] Robal, T., & Kalja, A. (2008) A Model for Users' Action Prediction Based on Locality Profiles. In Lang,M.; Wojtkowski,W.; Wojtkowski,G.; Wrycza,S.; Zupancic,J. (eds). The Inter-Networked World: ISD Theory, Practice, and Education, Springer-Verlag: New York, ISBN 978-0387304038, to appear

[17] Kosala, R., & Blockeel, H. (2000) Web Mining Research: A Survey, ACM SIGKDD Explorations, 2(1): 1-15

[18] Li, Y., & Zhong, N. (2006) Mining Ontology for Automatically Acquiring Web User Information Needs. IEEE Transactions on Knowledge and Data Engineering, 18(4): 554-568

[19] Robal, T., Kalja, A., & Põld, J. (2006) Analysing the Web Log to Determine the Efficiency of Web Systems. In Vasilecas, O., Eder, J., & Caplinskas, A. (eds) Proceedings of the 7th International Baltic Conference on Databases and Information Systems (DB&IS'2006), Communications, July 03-06, Vilnius, Lithuania, pp. 264-275.

[20] Zhang, P., & Dran, G. (2001) Expectations and Rankings of Website Quality Features: Results of Two Studies on User Perceptions. In Proceedings of the 34th Annual Hawaii international Conference on System Sciences (Hicss-34)-Volume 7, January 03-06, HICSS, IEEE Computer Society, Washington, DC, p.7019

[21] Farzan, R., & Brusilovsky, P. (2005) Social navigation support in e-learning: What are real footprints? In Proceedings of IJCAI'05 Workshop on Intelligent Techniques for Web Personalization, July 30-August 5, Edinburgh, Scotland, pp 49–56.

[22] Pan, B., Hembrooke, H. A., Gay, G. K., Granka, L. A., Feusner, M. K., & Newman, J. K. (2004) The determinants of web page viewing behavior: an eye-tracking study. In Proc. of the 2004 Symposium on Eye Tracking Research & Applications, March 22 – 24, San Antonio, Texas, USA, pp.147-154.

[23] Weinreich, H., Obendorf, H., Herder, E., & Mayer, M. (2006) Off the Beaten Tracks: Exploring Three Aspects of Web Navigation. In Proceedings of the 15th International Conference on World Wide Web (WWW '06), May 23 - 26, Edinburgh, Scotland, pp. 133-142.

[24] Rafter, R., & Smyth, B. (2001). Passive Profiling from Server Logs in an Online Recruitment Environment. In Proceedings of the IJCAI Workshop on Intelligent Techniques for Web Personalization (ITWP 2001), August 4-10, Seattle, WA, USA, pp. 35-41.

Databases and Information Systems V
H.-M. Haav and A. Kalja (Eds.)
IOS Press, 2009

doi:10.3233/978-1-58603-939-4-53

Domain Ontology Based Support to Navigation in Distance Study Course Structure

Lina TANKELEVICIENE[1] and Dale DZEMYDIENE
Software Engineering Department, Institute of Mathematics and Informatics

Abstract. We explore the possibility to improve typical Learning management system (LMS) by integrating modern achievements in the fields of semantic web, and especially, ontology engineering. Ontologies gain its popularity due to ability 1) to implement reuse on knowledge level; and 2) to enhance information retrieval processes. Automatically conducted information retrieval allows to increase effectiveness of human-computer interaction processes, which is also important in e-Learning processes. In this article, we analyse the possibilities and types of reasoning over different ontology elements. Then we explore a theoretically proposed framework for conceptual linking of educational resources, which is intended to support learners' navigation in Distance Study Course (DSC). We demonstrate the application of the proposed framework by the means of a designed scenario with real domain ontology and concrete pedagogical goals in mind: to automatically form a dynamical navigational menu in order to foster predictable learning paths.

Keywords. domain ontology, e-Learning, reasoning, knowledge engineering, linking educational resources

Introduction

The technical infrastructure for distance studies has increased rapidly in Lithuania during the last years, including Siauliai University and Lithuanian Virtual University, established in 2007. Despite of that, we still lack enough distance study courses (DSC) of high quality and corresponding activities for promoting e-Learning processes. Besides of clear view of leadership of organisation towards e-learning, well formulated strategy and explicitly expressed supporting activities, we need to develop and employ scientific engineering methods in order to achieve more effective development/delivery processes. These methods must be based both on sound technological and pedagogical theories.

From the technological point of view, we explore the possibility to improve a typical Learning management system (LMS) by integrating modern achievements in the fields of semantic web, and especially, ontology engineering and querying. In [1], we presented the scope and purpose of ontology for 'E-learning technologies' DSC and analysed our experience in the ontology development process. In [2], we analysed deductive reasoning over ontology components (concepts, properties, instances) and

[1] Corresponding Author: Lina Tankeleviciene, Institute of Mathematics and Informatics, Akademijos str. 4, LT-08663 Vilnius, Lithuania; E-mail: lina.tankeleviciene@gmail.com.

proposed a conceptual view, how these reasoning mechanisms can be employed at run-time. In this article, we consider the importance of navigation of learners throughout DSC structure, deepen the specification of our approach and explain how our approach of incorporating of domain ontology and implementing reasoning over it can enhance functionality of a LMS.

There are four main ways to organise information chunks in any information intensive environments, including e-Learning environments: 1) sequence, where information is presented linearly; 2) grid, where information is explored using two axes and where information chunks have quite uniform structure; 3) hierarchy, which is a typical structure for web sites; and 4) web-based, where information chunks are associated each with another according to relations of overall topic or separate words. DSC can support different information organisation structures at different levels. Requirements for information structure at the highest level depend on the final goal of DSC, for example, it can be expressed as '*support learners at their workplaces*' or '*present formal University level study course*'. DSCs usually use modular structure. For example, the *Topics* course format is used most often in our courses, delivered using MOODLE LMS. This format encourages students to work with material and learning activities sequentially. The *Weekly* format even stronger defines leaning process, because it determines dates for each topic. These formats sometimes don't correlate with pedagogical strategy or teaching/learning methods used, for example, where free exploration, long-term project-based activities are preferred. However, they don't forbid jumping from one chunk to another, if they are linked, or from the global content. On the other hand, the overused possibility to link any two chunks makes the overall information structure more complex, and usability and easiness to manage the learning process decreases. Therefore, the aim of our approach is to find a *golden mean* between flexibility and usability from one side, and control, provided by the system, from another side.

The aim of this paper is to explore a theoretically proposed framework for the conceptual linking of educational resources, substantiate it by scenario design, and show its implementation by illustrative running examples.

The structure of the paper is as follows. In Section 1 we present related works. Section 2 presents some remarks on interoperability of ontology and current web technologies. Section 3 analyses the background on domain ontology based reasoning and information retrieval. Section 4 explores theoretically proposed framework for conceptual linking of educational resources, which is intended to support learners' navigation in DSC. Section 5 demonstrates the application of the proposed framework by the means of a designed scenario with real domain ontology and concrete pedagogical goals in mind: to automatically form dynamical navigational menu in order to foster predictable learning paths. Finally, Section 6 presents conclusions and plans for future research.

1. Related Works

The topics of ontology engineering are comprehensively described in [3, 4, 5], including methods and methodologies for the development of ontologies, ontology development process and lifecycle, ontology tools and languages. The importance of methodology based ontology engineering is recognized, but applications of ontology are still analysed more widely than ontology engineering itself. Therefore there are not plenty of widely acceptable domain ontologies and the multiple-ontology approach still remains popular.

Besides other different areas of applicability, semantic web technologies – ontologies, agents, web services – can help in engineering of e-Learning and intensive research is carried in this field. The overviews of new possibilities of semantic web technologies for e-Learning are presented in [6, 7, 8]. Domain ontologies play an important role in approaches, presented in [9, 10]. Students' modelling and adaptation processes, based on ontologies, are analysed in [11, 12, 13, 14]. Several authors analyse the development of domain ontologies for specific subjects such as teaching programming in C [15], improving the English financial language studies [9], secondary school mathematics [16]. Other papers deal with frameworks or recommendations for ontology development [17, 18], intended for domain experts.

Analysis of scientific publications, projects documents and publicly accessible ontology libraries uncover two aspects:

- In most cases new architectural solutions are proposed. But in the same time the achievements in the design of virtual learning environments are not considered. Therefore, we aim at improving a LMS while integrating modern achievements in the fields of semantic web, and especially, ontology engineering.
- The development of domain ontology manually remains actual problem due to the lack of the existing ontologies or the lack of accessibility to them. Therefore, we need to get more effectiveness from the use of ontology at run-time.

2. Some Remarks on Interoperability of Ontology and Current Web Technologies

Some remarks must be made on interoperability of ontology and current web technologies. In order to gain better popularity and adoption, ontologies must be integrated into the current web technologies. Therefore, analysis and selection of the better tools for ontology modelling and managing at run-time is very important issue.

The choice of technologies for the development phase is conducted as a two-part process: we have to pick a language for ontology representation and for ontology reasoning/querying. In both cases, we turned our attention to standards, because the adoption of standards is very important for widely spreading an approach, framework or methodology. The first ontology languages were introduced in about 1990. The spread of Internet influenced other generation of ontology languages, so called Web-based ontology languages, including SHOE, XOL, DAML+OIL, RDF, RDF Schema, OWL. The last one, Ontology Web Language (OWL) was proposed as W3C recommendation in 2004 [19] and now it is actively used. On the other hand, Unified Modeling Language (UML) is very popular and widely adopted in the software engineering field. Arguments for choosing UML are clearly stated in [20, 21]. We think that UML is oriented and is better for ontology modelling, and OWL – for ontology engineering, therefore, we choose OWL.

According to the levels of expressiveness, OWL provides three sublanguages [19]: 1) OWL Lite supports classification hierarchies and simple constraints. It is intended to support in different tools and easier migration. 2) OWL DL supports more expressiveness, but still supports computational completeness and decidability. OWL DL allow us to use all possible OWL language constructs, but some use cases are additionally restricted (for example, a class cannot be an instance of another class). 3) OWL Full provides maximum expressiveness with no computational guarantees. The less expressiveness the language provides, the better reasoning mechanisms are implemented. This is very important in the context of immediate feedback generation and increasing the efficiency of a system in common and simple tasks. We choose OWL DL for our implementation of the framework.

Also we have to choose a Semantic Web toolkit. The last standard for querying ontology is SPARQL – Simple Protocol and RDF Query Language [22]. We need to integrate it with typical LAMP (Linux+Apache+MySQL+PHP) system, as it is LMS MOODLE. Therefore, we choose RAP – a software package for parsing, querying, manipulating, serializing and serving RDF models [23]. It is a Semantic Web toolkit for PHP developers. Further the extending of this tool is foreseen by pOWL – web-based OWL editor [24], which incorporates RAP.

3. Domain Ontology Based Reasoning and Information Retrieval

3.1. Concepts of Ontology and Reasoning

Ontology concept has a various meanings in different sources. Some of the definitions, used in computer science field, are presented in [25]. We assume the following definition of ontology: 'Ontology is a conceptual specification that describes knowledge about a domain in a manner that is independent of epistemic states and state of affairs' [26]. This definition emphasizes that ontologies are universal models of domains or models of known knowledge in a domain.

Our research concerns using of domain ontology in order to acquire a common understanding of the learning subject domain among users of a LMS and software components. In this case, ontology must satisfy two main requirements: 1) It must be formalised in order a computer could process it; 2) It must be shared in order a community of experts of some field could agree with it and use it in applications. Therefore, we adopt a formal definition of ontology from [25], derived from logic and set theory. Ontology is a 4-tuple $<C, R, I, A>$, where C is a set of classes (concepts), R is a set of relations, I is a set of instances, and A is a set of axioms. ***Classes*** represent important concepts of the domain. Classes in the ontology are usually organised in taxonomies, where generalisation-specification mechanisms are applied. ***Relations*** represent associations between the concepts of a domain. Most often the *is-a* and *consist-of* relationships are used. However, the taxonomical structure is not the only one possible. Ontologies usually contain binary relations. The attributes are sometimes distinguished from relations. ***Instances*** (individuals) represent individuals in ontology. Instances can be defined in ontology or in database of factual data. ***Formal axioms*** are used for expressing propositions that are always true, e.g., in the *eLearning* course the same person can not be in the lecturer and in the student role at the same time. Formal axioms are used to infer new knowledge. If axioms are not included into ontology itself, reasoning mechanisms must be implemented in program side of the system.

One of the commonly used reasoning definitions is as follows: 'Reasoning is computing the implied relations' [27]. We restrict ourselves with reasoning, oriented towards Semantic Web. It means that we are planning to reason using knowledge, represented by the means of ontologies. And differently from the traditional AI systems, which use a 'closed-world' assumption, the Semantic Web uses an 'open-world' assumption. Therefore, while working in the Semantic Web domain, we restrict ourselves with monotonic reasoning. 'Open-world' consumption means, that context is open-ended: we don't know about what new information might appear (for example, what tools for e-Learning will be offered).

Also differently from traditional AI systems, reasoning over ontologies tends to be deductive, not inductive. It is a limitation, because deductive reasoning does not allow to learn something new. However, the purpose of domain ontologies is to represent domain and support retrieval of data. Therefore, the use of ontology unconsciously provides better capabilities and ontology driven information system differs qualitatively.

3.2. Reasoning Over Different Ontology Elements

Usually the reasoning must be conducted over two elements: the ontology itself (TBox) and the knowledge base, in which instances are described (ABox). TBox part contains terminology, and ABox part contains assertions.

For example, we want to get answers to the following questions, while teaching/learning about e-Learning tools:

- What kinds of Web site authoring tools are?
- Are there free tools for Web site authoring?

The first question requires only reasoning over TBox, where concepts, their classifications and other relations among concepts are represented. The second question requires reviewing of ABox, to extract records about Web site authoring tools and pay attention to the value of property *free*.

In [2], we analysed shortly two main approaches for reasoning in the Semantic Web: a) Query languages; and b) Logic-based formalisms. We have chosen query based reasoning due to the following reasons:

- It is simpler and easier to implement. And we argue that it is more efficient to implement if we consider typical and usual tasks of the user.
- It employs the main idea used in RDBMS (Relational Data Base Management Systems): the use of structured query language in order to extract data, which matches given pattern. Our solution is oriented towards extending present LMS, which already uses current web technologies, including Relational Databases.

The categorisation of reasoning over ontologies also can be conducted considering formalisms used. The types of reasoning according to [27] are listed in Table 1.

Table 1. Types of reasoning.

Type of reasoning	**Meaning**
Property level reasoning	Inferring implied triples *(subject, predicate, object)* from the stated ones.
Class level reasoning	Checking whether a class B is a subclass of class A. A separate case is classification - constructing a class hierarchy.
Individual level reasoning	Checking if an individual can exist in some model (consistency check). Two separable cases are: – Realisation is finding the classes of which an individual is a member. – Instance retrieval is finding all the known instances from the class.

Antoniou [28] lists the main reasoning tasks as follows: 1) Class membership; 2) Equivalence of classes; 3) Consistency; 4) Classification.

Also we consider that reasoning, as domain ontologies, can be used at development-time and at run-time. These two main processes of the e-Learning life cycle – development and delivering – are shown in Table 2, and the goals for implementing reasoning are listed in the second column. Mainly, harder support is required during the development, for example, verifying consistency. And during delivery, at run-time, it is enough of simpler querying over ontology components. In both cases, the approach allows to automatically perform functions previously performed by the lecturer.

Table 2. Ontology and reasoning at development-time and at run-time.

Entitlement	**Description**
Development of learning materials/activities using subject domain and instructional ontology (optional).	Constitutes from two different parts: 1) Content and services discovery and assembly; 2) Development of their own materials and/or activities. Tasks that can be realised: verifying completeness, consistency, timeliness, compatibility, linking of learning materials.
Teaching/learning process.	Includes adaptive course delivery, adaptive sequencing, adaptive presentation, adaptive interaction, and adaptive support. For example: 1) Adapting educational resources for students with different levels of learning progress; 2) Different starting point. Concepts belong to overlapped groups, which are important differently to different students; 3) Concept mapping, development of topics map (as evaluated task); 4) Free exploration of content, based on conceptual linking.

4. Domain Ontology Based Support to Navigation in Distance Study Course Structure

The description of our proposed framework for the conceptual linking of educational resources consists from several parts:

- The goals and preconditions. It describes the motivation based on pedagogical strategy used, and organisational aspects of context in which the framework can be used.
- Static view. It describes the static architecture of resources used. Separation of domain and media spaces is emphasized.
- Dynamic view. It presents activities in time. In our case, we develop the sequence for defining process dynamic rather than identify the process itself. The concrete process is presented in the case study.

4.1. Navigation in Distance Study Course Structure

Usually in DSC all educational resources and links to external resources are compiled by a lecturer. This is called manual linking. Ontology as a formal description of relations between different concepts allows to link resources automatically. It ensures, that the humans and the computer accept a) common vocabulary of some domain; and b) the meanings of syntactical elements.

The goal of our framework is the automated support in e-Learning activities based on pedagogical background. We follow these instructional requirements: 1) Provide learners with the learning material and guidance towards the accomplishment of their goals; 2) Stimulate learners for active participation in learning and to take control over learning results; 3) Support adaptivity, personalisation and information retrieval. Often adaptivity is analysed in the context of learning, and is oriented towards knowledge transfer. For example: 'The main goal of adaptation in educational systems is to guide the students through the course material in order to improve the effectiveness of the learning process' [29]. It means that the constructivistic view is not taken into account. On the other hand, we can consider adaptivity and personalisation as 'guiding students' rather than forced intervention, but also support in simple and time consuming tasks, and provision of learners with alternative ways of learning process.

The organisational aspects of context in which the framework can be used are as follows: 1) Educational resources are prepared and integrated into a LMS (in our case - MOODLE). 2) Other necessary functions for delivering distance study courses are implemented in a LMS: authorisation, assessment tools, communication tools, etc. 3) We need to integrate our solution into the existing infrastructure.

4.2. Separation of Domain and Media Spaces

DSC, as a specific form of e-Learning, can be defined as a module of study programme, prepared according to the distance learning methodology and delivered in a virtual learning environment using information and communication technologies. Both study module and distance learning course are based on study goals and expected competences. Ontologies are universal models of known knowledge in a domain. It is desirable, that they would be developed by experts in the field and would match existing requirements in the country, for example, adopted regulations in a study area. Educational resources represent that knowledge to the learner in a form that is suitable for learning. Despite of increased research on open resource repositories and interoperability of learning resources, educational resources practically are still obtained after authorisation mechanisms. Therefore, we analyse restricted amount of educational resources, used in stand-alone DSC.

In the static view, we can distinguish two levels:

- Domain level, which concerns the domain knowledge. It is called *Domain Space.*
- Course level, which concerns the practical implementation of distance studies. The DSC consists of a set of educational resources, including both teaching/learning materials and activities. This level is called *Media Space.*

It is very important, that the subject domain ontology can be developed despite of educational resources and services, which may vary at different moments in different contexts.

4.3. Workflow

The design/development time processes are presented in Figure 1. First two steps, i.e. development of domain ontology and development of educational resources, can be performed independently. Either of these two steps can be done first. Also, the ontology and the resources can evolve over time, and they both can be augmented independently. Both ontology and resources can be reused in other context, too.

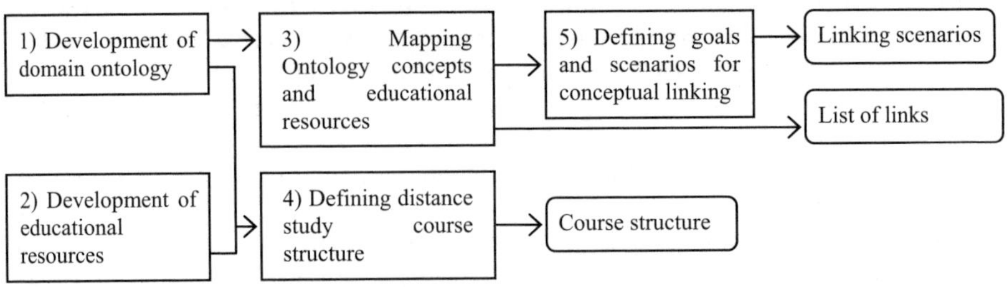

Figure 1. Workflow of processes at design/development time

Mapping of ontology concepts and educational resources allow us to conduct only elementary operations: to get class from its name, to get resource identifier from class name. Therefore, in step 5 further scenarios for reasoning over ontology must be defined. The scenarios that can be developed depend on 1) Pedagogical goal; 2) Ontology structure; 3) Technology (reasoner) used.

The run-time processes are presented in Figure 2.

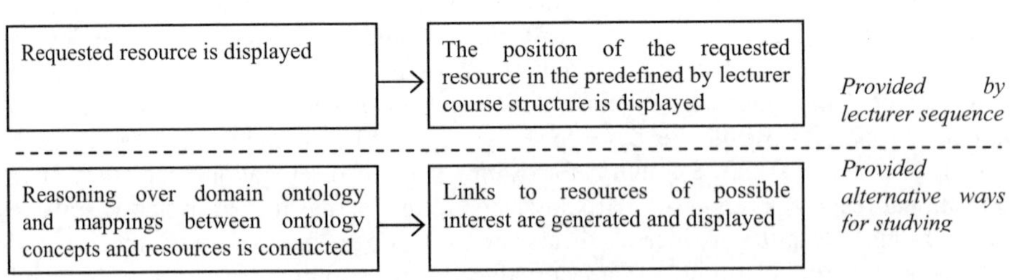

Figure 2. Workflow of processes at run time

4.4. Analysis of Advantages and Shortcomings of the Framework

Instructional engineering in general and our framework in particular try to focus on two important processes [30]:

- Knowledge extraction – the process of transforming the knowledge of experts into structured information, suitable for learning. Knowledge extraction is supported in our framework by separation of domain and media spaces, and possibilities for reuse on a separate level.
- Knowledge dissemination – the process of transforming information into knowledge that is internalised by the learner as new competencies. Knowledge dissemination is supported by the conceptual linking of educational resources at

run time, helping to deal with information overload and providing extra means for metacognitive support.

The limitations of the framework are as follows:

- We use only local context. Interaction between different LMSs is an unsolved problem, and it goes beyond our research. Therefore, educational resources will be distributed among different and possibly not linked systems. But in the future, domain ontologies can be prepared for global use.
- Ontology development and linking of ontology concepts and resources remains a manual process. The problems of relevance and trust are solved, because all parts are designed and developed by experts in the field. However, still much of manual work remains.

The framework fits to any country and language, but in this case alignment of ontologies in several languages must be conducted.

5. A Case Study: Dynamical Navigational Menu Formation in Order to Foster Predictable Learning Paths

In order to realise the ontology-based conceptual linking, the experimental domain ontology was developed, a pedagogical goal was formulated and a scenario was designed. This case study instantiates the framework, described in section 4.

In a case study, we demonstrate the application of the proposed framework by the means of a designed scenario considering real domain ontology for the '*E-Learning Technologies*' DSC and concrete pedagogical goals in mind. As the main goal for designing scenario, we choose metacognitive support during browsing, because it correlates well with modern didactic strategies.

5.1. Domain Ontology Explained

The domain of *E-learning tools* was chosen for implementation, in order to implement the ontology and the framework while working with the distance study course '*E-Learning Technologies*'. The course is implemented using MOODLE: a free, open source course management system. Therefore, we already have learning material, which shall be further linked to the concepts from domain ontology.

The main general concepts in our domain are: *SoftwareProduct*, *Manufacturer*, *Purpose*, *CurriculumLevel*. The more specific concepts are: *MultimediaProcessingTool*, *LMS*, *WebBrowser*, etc. A fragment of a taxonomical hierarchy from general concept *SoftwareProduct* is presented in Figure 3.

Also we employ a *whole-part* relationship in order to represent aggregation. The most general concepts are related with relationships *provides*, *isProvided*, *isSuitableFor*, *canBeAchievedWith*.

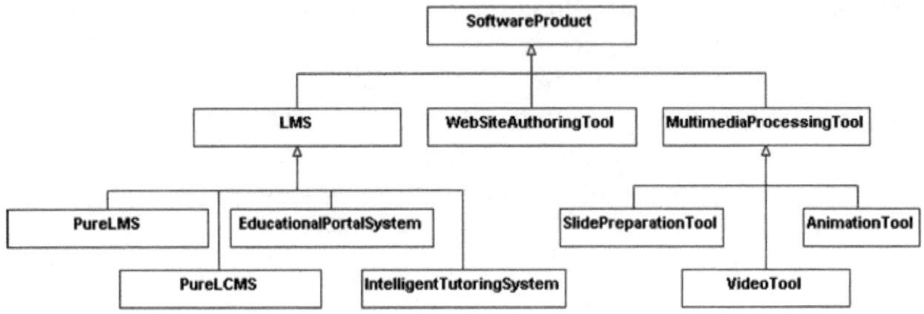

Figure 3. A fragment of a taxonomical structure

5.2. Pedagogical Goal

Among others, the expected ability of this course is formulated as follows: students will be able to analyse, compare and in the real context to choose the most suitable tools for development of study materials, delivering distance learning course or making other decision in e-Learning context.

Concrete tools, discussed in the course and treated as instances from the ontology-based view, are selected from a variety of tools from two types: 1) Best industry-leading tools in the field; 2) Free tools. The lists of important properties are defined considering what type of information is useful when we want to choose a tool for some job in the e-Learning field.

5.3. Scenario for Automated Linking of Educational Resources at Run-time

The systematic approach to choosing a tool suggests several steps of filtering, beginning from all possible alternatives. We may begin our analysis from defining a manufacturer, if we use some other its products; we can restrict ourselves only to the free tools or easy to use tools, if our competencies are on quite low level. The possible scenario is presented in Figure 4.

Learner acquires information about Adobe FlashCS3	Learner acquires information about some software product	*Human part*
1) The class of tools is founded – *AnimationTools* 2) Other tools for animation creation are found: *GifConstructionSetProfessional, CoffeeCupGIF, UleadGifAnimator* 3) Other tools from the same manufacture (Adobe) are found: *AdobeFlashPlayer, AdobeDreamweaverCS3*, etc.	1) Realisation: finding the most specific concept, which describes it. 2) Instance retrieval: finding all instances, that are described by a given class. 3) Querying over triples <Manufacturer, Provides, SoftwareProduct>, where Manufacturer is given.	*System part*
Concrete example	*Abstract example*	

Figure 4. Scenario for automated linking of educational resources

6. Discussion and Conclusions

Ontologies have a great potential in the e-Learning domain, but the methodologies, describing how to do that are rather underdeveloped from the instructional design viewpoint.

The query based reasoning over ontologies is simpler and more efficient than logic based reasoning, therefore it is suitable to choose in hybrid information systems, where current web technologies and ontology engineering are combined. We need a reasoner, which provides API for integration with external parts of the system.

The conceptual linking of educational resources and displaying different ways of reaching the learning goal provide us with better trade-off between control and self-responsibility. There is enough to apply simpler reasoning mechanisms over domain ontology in order to support learner in simple tasks.

In this paper, we have proposed a framework for the conceptual linking of educational resources. The framework is based on reasoning over structural parts of ontology: classes, instances and properties. We have demonstrated the applicability of this framework in a case study, where the domain of *E-learning tools* was chosen as a problem domain, and supporting browsing and searching of the most suitable tools for realising project work was formulated as a pedagogical goal. The same framework can be reused in other context for realising other pedagogical goals.

The social impact of our proposed solution can be identified as supporting knowledge building process. From the managerial view to e-Learning, it increases interactivity on student–study-material level and decreases the amount of repeatable workload of academic staff.

The analysis of the domain, the proposed framework and practical experiments allowed us to formulate open research problems: 1) The need for collaboration of experts in instructional design and ontology engineering fields exists, because design of scenarios must be based on sound pedagogic strategies. 2) Techniques for measurement the scope of improvement of eLearning system, while using innovative approaches, for example, the proposed framework, are underdeveloped. 3) Compatibility of the LMS (Moodle, in our case) with the ontology development tools and reasoners over ontology is problematical due to interoperability problems between ontology and current web technologies. These problems shall be a subject of our further research.

References

[1] Dzemydiene, D., & Tankeleviciene, L. (2008) On the development of domain ontology for distance learning course. In Sakalauskas, L., Weber, G.W., & Zavadskas, E.K. (eds.), The 20th International Conference EURO Mini Conference on Continous Optimization and Knowledge-Based Technologies EurOPT-2008, May 20-23, Neringa, Lithuania, pp. 474-479.

[2] Dzemydiene, D., & Tankeleviciene, L. (2008) Conceptual Linking of Educational Resources Based on Reasoning over Domain Ontology. In Haav, H-M., & Kalja, A. (eds), Databases and Information Systems. Proceedings of the Eighth International Baltic Conference Baltic DB&IS 2008, June 2-5, Tallinn, Estonia, pp. 241-252.

[3] Guarino, N. (1998) Formal Ontology and Information Systems. In Guarino, N. (ed), Formal Ontology in Information Systems. Proceedings of FOIS'98, Italy. Amsterdam: IOS Press, pp. 3-15.

[4] Devedzic, V. (2002) Understanding Ontology engineering, Communications of the ACM, 45(4): 136-144

[5] Corcho, O., Fernández-López, M., & Gómez-Pérez, A. (2007) Ontology engineering: what are ontologies and how can we build them. In Cardoso, J. (ed), Semantic Web: Theory, Tools and Applications, Information Science Reference, London, pp. 44-70.

[6] Stojanovic L., Staab S., & Studer R. (2001) eLearning based on the Semantic Web. WebNet2001 - World Conference on the WWW and Internet, Proceedings of the Conference.
[7] Allert, H., Markannen, H., & Richter, C. (2006) Rethinking the Use of Ontologies in Learning. In Memmel, M., & Burgos, D. (eds), Proceedings of the 2nd International Workshop on Learner-Oriented Knowledge Management and KM-Oriented Learning (LOKMOL 06), pp. 115–125.
[8] Alsultanny, Y. (2006) e-Learning System Overview based on Semantic Web, Electronics Journal of e-Learning, 4(2): 111-118
[9] Angelova, G., Kalaydjiev, O., & Strupchanska, A. (2004) Domain Ontology as a Resource Providing Adaptivity in eLearning. Proceedings 'On the Move to Meaningful Internet Systems 2004', OTM 2004 Workshops, Springer, (LNCS), pp. 700-712.
[10] Deline, G., Lin, F., Wen D., & Gasevic D. (2007) Ontology-Driven Development of Intelligent Educational Systems. IEEE Pacific Rim Conference on Communications, Computers and Signal Processing, August 22-24, pp. 34-37.
[11] Muñoz, L.S., & de Oliveira, J. P. M. (2004) Applying Semantic Web Technologies to Achieve Personalization and Reuse of Content in Educational Adaptive Hypermedia Systems. In Proceedings of the SWEL Workshop at Adaptive Hypermedia 2004, pp. 348-353.
[12] Dolog, P., Henze, N., Nejdl, W., & Sintek, M. (2004) Personalization in distributed e-learning environments. In Proceedings of WWW2004 - The Thirteen International WWW Conference, New York, pp. 170 - 179.
[13] Cristea, A. I. (2004) What can the Semantic Web do for Adaptive Educational Hypermedia? Educational Technology & Society, 7 (4): 40-58
[14] Karampiperis, P., & Sampson, D. (2005) Adaptive Learning Resources Sequencing in Educational Hypermedia Systems, Educational Technology & Society, 8(4): 128-147
[15] Sosnovsky, S., & Gavrilova, T. (2006) Development of Educational Ontology for C-Programming, Information Theories & Applications, 13(4): 303-308
[16] Cho, Y. S., Cha, J. H., & Chang, B. C. (2007) Potential Use of Ontology in Support of Educational Metadata. Presentation at WG4 Meeting.
[17] Gavrilova, T., Farzan, R., & Brusilovsky, P. (2005) One Practical Algorithm of Creating Teaching Ontologies. In Proceedings of Network Based Education (NBE), pp. 29-37.
[18] Boyce, S., & Pahl, C. (2007) Developing Domain Ontologies for Course Content, Educational Technology & Society, 10(3): 275-288
[19] OWL Web Ontology Language Overview. (available at http://www.w3.org/TR/owl-features/)
[20] Kogut, P., Cranefield, S., Hart, L., Dutra, M., Baclawski, K., Kokar, M., & Smith, J. (2002) UML for Ontology Development, The Knowledge Engineering Review, 17(1): 61-64
[21] Mika, P. (2007) Social Networks and the Semantic Web. Springer Science+Business Media, LLC, Barselona, Spain.
[22] SPARQL Query Language for RDF. (available at http://www.w3.org/TR/rdf-sparql-query/)
[23] RAP - RDF API for PHP V0.9.6. (available at http://sites.wiwiss.fu-berlin.de/suhl/bizer/rdfapi/index.html)
[24] pOWL. (available at http://sourceforge.net/projects/powl)
[25] Guizzardi, G. (2005) Ontological Foundations for Structural Conceptual Models. PhD thesis, Telematica Instituut Fundamental Research Series, vol. 015. Enschede, the Netherlands.
[26] Guizzardi, G. (2007) On Ontology, ontologies, Conceptualizations, Modeling Languages, and (Meta)Models. In Vasilecas, O., Edler, J., & Caplinskas, A. (eds), Frontiers in Artificial Intelligence and Applications, Databases and Information Systems IV, IOS Press, Amsterdam.
[27] Brusse, R., & Pokraev, S. (2007) Reasoning on the Semantic Web. In Cardoso, J. (ed), Semantic Web Services: Theory, Tools and Applications, IGI Global.
[28] Antoniou, G. (2007) Web Ontology Languages. In Cardoso J. (ed), Semantic Web Services: Theory, Tools and Applications, IGI Global.
[29] Gaudioso, E., & Montero, M. (2005) Adaptable and Adaptive Web-Based Educational Systems. In Ghaoui, C. (ed), Encyclopedia of human computer interaction, IGI Global, pp. 8-11.
[30] Paquette, G. (2004) Instructional Engineering in Networked Environments. Pfeiffer, San Francisco, 304 p.

Requirements Engineering for Information Systems

Databases and Information Systems V
H.-M. Haav and A. Kalja (Eds.)
IOS Press, 2009

doi:10.3233/978-1-58603-939-4-67

Development of the Plagiarism Detection Tool for Processing Template-Based Documents

Alla ANOHINA [1], Antons MISLEVICS and Janis GRUNDSPENKIS
Department of Systems Theory and Design, Riga Technical University, Latvia

Abstract. The paper presents the plagiarism detection tool for processing template-based documents specifying its conception, the method chosen for the plagiarism detection, the process of the checking of the originality of a submitted student's work, tool's users and requirements. Logical level of the architecture is given as well. Software needed for the implementation and the use of the tool is described.

Keywords. plagiarism detection, Microsoft SharePoint

Introduction

Rapid development of information and communication technologies and growing role of the Internet makes easy available different digital documents inter alia educational materials such as reports and presentations on various topics, full solutions of tasks given in text books, answers of examination questions and even completed course papers and individual works. In this context a serious challenge for the staff of educational institutions is the dissemination of plagiarism. Reasons are threefold [1]. Firstly, this phenomenon is in contradiction to the process of learning which demands from a learner to take certain intellectual and physical efforts in order to acquire knowledge and skills necessary for the further social and professional activities. Secondly, plagiarism reduces the value of a qualification received from an educational institution. Thirdly, it demotivates other students to work independently and to put efforts to learning in case of impunity of plagiarism. In reality students think that those who cheat are rarely caught because their teachers are reluctant to investigate plagiarism. The latter often is true due to the time it takes and burden of proof. And last, but not least, universities apply a wide scale of penalties such as resubmission of the work, reduced mark, or such severe penalty as suspension. All abovementioned sketches the complexity of the plagiarism problem.

The problem of plagiarism is more complicated for teachers teaching courses where individual works are included and the number of students registered for the mentioned courses each year is around several hundreds. So, to avoid plagiarism the teachers must generate several hundreds truly original tasks yearly. Of course, there are some options [2]: random selection of tasks for an individual work from a set of tasks,

[1] Corresponding Author: Alla Anohina, Riga Technical University, Kalku 1, LV-1658 Riga, Latvia; E-mail: alla.anohina@rtu.lv.

variation of input data for each task, permission for students to choose their own problem domains or the use of essay-form assignments. Our experience to use the mentioned approaches simultaneously gives good results: it is possible to generate several hundreds different individual tasks each year, but there are some serious drawbacks, as well. The growing number of individual tasks causes dramatic increase of workload of teachers for checking and assessment of submitted students' works. Moreover, the use of essays puts high cognitive load on learners. These are reasons why we propose to use a template for students' works and a corresponding tool for the detection of plagiarism.

Many different software tools for automated plagiarism detection have been already developed and used, for example, Turnitin, Eve2, CopyCatchGold, WordCheck, Glatt, Moss, JPlag [3, 4, 5, 6, 7, 8]. In general, they provide excellent service for detecting matching text in documents [8]. However our analysis of the mentioned plagiarism detection tools shows that they are inefficient in processing of documents based on a template. In brief, there are two main problems [2]. First, typically plagiarism detection tools check a whole document and as a result legally identical text areas, for example, tasks statements which are the same in all documents are identified as plagiarized parts. It distorts the overall results of the plagiarism detection process and causes difficulties to make decisions about real amount of plagiarism in the document. Second, known plagiarism detection tools compare all parts of a document with all parts of an another document for mutual similarities and as a result semantically unrelated parts of two documents, for example, two solutions of absolutely different tasks are processed unnecessarily. It increases the overall computational time of the document processing.

Previously we have introduced the conception [1] and have gathered and described detailed requirements [2] for a plagiarism detection tool for processing template-based documents. This paper focuses on the architecture of the tool and technologies used for its implementation, and is organized as follows. The first section describes the main idea of the tool, its users, requirements and the checking process of students' works. The second section identifies software needed for the implementation and for the use of the mentioned tool, as well as discusses the logical level of the architecture. Conclusions are given at the end of the paper.

1. Conception and Requirements for the Tool

We define a template is an e-document of pre-designed layout which provides consistent format and content of data put into it and is based on tables and text fields with unique identifiers for input of student's data corresponding to an individual task version. Open XML document format [9] is chosen for templates because it is approved as ISO/IEC International Standard [10] and data in this format can be easily subjected to automated analysis [11].

The main idea of the plagiarism detection tool for processing template-based documents is to make only necessary comparisons according to semantics of document content [1], that is, to compare only semantically correlated parts of documents which potentially can contain identical regions (Figure 1).

1.1. Method of the Plagiarism Detection

One of the popular purely statistical methods, that is, N-gram technique [12, 13] is chosen for the plagiarism detection process in the tool. Before describing the mentioned technique two definitions should be given. A *gram* is a sub-string which has a definite length. A *pattern* is a list of grams extracted from a text.

The comparison of two chunks of text includes two steps: the obtaining of patterns from both chunks of text and the comparison of the acquired patterns.

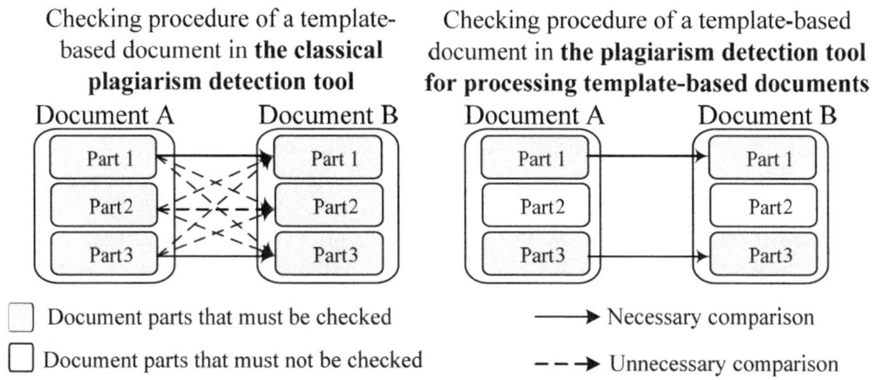

Figure 1. Comparison of documents in classical and template-based approaches to the plagiarism detection (adopted from [1])

The obtaining of a pattern is a process in which sub-strings of a definite length (grams) are extracted from the text. The sub-strings further are used for the comparison of two chunks of text and making of conclusions about their similarity: texts are similar if they have similar grams. Before the extraction of sub-strings the text must be modified in the following way:

- All symbols which do not belong to the alphabet (blank characters, numbers, punctuation signs, and special symbols) must be eliminated from the text.
- All uppercase letters must be replaced by lowercase letters.

For example, in order to extract all 5-grams (sub-strings of 5 symbols) for the sentence "May 15 is my birthday!" the following steps should be performed:

1. Elimination of symbols which do not belong to the alphabet: "Mayismybirthday".
2. Replacing of letters: "mayismybirthday".
3. Extraction of grams: "mayis", "ayism", "yismy", "ismyb", "smybi", "mybir", "ybirt", "birth", "irthd", "rthda", "thday".

When the lists of grams are acquired for both chunks of text they must be compared. This process gives the list with identical grams in both chunks. After that the similarity degree between two texts is calculated using the following equation:

$$SD = ((LP) / (LT)) * 100, \tag{1}$$

where SD is a similarity degree in percentage, LP- the number of identical grams, LT- the number of grams for the document under checking.

1.2. Users of the Tool

In general, the tool must support three groups of users with appropriate access rights and permissions [2]:

- A tool administrator is responsible for the administration of the tool configuration and access rights of other users. The standard functions of the user management, i.e., adding and deleting users, as well as granting them privileges, are widely used in other software systems and therefore are not specified in this paper. Usually administrators of computer classes or departments' laboratory assistants correspond to this group.
- A teacher provides the definition of meta-data and checks the originality of each submitted student's work. As a rule, the role of the teacher plays professors, lecturers or assistants.
- A secretary registers submitted students' works and makes the checking of their formatting against the required format of the template. Typical examples of users of this group are a secretary of the department or of a particular professor, as well as assistants.

However, in the future apart from the three mentioned user groups there are plans to give students an access to the tool in order to reduce the workload of a secretary. Thus, the user groups can be integrated in two main classes: internal users (an administrator, a teacher and a secretary) and external users (students). Figure 2 displays existing and potential users of the tool. All users use a web browser to access the tool.

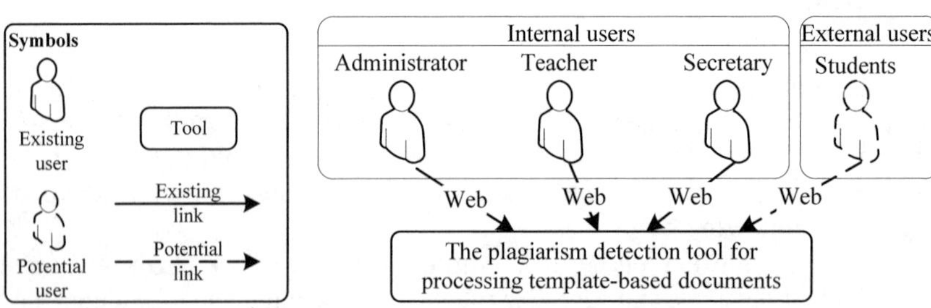

Figure 2. The users of the tool

1.3. Checking of a Student's Work

In general, the checking procedure of a template-based document consists of two stages. Firstly, the document formatting must be checked against the required format of the template. All documents must have the same formatting as defined in the template, otherwise it will not be possible to conduct mutual comparison of documents. Secondly, plagiarized parts of the document under checking must be detected by comparing parts from the document with corresponding parts from other documents.

The detailed steps of the use of the tool are the following [2]:

1. In the preparation step the teacher must describe the structure of the template by defining how many elements (text fields and tables) and with what identifiers the submitted document must contain, as well as, what elements must be compared in documents created on the basis of the same template.

The description of this step can be found in [1]. It will be elaborated after the implementation and evaluation of the first prototype of the tool.

2. The secretary must register the student's submitted work in the tool and must perform the checking of its formatting. As a result of this process the student's work can be recognized as consistent or inconsistent with the required format of the template. In the first case it must be excluded from the further processing. Otherwise, the subsequent steps described below must be applied to the student's work.
3. The teacher must define meta-data of the student's submitted work.
4. The teacher must perform the checking of the originality of the student's submitted work. As a result of this process the student's work can be recognized as containing or not containing plagiarized parts. In the first case the work must be excluded from the further processing. Otherwise, the last step must be applied to the student's work.
5. The teacher must assess the student's work and assign it a mark.

Going through the process described above the student's submitted work can have different statuses [2]:

- "Inconsistent formatting"- the student's submitted work has been recognized as inconsistent with the required format of the template and therefore is excluded from the further processing.
- "Meta-data input"- the student's submitted work has been recognized as consistent with the required format of the template and is waiting when the teacher will define its meta-data.
- "Originality checking"- the student's submitted work has been recognized as consistent with the required format of the template, its meta-data have been defined and it is waiting when the teacher will check it for plagiarism.
- "Plagiarism" - the student's submitted work has been recognized as plagiarism.
- "Non-plagiarism"- the student's submitted work has been recognized as an original work.

Figure 3 displays all processes related to the use of the tool and their actors.

1.4. Requirements for the Tool

Table 1 presents a summary of tool's main functions specifying function purpose, input data, their necessity (mandatory or optional) and source (from the user or from the tool), output data, their necessity (mandatory or optional) and destination (on display or within the tool). Detailed description containing also step-by-step processing of each function is given in [2].

Two main functions of the tool are: the registration of a student's work and checking of its formatting and originality. The first function is performed in the following way [2]:

1. Choosing of the student's work by using a standard file dialog.
2. Input of the date when the student's work was submitted.
3. Checking of the formatting of the submitted work against the required format of the template:
   a) checking of the student's data within the corresponding text fields on the title-page of the student's work: first name, last name, and the number of the student's identity card;

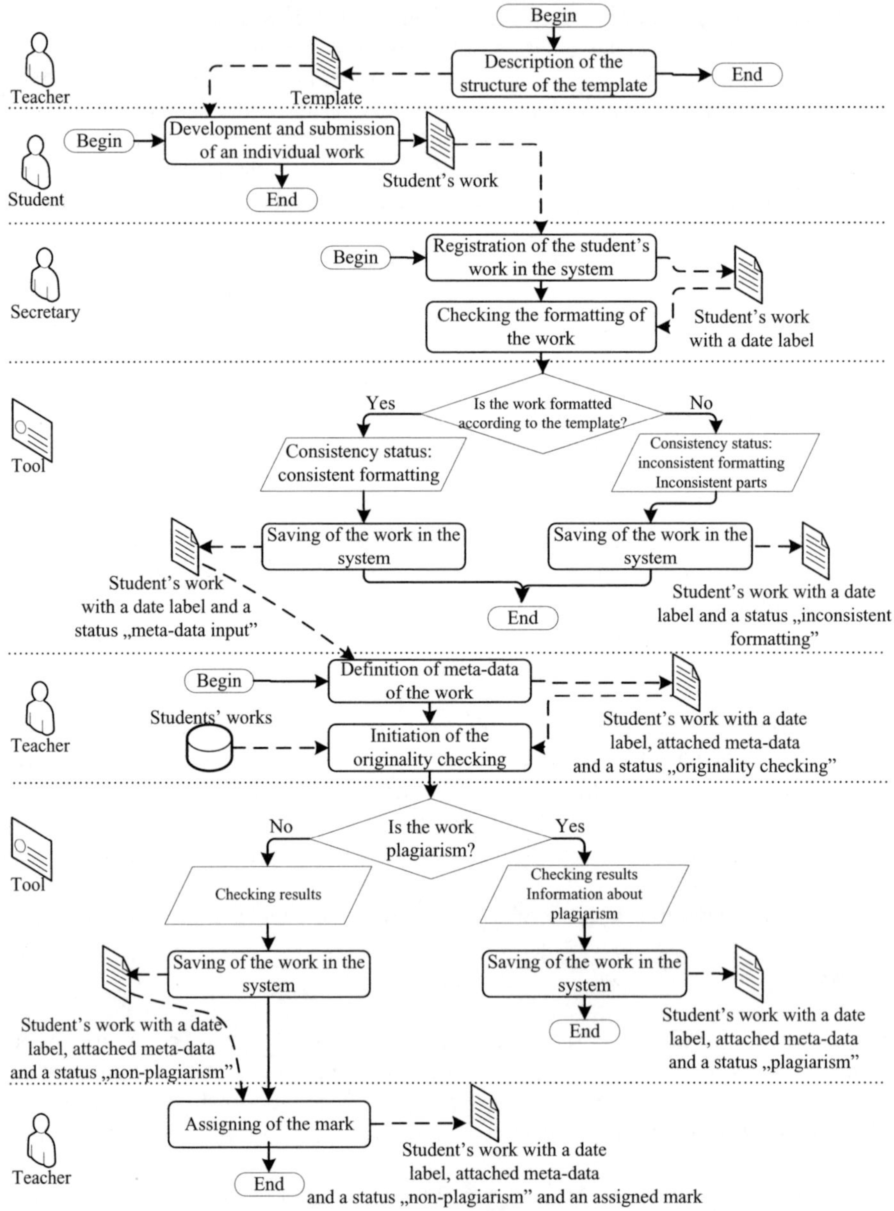

Figure 3. Main processes related to the use of the tool

b) checking whether the student's work contains text fields or tables which are not defined within the template. At this point it is necessary to give additional explanations. As it was mentioned earlier in the paper, the template consists from tables and text fields (elements) with unique

Table 1. Summary of requirements for the tool.

User	Function	Purpose	Input	Output
Teacher	Definition of meta-data	To specify meta-data that give additional information about the student's work and may help in the process of the originality checking	Keywords both for the whole student's work and its particular parts (optional; from the user)	Keywords both for the whole student's work and its particular parts (optional; within the tool)
	Originality checking	To detect either the student's submitted work is an original work or it contains plagiarized parts	Search criteria (optional; from the user) Selected student's works or all students' works registered in the tool (mandatory; from the tool) Student's work under checking (mandatory; from the tool)	Checking results (mandatory; on display): information about the work under checking (student's first name and last name, submission date, and version number) and a list of other students' works which parts are similar to the work under checking Information about plagiarism (optional; within the tool): name of the work which parts are similar with the work under checking and parts of the work where the similarity was detected Status of the student's work under checking: either "plagiarism" or "non-plagiarism" (mandatory; within the tool)
	Archiving/ dearchiving of registered works	To decrease/increase the number of students' works participating in the originality checking	Search criteria (optional; from the user)	Students' works (optional; within the tool)
	Assigning of a mark	To assign a mark to the student's work which is not recognized as plagiarism	Student's work (mandatory; from the tool) Mark (mandatory; from the user)	Student's work (mandatory; within the tool) Mark (mandatory; within the tool)
	Generation of the report on submitted works	To generate the report of students' submitted works selected by using different searching criteria	Search criteria (optional; from the user)	Report on students' submitted works (mandatory; on display)
	Description of the structure of the template	To describe structure of the template	Number and identifiers of elements, as well as comparable pairs of elements (mandatory; from the user)	Description of the structure of the template (mandatory; within the tool)

Table 1 (continued). Summary of requirements for the tool.

User	Function	Purpose	Input	Output
Secretary	Registration of a student's work and checking of its formatting	To register a student's submitted work in the tool and to check its formatting against the formatting of the template. As a result of this process works which have inconsistent formatting are excluded from the further processing	Student's work (mandatory; from the user) Date when the student's work was submitted (mandatory; from the user)	Summary of checking results (mandatory; on display): consistency status (either inconsistent or consistent formatting) and an identification of inconsistent parts of the work Student's work with the status either "inconsistent formatting" or "meta-data input" and date when it was submitted (mandatory; within the tool)
	Generation of the report on submitted works	To generate the report of students' submitted works selected by using different searching criteria	Search criteria (optional; from the user)	Report on students' submitted works (mandatory; on display)

identifiers. The process of the originality checking must compare content of elements with identical identifiers within a pair of documents. If the student replaces some elements in his/her work with new ones or with ones taken from another student's work, identifiers will differ from identifiers of the template. In this case it will not be possible to check the originality of their content in comparison with other documents. Therefore, it is necessary to verify that the student's work does not contain elements with different identifiers before the checking of the originality.

4. Displaying the summary of the checking results by providing information about the student's work consistency with the required format of the template. In case of inconsistency the identification of inconsistent parts of the work must be given.
5. Saving the student's work in the tool's data base:
   a) if the student's work is inconsistent with the required format of the template, it must be stored in the tool's data base by attaching it to the corresponding student with the status "inconsistent formatting";
   b) if the student's work is consistent with the formatting of the template, the tool must generate a unique name for each submission in the form of NoOfStudentIdentityCard_DataOfSubmission_VersionNumber.doc, where NoOfStudentIdentityCard must be taken from the corresponding text fields on the title-page of the student's work, DataOfSubmission is the date provided in the 2nd step of this function, and VersionNumber is a version number of the work for a particular student that the tool must acquire automatically from the data base, taking into account the number of the student's identity card. The student's work must be stored in the

tool's data base by attaching it to the corresponding student with the status "meta-data input".

The originality checking includes the following steps [2]:

1. Selection of students' works which will participate in the checking process. The following criteria can be used: number of the student's identity card, first name and last name, interval of dates when students' works were submitted or a particular date, status of students' works, and a mark. The selection results must be displayed as a list. The user must have the possibilities to select all works from the list or only some of them. The user must have the possibility not to make the selection. In this case the student's work will be compared with all other works registered in the tool.
2. The one-to-one comparison of the documents (the submitted student's work with the selected works) will be made on the basis of the teacher's provided information about what fields must be compared in two documents created on the basis of the same template. The comparison will be performed on the basis of N-gram technique described earlier in the paper (Sub-section 1.1).
3. After the checking process, the tool must display checking results for the user. The results must include information about the work under checking (student first name and last name, number of the identity card, submission date, and version number) and the list of other students' works which parts are similar to the work under checking. The list must contain the information about the name of the work, work parts which are similar with the work under checking, and the similarity degree calculated in accordance with Eq. (1).
4. The possibility to compare students' submissions manually must be provided. In this case the teacher must choose one of the works from the list described in Step 3. The work under checking and the selected work must be displayed in a separate window.
5. The user can mark the students' works in the list described in Step 3 as "source of plagiarism" or "not source of plagiarism". If the work under checking is recognized as plagiarism, the following information must be stored in the tool's data base: name of the work which parts are similar to the work under checking, parts where the similarity was detected, as well as the status of the work under checking must be changed to "plagiarism". Otherwise, the work will acquire the status “non-plagiarism”.
6. The possibilities to print out or to save the checking results must be provided.
7. The user will not be allowed to start the checking of another work until all works in the list described in Step 3 will not be marked as "source of plagiarism" or "not source of plagiarism".

2. Design of the Tool

2.1. Software

Microsoft Windows SharePoint Services 3.0 (WSS 3.0) platform is chosen for the implementation of the tool. The platform includes all necessary basic functionality: user authentication, Web access, storing lists of custom information, managing access rights and permissions, search facilities, backup and recovery, document versioning, and workflows. Moreover, the platform provides different integration mechanisms such as WebDAV, Web services, RSS, as well as a rich application programming interface (API) for Microsoft .NET Framework [14, 15]. Additionally, in the future it will be possible to perform the migration of the tool to Microsoft Office SharePoint Server 2007 (MOSS 2007), which extends the WSS 3.0 platform, providing additional features [16, 17].

Figure 4 shows which software must be installed on the server and on clients' computers. The use of WSS 3.0 platform demands the installation of Windows Server 2003 operating system, IIS 6.0 Internet server, Microsoft .NET Framework 3.0, Microsoft SQL Server 2005 and WSS 3.0, or MOSS 2007 on the server side. Most of the popular Web browsers can be used on clients' computers. However, a text editor which supports Open XML document format must be installed in order to provide that students can develop their individual works using the offered template and teachers can create templates.

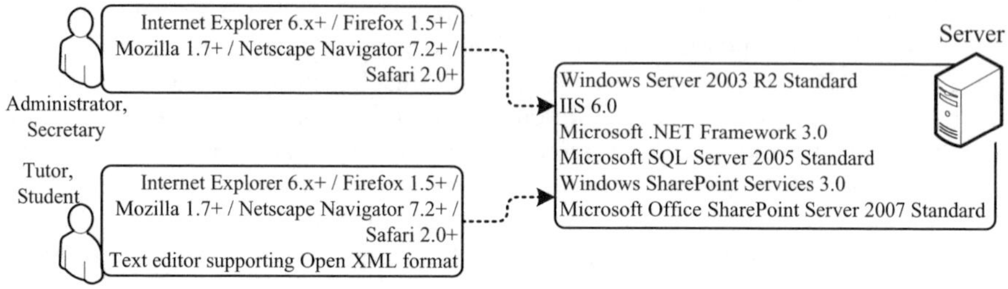

Figure 4. Used software

2.2. Logical Level of the Architecture

Figure 5 displays the logical level of the tool's architecture. All users access the tool through a WSS 3.0 provided authentication layer (2). Internal users (Figure 2) access the tool in the same way as their work computers, by using active directory credentials. Credentials for external users are stored in the database (1) and authentication mechanism validates provided credentials against this database during login procedure. For each class of users (internal or external) a separate WSS zone should be created to ensure the described functionality. All users will work with the tool through the Web interface (3) which also is out of the box WSS 3.0 functionality.

The layer of business logic (5) provides an abstraction from physical elements such as database records and files to logical ones such as objects and documents. This layer will be implemented using WSS objects and API.

Data adapters (6) provide an abstraction of data sources. Here default WSS 3.0 adapters will be used in order to access WSS 3.0 databases, as well as WSS or ADO.NET adapters for accessing the index database. Data will be stored in several storages: students' works (7) and other tool's data in the WSS 3.0 database, indexes of students' works (9) in the WSS 3.0 or an external database (moving indexes to an external database could potentially increase overall performance of the solution).

The work indexer (10) retrieves students' works (7), generates an index needed to search for plagiarism and stores the index in the database (9). This component is a part of the works analyzing agent's functionality (12), thus, links to storages shown in Figure 5 are informative only: data sources will be accessed through an integration layer (4), business logic (5) and data adapters (6).

The searcher of similar works (11) must compare a particular student's work with similar works (7) on the basis of keywords included in meta-data. Indexes of works (9) must be used for the comparison. Similar to the work indexer (10) this component is a part of the works analyzing agent's functionality (12), so the displayed links are informative only.

The integration layer (4) serves as an interface for external systems. In this case WSS 3.0 provided integration mechanisms through API or Web services will be used. API can be used if an external system physically is deployed on the same server, but Web services support integration with systems deployed on other servers as well.

The works analyzing agent (12) searches plagiarism in students' works. The agent will be implemented using C# programming language and will connect to the tool through WSS 3.0 API, because at the first stage of the tool's development it will be deployed on the same server as the tool. The component will be implemented as an external agent that gives the following advantages. First, the agent will access the tool through the authentication layer (2) with its own user name and password. Thus, the tool's administrator will be able to control which data the agent can access. Second, logic of the agent will be fully independent from the tool and it will allow the improvement or the changing of algorithms for the detection of plagiarism without influencing the overall workflow. Third, in case if the number of students' works increases it will be possible to move the agent to another server in order to improve the overall process performance. Fourth, technology for the implementation of the agent is fully independent of technologies used for the development of the tool that provides further improvement of the tool more flexible.

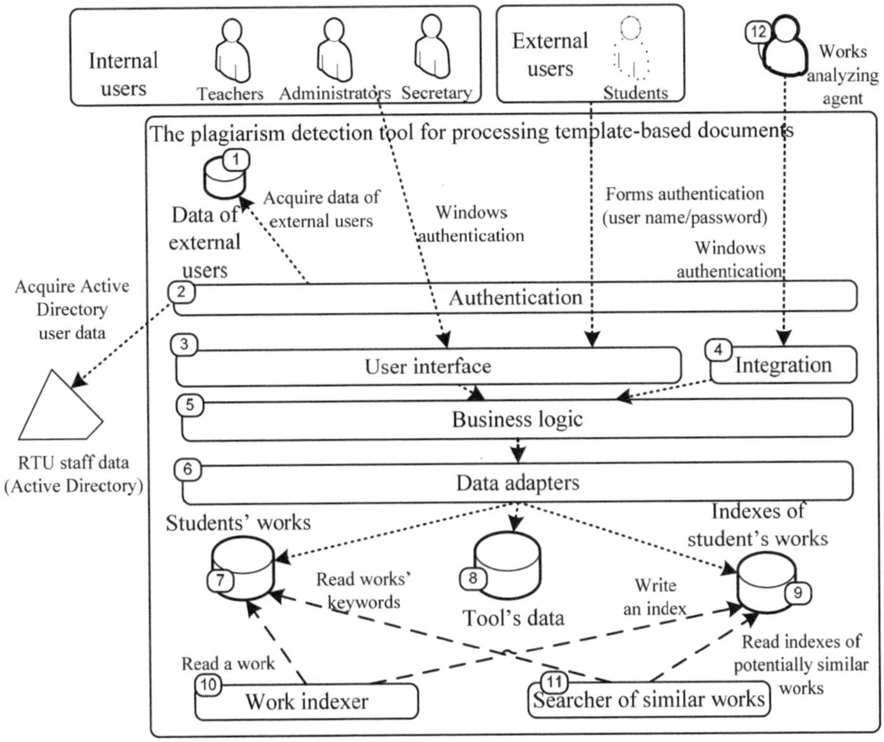

Figure 5. The logical level of the architecture of the tool

3. Conclusions

The problem of plagiarism is investigated in many higher education institutions. Researchers have found wide variations both in rates and in penalties applied. They are trying to find efficient solutions by developing plagiarism detection tools. The analysis of known plagiarism detection tools shows that they are inefficient in processing of documents based on templates. The use of templates is a reasonable approach for decrease of workload of teachers in situations where the number of students who submit their individual works is around several hundreds.

The paper discusses the conception, requirements and design of the plagiarism detection tool which purpose is to process template-based documents. Future work is related to the implementation of the designed tool. The tool will be evaluated experimentally in the study course "Fundamentals of artificial Intelligence".

References

[1] Lukashenko, R., Anohina, A., & Grundspenkis, J. (2007) A Conception of a Plagiarism Detection Tool for Processing Template-Based Documents. In Annual Proceedings of Vidzeme University College, Valmiera, Latvia (in print).
[2] Anohina, A., & Grundspenkis, J. (2008) Requirements of the Plagiarism Detection Tool for Processing Template-Based Documents. In Proceedings of the 8th International Baltic Conference on Databases and Information Systems (Baltic DB&IS 2008), Tallinn, Estonia, June 2-5, pp. 51-62.
[3] Maurer, H., Kappe, F., & Zaka, B. (2006) Plagiarism-A Survey, Journal of Universal Computer Sciences, 12 (8): 1050-1084
[4] Delvin, M. (2002) Plagiarism Detection Software: How Effective is it? Assessing Learning in Australian Universities (available at http://www.cshe.unimelb.edu.au/assessinglearning/docs/PlagSoftware.pdf)
[5] Lancaster, T., & Culwin, F. (2000) A Review of Electronic Services for Plagiarism Detection in Student Submissions. In Proceedings of the 8th Annual Conference on the Teaching of Computing, Edinburgh, UK, July 23-25, pp. 54-61.
[6] Lancaster, T., & Culwin, F. (2005) Classifications of Plagiarism Detection Engines, ITALICS, 4 (2) (available at http://www.ics.heacademy.ac.uk/italics/Vol4-2/Plagiarism%20-%20revised%20paper.pdf)
[7] Neill, C.J., Shanmuganthan, G. (2004) A Web-enabled Plagiarism Detection Tool, IT Professional, 6 (5): 19–23
[8] Plagiarism Detection Software Report. (2003) The University of Sydney Teaching and Learning Committee. Draft One (available at http://www.usyd.edu.au/su/ab/docs/2003/ABAgAug03.pdf)
[9] Introducing the Office (2007) Open XML File Formats, (available at http://msdn.microsoft.com/en-us/library/aa338205.aspx)
[10] Open XML Community, (available at http://www.openxmlcommunity.org/)
[11] Open XML Developer, (available at http://openxmldeveloper.org/default.aspx)
[12] Brin, S., Davis, J., & Garcia, M.H. (1995) Copy Detection Mechanisms for Digital Documents. In Proceedings of the 1995 ACM SIGMOD International Conference on Management of Data, San Jose, California, USA, May 22-25 pp. 398-409.
[13] Tan, C.L, Huang, W., Sung, S.Y., Yu, Z., & Xu, Y. (2003) Text Retrieval from Document Images Based on Word Shape Analysis, Applied Intelligence, 18: 257–270
[14] Windows SharePoint Services 3.0 (available at http://msdn.microsoft.com/en-us/library/bb931737.aspx)
[15] Windows SharePoint Services Developer Center (available at http://msdn.microsoft.com/en-us/sharepoint/default.aspx)
[16] Microsoft Office SharePoint Server 2007 (available at http://msdn.microsoft.com/en-us/library/bb931736.aspx)
[17] SharePoint Server 2007 Developer Portal (available at http://msdn.microsoft.com/en-us/office/aa905503.aspx)

Databases and Information Systems V
H.-M. Haav and A. Kalja (Eds.)
IOS Press, 2009

doi:10.3233/978-1-58603-939-4-79

Extended Method for Transforming Requirements to Conceptual Model of a Data Warehouse

Natalija KOZMINA[1], Laila NIEDRITE and Darja SOLODOVNIKOVA
Department of Computer Science, University of Latvia

Abstract. Business requirements are essential for developing any information system, including a data warehouse. However, the requirements, written in natural language, may be ambiguous and imprecise. This paper offers business requirement formalization metamodel, which defines business requirements according to a certain pattern, specific to data warehouse systems. We also propose a method to create a conceptual model of a data warehouse, based on the knowledge about requirements and conceptual models of previously developed projects. The method is extended by providing evaluation of possible ways of selecting conceptual model of existing data warehouse projects.

Keywords. data warehouse, requirements, metamodel, conceptual model

Introduction

One of the starting points in development of a data warehouse is the construction of a conceptual model of a data warehouse. To make a data warehouse model that satisfies customer's needs, according to the software development lifecycle well-known in the software engineering, at first requirements should be stated, for example, by interviewing users. In case of a data warehouse, not discarding awareness of users' needs, existing data and their models have much bigger influence on the final result.

There are several approaches how to determine the requirements for the conceptual model of a data warehouse. The requirements for data warehouses are different than those which apply to other types of systems. In the data warehousing field we can speak about information requirements [1] as opposed to the functional requirements that are usually used.

The methods for developing of conceptual models for data warehouses can be split up into several groups on the basis of the approach that is taken. The data-driven approach [2], [3] is based on exploration of the models and data of data sources. The conceptual model for a data warehouse comes from models of data sources via transformation. The analysis needs of an organisation are not identified at all, or are identified only partly. The requirement-driven approach [1] is based on the elicitation of requirements in different ways. Some authors speak about more detailed subgroups

[1] Corresponding Author: Natalija Kozmina, University of Latvia, Raina blvd. 19, LV-1586, Riga, Latvia; E-mail: natalija.kozmina@lu.lv.

that are based on various ways of requirements elicitation. For example, [2] speaks of a measurement-driven approach, but [3] refers to user-driven and goal-driven approaches.

There are many methods to define the requirements for the development of the most appropriate conceptual model of the data warehouse. There is no consensus about the best method. There exists a challenge to develop new approaches and methods.

The rest of the paper is organized as follows: related work presents different methods used in development of conceptual models of data warehouses. The 2nd section introduces a method for new conceptual model creation. This section describes business requirement pattern for data warehouses, formalized requirements metamodel, knowledge base for storing conceptual models as well as transition algorithm, which is based on the knowledge about similar existing models. The 3rd section introduces as idea of expansion of metamodel for description of conceptual models of data warehouse. The paper ends with conclusions and the description of the future work.

1. Related Work

There exist many methods, how to use the approaches for the development of a conceptual model of a data warehouse. The user-driven approach is described and formalized to a greater extent: [4], [5]. For example, Poe [5] proposes a catalogue for storage of users' interviews to collect end-users' requirements.

In case of the process-driven approach a business process is analyzed: [3], [6]. For example, in [6] the process models are constructed, including the analyzed processes, as well as the corresponding data models.

In case of the goal-driven approach goals of an enterprise, goals of analyzed business processes are analyzed and data, that should be analyzed to achieve these goals, are identified: [7], [8], and [9].

We have also used the aforementioned approaches in our data warehousing projects, our corresponding methods are presented in [10], [11], and [12].

A new approach and a method are presented in [13]. The authors introduce Dimensional Design Patterns (DDPs) and develop dimensional models using a known practice. The DDPs cover temporal, action, location, object, stakeholder, qualifier, and combination patterns. This approach may help construct dimensional objects, but the method does not describe how the requirements in particular data warehousing projects affect the construction of a model.

The existing conceptual models of data warehouses are based on the E/R model, e.g., ME/R [14], based on the UML [15], or independent conceptual models, e.g., Dimensional Fact Model [16]. The variety of elements and features in the conceptual models reflect differences in opinion about the best model for data warehouses, and that means that there is no universal agreement about the relevant standard [17]. So many conceptual models were developed because the existing models used for the conceptual modeling of information systems, e.g. UML or ER model, do not properly express the features of the multidimensional paradigm. One of these features is the existence of two kinds of data that should be modeled – the quantifying and qualifying data. Also the other well known elements of data warehouses – dimensions, hierarchies, cubes should be represented in more intuitive way.

2. Method Description

When a data warehouse for the particular specific business area is developed, the experience of similar projects is often taken into account, for example, the solutions of data models that were previously used. Therefore it is possible to develop a knowledge base, where formally described requirements from previous projects and corresponding multidimensional models are stored.

In our case study, knowledge base consists of knowledge about business requirements and conceptual models of existing data warehouse projects as well as knowledge about business requirements of new data warehouse project. The first version of a data mart for the assessment of the usage of an e-learning environment was developed in 2004. In different periods of time two e-learning systems were used at the University of Latvia – WebCT from year 2002 to 2008 and Moodle since year 2007. During the implementation of the new e-learning system Moodle the need to evaluate the usage of the e-learning environment remained the same. We had now a possibility to get from data warehouse users precise definitions of the information requirements based on their previous experience with WebCT data mart.

Let’s call WebCT data mart an Old System and Moodle data mart – a New System. It is clear that for a New System a new conceptual model should be created, that’s why the analysis of the existing Old System requirements and conceptual model based on these requirements is essential.

The method of the New System conceptual model creation is depicted in Figure 1. Firstly, there should be a check made – whether business requirements of the Old System correspond to the Old System conceptual model (Figure 1, 1). Then business requirements of the Old and the New System as well as conceptual model of the Old System are passed as input parameters (Figure 1, arrow 2) to the algorithm, described in Sections 2.3-2.4. The result of algorithm execution is the New System conceptual mode (Figure 1, arrow 3). Afterwards mapping is being made, which denotes correspondence of business requirements of the Old or the New System to conceptual model of the New System (Figure 1, 4). Finally, the New System conceptual model is reviewed: candidate attributes (see Section 2.2) are either approved or eliminated. After that the New System conceptual model is added to a set of conceptual models in the knowledge base (Figure 1, arrow 5).

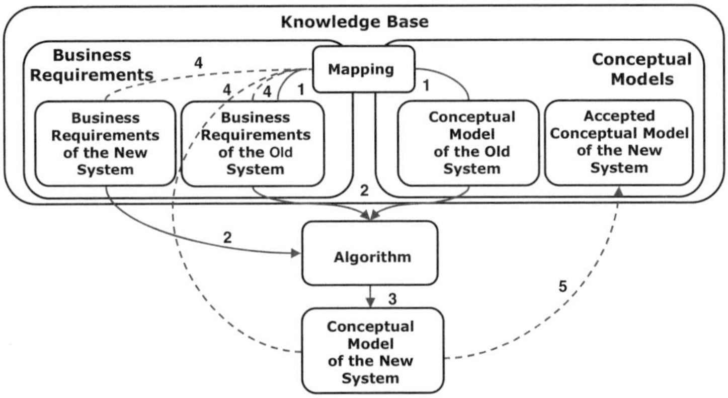

Figure 1. The scheme of the New System conceptual model creation

2.1. Requirement Pattern Description

Software requirements are usually described using a requirement specification language with various levels of formality [18]. The approach that we are going to use is based on extracting necessary information out of business requirements, defined in natural language, thus making business requirements more precise and formal. Business requirements for data warehouses could be represented by sentences that are used to specify what action(-s) the system should perform and which object(-s) it will affect. Our experience shows that all data warehouse requirements have common structure, for that reason we propose a pattern for re-writing these business requirements formally. The idea of requirement formalization is represented as metamodel, designed using UML 2.0 class diagram notation (Figure 2).

In Figure 2 business requirements consist of one or more simple requirements with zero or one condition. Simple requirements consist of a verb (*operation*) that denotes a command which refers to an *object*. In Data Warehousing there are two kinds of data – *quantifying* (measurements) and *qualifying* (properties that characterize measurements). An object is either an instance of quantifying or qualifying data, depending on the requirement. The term „operation" describes the kind of *action(-s)* to be performed. If some kind (or different kinds) of action should be performed more than once, then it is called a *complex operation*. There are two possible kinds of action: *aggregation* (commands, used for calculation and grouping, "roll-up") and *refinement* (commands, used for information selection, "roll-down" as an opposite to aggregation). Information refinement is either showing details, that is selecting information about one or more objects, or slicing, that means showing details, according to a certain constraint (*typified condition*). If there is a restriction in the requirement, then it is represented by a typified condition.

There are two types of conditions: *simple* and *complex*. If there is only one condition defined in business requirement, it is called a simple condition (for example, "time is greater than last_access_time – 1 second"), consisting of *comparison* of two *expressions*. Expressions are divided in two groups – qualifying data (for example, last_access_time) and *constant* (for example, "1 second").

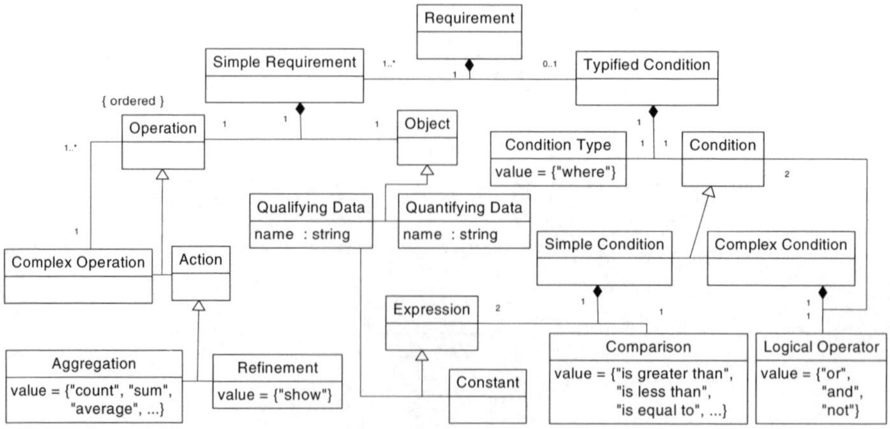

Figure 2. Formalized requirements metamodel (UML)

Arithmetical operations (if it is necessary) may also be used in expressions together with qualifying data and constants. Complex condition joins two or more simple conditions by *logical operators* (such as "and", "or", "not").

Let's see the examples of WebCT and Moodle formalized business requirements. The amount of downloaded and uploaded data (Kb) per study program (in WebCT): "show study program name, sum (data amount) where date is greater than '01.09.2007' and date is less than '01.02.2008' ". The total amount of user hits per e-course per study program (in WebCT, Moodle): "show e-course name, sum (hits) where study program name is equal to 'Computer Science' and date is greater than '01.09.2007' and date is less than '01.02.2008' ". The average amount of user hits per Moodle category per study program level (in Moodle): "show Moodle category name, avg(hits) where study program level is equal to 'Bachelor' ".

Mentioned business requirement examples are illustrated in [19].

2.2. Knowledge Base for Conceptual Models

We use OLAP package of Common Warehouse Metamodel (CWM) [20] as a representation of a conceptual model of a data warehouse (see Figure 7). According to CWM, the root of the conceptual model is a *schema* which usually is created for each data mart. It contains *dimensions* and *cubes* which are connected by *cube dimension association*. Cubes have *measures*, presented by numerical values. Cubes can have default hierarchy which is used for grouping measures. Dimensions can include several *hierarchies*, one of which is a default hierarchy. Hierarchies describe relationships between dimension *levels*. Levels consist of dimension *attributes* that are specified in CWM Core package. We will not describe all attributes, depicted in Figure 7, but only those which are used in transition algorithm (see Section 2.3). According to CWM, time dimension is specially marked with property *isTime*. Each dimension attribute has a property *isCandidate*. This property is not present in CWM and is added by authors. It indicates whether the attribute is mentioned in the new business requirements or is mentioned only in the business requirements of existing projects (see Section 2.4). The example model of the WebCT data mart from our case study can be represented by instance diagrams of the OLAP package of CWM. The instance diagram in Figure 3 represent the cube *Activity* and its properties - measures (*Hit number*, *Data amount*, *Time*) and dimensions - *Time*, *Course*, *Tool*, *Person*, *Program*, *Session* etc.

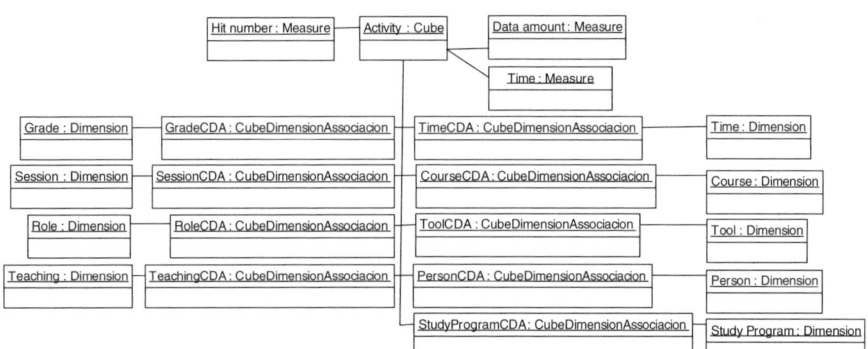

Figure 3. The instance diagram of the cube elements according to CWM

2.3. Transition Algorithm

We propose an algorithm for creating cubes and dimensions which are defined in the New System requirements. Conceptual models of the New and the Old System will be further called the *New* and *the Old Schema* correspondingly.

The algorithm is based on "building" a data mart from "bricks", that is from such New System requirement components as objects and expressions. Both of these components provide information about cube and dimension attributes of the New Schema. All attribute names should be precise in order not to create confusion. For example, if there is an attribute "Status" in "Person" dimension and in "E-course" dimension, then in the requirements a status should be unambiguously defined either as "person status" or "e-course status".

2.4. The Algorithm Body and Description

The algorithm, written in pseudocode, describes the main ideas of a data mart construction process. It is based on the Old System and the New System business requirements comparison.

The Old and the New System requirements are the parameters for *BuildNewSchema* procedure (Figure 4). All New Schema requirements are analyzed in turn (line 2). The main cycle is split in two parts: Simple Requirements (lines 3-25) and Typified Condition (lines 26-35) analysis.

Searching for an element in the Old System that corresponds to that in the New System, we check quantifying or qualifying data, presented by one or more operations applied to an object (for example, "avg(sum(hits))"). The function *mappingReq* is searching for the New System's business requirement element value among the Old System's elements. The function gets as the 1st parameter the value of the element, which we are looking for in the Old System requirements, presented by the 2nd parameter. The function returns the value of the Old System element that maps the 1st parameter (if anything is found). If function execution result (*mapElement*) is not null, then quantifying data as the dimension attribute or qualifying data as the fact table measure are added to the New Schema (lines 7-10). The function *createDimAttribute* (lines 8, 29) gets as the 1st parameter the name of the schema and as the 2nd parameter – *mapElement*. Function adds an attribute, which name is contained in *mapElement*, to the dimension in the New Schema. This function sets an attribute property *isCandidate* to 'no' by default. The function *createCubeMeasure* (line 10) gets as the 1st parameter the name of the New Schema and as the 2nd parameter the name of fact table measure, contained in *mapElement*, and adds it to the cube. If nothing is found, then the "outer" operation (in our example: "avg") is removed (line 13) and the check is repeated (line 4). Finally, when all aggregations are consequently eliminated and the element is found, then the dimension attribute or fact table measure (described in *mapElement*) is added to the New Schema (lines 7-10). If there was no aggregation applied to Simple Requirement object, then the new attribute or measure is added to the New Schema (lines 19-23). The function *createNewDimAttribute* (lines 20, 31) gets similar parameters as function *createDimAttribute*. It is used to add an attribute that is not in the New Schema. If there is no corresponding dimension found, then a new dimension with the same name as the attribute is created and the attribute is added to it. The function *createNewCubeMeasure* (line 22) gets similar parameters as procedure *createCubeMeasure*. This function adds a new measure to the New Schema cube.

```
{1} Procedure BuildNewSchema (NewRequirement, OldRequirement) {
{2} for each newReq in NewRequirement.Requirement {
{3}    for each newSimpleReq in NewRequirement.SimpleRequirement {
{4}       do {
{5}             mapElement = mappingReq (newSimpleReq, OldRequirement);
{6}             if mapElement is not null {
{7}                if mapElement is QualifyingData
{8}                   map = createDimAttribute (NewSchema, mapElement);
{9}             else
{10}                  map = createCubeMeasure (NewSchema, mapElement);
{11}         else
{12}            if newSimpleReq.Operation is not null
{13}                  remove outer Action from newSimpleReq;
{14}            else
{15}               exit;
{16}         }
{17}      } while mapElement is null
{18}         if mapElement is null {
{19}            if newSimpleReq is QualifyingData
{20}               map = createNewDimAttribute (NewSchema, newSimpleReq);
{21}            else
{22}               map = createNewCubeMeasure (NewSchema, newSimpleReq);
{23}         }
{24}      mapping(map, mapElement);
{25}   }
{26}   for each qualData in newReq.TypifiedCondition.SimpleCondition.QualifyingData {
{27}      mapElement = mappingReq (qualData, OldRequirement);
{28}         if mapElement is not null
{29}            map = createDimAttribute (NewSchema, mapElement);
{30}         else
{31}            map = createNewDimAttribute (NewSchema, qualData);
{32}      mapping(map, mapElement);
{33}   }
{34} }
{35} }
```

Figure 4. Listing of BuildNewSchema procedure

Dimension attributes may be described by qualifying data in Simple Conditions. The function *mappingReq* searches for an element in the New System requirements that corresponds to that in the Old System requirements. If element is found, then a copy of it appears in the New Schema, if not – a new element is created (lines 26-33).

```
{36} Procedure AddCandidateAttribute (NewSchema, OldSchema) {
{37}    for each dim in NewSchema {
{38}       for each oldAttr in OldSchema.Dimension.Attribute where OldSchema.Dimension = dim {
{39}          if oldAttr is not present in dim {
{40}             attr = createCandidateAttribute (NewSchema, dim, oldAttr);
{41}             setCandidate (attr, 'yes');
{42}          }
{43}       }
{44}    }
{45} }
```

Figure 5. Listing of AddCandidateAttribute procedure

When all necessary dimensions are created in the New Schema, there may be some elements in the Old System business requirements that are not in the New System business requirements. That's why there may be attributes that are used in the Old Schema and absent in the New Schema. By means of *AddCandidateAttribute* procedure (Figure 5) we have to add such attributes from corresponding Old Schema dimensions. The added attribute property *isCandidate* is set to 'yes', because there is no guarantee that this attribute will not be used in the future in the New Schema (line 41). Creating a new data mart, using knowledge about the previous schemas, only attributes with *isCandidate* property equal to 'no' will be considered as potential dimension attributes.

```
{46} Procedure AddHierarchyLevels (NewSchema, OldSchema) {
{47}    for each attr in NewSchema.Dimension.Attribute {
{48}       mapElement = mappingAttr (attr, OldSchema);
{49}       if mapElement is not null {
{50}          level = checkLevel (mapElement, OldSchema);
{51}            if level = 'yes' {
{52}               oldHierarchy = getHierarchyName (mapElement, oldSchema);
{53}                  if repeats (oldHierarchy, NewSchema) = 'no' {
{54}                     newHierarchy = createNewHierarchy (NewSchema, oldHierarchy);
{55}                        for each oldLevel in OldHierarchy.Level
{56}                           assignLevel (newHierarchy, oldLevel);
{57}                  }
{58}            }
{59}       }
{60}    }
{61} }
```

Figure 6. Listing of AddHierarchyLevels procedure

Final step of the algorithm is creating hierarchies in the New Schema (Figure 6). For each attribute in the New Schema we are trying to find a corresponding attribute in the Old Schema (line 48), using function *mappingAttr*. If such attribute is found, then we have to check whether this attribute is a level of any hierarchy or not (line 50). Suppose it is. After finding out by means of *getHierarchyName* procedure which Old Schema hierarchy the current attribute belongs to (line 52), we have to check if the hierarchy with such name already exists in the New Schema. If it doesn't (line 53), then, using the procedure *createNewHierarchy*, in the New Schema a copy of the foregoing hierarchy from the Old Schema is created (line 54). Finally, we have to assign hierarchy levels from the Old Schema hierarchy to that in the New Schema (line 55).

3. Selecting Conceptual Model for Transition Algorithm

Procedures of transition algorithm (see Section 2.3) get as input parameters either business requirements of the Old and The New System or the New and the Old Schema. However, if there is available knowledge about more than one data warehouse project in the same business area, then there is a question – which system should be considered as 'the Old System' for transition algorithm? Let's name conceptual models of similar data warehouse projects as *related data mart schema collections*.

We propose 3 options for selecting one data mart conceptual model from a related data mart schema collection in the same business area – 1) the newest conceptual model from related data mart schema collection, 2) the mixed conceptual model and 3) the conceptual model which matches the New Schema best of all, according to the set of requirements. Each option is analyzed by getting answers to the following questions:

- what is the way of selecting the Old Schema?
- what is the expected number of differences between the New Schema and selected Old Schema?
- what are the additional requirements for transition algorithm modification?

Let's start with *the newest of the existing conceptual models.*

- The way of selecting the Old Schema:

All existing conceptual models in knowledge base are arranged by date and time of its creation and the newest conceptual model is selected as the Old Schema.

- The expected number of differences between the New Schema and selected Old Schema:

The number of differences is between "slight difference" and "striking difference" – depends on how similar business requirements of the corresponding Old System and the New System are.

- Additional requirements:

The metamodel for description of data warehouse conceptual model has to be modified in order to ensure keeping information about date and time of creation of data mart schema. No changes required to transition algorithm.

It is possible that the selected Old System's business requirements will have very little in common with the New System requirements, meaning that knowledge about previous project will not be efficiently used during the process of creation of the New Schema.

The next is *mixed conceptual model (or all existing conceptual models united into one).*

- The way of selecting the Old Schema:

The oldest conceptual model of related data mart schema collection is supplemented with elements of newer conceptual models. The obtained mixed conceptual model is called 'the Old Schema' in transition algorithm.

- The expected number of differences between the New Schema and the selected Old Schema:

Difference between the New Schema and the chosen Old Schema will be minimal, but the Old Schema is complicated, meaning that in the New Schema will appear many candidate attributes which might not be used afterwards.

- Additional requirements:

An algorithm for merging all conceptual models into one should be created. No changes required to transition algorithm.

Finally, let's analyze *the conceptual model which has the biggest number of matches between corresponding system business requirements and business requirements of the New System.*

- The way of selecting the Old Schema:

Business requirements of all existing Old Systems in the same business area are consequently compared with business requirements of the New System. The Old Schema is the one that refers to the system which has the smallest number of differences when comparing to the New System business requirements. Detection of similarity is the following: business requirements are re-written formally, according to the metamodel (Figure 2). Each business requirement of existing systems is compared by each element to business requirements of the New System. Compared business requirements are similar (the requirements are identical), partly similar ((i) one or more simple requirements or typified condition of the requirements are identical, (ii) separate requirement elements (e.g. object, operation, etc.) are identical) or different (there are no identical elements).

If there are two or more existing systems with the same number of business requirements that are similar/partly similar to business requirements of the New System, then the newest conceptual model of existing systems is called 'the Old Schema' in transition algorithm.

If the New System business requirements and business requirements of existing systems do not have similar elements at all, then the way of selecting the Old Schema is the same as in the first approach – conceptual model of the newest existing system is called 'the Old Schema' in transition algorithm.

- The number of differences between the New Schema and the selected Old Schema:

Difference between the New Schema and the chosen Old Schema will be minimal.

- Additional requirements:

The metamodel for description of data warehouse conceptual model should be modified in order to (i) ensure keeping information about date and time of creation of data mart schema, (ii) to store number of similar elements for each pair of business requirements (New System business requirements and existing system business requirements).

We prefer 3rd approach to others for several reasons. The 1st approach is useful only if business requirements of the New System are completely or partly included into business requirements of the Old System. The 2nd approach is more universal, but a lot of analysis is demanded to decide which candidate attributes should or should not be eliminated. The 3rd approach includes the 1st approach in case, if the latest Old System has the biggest number of similar elements, comparing business requirements of the Old and the New System. This approach is based on re-using conceptual model of the Old Schema most effectively.

An algorithm for selection of the most matching conceptual model to the New Schema has to be created. For instance, 1) compare consequently all business requirements of the New System to business requirements of each of the Old Systems; 2) find business requirements of the Old System which are the most similar to the business requirements of the New System that is with the largest number of similar elements; 3) pick the Old Schema which refers to the chosen Old System.

In order to store information about multiple data mart schemas, which refer to similar data warehouse projects, some changes to metamodel for data warehouse conceptual model description are necessary (Figure 7).

We extended metamodel for description of data warehouse conceptual model (based on CWM) by attributes: *Business area* – business area of the corresponding data warehouse project (for example, finance, education, etc.), *Created* – the date and time when the Schema was created, *Matching schema ID* – each schema has from zero to many matching schemas – it depends on the quantity of conceptual models in related data mart schema collection, *NSE* – number of similar elements, according to metamodel in Figure 2, and *isNew* – indicates whether the Schema is in related data mart schema collection or not (to avoid comparison of two Old Schemas).

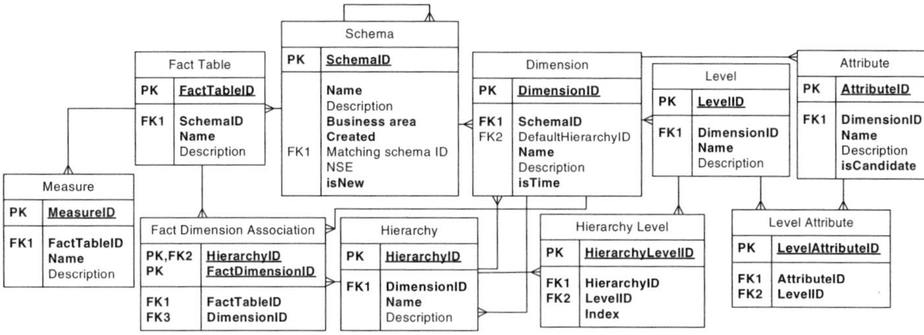

Figure 7. Extended metamodel for data warehouse conceptual model description

4. Conclusion and Future Work

The main contribution of this paper is the method for constructing a conceptual model of a data warehouse using the transition algorithm, which takes advantage of the existing information about requirements and a conceptual model of a successful data warehouse project. The method is applicable in situations when the knowledge base of other data warehouse projects with similar requirements in related areas is available.

We used CWM to describe conceptual models of data warehouses. It reflects only models that are composed of basic elements of data warehouses, but the possibility of using other, more complicated conceptual models of data warehouses (for example, discussed in [21]) should be also considered.

The proposed method was successfully applied in the case study project of the development of the data warehouse for e-learning assessment, using the knowledge of one existing project. Evaluation of our approach in situations when the knowledge about several similar data warehouses is available as well as extended metamodel for data warehouse conceptual model description is proposed in this paper. In order to measure the applicability of our approach, it would be desirable to utilize the proposed method for building conceptual models of data warehouses in areas other than education (e.g., finance).

Acknowledgements

This research was partly supported by the European Social Fund (ESF).

References

[1] Winter, R., & Strauch, B. (2003) A Method for Demand-driven Information Requirements Analysis in Data Warehousing Projects. In Proceedings of 36th Annual Hawaii International Conference on System Sciences (HICSS '03), January 6-9, Waikoloa, Hawaii, USA, IEEE, p. 231.1. (available at http://www.hicss.hawaii.edu/HICSS36/HICSSpapers/OSDWH01.pdf)

[2] Artz, J. M. (2005) Data Driven vs. Metric Driven Data Warehouse Design, Encyclopedia of Data Warehousing and Mining, 2(1): pp. 223-227.

[3] List, B., Bruckner, R. M., Machaczek, K., & Schiefer, J. (2002) A Comparison of Data Warehouse Development Methodologies Case Study of the Process Warehouse. In Hameurlain, A., et. Al. (eds)

Database and Expert Systems Applications (DEXA 2002), September 2-6, Aix-en-Provence, France, London:Springer, (LNCS), pp. 203-215.
[4] Westerman, P. (2000) Data Warehousing using the Wal-Mart Model. Morgan Kaufmann, 2000, 1st ed., 297 p.
[5] Poe, V., Klauer, P., & Brobst, S. (1996) Building a Data Warehouse for Decision Support. Prentice Hall, 1996, 2nd ed., 285 p.
[6] Kaldeich, C., & Oliveira, J. (2004) Data Warehouse Methodology: A Process Driven Approach. In Persson, A., & Stirna, J. (eds) 16th Conference on Advanced Information Systems Engineering (CAiSE 2004), June 7-11, Riga, Latvia, Berlin:Springer, (LNCS), pp. 536-549.
[7] Giorgini, P., Rizzi, S., & Garzetti, M. (2005) Goal-Oriented Requirement Analysis for Data Warehouse Design. In Song, I.-Y. & Trujillo, J. (eds) 8th ACM International Workshop on Data Warehousing and OLAP (DOLAP 2005), November 4-5, Bremen, Germany, pp. 47-56.
[8] Bonifati, A., Cattaneo, F., Ceri, S., Fuggetta, A., & Paraboschi, S. (2001) Designing Data Marts for Data Warehouses, ACM Transactions on Software Engineering and Methodology (TOSEM), 10(4): 452-483
[9] List, B., & Machaczek, K. (2004) Towards a Corporate Performance Measurement System. In Haddad, H. et. Al. (eds) ACM Symposium on Applied Computing (SAC), March 14-17, Nicosia, Cyprus, pp. 1344-1350.
[10] Benefelds, J., & Niedrite, L. (2004) Comparison of Approaches in Data Warehouse Development in Financial Services and Higher Education. In Seruca, I., et. Al (eds) 6th International Conference of Enterprise Information Systems (ICEIS 2004), April 14-15, Porto, Portugal, pp. 552-557.
[11] Solodovnikova, D., Niedrite, L. (2005) Using Data Warehouse Resources for Assessment of E-Learning Influence on University Processes. In Eder, J., et. Al. (eds) 9th East-European Conference on Advances in Databases and Information Systems (ADBIS 2005), September 12-15, Tallinn, Estonia, pp. 233-248.
[12] Niedrite, L., Solodovnikova, D., Treimanis, M., & Niedritis, A. (2007) The Development Method for Process-Oriented Data Warehouse, WSEAS Transactions on Computer Research, 2(2): pp. 183-90.
[13] Jones, M. E., Song I.-Y. (2005) Dimensional Modeling: Identifying, Classifying & Applying Patterns. In Song, I.-Y. & Trujillo, J. (eds) 8th ACM International Workshop on Data Warehousing and OLAP (DOLAP 2005), November 4-5, Bremen, Germany, pp. 29-37.
[14] Sapia, C., Blaschka, M., Höfling, & G., Dinter, B. (1998) Extending the E/R Model for the Multidimensional Paradigm. In Kambayashi, Y., et. Al. (eds) Workshops on Data Warehousing and Data Mining: Advances in Database Technologies, November 19-20, Singapore, London:Springer, (LNCS), vol. 1552, pp. 105-116.
[15] Lujan-Mora, S., Trujillo, J., & Song, I. (2002) Extending the UML for Multidimensional Modeling. In Jézéquel, J.-M., et. Al. (eds) 5th International Conference, UML 2002 – The Unified Modeling Language, September 30 – October 4, Dresden, Germany, Springer, (LNCS), pp. 290-304.
[16] Golfarelli, M., Maio, D., & Rizzi, S. (1998) Conceptual Design of Data Warehouses from E/R Schemes. In Proceedings of 31st Annual Hawaii International Conference on System Sciences (HICSS '98), January 6-9, Kona, Hawaii, USA, IEEE, vol. VII, pp. 334-343. (available at http://www-db.deis.unibo.it/~srizzi/PDF/hicss98.pdf)
[17] Rizzi, S., Abelló, A., Lechtenbörger, J., & Trujillo, J. (2006) Research in data warehouse modeling and design: dead or alive? In Song, I.-Y., & Vassiliadis, P. (eds) 9th ACM International Workshop on Data Warehousing and OLAP (DOLAP 2006), Arlington, Virginia, USA, pp. 3-10.
[18] Videira, C., & Silva A. R. (2005) Patterns and Metamodel for a Natural-language-based requirements specification language. In Belo, O., et. Al. (eds) 17th Conference on Advanced Information Systems Engineering (CAiSE '05), June 13-17, Porto, Portugal, pp. 189-194.
[19] Kozmina, N., Niedrite, L., & Solodovnikova, D. (2008) A Knowledge-based Method for Transforming Requirements to Conceptual Model of a Data Warehouse. In Haav, H.-M., & Kalja, A. (eds) 8th International Baltic Conference on Databases and Informational Systems (DBIS '08), June 2-5, Tallinn, Estonia, pp. 63-74.
[20] Poole, J., Chang, D., Tolbert, D., & Mellor, D. (2003) Common Warehouse Metamodel Developers Guide. Wiley Publishing, 2003, 1st ed., 704 p.
[21] Abelló, A., Samos, J., & Saltor, F. (2001) A Framework for the Classification and Description of Multidimensional Data Models. In Mayr H. C., et. Al. (eds) 12th International Conference, Database and Expert Systems Applications (DEXA 2001), September 3-5, Munich, Germany, Berlin:Springer, (LNCS), pp. 668-677.

Databases and Information Systems V
H.-M. Haav and A. Kalja (Eds.)
IOS Press, 2009

doi:10.3233/978-1-58603-939-4-91

The Formal Model for Multiversion Data Warehouse Evolution

Darja SOLODOVNIKOVA[1]
Department of Computer Science, University of Latvia

Abstract. Schemata of data warehouses often need to be adapted because of evolving business requirements or changes in data sources. To accumulate the history of schemata and data, it is possible to maintain multiple versions of data warehouse schemata. We propose the formal model to store the data about data warehouse logical and physical schemata and their versions. For each modification of a data warehouse schema, we outline the changes that need to be made to the formal model. We present the data warehouse framework that is able to track evolution process and adapt data warehouse schemata and data extraction, transformation and loading (ETL) processes.

Keywords. data warehouse evolution, schema versioning, formal model

Introduction

Changes in data sources and business requirements of a data warehouses can invalidate existing schemata and data extraction, transformation and loading (ETL) processes of the data warehouse. This is why these changes need to be handled properly. In many cases the existing data warehouse schema and ETL processes can be adapted to changes automatically or with minimal manual work. Simple adaptation of the data warehouse schema can cause a loss of history. This is why, it is necessary to keep versions of data warehouse schemata. According to [1], 'schema version is a schema that reflects the business requirements during a given time interval, called its validity, that starts upon schema creation and extends until the next version is created.'

In this paper the formal model of the multiversion data warehouse is discussed. The model includes physical and logical information about data warehouse schema versions. At the physical level an implementation of a data warehouse in RDBMS is specified, bet the logical level describes schema versions of a data warehouse. These two levels are connected by special mappings. The impact of changes of data warehouse schema on the physical and logical level of the model is also discussed.

The rest of this paper is organized as follows. In Section 1 the related work is presented. In Section 2 the proposed data warehouse evolution framework is outlined. The main contribution of this paper is presented in Sections 3 and 4 where the formal model for a multiversion data warehouse is described, and changes of the data warehouse schema that are supported by the proposed framework and their results are discussed. We conclude with directions for future work in Section 5.

[1] Corresponding Author: Darja Solodovnikova, University of Latvia, Raina blvd. 19, Riga, LV 1586, Latvia; E-mail: darja.solodovnikova@lu.lv.

1. Related Work

In the literature there are various solutions for the data warehouse evolution problems, which are the data warehouse adaptation after the changes in source data and schemata as well as business requirements.

Changes in dimensions of a data warehouse are discussed in [2]. Dimension structural and instance update operators are formally specified, and their effect is studied over materialized views over dimension levels. In [3] a temporal multidimensional data model is proposed to track history of dimension updates.

In [4], [5] the primitive evolution operations that occur over the data warehouse schema are defined. The necessary adaptation activities of the data warehouse schema and instances are formally specified for each operation. In [5] the formal semantics of the changes for star and snowflake schemata are given for each operation.

The above mentioned papers do not address the problems of the data warehouse adaptation after changes in data sources. Several approaches have been proposed for solving these problems [6], [7], [8]. These approaches are based on mappings or transformations that specify how one schema is obtained from the other schema. This specification is used to adapt one schema after changes in the other schema.

In several papers [9], [10] a data warehouse is defined as a set of materialized views over data sources. These papers study the problems of how to rewrite a view definition and adapt view extent after changes in source data and schemata.

In all these approaches schema versioning is not supported. Several authors [1], [11], [12] propose the data warehouse schema versioning approach to solve the problems of schema evolution. The main idea in [1] is to store augmented schemata together with schema versions to support cross-version querying. When a new version is created, for all previous versions, augmented schemata are created and populated with data. Though the metadata of schema versions is mentioned, the details are not explored. In [11] the definition of a multidimensional schema that supports schema versioning is given. This definition is very similar to the one given in [13], the difference is that the first one supports versioning. In [14] a method to support data and structure versions of dimensions is proposed. The method allows tracking history and comparing data using temporal modes of presentation that is data mapping into the particular structure version. In [12] metadata management solutions in a multiversion data warehouse are proposed, where one of the discussed issues is metadata support for detection of changes in sources and propagation of them to the designated data warehouse version. Issues related to queries over a multiversion data warehouse are considered in [15], but the translation of queries to SQL is not discussed.

The above mentioned papers consider only one kind of evolution problems, for example, changes in a schema of a data warehouse raised by evolving business requirements, adaptation of a data warehouse after changes in data sources or data warehouse versioning and querying multiversion data warehouse. In our approach we propose the framework that is able to solve all these kinds of evolution problems.

2. Data Warehouse Evolution Framework

To handle data warehouse evolution problems, we propose the data warehouse framework depicted in Figure 1. In this section only the general issues of the framework are discussed. The detailed description of the framework is given in [16].

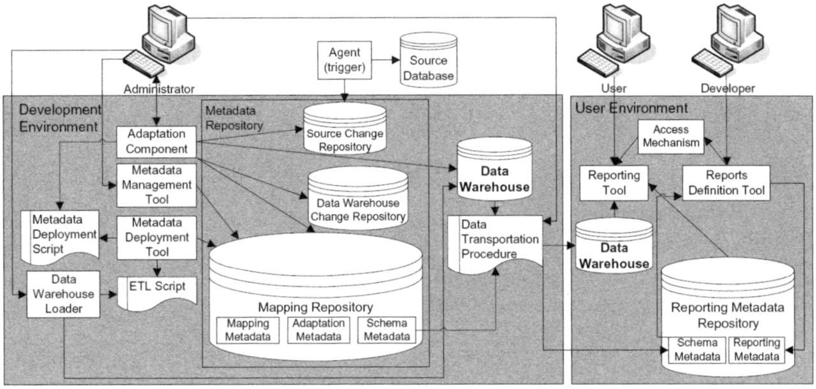

Figure 1. Data warehouse evolution framework

The framework is composed of the development environment and user environment. In the development environment the data warehouse metadata repository and other metadata management components are located and ETL processes and change processing is conducted. In the user environment reports on one or several data warehouse versions are defined and executed by users.

The metadata of the logical data warehouse schema versions and physical database structure are stored in the mapping repository. Also the repository includes mapping metadata, which define the logics of ETL processes, and the adaptation metadata, which are used for data warehouse adaptation. The detailed description of the mapping and adaptation metadata as well as the operation of the adaptation component is found in the paper [17]. The schema metadata are based on the formal model of a data warehouse presented in sections 3.1, 3.2 and 3.3.

In addition to the data warehouse, in the user environment there is also the reporting metadata, which are used by the reporting tool for generation of reports. These metadata are presented in [18]. Using links between data warehouse versions in the metadata repository, the reporting tool can run queries on multiple data warehouse schema versions or one version. In the user environment an access mechanism is also implemented. It is the metadata that defines which elements of a data warehouse schema and information can be accessed by the particular user.

3. Formal Model of Multiversion Data Warehouse

Using the following formal model, it is possible to desigm a data warehouse schema at physical and logical level. The logical level describes the data warehouse schema. The physical level describes relational database schema. The physical level does not include versioning information, because versioning is implemented at the logical level.

3.1. Logical Level

At the logical level a data warehouse is a set of schemata and their versions.

A *schema* is a tuple $DWS=<F,D,FDA,V,MAP>$, where $F=\{fact_1,...,fact_a\}$ is a set of fact tables, $D=\{dim_1,...,dim_b\}$ is a set of dimensions, $FDA=\{fda_1,...,fda_c\}$ is a set of fact dimension associations, $V=\{v_1,...,v_u\}$ is a set schema versions, where $v_u \in V$ is a currently valid schema version, and $MAP=\{map_1,...,map_e\}$ is a set of attribute and measure mappings.

Fact dimension association fda∈FDA is a tuple $<dim,fact>$, which associates dimension $dim \in D$ with fact table $fact \in F$.

Dimension dim∈D is a tuple $<ATT,LEV,H,AL,HL>$, where $ATT=\{att_1,...,att_f\}$ is a set of *attributes*, $LEV=\{lev_1,...,lev_g\}$ is a set of *levels*, $H=\{h_1,...,h_k\}$ is a set of *hierarchies*, $AL=\{al_1,...,al_l\}$ is a set of attribute level associations and $HL=\{hl_1,...,hl_m\}$ is a set of hierarchy level associations.

Attribute level association al∈AL is a tuple $<att,lev>$, which associates attribute $att \in ATT$ with level $lev \in LEV$.

Hierarchy level association hl∈HL is a tuple $<lev,h>$, which associates level $lev \in LEV$ with hierarchy $h \in H$.

Fact table fact∈F is a tuple $<MS>$, where $MS=\{ms_1,...,ms_n\}$ is a set of *measures*.

Schema version v∈V is a tuple $<\tau_{from}, \tau_{to}, VT>$, where τ_{from} and τ_{to} are times, which define the validity period of the schema version, $VT=\{vt_1,...,vt_r\}$ is a set of version transformations.

Version transformation vt∈VT is a tuple $<el,conv,E>$, which states that an element $el \in ELEM$ ($ELEM=F \cup D \cup FDA \cup ATT \cup LEV \cup H \cup AL \cup HL \cup MS$) is obtained from a set of elements $E \subseteq ELEM$ by a conversion function *conv*. If an element *el* is obtained from directly from the database, then $vt=<el,null,null>$.

3.2. Physical Level

At the physical level a relational database schema of a data warehouse is described.

A *relational database schema* is a tuple $DBS=<CS>$, where $CS=\{cs_1,...,cs_s\}$ is a set of column sets. A column set reflects a database table, view or query.

Column set cs∈CS is a tuple $<C,KEY,DOMA>$, where $C=\{c_1,...,c_y\}$ is a set of *columns*, $KEY=\{key_1,...,key_m\}$ is a set of keys and $DOMA=\{doma_1,...,doma_z\}$ is a set of column domain associations.

Key key∈KEY is a tuple $<type,KC,pk>$, where $type \in \{$'PRIMARY', 'FOREIGN'$\}$, $KC \subset C$ is a set of key columns and, if *type='FOREIGN'* then $pk \in KEY'$ is a primary key, *KEY'* is a set of keys of any column set.

Column domain association doma∈DOMA is a tuple $<c,dom>$, which associates domain *dom* with column $c \in C$.

3.3. Mappings

A *mapping* of measures and attributes of a data warehouse map∈MAP is a tuple $<el,mapfun,EC>$, where $el \in ATT \cup MS$ is a mapped element, mapfunc is a function, which specifies how the element el is obtained from a set of columns $EC \subseteq C$. In this paper it is assumed that attributes and measures are obtained directly from columns by the mapping function "copy", i.e. $map=<el,'copy',\{c\}>$, where $c \in C$.

4. Supported Changes

The data warehouse evolution framework supports physical and logical changes that create a new data warehouse schema version. Physical changes operate with database objects (tables, columns), but logical changes modify mainly the logical level of the model. As a result of a logical change, logical level is adapted and there may be no changes at the physical level, except for new keys or key columns. As a result of a physical change, both logical and physical levels are modified.

As a result of every change a new schema version v' is constructed from the previous version v_u. Each change procedure is describes as a sequence of steps, which modify the data warehouse schema $DWS=<F,D,FDA,V,MAP>$ and the database schema $DBS=<T,VW,Q,CS>$. The output of the change procedure is a new data warehouse schema $DWS'=<F',D',FDA',V',MAP'>$ at the logical level and a new database schema $DBS'=<T',VW',Q',CS'>$ at the physical level. If the physical schema is not changed, then the description the physical level is omitted.

4.1. Common Procedures

The following common procedures are used in change procedures:

$v'=duplicate(v)$ is a function, which creates a version v', which contains the same elements as a version v. If $v=<\tau_{from},\tau_{to},VT>$, then $v'=<\tau_{now},null,VT'>$, where τ_{now} is the current time and VT' is a set of version transformations, where for each $vt=<el,conv,E>\in VT$ a corresponding version transformation is constructed $vt'=<el,conv,E>\in VT'$. If τ_{to} is null then $v=<\tau_{from},\tau_{now}\text{-}1,VT>$.

$VT=vtrans(elem)$ is a recursive function, which returns the set of version transformations $\{vt_1,\ldots,vt_i\}$, which require an element $elem\in ELEM$. The transformations returned by this functions are the following $vt=<elem,null,null>$ or $vt=<el,conv,E>$ and $elem\in E$, where $el\in ELEM$, $conv$ is any conversion function. In the last case the function $vtrans(elem)$ returns also $vtrans(el)$.

$key=primary(cs)$ is a function, which returns the primary key of the column set cs. If $cs=<C,KEY,DOMA>$ then $key=<'PRIMARY',KC,null>\in KEY$.

4.2. Physical Changes

4.2.1. New Dimension Attribute

A new attribute att is added to the dimension $dim=<ATT,LEV,H,AL,HL>$. The column set $cs=<C,KEY,DOMA>$ corresponds to the dimension dim.

Physical level: A new column c' is created in the column set cs.

1. c'=new Column;
2. Set $cs=<C\cup\{c'\},KEY,DOMA\cup\{<c',dom_{att}>\})>$, where dom_{att} is a domain, which corresponds to att;
3. return $DBS'=<T,VW,Q,CS>$.

Logical level: A new attribute att is attached to the dimension dim. A mapping is created to connect c' with att. The version transformation for v_u can be constructed for att, if it can be calculated from other attributes.

1. $v'=duplicate(v_u)=<\tau_{now},null,VT'>$;
2. Set $dim=<ATT\cup\{att\},LEV,H,AL,HL>$;

3. Set $v'=<\tau_{now},null,VT'\cup\{<att,null,null>\}>$;
4. If *att* can be calculated from other attributes $\{att_i,\ldots,att_j\}$ of the dimension *dim* by the function *conv*, then set $v_u=<\tau_{from},\tau_{to},VT_u\cup\{<att,conv,\{att_i,\ldots,att_j\}>\}>$;
5. return $DWS'=<F,D,FDA,V\cup\{v'\},MAP\cup\{<att,'copy',\{c'\}>\}>$.

4.2.2. Deletion of Dimension Attribute

An attribute *att* is deleted from the dimension $dim=<ATT,LEV,H,AL,HL>$. An attribute can be deleted only if in the current version it is not connected to any level. If a connection persists, at first an attribute must be disconnected from all levels. It is not allowed to delete an attribute that corresponds to a primary key column.

Logical level: The version transformation for *v'* can be constructed for *att*, if it can be calculated from other attributes. In other case the attribute *att* and other dependant attributes are removed from the version *v'*.

1. $v'=duplicate(v_u)=<\tau_{now},null,VT'>$;
2. If the attribute *att* can be calculated from the remaining attributes $\{att_i,\ldots,att_j\}$ of the dimension *dim* by the function *conv*, then Set $v'=<\tau_{now},null,VT'\cup\{<att,conv,\{att_i,\ldots,att_j\}>\}>$;
   otherwise Set $v'=<\tau_{now},null,VT'\backslash vtrans(att)>$;
3. return $DWS'=<F,D,FDA,V\cup\{v'\},MAP>$.

4.2.3. Change of Domain of Column

A domain *dom* of the column *c* of the column set $cs=<C,KEY,DOMA>\in CS$ is changed to *dom'*. The element $el\in ATT\cup MS$ of the dimension or fact table $tab\in D\cup F$ is obtained from column *c* by mapping $map=<el,'copy',\{c\}>$. The functions $conv_{dom\text{->}dom'}$ and $conv_{dom'\text{->}dom}$ are function, which convert values between corresponding domains.

Physical level: A new column *c'* is created in the column set *cs*.

1. c'=new Column;
2. Set $cs=<C\cup\{c'\},KEY,DOMA\cup\{<c',dom'>\}>$;
3. return $DBS'=<T,VW,Q,CS>$.

Logical level: A new attribute or measure *el'* is added to *tab*. A mapping is created to connect *c'* with *el'*. Both version v' and v_u are supplemented by version transformations to covert values between versions of the element.

1. $v'=duplicate(v_u)=<\tau_{now},null,VT'>$;
2. el'=new Attribute or Measure;
3. Set $tab=<ATT\cup\{el'\},LEV,H,AL,HL>$ or $tab=<MS\cup\{el'\}>$;
4. Set $v_u=<\tau_{from},\tau_{to},VT_u\cup\{<el',conv_{dom\text{->}dom'},\{el\}>\}>$;
5. Set $v'=<\tau_{now},null,VT'\cup\{<el,conv_{dom'\text{->}dom},\{el'\}>\}>$;
6. return $DWS'=<F,D,FDA,V\cup\{v'\},MAP\cup\{<el','copy',\{c'\}>\}>$.

4.2.4. New Dimension

A new dimension *dim* with attributes $\{att_1,\ldots,att_i\}$ is added.

Physical level: A new column set *cs* is created with its' columns and domains.

1. cs=new Column set;
2. For each $att_j\in\{att_1,\ldots,att_i\}$ do c_j=new Column;
3. Set $cs=<\{c_1,\ldots,c_i\},null,\{<c_1,dom_1>,\ldots,<c_i,\ldots,dom_i>\}>$, where $dom_1,\ldots,dom_i$ are domains, which correspond to attributes $\{att_1,\ldots,att_i\}$;

4. return $DBS'=\langle T,VW,Q,CS\cup\{cs\}\rangle$.

Logical level: A new dimension with attributes is added. Mappings are created to connect columns of the column set *cs* with attributes of the dimension *dim*.

1. $v'=duplicate(v_u)=\langle \tau_{now},null,VT'\rangle$;
2. Set $dim=\langle\{att_1,\ldots,att_i\},null,null,null,null\rangle$;
3. For each $att_j\in\{att_1,\ldots,att_i\}$ do $map_j=$new Mapping($\langle att_j,'copy',\{c_j\}\rangle$);
4. Set $v'=\langle \tau_{now},null,VT'\cup\{\langle dim,null,null\rangle,\langle att_1,null,null\rangle,\ldots,\langle att_i,null,null\rangle\}\rangle$;
5. return $DWS'=\langle F,D,FDA,V\cup\{v'\},MAP\cup\{map_1,\ldots,map_i\}\rangle$.

4.2.5. Deletion of Dimension

A dimension *dim* is deleted. A dimension can be deleted only if in the current version it does not contain levels and hierarchies and is not connected to any fact table. If a connection persists, at first a dimension must be disconnected from all fact tables.

Logical level: The attributes of the dimension *dim* and other dependant attributes are removed from the version *v'*.

1. $v'=duplicate(v_u)$;
2. $v'=\langle \tau_{now},null,VT'\backslash(vtrans(att_1)\cup\ldots\cup vtrans(att_i))\rangle$;
3. return $DWS'=\langle F,D,FDA,V\cup\{v'\},MAP\rangle$.

4.2.6. New Measure

A new measure *ms* is added to the fact table $fact=\langle MS\rangle$. The column set $cs=\langle C,KEY,DOMA\rangle$ corresponds to the fact table *fact*.

Physical level: A new column *c'* is created in the column set *cs*.

1. c'=new Column;
2. Set $cs=\langle C\cup\{c'\},KEY,DOMA\cup\{\langle c',dom_{ms}\rangle\}\rangle$, where dom_{ms} is a domain, which corresponds to *ms*;
3. return $DBS'=\langle T,VW,Q,CS\rangle$.

Logical level: A new measure *ms* is attached to the fact table *fact*. A mapping is created to connect *c'* with *ms*. The version transformation for v_u can be constructed for *ms*, if it can be calculated from other measures.

1. $v'=duplicate(v_u)=\langle \tau_{now},null,VT'\rangle$;
2. Set $fact=\langle MS\cup\{ms\}\rangle$;
3. Set $v'=\langle \tau_{now},null,VT'\cup\{\langle ms,null,null\rangle\}\rangle$;
4. If *ms* can be calculated from other measures $\{ms_i,\ldots,ms_j\}$ of the fact table *fact* by the function *conv*, then set $v_u=\langle \tau_{from},\tau_{to},VT_u\cup\{\langle ms,conv,\{ms_i,\ldots,ms_j\}\rangle\}\rangle$;
5. return $DWS'=\langle F,D,FDA,V\cup\{v'\},MAP\cup\{\langle ms,'copy',\{c'\}\rangle\}\rangle$.

4.2.7. Deletion of Measure

A measure *ms* is deleted from the fact table *fact*.

Logical level: The version transformation for *v'* can be constructed for *ms*, if it can be calculated from other measures. In other case the measure *ms* and other dependant measures are removed from the version *v'*.

1. $v'=duplicate(v_u)=\langle \tau_{now},null,VT'\rangle$;
2. If the measure *ms* can be calculated from the remaining measures $\{ms_i,\ldots,ms_j\}$ of the fact table *fact* by the function *conv*, then set $v'=\langle \tau_{now},null,VT'\cup\{\langle ms,conv,\{ms_i,\ldots,ms_j\}\rangle\}\rangle$,

otherwise set $v'=\langle\tau_{now},null,VT'\setminus vtrans(ms)\rangle$.

3. return $DWS'=\langle F,D,FDA,V\cup\{v'\},MAP\rangle$.

4.2.8. New Fact Table

A new fact table *fact* with measures $\{ms_1,\ldots,ms_i\}$ is added.

Physical level: A new column set *cs* is created with its' columns and domains.

1. cs=new Column set;
2. For each $ms_j\in\{ms_1,\ldots,ms_i\}$ do c_j=new Column;
3. Set $cs=\langle\{c_1,\ldots,c_i\},null,\{\langle c_1,dom_1\rangle,\ldots,\langle c_i,\ldots,dom_i\rangle\}\rangle$, where $dom_1,\ldots,dom_i$ are domains, which correspond to measures $\{ms_1,\ldots,ms_i\}$;
4. return $DBS'=\langle T,VW,Q,CS\cup\{cs\}\rangle$.

Logical level: A new fact table with measures is added. Mappings are created to connect columns of the column set *cs* with measures of the fact table *fact*.

1. $v'=duplicate(v_u)=\langle\tau_{now},null,VT'\rangle$;
2. Set $fact=\langle\{ms_1,\ldots,ms_i\},null,null,null,null\rangle$;
3. For each $ms_j\in\{ms_1,\ldots,ms_i\}$ do map_j=new Mapping($\langle ms_j,\text{'copy'},\{c_j\}\rangle$);
4. Set $v'=\langle\tau_{now},null,VT'\cup\{\langle ms_1,null,null\rangle,\ldots,\langle ms_i,null,null\rangle\}\rangle$;
5. return $DWS'=\langle F,D,FDA,V\cup\{v'\},MAP\cup\{map_1,\ldots,map_i\}\rangle$.

4.2.9. Deletion of Fact Table

A fact table *fact* is deleted. A fact table can be deleted only if in the current version it is not connected to any dimension. If a connection persists, at first a fact table must be disconnected from all dimensions.

Logical level: The measures of the fact table *fact* and other dependant measures are removed from the version *v'*.

1. $v'=duplicate(v_u)=\langle\tau_{now},null,VT'\rangle$;
2. Set $v'=\langle\tau_{now},null,VT'\setminus(vtrans(ms_1)\cup\ldots\cup vtrans(ms_i))\rangle$;
3. return $DWS'=\langle F,D,FDA,V\cup\{v'\},MAP\rangle$.

4.3. Logical Changes

4.3.1. Connection of Dimension to Fact Table

A dimension $dim=\langle ATT,LEV,H,AL,HL\rangle$ is connected to a fact table $fact=\langle\{ms_1,\ldots,ms_i\}\rangle$, the measures $\{ms_1,\ldots,ms_i\}$ are mapped to columns $\{c_1,\ldots,c_i\}$. The column sets cs_d and $cs_f=\langle C,KEY,DOMA\rangle$ correspond to *dim* and *fact*.

Physical level: A foreign key columns are added to the column set cs_f, which are connected to the primary key columns of the column set cs_d. The columns $c'_1,\ldots,c'_i$ are included in the primary key of the column set cs_f.

1. $pkey_d=primary(cs_d)=\langle\text{'PRIMARY'},\{kc_1,\ldots,kc_i\},null\rangle$;
2. For each $kc_j\in\{kc_1,\ldots,kc_i\}$ do c'_j=new Column;
3. fkey=new Key($\langle\text{'FOREIGN'},\{c'_1,\ldots,c'_i\},pkey\rangle$);
4. $pkey_f=primary(cs_f)=\langle\text{'PRIMARY'},KC,null\rangle$;
5. Set $pkey_f=\langle\text{'PRIMARY'},KC\cup\{c'_1,\ldots,c'_i\},null\rangle$;
6. Set $cs_f=\langle C\cup\{c'_1,\ldots,c'_i\},KEY\cup\{fkey\},DOMA\cup\{\langle c'_1,dom_1\rangle,\ldots,\langle c'_i,\ldots,dom_i\rangle\}\rangle$, where $dom_1,\ldots,dom_i$ are domains, which correspond to columns $\{kc_1,\ldots,kc_i\}$;

7. return $DBS' = \langle T, VW, Q, CS \rangle$.

Logical level: A fact dimension association is created between the fact table *fact* and dimension *dim*. Version transformations are created for measures of the fact table *fact* if it is possible.

1. $v' = duplicate(v_u) = \langle \tau_{now}, null, VT' \rangle$;
2. $fda' = $ new Fact dimension association($\langle dim, fact \rangle$);
3. For each $ms_j \in \{ms_1, \ldots, ms_i\}$ do $ms'_j = $ new Measure;
4. Set $fact = \langle \{ms_1, \ldots, ms_i, ms'_1, \ldots, ms'_i\} \rangle$;
5. For each $ms_j \in \{ms_1, \ldots, ms_i\}$ do $map'_j = $ new Mapping($\langle ms'_j, 'copy', \{c_j\} \rangle$);
6. If it is possible to transform (divide) values of measures $\{ms_1, \ldots, ms_i\}$ with respect to dimension *dim* by the function *conv*, then version transformations are constructed:
   - For each $ms'_j \in \{ms'_1, \ldots, ms'_i\}$ do
     $vt'_j = $ new Version transformation($\langle ms'_j, conv, \{ms_j\} \rangle$);
   - Set $v_u = \langle \tau_{now}, null, VT_u \cup \{vt'_1, \ldots, vt'_i\} \rangle$;
7. If it is possible to transform (aggregate) values of measures $\{ms'_1, \ldots, ms'_i\}$ with respect to dimension *dim* by the function *conv'*, then version transformations are constructed:
   - For each $ms_j \in \{ms_1, \ldots, ms_i\}$ do
     $vt_j = $ new Version transformation($\langle ms_j, conv, \{ms'_j\} \rangle$);
   - Set $v' = \langle \tau_{now}, null, VT' \cup \{vt_1, \ldots, vt_i\} \cup \{\langle fda', null, null \rangle\} \rangle$;

   Otherwise: Set
   $v' = \langle \tau_{now}, null, VT' \setminus (vtrans(ms_1) \cup \ldots \cup vtrans(ms_i)) \cup \{\langle fda', null, null \rangle\} \rangle$;
8. return $DWS' = \langle F, D, FDA \cup fda', V \cup \{v'\}, MAP \cup \{map'_1, \ldots, map'_i\} \rangle$.

4.3.2. Disconnection of Dimension from Fact Table

A dimension $dim = \langle ATT, LEV, H, AL, HL \rangle$ is disconnected from a fact table $fact = \langle \{ms_1, \ldots, ms_i\} \rangle$, the measures $\{ms_1, \ldots, ms_i\}$ are mapped to columns $\{c_1, \ldots, c_i\}$.

Logical level: Version transformations are created for measures of the fact table *fact* if it is possible. In other case the fact dimension association between *fact* and *dim* is removed from the version *v'*.

1. $v' = duplicate(v_u) = \langle \tau_{now}, null, VT' \rangle$;
2. For each $ms_j \in \{ms_1, \ldots, ms_i\}$ do $ms'_j = $ new Measure;
3. Set $fact = \langle \{ms_1, \ldots, ms_i, ms'_1, \ldots, ms'_i\} \rangle$;
4. For each $ms_j \in \{ms_1, \ldots, ms_i\}$ do $map'_j = $ new Mapping($\langle ms'_j, 'copy', \{c_j\} \rangle$);
5. If it is possible to transform (divide) values of measures $\{ms'_1, \ldots, ms'_i\}$ with respect to dimension *dim* by the function *conv*, then version transformations are constructed:
   - For each $ms_j \in \{ms_1, \ldots, ms_i\}$ do
     $vt_j = $ new Version transformation($\langle ms_j, conv, \{ms'_j\} \rangle$);
   - Set $v' = \langle \tau_{now}, null, VT' \cup \{vt_1, \ldots, vt_i\} \rangle$;

   Otherwise: Set
   $v' = \langle \tau_{now}, null, VT' \setminus vtrans(ms_1) \cup \ldots \cup vtrans(ms_i)) \setminus \{\langle fda', null, null \rangle\} \rangle$;
6. If it is possible to transform (aggregate) values of measures $\{ms_1, \ldots, ms_i\}$ with respect to dimension *dim* by the function *conv'*, then version transformations are constructed:
   - For each $ms'_j \in \{ms'_1, \ldots, ms'_i\}$ do

vt'$_j$= new Version transformation(<ms'$_j$,conv,{ms$_j$}>);

- Set v$_u$=<τ_{now},null,VT$_u$∪{vt'$_1$,…,vt'$_i$}>;

7. return DWS'=<F,D,FDA∪fda',V∪{v'},MAP∪{map'$_1$,…,map'$_i$}>.

4.3.3. New Dimension Hierarchy

A new hierarchy *h* is added to the dimension *dim=<ATT,LEV,H,AL,HL>*.

Logical level: A new hierarchy *h* is attached to the dimension *dim*.

1. v'=duplicate(v$_u$)=<τ_{now},null,VT'>;
2. Set dim=<ATT,LEV,H∪h,AL,HL>;
3. Set v'=<τ_{now},null,VT'∪{<h,null,null>}>;
4. return DWS'=<F,D,FDA,V∪{v'},MAP>.

4.3.4. Deletion of Dimension Hierarchy

A hierarchy *h* is deleted from the dimension *dim=<ATT,LEV,H,AL,HL>*.

Logical level: The hierarchy *h* is removed from the version *v'*.

1. v'=duplicate(v$_u$)=<τ_{now},null,VT'>;
2. Set v'=<τ_{now},null,VT'\{<h,null,null>}>.
3. return DWS'=<F,D,FDA,V∪{v'},MAP>.

4.3.5. New Dimension Level

A new level *lev* is added to the dimension *dim=<ATT,LEV,H,AL,HL>*.

Logical level: A new level *lev* is attached to the dimension *dim*.

1. v'=duplicate(v$_u$)=<τ_{now},null,VT'>;
2. Set dim=<ATT,LEV∪{lev},H,AL,HL>;
3. Set v'=<τ_{now},null,VT'∪{<lev,null,null>}>;
4. return DWS'=<F,D,FDA,V∪{v'},MAP>.

4.3.6. Deletion of Level from Hierarchy

A level *lev* is deleted from the hierarchy *h* of the dimension *dim*.

Logical level: The association between *h* and *lev* is removed from the version *v'*.

1. v'=duplicate(v$_u$)=<τ_{now},null,VT'>;
2. Set v'=<τ_{now},null,VT'\{<<lev,h>,null,null>}>;
3. If there are any other levels in the hierarchy *h* that have the index which is bigger than the index of the level *lev*, their index is decreased by 1;
4. return DWS'=<F,D,FDA,V∪{v'},MAP>.

4.3.7. Deletion of Level from Dimension

A level *lev* is deleted from a dimension *dim*. Level *lev* must be deleted from all hierarchies where it is used.

Logical level: The level *lev* is removed from the version *v'*.

1. v'=duplicate(v$_u$)=<τ_{now},null,VT'>;
2. Set v'=<τ_{now},null,VT'\{<lev,null,null>}>;
3. return DWS'=<F,D,FDA,V∪{v'},MAP>.

4.3.8. Connection of Level to Hierarchy

An existing level *lev* is connected to a hierarchy *h* of the dimension $dim=<ATT,LEV,H,AL,HL>$.

Logical level: A new association between *lev* and *h* is attached to the dimension *dim*.

1. $v'=duplicate(v_u)=<\tau_{now},null,VT'>$;
2. Set $dim=<ATT,LEV,H,AL,HL\cup\{<lev,h>\}>$;
3. Set $v'=<\tau_{now},null,VT'\cup\{<<lev,h>,null,null>\}>$;
4. If there are any other levels in the hierarchy *h* that have the index, which is the same or bigger than the index of the level *lev*, their index is increased by 1.
5. return $DWS'=<F,D,FDA,V\cup\{v'\},MAP>$.

4.3.9. Connection of Attribute to Level

An existing attribute *att* is connected to a level *lev* of the dimension $dim=<ATT,LEV,H,AL,HL>$.

Logical level: A new association between *att* and *lev* is attached to the dimension *dim*.

1. $v'=duplicate(v_u)=<\tau_{now},null,VT'>$;
2. Set $dim=<ATT,LEV,H,AL\cup\{<att,lev>\},HL>$;
3. Set $v'=<\tau_{now},null,VT'\cup\{<<att,lev>,null,null>\}>$;
4. return $DWS'=<F,D,FDA,V\cup\{v'\},MAP>$.

4.3.10. Disconnection of Attribute from Level

An attribute *att* is disconnected from a level *lev*.

Logical level: The association between *att* and *lev* is removed from the version *v'*.

1. $v'=duplicate(v_u)=<\tau_{now},null,VT'>$;
2. Set $v'=<\tau_{now},null,VT'\setminus\{<<att,lev>,null,null>\}>$;
3. return $DWS'=<F,D,FDA,V\cup\{v'\},MAP>$.

5. Conclusions and Future Work

The main contribution of this paper is a formal model that describes data warehouse schema at the logical and physical level. The model was based on the CWM standard, which was supplemented with a data to describe data warehouse schema versions. The proposed model is used in the framework that supports data warehouse evolution caused by changes of business requirements and data sources. The implementation of the proposed model as a data warehouse repository, as well as the algorithm for construction of SQL queries based on the proposed formal model is described in [18].

Changes that can happen with multidimensional data warehouse and create new schema versions are discussed. Necessary modifications in the proposed model are given. It would be desirable to evaluate the completeness of the supported changes.

It is planned to develop a reporting system to allow to execute reports on one or several data warehouse versions. A user would select data elements to display in a report and create conditions and these data will be translated into an SQL query on several schema versions using version transformations.

Acknowledgements

This research was partially funded by the European Social Fund (ESF).

References

[1] Golfarelli, M., Lechtenbörger, J., Rizzi, S., & Vossen, G. (2006) Schema versioning in data warehouses: Enabling cross-version querying via schema augmentation, Data Knowl. Eng. 59(2): 435—459

[2] Hurtado, C.A., Mendelzon, A.O., & Vaisman, A.A. (1999) Maintaining Data Cubes under Dimension Updates. In Kitsuregawa, M., et. Al (eds) 15th International Conference on Data Engineering (ICDE 1999), March 23-26, Sydney, Australia, pp. 346-357.

[3] Mendelzon, A.O., & Vaisman, A.A. (2000) Temporal Queries in OLAP. In Abbadi, A.E., et. Al (eds) 26th International Conference on Very Large Data Bases (VLDB 2000), September 10-14, 2000, Cairo, Egypt, pp. 242-253.

[4] Blaschka, M. (2000) FIESTA: A Framework for Schema Evolution in Multidimensional Databases, PhD thesis, Technische Universität München, Germany, 214 p.

[5] Kaas, C.E., Pedersen, T.B., & Rasmussen, B.D. (2004) Schema Evolution for Stars and Snowflakes. In Seruca, I., et. Al (eds) 6th Internatioanl Conference on Enterprise Information Systems (ICEIS 2004), Porto, Portugal, pp. 425-433.

[6] Marotta, A. (2000) Data Warehouse Design and Maintenance through Schema Transformations. Master thesis, Universidad de la República Uruguay.

[7] McBrien, P., & Poulovassilis, A. (2003) Data Integration by Bi-Directional Schema Transformation Rules. In Dayal, U., Ramamritham, K., & Vijayaraman, T.M. (eds) 19th International Conference on Data Engineering (ICDE 2003), March 5-8, Bangalore, India, pp. 227—238.

[8] Velegrakis, Y., Miller R.J., & Popa, L. (2003) Mapping Adaptation under Evolving Schemas. In Freytag, J.C., et. Al (eds) 29th International Conference on Very Large Data Bases (VLDB 2003), September 9-12, Berlin, Germany, pp. 584-595.

[9] Bellahsene, Z. (2002) Schema Evolution in Data Warehouses, Knowl. Inf. Syst. 4(3): 283–304

[10] Rundensteiner, E.A., Koeller, A., & Zhang, X.: Maintaining Data Warehouses over Changing Information Sources, Commun. ACM. 43(6): 57—62

[11] Shahzad, M.K., Nasir, J.A., & Pasha, M.A. (2005) CEV-DW: Creation and Evolution of Versions in Data Warehouse, Asian Journal of Information Technology 4(10), 910—917

[12] Wrembel, R., & Bebel, B. (2005) Metadata Management in a Multiversion Data Warehouse. In Meersman, R., et. Al (eds) On the Move to Meaningful Internet Systems 2005: CoopIS, DOA, and ODBASE, OTM Confederated International Conferences, CoopIS, DOA, and ODBASE 2005, October 31 – November 4, Agia Napa, Cyprus, (LNCS), pp. 1347-1364.

[13] Blaschka, M., Sapia, C., & Höfling, G. (1999) On Schema Evolution in Multidimensional Databases. In Mohania, M.K., & Tjoa, A.M. (eds) Data Warehousing and Knowledge Discovery, First International Conference, DaWaK '99, August 30 – September 1, Florence, Italy, (LNCS), pp. 153–164.

[14] Body, M., Miquel, M., Bedard, Y., & Tchounikine, A. (2003) Handling Evolutions in Multidimensional Structures. In Dayal, U., Ramamritham, K., & Vijayaraman, T.M. (eds) 19th International Conference on Data Engineering (ICDE 2003), March 5-8, Bangalore, India, pp. 581.

[15] Morzy, T., & Wrembel, R. (2004) On Querying Versions of Multiversion Data Warehouse. In Song, I., & Davis, K.C. (eds) ACM Seventh International Workshop on Data Warehousing and OLAP, November 12-13, Washington, DC, USA, pp. 92–101.

[16] Solodovnikova, D. (2007) Data Warehouse Evolution Framework. In Kuznetsov, S.D., et. Al (eds) Colloquium on Database and Information Systems (SYRCoDIS 2007), May 31-June 1, Moscow, Russia.

[17] Solodovnikova, D., & Niedrite, L. (2006) Data Warehouse Adaptation after the Changes in Source Schemata. In Vasilecas, O., Eder, J., & Caplinskas, A. (eds) 7th International Baltic Conference on Databases and Information Systems (Baltic DB & IS 2006), July 3-6, Vilnius, Lithuania, pp. 52—63.

[18] Solodovnikova, D. (2008) Building Queries on Multiple Versions of Data Warehouse. In Haav, H.-M., & Kalja, A. (eds) 8th International Baltic Conference on Databases and Information Systems (Baltic DB & IS 2008), June 2-5, Tallinn, Estonia, pp. 75–86.

Semantic Interoperability of Information Systems

Databases and Information Systems V
H.-M. Haav and A. Kalja (Eds.)
IOS Press, 2009

doi:10.3233/978-1-58603-939-4-105

Ontology Enabled Graphical Database Query Tool for End-Users

Guntis BARZDINS[1], Edgars LIEPINS, Marta VEILANDE and Martins ZVIEDRIS
Institute of Mathematics and Computer Science, University of Latvia

Abstract. In this paper we show how semantic web technologies are used in a real application in the domain of national medical databases where an important technological gap between the legacy relation databases and OWL ontologies is bridged by the recently standardized UML profile for OWL. After data has been exported from multiple relational databases into a single shared RDF database structured according to an integrated OWL ontology there emerges a need for a convenient end-user query tools. We describe a fully graphical access to the exported data through the graphical front-end tool (named "DEMO" tool) based on the UML profile for OWL and SPARQL query language.

Keywords. semantic web, ontologies, information system design, database design, RDF data stores, modeling languages, data semantics

Introduction

Semantic web technologies such as RDF and OWL are lately starting to find promising and somewhat unexpected applications also in the field of information system engineering which traditionally has been based on the SQL driven relational databases [1, 2]. Despite relative inefficiency of RDF databases and SPARQL [3] query language (compared to the more mature relational databases) the flexibility of RDF to directly integrate data with its conceptual model (OWL domain ontology) removes a historic barrier from the databases – the end-users now can query data from the database themselves by knowing the OWL ontology only, rather than rely on the "man in the middle" (a programmer, who creates the application-specific user interface for the database) to reformulate the end-user queries into the SQL statements over the hidden, implementation-specific normalized relational database schema. The problem is that in the legacy relational databases the initial conceptual model of the domain (often modeled as UML class diagram or ER-diagram) tends to disappear during conversion into the normalized database schema thus leading to database being inaccessible for direct query by domain experts familiar only with the conceptual model.

Additional benefit added by RDF and OWL is the hierarchical scalable URI namespace, which eases the integration of previously separate databases. Such integration is aided also by the rich and yet strictly formal semantics of OWL DL. The richness of OWL DL provides means for modular abstraction levels over narrower domain ontologies during the database integration such as *subClassOf, subPropertyOf,*

[1] Corresponding Author: Guntis Barzdins, Institute of Mathematics and Computer Science, University of Latvia, Rainis Blvd. 29, Riga LV-1459, Latvia; E-mail: guntis.barzdins@mii.lu.lv.

sameAS, equivalentClass, equivalentProperty and similar constructs. Meanwhile formal semantics of OWL DL and its sub-languages maintains complete "computability" of such expressive ontologies.

In this paper through the simple example derived from the real-life case-study in the medical domain we demonstrate the data access benefits made possible by the above mentioned semantic web technologies. We are largely omitting details of the actual relational databases conversion into OWL ontology and RDF data – this subject is already covered in detail in our paper [1], as well as in D2RQ related papers [4]. Therefore the focus of this paper is on the "syntactic sugar" for fully graphical representation of both the ontologies (OWL) and the query language (SPARQL) thus making them directly accessible to the end-users, as it has long been acknowledged that the rather verbose nature of RDF, OWL, URI and SPARQL default serialization formats makes them unsuitable for the direct manipulation by the end-users. By "end-users" here we do not mean casual web surfers, but rather the domain specialists, such as medical researchers, who need to extract various data subsets from the databases in their expertise domain.

Methods for graphical SPARQL query formulation with user-friendly GUI have been discussed by other authors earlier [5]. There are already some tools developed that support graphical query formulation such as Tabulator [6] and Longwell [7]. Meanwhile these tools are mainly based on query formulation by exploration. One problem what can arise with this approach is that user must know which way to explore. If user does not know given ontology well (and the query tool does not provide appropriate ontological assistance) then it could also be hard to know precise path for exploration. In our approach we are trying to avoid this problem by relying on the graphical ontology as the central concept.

The graphical representation of ontologies is defined by the recently adopted UML profile for OWL [7] standard, therefore the proposed graphical SPARQL query tool ("DEMO" tool) is modeled along the same graphical primitives to provide an unified, fully graphical end-user interface. In Section 1 we illustrate the crucial role of UML profile for OWL and how data from multiple databases can be integrated into a single shared RDF database structured according to the integrated OWL ontology. In Section 2 we describe a graphical end-user friendly SPARQL front-end that makes exported RDF data easy accessible to the end-user familiar only with the domain ontology. To demonstrate our approach as an example we use two simplified medical databases – Oncologic Disease register and Trauma/Injury register from the earlier case-study [9] which was inspired by "Semantic Latvia" vision [10].

1. OWL Ontology and Preparation of RDF Data

The database export to RDF data triples (so-called Abox – the data part of the ontology) structured according to the given OWL ontology (so-called Tbox – the schema part of the ontology, without data) is typically implemented through the mapping process illustrated in Figure 1. In this paper we are not elaborating this conversion in detail as it is already covered in other papers [1, 4]. Nevertheless, by Figure 1 we want to stress that the below discussed OWL ontologies and RDF data are typically obtained from the legacy relational databases.

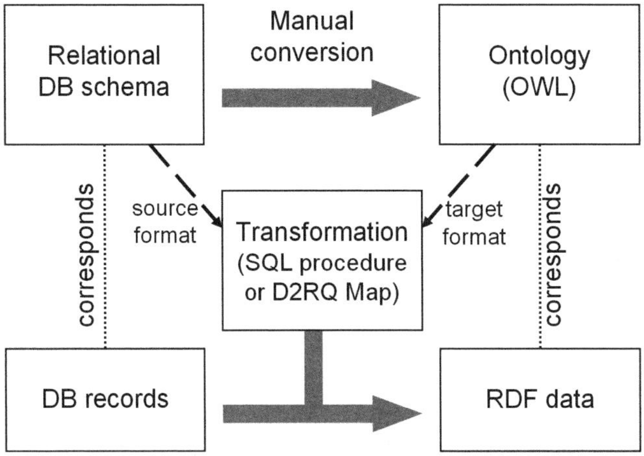

Figure 1. The relation database to RDF/OWL mapping process

The key enabling technique for the described approach is the UML profile for OWL [8] which formally is a syntactic dialect of the W3C standard Semantic Web ontology language OWL. The outstanding characteristic of this dialect is that from one side it is fully compatible with the OWL language used for describing semantic web ontologies, but from the other side it is compatible with the UML class diagrams widely accepted for the design of traditional information systems. Since UML OWL profile diagrams correspond to regular OWL ontologies, they can be universally exchanged with other semantic web tools (Protégé editor, RDF databases, reasoners, etc.) through the W3C standard OWL serialization formats such as OWL/XML or OWL/N-TRIPLES. In other words, UML profile for OWL allows to view UML class diagrams as OWL ontology diagrams under the assumption that UML class is perceived as OWL class and UML property is perceived as OWL property (details see in [8]).

We will use a small but representative fragment of the medical ontology derived from the Oncologic Disease register and Trauma/Injury register in our earlier case-study [9] as a running example for the rest of this paper. In Figure 2 the example ontology is presented in the form of UML class diagram. This diagram illustrates the key features we have found to be the most relevant when mapping legacy relational database schemas into OWL ontologies via UML class diagrams:

- Generally class attributes correspond to datatype properties in OWL, while associations between classes correspond to object properties in OWL. Although UML profile for OWL allows overriding this "rule", in our case-study it was not necessary.
- Subclass relationship (inheritance between classes in UML). Due to formal semantics of OWL DL, subclasses may be marked to be *owl:disjointWith* each other, or they may be left potentially overlapping. In Figure 2 *Injury* and *Cancer* are examples of disjoint subclasses of *Disease* while *TransportAccident* and *BrokenBone* are potentially overlapping subclasses of *Injury*. This difference is further illustrated by the data sample in Figure 4, where individual *i00008* belongs to the subclasses *TransportAccident* and

BrokenBone simultaneously and therefore has attributes of both of these classes.

- Subproperty relationship ("redefines" for association ends in UML). Along with subclass relationship, this provides a powerful mechanism for integrating overlapping ontologies from different abstraction levels. In Figure 2 the grey background highlights a portion of the integrated ontology which effectively is a high-level abstraction of the more fine-grained "domain" ontology fragments outside the highlighted area. Thanks to formal semantics of OWL DL, these various abstraction levels later will be usable also in queries (e.g., end-user may ask for *Persons* having any *Disease*, although the raw data for *Persons* might have links only to *Injury* or *Cancer* classes).
- Enumeration datatype. This is a widely used feature in legacy relational databases – in UML it is depicted by <<*enum*>> class, which effectively enumerates all individuals belonging to this class. Enumeration datatype in OWL is supported through the *owl:oneOf* feature.

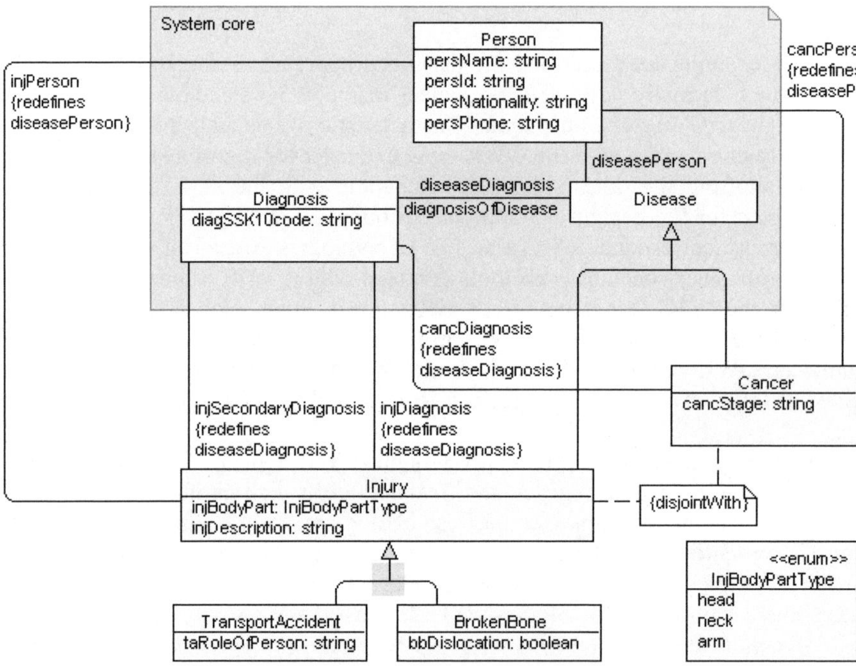

Figure 2. An example of medical ontology as UML class diagram

The graphical ontology in Figure 2 corresponds to the OWL/N-TRIPLES serialization ontology shown in Figure 3. To execute this conversion one option is to rewrite the UML class diagram shown in Figure 2 into correct[2] UML OWL profile diagram supported by the Eclipse-based IODT (EODM) tool. This tool can save UML

[2] For example, UML profile for OWL does not include „redefines" feature; in this example we model it as a subproperty although formally it should be modelled using restriction classes

OWL profile diagrams into the standard OWL/XML serialization further convertible into OWL/N-TRIPLES serialization (used in this paper). Unfortunately, the available IODT (EODM) tool has a rather limited functionality and therefore authors currently suggest using Protégé editor to manually convert between these two formats.


```
<http://lumii.lv/preda> <http://www.w3.org/1999/02/22-rdf-syntax-ns#type> <http://www.w3.org/2002/07/owl#Ontology> .
<http://lumii.lv/preda#diseaseDiagnosis> <http://www.w3.org/1999/02/22-rdf-syntax-ns#type> <http://www.w3.org/2002/07/owl#ObjectProperty> .
<http://lumii.lv/preda#diseaseDiagnosis> <http://www.w3.org/2000/01/rdf-schema#range> <http://lumii.lv/preda#Diagnosis> .
<http://lumii.lv/preda#diseaseDiagnosis> <http://www.w3.org/2000/01/rdf-schema#domain> <http://lumii.lv/preda#Disease> .
<http://lumii.lv/preda#diseaseDiagnosis> <http://www.w3.org/2002/07/owl#inverseOf> <http://lumii.lv/preda#diagnosisOfDisease> .
<http://lumii.lv/preda#diagnosisOfDisease> <http://www.w3.org/2002/07/owl#inverseOf> <http://lumii.lv/preda#diseaseDiagnosis> .
<http://lumii.lv/preda#diagnosisOfDisease> <http://www.w3.org/2000/01/rdf-schema#domain> <http://lumii.lv/preda#Diagnosis> .
<http://lumii.lv/preda#diagnosisOfDisease> <http://www.w3.org/1999/02/22-rdf-syntax-ns#type> <http://www.w3.org/2002/07/owl#ObjectProperty> .
<http://lumii.lv/preda#diagnosisOfDisease> <http://www.w3.org/2000/01/rdf-schema#range> <http://lumii.lv/preda#Disease> .
<http://lumii.lv/preda#TransportAccident> <http://www.w3.org/2000/01/rdf-schema#subClassOf> <http://lumii.lv/preda#Injury> .
<http://lumii.lv/preda#TransportAccident> <http://www.w3.org/1999/02/22-rdf-syntax-ns#type> <http://www.w3.org/2002/07/owl#Class> .
<http://lumii.lv/preda#injDiagnosis> <http://www.w3.org/2000/01/rdf-schema#range> <http://lumii.lv/preda#Diagnosis> .
<http://lumii.lv/preda#injDiagnosis> <http://www.w3.org/1999/02/22-rdf-syntax-ns#type> <http://www.w3.org/2002/07/owl#ObjectProperty> .
<http://lumii.lv/preda#injDiagnosis> <http://www.w3.org/2000/01/rdf-schema#subPropertyOf> <http://lumii.lv/preda#diseaseDiagnosis> .
<http://lumii.lv/preda#injDiagnosis> <http://www.w3.org/2000/01/rdf-schema#domain> <http://lumii.lv/preda#Injury> .
<http://lumii.lv/preda#persName> <http://www.w3.org/2000/01/rdf-schema#domain> <http://lumii.lv/preda#Person> .
<http://lumii.lv/preda#persName> <http://www.w3.org/2000/01/rdf-schema#range> <http://www.w3.org/2001/XMLSchema#string> .
<http://lumii.lv/preda#persName> <http://www.w3.org/1999/02/22-rdf-syntax-ns#type> <http://www.w3.org/2002/07/owl#DatatypeProperty> .
<http://lumii.lv/preda#injSecondaryDiagnosis> <http://www.w3.org/2000/01/rdf-schema#domain> <http://lumii.lv/preda#Injury> .
<http://lumii.lv/preda#injSecondaryDiagnosis> <http://www.w3.org/1999/02/22-rdf-syntax-ns#type> <http://www.w3.org/2002/07/owl#ObjectProperty> .
<http://lumii.lv/preda#injSecondaryDiagnosis> <http://www.w3.org/2000/01/rdf-schema#subPropertyOf> <http://lumii.lv/preda#diseaseDiagnosis> .
<http://lumii.lv/preda#injSecondaryDiagnosis> <http://www.w3.org/2000/01/rdf-schema#range> <http://lumii.lv/preda#Diagnosis> .
<http://lumii.lv/preda#BrokenBone> <http://www.w3.org/2000/01/rdf-schema#subClassOf> <http://lumii.lv/preda#Injury> .
<http://lumii.lv/preda#BrokenBone> <http://www.w3.org/1999/02/22-rdf-syntax-ns#type> <http://www.w3.org/2002/07/owl#Class> .
<http://lumii.lv/preda#persPhone> <http://www.w3.org/2000/01/rdf-schema#domain> <http://lumii.lv/preda#Person> .
<http://lumii.lv/preda#persPhone> <http://www.w3.org/2000/01/rdf-schema#range> <http://www.w3.org/2001/XMLSchema#string> .
<http://lumii.lv/preda#persPhone> <http://www.w3.org/1999/02/22-rdf-syntax-ns#type> <http://www.w3.org/2002/07/owl#DatatypeProperty> .
<http://lumii.lv/preda#Cancer> <http://www.w3.org/1999/02/22-rdf-syntax-ns#type> <http://www.w3.org/2002/07/owl#Class> .
<http://lumii.lv/preda#Cancer> <http://www.w3.org/2000/01/rdf-schema#subClassOf> <http://lumii.lv/preda#Disease> .
<http://lumii.lv/preda#Cancer> <http://www.w3.org/2002/07/owl#disjointWith> <http://lumii.lv/preda#Injury> .
<http://lumii.lv/preda#Disease> <http://www.w3.org/1999/02/22-rdf-syntax-ns#type> <http://www.w3.org/2002/07/owl#Class> .
<http://lumii.lv/preda#Injury> <http://www.w3.org/2000/01/rdf-schema#subClassOf> <http://lumii.lv/preda#Disease> .
<http://lumii.lv/preda#Injury> <http://www.w3.org/1999/02/22-rdf-syntax-ns#type> <http://www.w3.org/2002/07/owl#Class> .
<http://lumii.lv/preda#Injury> <http://www.w3.org/2002/07/owl#disjointWith> <http://lumii.lv/preda#Cancer> .
<http://lumii.lv/preda#cancDiagnosis> <http://www.w3.org/2000/01/rdf-schema#subPropertyOf> <http://lumii.lv/preda#diseaseDiagnosis> .
<http://lumii.lv/preda#cancDiagnosis> <http://www.w3.org/1999/02/22-rdf-syntax-ns#type> <http://www.w3.org/2002/07/owl#ObjectProperty> .
<http://lumii.lv/preda#cancDiagnosis> <http://www.w3.org/2000/01/rdf-schema#domain> <http://lumii.lv/preda#Cancer> .
<http://lumii.lv/preda#cancDiagnosis> <http://www.w3.org/2000/01/rdf-schema#range> <http://lumii.lv/preda#Diagnosis> .
<http://lumii.lv/preda#Person> <http://www.w3.org/1999/02/22-rdf-syntax-ns#type> <http://www.w3.org/2002/07/owl#Class> .
<http://lumii.lv/preda#injBodyPart> <http://www.w3.org/1999/02/22-rdf-syntax-ns#type> <http://www.w3.org/2002/07/owl#DatatypeProperty> .
<http://lumii.lv/preda#injBodyPart> <http://www.w3.org/2000/01/rdf-schema#domain> <http://lumii.lv/preda#Injury> .
<http://lumii.lv/preda#injBodyPart> <http://www.w3.org/2000/01/rdf-schema#range> _:AX40XX5fXX3aXUA3 .
_:AX40XX5fXX3aXUA3 <http://www.w3.org/1999/02/22-rdf-syntax-ns#type> <http://www.w3.org/2002/07/owl#DataRange> .
_:AX40XX5fXX3aXUA3 <http://www.w3.org/2002/07/owl#oneOf> _:AX40XX5fXX3aXUA0 .
_:AX40XX5fXX3aXUA0 <http://www.w3.org/1999/02/22-rdf-syntax-ns#first> "head"^^<http://www.w3.org/2001/XMLSchema#string> .
_:AX40XX5fXX3aXUA0 <http://www.w3.org/1999/02/22-rdf-syntax-ns#rest> _:AX40XX5fXX3aXUA1 .
_:AX40XX5fXX3aXUA1 <http://www.w3.org/1999/02/22-rdf-syntax-ns#first> "neck"^^<http://www.w3.org/2001/XMLSchema#string> .
_:AX40XX5fXX3aXUA1 <http://www.w3.org/1999/02/22-rdf-syntax-ns#rest> _:AX40XX5fXX3aXUA2 .
_:AX40XX5fXX3aXUA2 <http://www.w3.org/1999/02/22-rdf-syntax-ns#first> "arm"^^<http://www.w3.org/2001/XMLSchema#string> .
_:AX40XX5fXX3aXUA2 <http://www.w3.org/1999/02/22-rdf-syntax-ns#rest> <http://www.w3.org/1999/02/22-rdf-syntax-ns#nil> .
<http://lumii.lv/preda#cancPerson> <http://www.w3.org/2000/01/rdf-schema#domain> <http://lumii.lv/preda#Cancer> .
<http://lumii.lv/preda#cancPerson> <http://www.w3.org/2000/01/rdf-schema#subPropertyOf> <http://lumii.lv/preda#diseasePerson> .
<http://lumii.lv/preda#cancPerson> <http://www.w3.org/2000/01/rdf-schema#range> <http://lumii.lv/preda#Person> .
<http://lumii.lv/preda#cancPerson> <http://www.w3.org/1999/02/22-rdf-syntax-ns#type> <http://www.w3.org/2002/07/owl#ObjectProperty> .
<http://lumii.lv/preda#injPerson> <http://www.w3.org/2000/01/rdf-schema#domain> <http://lumii.lv/preda#Injury> .
<http://lumii.lv/preda#injPerson> <http://www.w3.org/2000/01/rdf-schema#subPropertyOf> <http://lumii.lv/preda#diseasePerson> .
<http://lumii.lv/preda#injPerson> <http://www.w3.org/2000/01/rdf-schema#range> <http://lumii.lv/preda#Person> .
<http://lumii.lv/preda#injPerson> <http://www.w3.org/1999/02/22-rdf-syntax-ns#type> <http://www.w3.org/2002/07/owl#ObjectProperty> .
<http://lumii.lv/preda#Diagnosis> <http://www.w3.org/1999/02/22-rdf-syntax-ns#type> <http://www.w3.org/2002/07/owl#Class> .
<http://lumii.lv/preda#persID> <http://www.w3.org/2000/01/rdf-schema#range> <http://www.w3.org/2001/XMLSchema#string> .
<http://lumii.lv/preda#persID> <http://www.w3.org/2000/01/rdf-schema#domain> <http://lumii.lv/preda#Person> .
<http://lumii.lv/preda#persID> <http://www.w3.org/1999/02/22-rdf-syntax-ns#type> <http://www.w3.org/2002/07/owl#DatatypeProperty> .
<http://lumii.lv/preda#cancStage> <http://www.w3.org/2000/01/rdf-schema#range> <http://www.w3.org/2001/XMLSchema#string> .
<http://lumii.lv/preda#cancStage> <http://www.w3.org/2000/01/rdf-schema#domain> <http://lumii.lv/preda#Cancer> .
<http://lumii.lv/preda#cancStage> <http://www.w3.org/1999/02/22-rdf-syntax-ns#type> <http://www.w3.org/2002/07/owl#DatatypeProperty> .
<http://lumii.lv/preda#bbDislocation> <http://www.w3.org/2000/01/rdf-schema#range> <http://www.w3.org/2001/XMLSchema#boolean> .
<http://lumii.lv/preda#bbDislocation> <http://www.w3.org/1999/02/22-rdf-syntax-ns#type> <http://www.w3.org/2002/07/owl#DatatypeProperty> .
<http://lumii.lv/preda#bbDislocation> <http://www.w3.org/2000/01/rdf-schema#domain> <http://lumii.lv/preda#BrokenBone> .
<http://lumii.lv/preda#diseasePerson> <http://www.w3.org/1999/02/22-rdf-syntax-ns#type> <http://www.w3.org/2002/07/owl#ObjectProperty> .
<http://lumii.lv/preda#diseasePerson> <http://www.w3.org/2000/01/rdf-schema#domain> <http://lumii.lv/preda#Disease> .
<http://lumii.lv/preda#diseasePerson> <http://www.w3.org/2000/01/rdf-schema#range> <http://lumii.lv/preda#Person> .
<http://lumii.lv/preda#persNationality> <http://www.w3.org/1999/02/22-rdf-syntax-ns#type> <http://www.w3.org/2002/07/owl#DatatypeProperty> .
```

```
<http://lumii.lv/preda#persNationality> <http://www.w3.org/2000/01/rdf-schema#range> <http://www.w3.org/2001/XMLSchema#string> .
<http://lumii.lv/preda#persNationality> <http://www.w3.org/2000/01/rdf-schema#domain> <http://lumii.lv/preda#Person> .
<http://lumii.lv/preda#diagSSK10code> <http://www.w3.org/1999/02/22-rdf-syntax-ns#type> <http://www.w3.org/2002/07/owl#DatatypeProperty> .
<http://lumii.lv/preda#diagSSK10code> <http://www.w3.org/2000/01/rdf-schema#domain> <http://lumii.lv/preda#Diagnosis> .
<http://lumii.lv/preda#diagSSK10code> <http://www.w3.org/2000/01/rdf-schema#range> <http://www.w3.org/2001/XMLSchema#string> .
<http://lumii.lv/preda#taRoleOfPerson> <http://www.w3.org/1999/02/22-rdf-syntax-ns#type> <http://www.w3.org/2002/07/owl#DatatypeProperty> .
<http://lumii.lv/preda#taRoleOfPerson> <http://www.w3.org/2000/01/rdf-schema#range> <http://www.w3.org/2001/XMLSchema#string> .
<http://lumii.lv/preda#taRoleOfPerson> <http://www.w3.org/2000/01/rdf-schema#domain> <http://lumii.lv/preda#TransportAccident> .
<http://lumii.lv/preda#injDescription> <http://www.w3.org/2000/01/rdf-schema#range> <http://www.w3.org/2001/XMLSchema#string> .
<http://lumii.lv/preda#injDescription> <http://www.w3.org/2000/01/rdf-schema#domain> <http://lumii.lv/preda#Injury> .
<http://lumii.lv/preda#injDescription> <http://www.w3.org/1999/02/22-rdf-syntax-ns#type> <http://www.w3.org/2002/07/owl#DatatypeProperty> .
```


Figure 3. OWL/N-TRIPLES serialization of the ontology from Figure 2

Finally, Figure 4 shows some RDF data structured according to the example ontology shown in Figure 2 and Figure 3. In the scenario depicted in Figure 1 such data would come from the legacy relational database through the transformation defined by the source database schema and the target OWL ontology. Such transformation most conveniently can be implemented either as an SQL procedure in the original database with appropriate output formatting or as a mapping file for D2RQ tool [11].


```
<http://lumii.lv/preda#i00001> <http://lumii.lv/preda#persPhone> "+37129651829"^^<http://www.w3.org/2001/XMLSchema#string> .
<http://lumii.lv/preda#i00001> <http://lumii.lv/preda#persID> "36819"^^<http://www.w3.org/2001/XMLSchema#string> .
<http://lumii.lv/preda#i00001> <http://www.w3.org/1999/02/22-rdf-syntax-ns#type> <http://lumii.lv/preda#Person> .
<http://lumii.lv/preda#i00001> <http://lumii.lv/preda#persName> "Janis Liepa"^^<http://www.w3.org/2001/XMLSchema#string> .
<http://lumii.lv/preda#i00001> <http://lumii.lv/preda#persNationality> "Latvian"^^<http://www.w3.org/2001/XMLSchema#string> .
<http://lumii.lv/preda#i00002> <http://lumii.lv/preda#cancPerson> <http://lumii.lv/preda#i00001> .
<http://lumii.lv/preda#i00002> <http://lumii.lv/preda#cancDiagnosis> <http://lumii.lv/preda#i00003> .
<http://lumii.lv/preda#i00002> <http://www.w3.org/1999/02/22-rdf-syntax-ns#type> <http://lumii.lv/preda#Cancer> .
<http://lumii.lv/preda#i00002> <http://lumii.lv/preda#cancStage> "1A"^^<http://www.w3.org/2001/XMLSchema#string> .
<http://lumii.lv/preda#i00003> <http://www.w3.org/1999/02/22-rdf-syntax-ns#type> <http://lumii.lv/preda#Diagnosis> .
<http://lumii.lv/preda#i00003> <http://lumii.lv/preda#diagSSK10code> "A00.0"^^<http://www.w3.org/2001/XMLSchema#string> .
<http://lumii.lv/preda#i00004> <http://lumii.lv/preda#diagSSK10code> "A00.1"^^<http://www.w3.org/2001/XMLSchema#string> .
<http://lumii.lv/preda#i00004> <http://www.w3.org/1999/02/22-rdf-syntax-ns#type> <http://lumii.lv/preda#Diagnosis> .
<http://lumii.lv/preda#i00005> <http://lumii.lv/preda#diagSSK10code> "A00.9"^^<http://www.w3.org/2001/XMLSchema#string> .
<http://lumii.lv/preda#i00005> <http://www.w3.org/1999/02/22-rdf-syntax-ns#type> <http://lumii.lv/preda#Diagnosis> .
<http://lumii.lv/preda#i00006> <http://lumii.lv/preda#injDescription> "fell from rock"^^<http://www.w3.org/2001/XMLSchema#string> .
<http://lumii.lv/preda#i00006> <http://lumii.lv/preda#injPerson> <http://lumii.lv/preda#i00001> .
<http://lumii.lv/preda#i00006> <http://lumii.lv/preda#bbDislocation> "true"^^<http://www.w3.org/2001/XMLSchema#boolean> .
<http://lumii.lv/preda#i00006> <http://lumii.lv/preda#injBodyPart> "arm"^^<http://www.w3.org/2001/XMLSchema#string> .
<http://lumii.lv/preda#i00006> <http://www.w3.org/1999/02/22-rdf-syntax-ns#type> <http://lumii.lv/preda#TransportAccident> .
<http://lumii.lv/preda#i00006> <http://lumii.lv/preda#diseasePerson> <http://lumii.lv/preda#i00001> .
<http://lumii.lv/preda#i00006> <http://lumii.lv/preda#injSecondaryDiagnosis> <http://lumii.lv/preda#i00005> .
<http://lumii.lv/preda#i00006> <http://www.w3.org/1999/02/22-rdf-syntax-ns#type> <http://lumii.lv/preda#BrokenBone> .
<http://lumii.lv/preda#i00006> <http://lumii.lv/preda#injDiagnosis> <http://lumii.lv/preda#i00004> .
<http://lumii.lv/preda#i00007> <http://lumii.lv/preda#persNationality> "Russian"^^<http://www.w3.org/2001/XMLSchema#string> .
<http://lumii.lv/preda#i00007> <http://www.w3.org/1999/02/22-rdf-syntax-ns#type> <http://lumii.lv/preda#Person> .
<http://lumii.lv/preda#i00007> <http://lumii.lv/preda#persID> "72256"^^<http://www.w3.org/2001/XMLSchema#string> .
<http://lumii.lv/preda#i00007> <http://lumii.lv/preda#persName> "Igor Valujev"^^<http://www.w3.org/2001/XMLSchema#string> .
<http://lumii.lv/preda#i00007> <http://lumii.lv/preda#persPhone> "+37126541967"^^<http://www.w3.org/2001/XMLSchema#string> .
<http://lumii.lv/preda#i00008> <http://www.w3.org/1999/02/22-rdf-syntax-ns#type> <http://lumii.lv/preda#BrokenBone> .
<http://lumii.lv/preda#i00008> <http://www.w3.org/1999/02/22-rdf-syntax-ns#type> <http://lumii.lv/preda#TransportAccident> .
<http://lumii.lv/preda#i00008> <http://lumii.lv/preda#injDiagnosis> <http://lumii.lv/preda#i00009> .
<http://lumii.lv/preda#i00008> <http://lumii.lv/preda#taRoleOfPerson> "victim"^^<http://www.w3.org/2001/XMLSchema#string> .
<http://lumii.lv/preda#i00008> <http://lumii.lv/preda#injDescription> "hit by car"^^<http://www.w3.org/2001/XMLSchema#string> .
<http://lumii.lv/preda#i00008> <http://lumii.lv/preda#injBodyPart> "head"^^<http://www.w3.org/2001/XMLSchema#string> .
<http://lumii.lv/preda#i00008> <http://lumii.lv/preda#bbDislocation> "false"^^<http://www.w3.org/2001/XMLSchema#boolean> .
<http://lumii.lv/preda#i00008> <http://lumii.lv/preda#injSecondaryDiagnosis> <http://lumii.lv/preda#i00010> .
<http://lumii.lv/preda#i00008> <http://lumii.lv/preda#injPerson> <http://lumii.lv/preda#i00007> .
<http://lumii.lv/preda#i00009> <http://www.w3.org/1999/02/22-rdf-syntax-ns#type> <http://lumii.lv/preda#Diagnosis> .
<http://lumii.lv/preda#i00009> <http://lumii.lv/preda#diagSSK10code> "A01.2"^^<http://www.w3.org/2001/XMLSchema#string> .
<http://lumii.lv/preda#i00010> <http://lumii.lv/preda#diagSSK10code> "A01.7"^^<http://www.w3.org/2001/XMLSchema#string> .
<http://lumii.lv/preda#i00010> <http://www.w3.org/1999/02/22-rdf-syntax-ns#type> <http://lumii.lv/preda#Diagnosis> .
```


Figure 4. RDF data triples corresponding to the ontology shown in Figure 2 and Figure 3

The data sample in Figure 4 illustrates an important aspect of the OWL „open-world" semantics (mentioned already in the beginning of this section), which is different from the traditional „closed-world" semantics of SQL databases: individual *i00008* via „type" relation belongs to two possibly overlapping classes *BrokenBone* and

TrafficAccident simultaneously – this describes a case, where broken bone injury is a result of a traffic accident. This is a perfectly legitimate (and necessary) situation in OWL as long as the involved classes are not explicitly declared to be *owl:disjointWith*.

This completes the steps required to present a database into the OWL/RDF format – now the prepared OWL ontology and RDF data can be loaded into RDF database such as Sesame [12] and accessed through the SPARQL [3] queries as it will be discussed in the next section. Nevertheless there is one important aspect involved without which the whole setup would not work properly – it is the need for reasoning (or entailment inference) support in the RDF database. Without that we would not be able to infer, for example, the RDF triple <http://lumii.lv/preda#i00008> <http://www.w3.org/1999/02/22-rdf-syntax-ns#type> <http://lumii.lv/preda#Disease> which is entailed by the OWL DL formal semantics, but is not explicitly present among RDF triples in Figure 3 and Figure 4. Full OWL DL entailment power is available only in OWL DL reasoners such as Pellet which technically can be used also as a limited-size RDF database with SPARQL access. Meanwhile for pure data access there is no need for full OWL DL reasoning, much of which deals with enforcing constraints such as satisfiability, *owl:disjointWith*, and cardinality restrictions which we can assume to be already enforced by other means in the provided RDF data. Therefore for pure data access it is sufficient to enable only RDF Schema and direct type hierarchy inferencing, which is much faster and more scalable to large data sets (for example, in Sesame RDF database this kind of entailment inferencing is enabled by applying *native-rdfs-dt* or *memory-rdfs-dt* template during Sesame repository creation). As a side note – lack of any reasoning support in D2RQ is the only reason why this otherwise convenient tool for on-the-fly SPARQL access to relational databases is not compatible with the approaches described in this paper.

2. Graphical Query Tool for End-Users

As it was mentioned in the Introduction, the key idea of our approach is to use the OWL ontology as the only guidance for SPARQL queries over the RDF database. To query relational database with SQL one needs to know physical database schema. To query RDF database with SPARQL one needs to know RDF database structure – a corresponding OWL ontology.

```
Query:
select ?name ?phone
where {?p <http://www.w3.org/1999/02/22-rdf-syntax-ns#type>
<http://lumii.lv/preda#Person> .
?t <http://lumii.lv/preda#injPerson> ?p .
?v <http://lumii.lv/preda#cancPerson> ?p .
?p <http://lumii.lv/preda#persName> ?name .
?p <http://lumii.lv/preda#persPhone> ?phone .}
-----------------------------------------------------
Query Results (1 answers):
name                     | phone
===================================================
"Janis Liepa"^^xsd:string | "+37129651829"^^xsd:string
```

Figure 5. SPARQL query executed over database of RDF triples from Figures 3, 4

Indeed we can formulate semantically clear queries in SPARQL using only the OWL ontology from Figure 2. For example, if we would like to find names and phone numbers of all persons having both an injury and a cancer, we could formulate this query in SPARQL by traversing the appropriate path in ontology – Figure 5 shows the resulting SPARQL query and its execution result on the RDF triples from Figure 3 (ontology) and Figure 4 (data).

Although it is now possible to formulate SPARQL queries as shown in Figure 5 manually from the ontology in Figure 2, the coding of such queries requires remembering of exact qualified URIs for involved concepts and is generally time-consuming for the potential end-user. Therefore we have developed a graphical frontend for generating such SPARQL queries via same graphical primitives used by UML OWL profile representation of the ontology – without the need for the end-user to digress into the textual SPARQL and technical RDF triples encoding of ontologies. This enables convenient querying by the end-user even in large ontologies which would otherwise be difficult to even comprehend textually.

The main idea of our query construction tool is that user first selects concepts (classes) in the ontology that are involved in his query and after that just says that these concepts should be somehow connected. Then a shortest path algorithm finds several most probable connection paths between the selected classes and returns them to the user so that he can choose the correct path intended or narrow the search space by selecting classes defining a partial path manually, if none of the returned paths is appropriate. This way we tackle the problem that user must be somewhat familiar with the ontology (is able to read it) but does not need to know it very well.

There are two main components in our query language – a class (concept) and a link (relation, property) representing an association between two classes. When user starts to formulate a query, first of all, he chooses classes that will be involved in the query as shown in Figure 5. The user does not need to remember exact class names, as these are automatically retrieved by the DEMO tool from the RDF database (by a simple SPARQL query) and presented to the user as a drop-down list. Note that the same class from the ontology may be represented with more than one class-icon in the graphical query if different subsets from the same class need to be considered (e.g. *Diagnoses* related to *Injuries* and *Diagnoses* related to *Cancer* as illustrated in Figure 11).

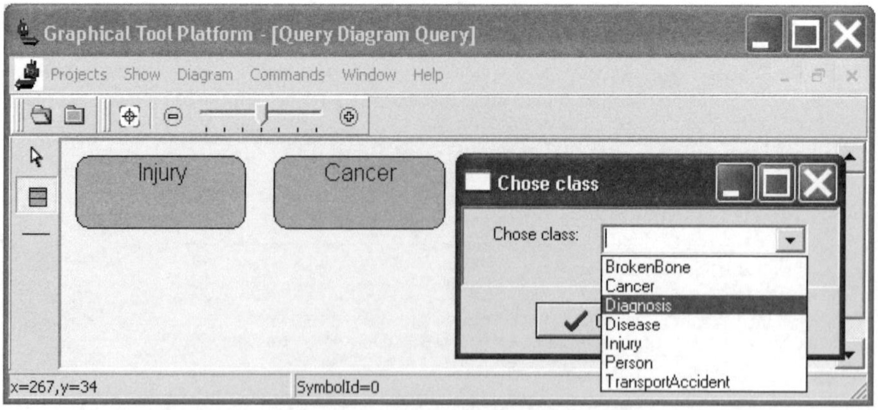

Figure 6. Choosing classes in DEMO tool

User can also draw links between the selected concepts (classes). The key idea of DEMO tool is that user can draw such links even between classes that are not directly connected in the ontology – the mentioned shortest path algorithm computes the most probable full paths in the ontology and shows them in the dialogue box from where the user chooses the appropriate actual path for his query (Figure 7). If there are some additional classes in the selected path then these classes are automatically added to the graphical picture.

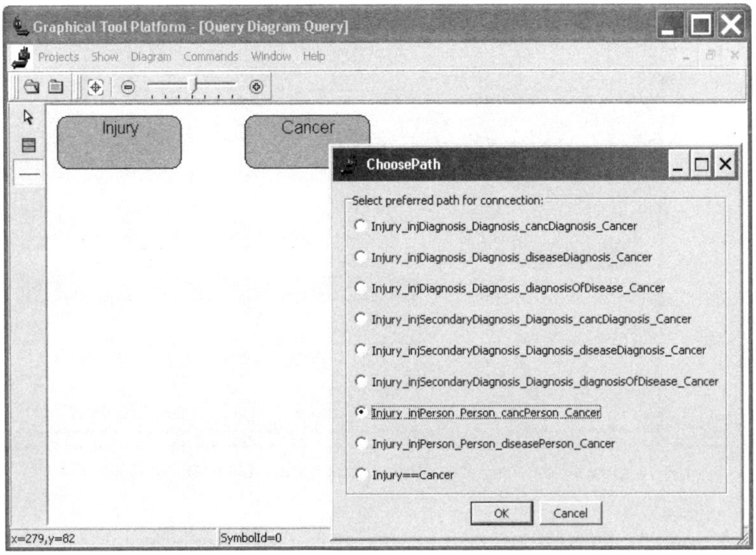

Figure 7. Choosing links between classes in DEMO tool

After user has selected all necessary classes and relations (selected classes and relations must form a connected graph) he can further narrow the query by optionally adding attribute conditions to some of the selected classes as shown in Figure 8.

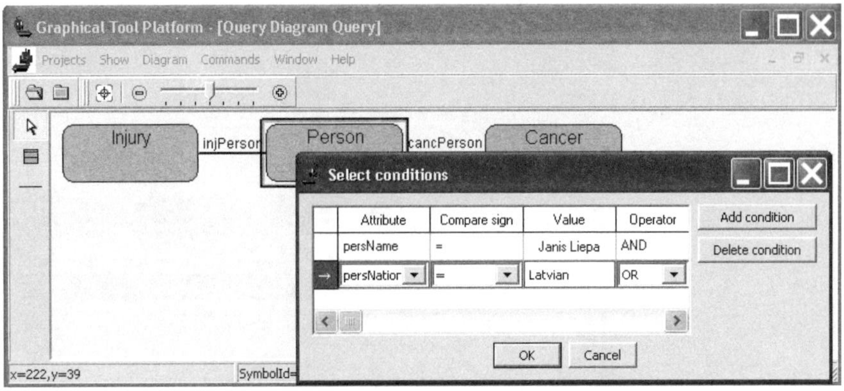

Figure 8. Adding attribute conditions in DEMO tool

After query has been formulated the next step is to get an answer. The tool could return as an answer a full table containing all attributes of all classes involved in the query. Meanwhile more often user is interested only in few attributes of few involved classes – in this case user must select which attributes of which class he would like to see in the result table (Figure 9).

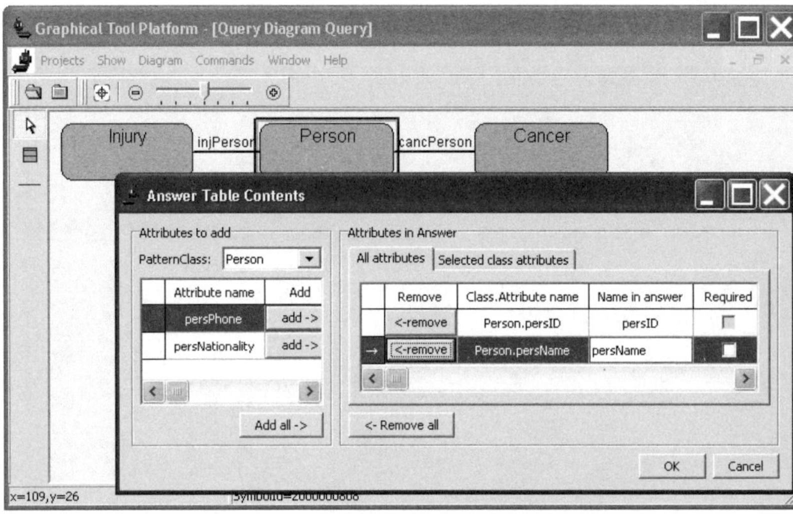

Figure 9. Choosing class attributes for result table in DEMO tool

At this point a SPARQL query is created from the designed graphical structure and is submitted to the RDF database for execution. After it has been processed by the RDF database the answer is received back and the result table is constructed as shown in Figure 10. The result table window includes also the actual SPARQL query constructed by the graphical query tool.

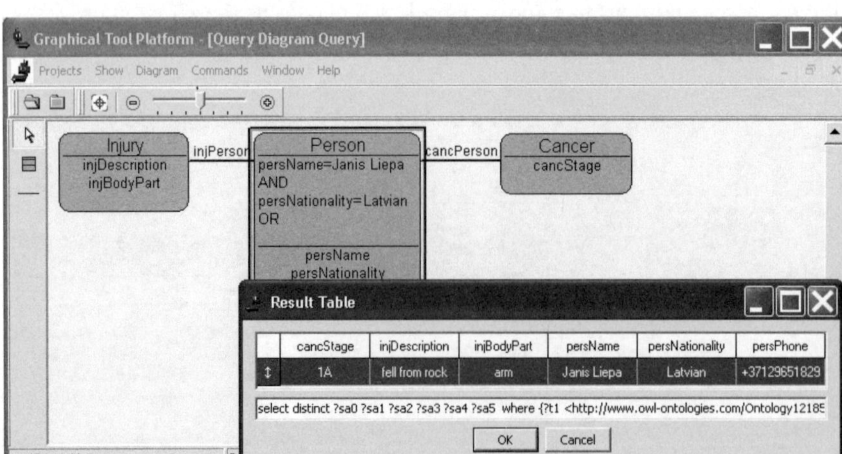

Figure 10. SPARQL answers in DEMO tool

Of course, further user interface and functionality improvements could be added to the illustrated DEMO tool. The tool could be extended to cover more complete set of OWL and SPARQL features besides the core features demonstrated in this example. At present only classes are considered as selectable concepts but sometimes user might want to select also a concept that actually is an attribute. Another advanced example in Figure 11 illustrates use of inheritance to specify that only injuries that are both *TransportAccident* and *BrokenBone* should be considered.

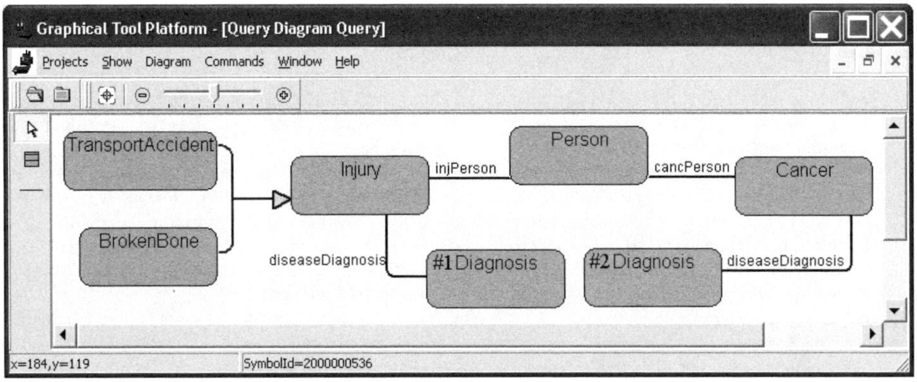

Figure 11. Advanced features in DEMO tool

Our graphical query construction tool (a "DEMO tool") is built using GrTP tool platform [13] and transformation language LX [14]. Graphically formulated queries are translated into SPARQL and then queried to Sesame RDF database with RDF Schema and direct type entailment inference enabled through the *native-rdfs-dt* template.

3. Conclusion

In this paper we have demonstrated a successful practical application of graphical semantic web technologies. The successful application relies on essential graphical techniques provided by UML OWL profile [8] both in ontology definition phase as well as in data access phase. The described project is work in progress, but even the current results provide highly useful fully graphical end-user interface with ontologies and data queries.

Acknowledgments

This work is supported by the National Research Programme projects "Multi-Disciplinary Research Consortium on Major Pathologies Threatening the Life Expectancy and Quality of Life of the Latvian Population" and "Research and Adaptation of Semantic Web Technologies in Latvia"

References

[1] Barzdins, J., Barzdins, G., & Cerans, K. (2008) From Databases to Ontologies. In Cardoso, J., & Lytras, M. (eds), Semantic Web Engineering in the Knowledge Society. IGI Global, pp. 247-271.

[2] Yuan, J., & Jones, G. H. (2007) Enabling Semantic Access to Enterprise RDB Data. In W3C Workshop on RDF Access to Relational Databases. (available at http://www.w3.org/2007/03/RdfRDB/papers/yuan.html)

[3] SPARQL Query Language for RDF. W3C Recommendation (2008). (available at http://www.w3.org/TR/rdf-sparql-query)

[4] Bizer, C., & Cyganiak, R. (2006) D2R Server - Publishing Relational Databases on the Semantic Web. Poster at the 5th International Semantic Web Conference (ISWC2006), November 5-9, Athens, GA, USA. (available at http://sites.wiwiss.fu-berlin.de/suhl/bizer/pub/Bizer-Cyganiak-D2R-Server-ISWC2006.pdf)

[5] Athanasis, N., Christophides, V., & Kotzinos, D. (2004) Generating On the Fly Queries for the Semantic Web: The ICS-FORTH Graphical RQL Interface (GRQL). In the 3rd International Semantic Web Conference (ISWC2004), November 7-11, Hiroshima, Japan, pp. 486-501. (available at http://dblp.uni-trier.de/rec/bibtex/conf/semweb/AthanasisCK04)

[6] Berners-Lee, T., et al. (2006) Tabulator: Exploring and Analyzing linked data on the Semantic Web. In the 3rd International Semantic Web User Interaction Workshop (SWUI 2006), November 6, Athens, GA, USA. (available at http://swui.semanticweb.org/swui06/papers/Berners-Lee/Berners-Lee.pdf)

[7] Longwell project page. SIMILE Project (2006). (available at http://simile.mit.edu/wiki/Longwell)

[8] Ontology Definition Metamodel. OMG Adopted Specification. Document Number: ptc/2007-09-09, November 2007. (available at http://www.omg.org/docs/ptc/07-09-09.pdf)

[9] Barzdins, G., Liepins, E., Veilande, M., & Zviedris, M. (2008) Semantic Latvia Approach in the Medical Domain. In Haav, H-M., & Kalja, A. (eds), Proceedings of the 8th International Baltic Conference (Baltic DB&IS 2008), June 2-5, Tallinn, Estonia, Tallinn University of Technology Press, pp. 89-102.

[10] Barzdins, J., Barzdins, G., Balodis, R., Cerans, K., et al. (2006) Towards Semantic Latvia. In Communications of the 7th International Baltic Conference on Databases and Information Systems (Baltic DB&IS 2006), July 3-6, Vilnius, Lithuania, pp. 203-218. (available at http://melnais.mii.lu.lv/audris/CReady_Barzdins_TowardsSemanticLatvia.pdf)

[11] Bizer, C., & Seaborne, A. (2004) D2RQ – Treating Non-RDF Databases as Virtual RDF Graphs. In the 3rd International Semantic Web Conference (ISWC2004), November 7-11, Hiroshima, Japan. (available at http://www4.wiwiss.fu-berlin.de/bizer/pub/Bizer-D2RQ-ISWC2004.pdf)

[12] Broekstra, J., Kampman, A., & Harmelan, F.v. (2002) Sesame: A Generic Architecture for Storing and Querying RDF and RDF Schema. In The Semantic Web - ISWC 2002, volume 2342 of Lecture Notes in Computer Science, pp. 54-68. (available at http://www.cs.vu.nl/~frankh/postscript/ISWC02.pdf)

[13] Barzdins, J., Zarins, A., Cerans, K., Kalnins, A., Rencis, E., Lace, L., Liepins, R., & Sprogis, A. (2007) GrTP: Transformation Based Graphical Tool Building Platform. In Proceedings of the MoDELS'07 Workshop on Model Driven Development of Advanced User Interfaces (MDDAUI-2007), CEUR Workshop Proceedings, Vol 297. (available at http://ftp.informatik.rwth-aachen.de/Publications/CEUR-WS/Vol-297/paper6.pdf)

[14] Barzdins, J., Kalnins, A., Rencis, E., & Rikacovs, S. (2008) Model Transformation Languages and Their Implementation by Bootstrapping Method. In LNCS, vol. 4800, Springer, pp. 130-145.

Databases and Information Systems V
H.-M. Haav and A. Kalja (Eds.)
IOS Press, 2009

doi:10.3233/978-1-58603-939-4-117

Ensuring Large-Scale Semantic Interoperability: The Estonian Public Sector's Case Study

Hele-Mai HAAV [a], Ahto KALJA [b], Peep KÜNGAS [c] and Martin LUTS [d,1]
[a] *Institute of Cybernetics at Tallinn University of Technology, Estonia*
[b] *Department of Computer Engineering, Tallinn University of Technology, Estonia*
[c] *SOA Trader, Ltd, Estonia*
[d] *Department of Informatics, Tallinn University of Technology, Estonia*

Abstract. E-services are built upon the exchange of information between several databases and institutions. The creation process of new e-services may be not an efficient one because the discovery, integration and reuse of appropriate information resources is time-consuming as the meaning of these information resources is not well-enough documented. In order to describe the meaning of information resources – being poured into hundreds of heterogeneous databases, distributed between several institutions – some coordination, principles, architecture and infrastructure are needed. This paper outlines proposed large-scale semantic interoperability architecture and its pilot implementation in the Estonian public sector's semantic interoperability initiative.

Keywords. semantic interoperability, ontology, web service annotation, XMI, XBRL

Introduction

E-services are built upon the exchange of information. Semantic or content interoperability is about ensuring that the meaning of the information exchanged is not lost in the process, that it is readable and understood by the involved people, applications, and institutions. In order to deliver cross-border services, the European institutions and member states will have to agree on a multitude of semantic specifications, such as descriptions of people, products, processes, forms, etc. They will also have to agree on how to formulate these descriptions and where to store them for public use [1].

Many member states of the European Union (MS) currently have some semantic interoperability initiatives ongoing, see for example German's initiative Deutschland Online [2], Italian' initiative in public administration [3], Finnish semantic initiative FinnONTO [2], and Semantic Latvia project [3]. The scope and accent of these initiatives are quite different – some MS focus on consolidating semantic assets in several governmental institutions already in place into semantic portals, some on

[1] Corresponding Author: Martin Luts, Tallinn University of Technology; E-mail: martin.luts@eesti.ee
[2] http://www.deutschland-online.de/DOL_en_Internet/broker.jsp
[3] http://www.cnipa.gov.it/site/it-IT/

building full-scale national semantic web infrastructures, others target syntactic or semantic descriptions of data schemas, some are on the level of human-oriented descriptions of assets, others try to reach automatic use.

There are also pan-European initiatives, which include SEMIC (SEMantic Interoperability Centre Europe)[4], led by the European Commission's IDABC program[5], and semanticGov, fully titled "Providing Integrated Public Services to Citizens at the National and Pan-European level with the use of Emerging Semantic Web Technologies" [4].

This paper outlines the Estonian semantic interoperability initiative in the public sector, describes its architecture and components used in the architecture, present state and future developments. The organisational, time, budget and project management viewpoints are not addressed in this paper.

The structure of the paper is as follows. In section 1 concepts related to semantic interoperability are considered in order to give needed background knowledge. Section 2 gives an overview of semantic interoperability architecture for state registries in Estonia and describes its most important components. Section 3 describes the semantic annotation of information assets, followed by a case study in section 4. In section 5 we make concluding remarks and outline planned future developments.

1. Concepts of Semantic Interoperability

Interoperability – as defined by IEEE – is the ability of two or more systems or components (i) to exchange information and (ii) to use the information that has been exchanged [5]. The European Interoperability Framework defines semantic interoperability as one of the three main dimensions of interoperability – besides organisational and technical interoperability [6]. Semantic interoperability refers to the ability of organisations to understand the exchanged data in a similar way. The semantic interoperability of information systems is the ability of software systems to make adequate use of data received from other software systems. All three dimensions of interoperability: organisational, technical and semantic are considered to be prerequisites for the seamless and user-centred delivery of pan-European e-government services.

Organisations are able to invest less in the production of data by integrating external data sources. However, integration does not come for free – the reuse of data has its price. It is necessary to maintain semantic descriptions (records), integrate different data structures and solve conflicts arising from semantic diversity e.g. terms with different fields of meaning [7].

[4] http://semic.eu/about_semantic_interoperability_centre_europe.html

[5] http://ec.europa.eu/idabc/

2. Semantic Interoperability Architecture for State Information System and Registries in Estonia

2.1. Interoperability Platform for State Information System in Estonia

The state information systems' data transport layer X-Road (X-tee in Estonian) [8, 9, 10] is a technical and organizational environment that enables secure data transfer between digital government databases and enables secure data transfer between individuals and government institutions. X-Road allows officials as well as legal and natural persons to search data from national databases over the Internet within the limits of their authority.

X-Road platform supports the technical interoperability of the components and registries of state information system. Currently, X-Road does not support semantic interoperability. In following we describe the extension of X-Road – the semantic layer to be built on top of X-Road infrastructure.

2.2. Overview of Semantic Interoperability Architecture for State Information System

Semantic interoperability – the ability to understand the exchanged data in a similar way and make adequate use of it – requires a system for the semantic description of several types of objects (infoware or information resources), like:

- Operations (e.g. web services): the input-output data, preconditions, effects, logical relation between input and output structures;
- Business processes;
- Data-structures in databases or data-structures to be exchanged;
- Official and other documents, web-pages;
- Other types of objects, in public or private sector.

The architecture that we provide in this paper for a system of semantic descriptions proceeds from the following principles:

- Principle of reuse – one concept or relation should be described only once and in any other use the initial description should be referred to. That brings us to the segregation of infoware's metadata and ontologies, that is, infoware's meaning in not described within metadata but a link is provided which points to the meaning of the infoware's element in ontology.
- Simple and standard compilation, management and search of the descriptions of objects and concepts.

The semantic interoperability architecture for state information system and registries of Estonia (see Figure 1) consists of the following interrelated components: ontologies, semantically annotated objects (contained in infoware's metadata), supported by policies and guidelines, several processes and workflows, tools, educational activities, PR, among others.

The Administration System for the State Information System (RIHA) [11] is the central tool in the semantic interoperability architecture for state information system. RIHA fulfils the following tasks in the semantic interoperability architecture:

- Hosting and publishing of ontologies.
- Hosting and publishing of infoware's metadata, including semantics.
- Serving as semantic search engine for semantic assets (resources).

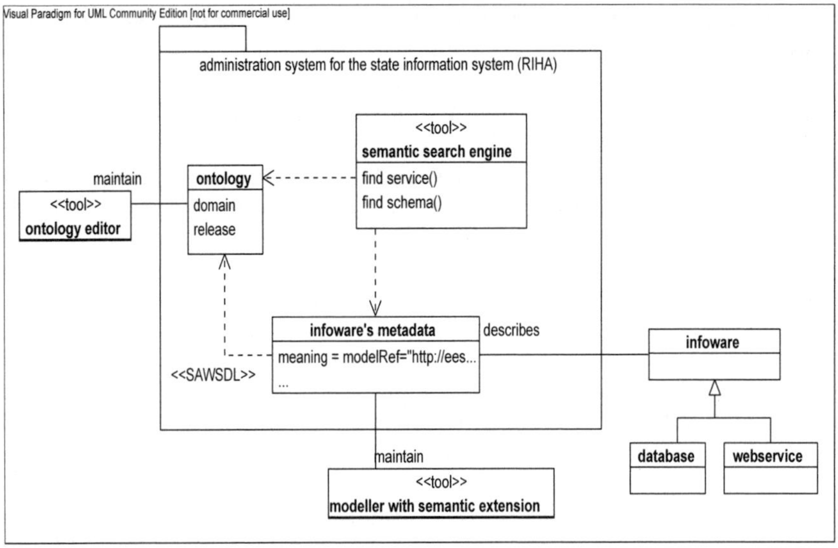

Figure 1. Semantic interoperability architecture for state information system and registries in Estonia

RIHA works to ensure the interoperability of public sector registries and the reuse of technical, organisational and semantic resources. For end-users, RIHA is the tool to:

- Obtain information about existing services, as well as about service descriptions and the principles of service provision.
- Apply for the right to use a service.
- Propose the creation of a new service.

2.3. Ontologies

2.3.1. Ontology Support for Semantic Interoperability

One of the main components of semantic interoperability architecture – as designed for Estonian state registries – are ontologies. We use the term 'ontology' meaning "a formal explicit specification of a shared conceptualization for a domain of interest" [12] and "information about how individuals are grouped and fit together in a particular domain"[6].

Currently, there are – as far as the authors know – no ontologies in Estonian, which could be used to annotate operations performed by state registries and other objects.

The ontology component in our architectural framework is not a monolithic structure – for the purposes of easier, domain-expert driven maintenance, it is divided into domains, e.g. "Environment", "Social Affairs". The initial tree for categorizing ontologies is based on the official naming of EU activities. The language used in the semantic description of ontology objects draws from W3C recommendation OWL (Web Ontology Language) [13]. The ontologies are developed and maintained in a distributed manner, the tools to be used are not prescribed as long as certain standards

---

[6] OWL 2 Web Ontology Language: Primer. W3C Working Draft 11 April 2008 (http://www.w3.org/TR/2008/WD-owl2-primer-20080411/).

are followed (for example, Collaborative Protégé, Semantic Media Wiki, IkeWiki and others may be in use), but stored and published centrally – in the administration system for the state information system [11].

Ontologies that support the semantic interoperability architecture are classified into 3 layers depending on how general they are i.e. how general concepts they cover (see Figure 2).

Most general is Estonian Top Ontology (possible several ontologies in future) that represents general concepts used in many different fields of human activities. On the bottom level, different domain ontologies represent domain specific concepts from domains of state IS and their services. On the middle, there is a need for interdomain ontology modules that capture common concepts from many domains of interest, but which are not general enough to be included in top ontology. There might be overlapping between domain, interdomain, and top ontologies.

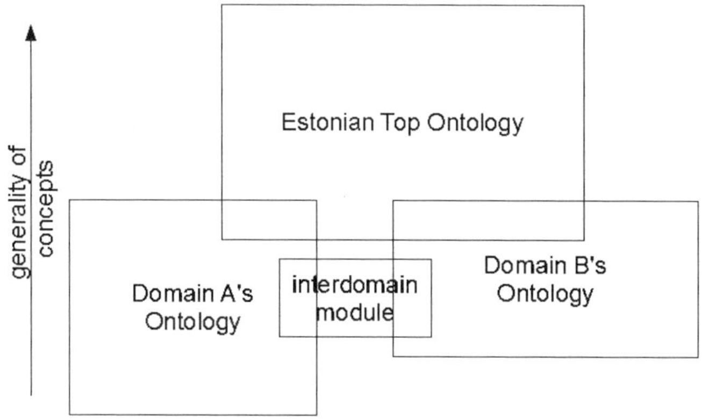

Figure 2. Modularity and layering of ontologies component in interoperability architecture

The reason for such a segregation of ontologies is that we foresee many different use-case scenarios of ontologies that go beyond the needs and borders of state information system. For example, top ontology can be used by many applications, including commercial. On the other hand, in order to meet specific needs of web services provided by state information system as well as possible, domain ontologies are built. Already now, it is clear that there are ontologies that capture concepts common to many domains and as such they may form a separate module used by many domains. This approach supports maximum reuse of ontologies and hopefully helps to avoid contradictions in defining same concepts by different domain experts.

2.3.2. Methodology for Ontology Creation and Maintenance

From the methodological point of view, development of ontologies is a complex task and a lot of ontology building experiences are needed in order to participate in the production of good ontologies. In this respect, Estonia is at the initial level of education and experience, both in the universities as well as in software companies. However, current semantic interoperability initiative is going to improve the situation by providing training and methodological aid for ontology development.

According to this, we decided to start the developing of domain ontologies in some chosen pilot fields of state information system. After lessons learnt in the pilot projects we plan to go further and create top ontologies based on already compiled glossaries like Estterm[7], thesauri Wordnet[8], EuroVoc[9] and others by converting them to machine processable OWL ontologies.

Concerning methods for building domain ontologies, we follow already accepted ontology development methodologies like METHONTOLOGY [14] but we are going to customise these methodologies to meet our specific needs.

The scope of domain ontologies in state information system is limited to inputs and outputs of web services provided by registries, both the services in production, but also services in design phase. The scope could be widened according to the needs of semantically annotating other types of objects – like data-schemas of registries, business processes, preconditions and effects of services, and others – in the same domain.

The ontology creation process is planned to be data-driven, following a mixture of bottom-up and middle-out approaches – we start with data-object used as input-output in web services offered by main state registries (i.e. population registry, land cadastre, vehicle registry). We are trying to partially automate this ontology-learning task, including extracting concept relations from the so-called query-type web services. As a formal representation we use OWL as ontology language. This makes it possible to use a number of existing ontology editors like Protégé and suitable reasoners like RacerPro or Pellet.

In our case, ontology maintenance is decentralised and publishing of ontologies is centralised (via RIHA). This approach will be supported by collaborative web-based ontology development and maintenance tool, codenamed SEHKE, under development.

An ultimate goal of ontology creation is its reuse by various bodies and applications. In current initiative, ontologies will be made publicly available via RIHA that gives opportunity to reuse them across many applications and in other ontologies.

We plan to use release-based publishing of ontologies, i.e. every single or minor change does not reflect on officially published ontologies. The number of the year and release number are encoded into URLs which are used to point to the elements of ontologies, so the versioning of ontologies is achieved.

3. Semantically Enriching State Registries

3.1. Semantic Description of Operations Performed by Databases

We see our first priority to semantically annotate operations performed by state registries – as it promises quick return of investment and we also consider it to solve the complex task of integrating state registries – and creating e-services more efficiently – to some extent.

Semantic annotation of operations includes the description of every single operation and its input-output data-structures, preconditions, effects, relation between input-output, in a form of reference to the respective entry in the domain ontology. The

---

[7] http://www.legaltext.ee/et/andmebaas/ava.asp?m=032
[8] http://www.cl.ut.ee/ressursid/teksaurus/index.php?lang=en
[9] http://europa.eu/eurovoc/

languages used for description are WSDL and SA-WSDL (Semantic Annotations for WSDL and XML Schema) [15]. The idea of W3C's SA-WSDL recommendation is simple – it standardises the way of semantically enriching web service descriptions by adding pointers to WSDL. These pointers refer to the semantic description of a web service element in a model outside the WSDL document. That model could be an OWL ontology, UML model created according to OUP (Ontology UML Profile [16]) or similar. For example, describing the "cadastral unit" input data element of a web service, instead of describing it in human-readable form in the WSDL document, a SA-WSDL pointer, which refers to the appropriate record in land survey ontology is used.

Excerpt from semantically annotated WSDL follows:

```
<wsdl:types>
   ...
   <xs:simpleType name="immovable" sawsdl:modelReference=
            "http://www.ee/onto/land/2008/release2/cadastralUnit">
   ...
   </xs:simpleType>
</wsdl:types>
```

One thing to consider is whether to store the semantic descriptions within the information resource – e.g. WSDL close to the organisation offering the service – or in a centralized pattern. We have chosen to store and publish the descriptions in the administration system for the state information system (RIHA) [11] – for easier access. Storing descriptions outside the information resource requires more work: creation and maintenance of repositories as well as motivating and supervising describers. On the other hand, with that approach describers might be more motivated, because there are more supervisors as the description is available for everyone.

3.2. Semantic Description of Databases and Data Structures

Semantic annotation of databases and data structure includes the description of every single data element, in a form of reference to the respective entry in the domain ontology. The languages used for description are XML for data structures, XMI for all types of database (relational, object-oriented or other) schemas combined with SA-WSDL (Semantic Annotations for WSDL and XML Schema) [15]. For XMI we have created a special UML profile for attaching SA-WSDL pointers into serialized UML (i.e. XMI).

In some cases a domain-specific standard is already in place in order to describe the semantics of data structures. For example, in financial domain business reports and statements are described using XBRL (eXtensible Business Reporting Language)[10], an XML based open standard which supports information modelling and the expression of semantic meaning commonly required in business reporting. For such cases, we try to build transformations from the domain-specific semantic descriptions, expressed in domain-specific languages, into OWL – extracting the semantics and publishing it using one common supradomain standard.

---

[10] see http://www.xbrl.org/.

3.3. Semantic Description of Other Assets

The architecture outlined above is not closed for annotating only web services or data structures. Adding semantics to business processes, documents, web pages, and other type of objects, expanding beyond public sector, can be carried out with relatively moderate effort. So the reuse of ontologies, knowledge, tools, etc is in the vision of the developers of this architecture.

3.4. Tools

To support large-scale (e.g. nation-wide or pan-European) systematic collaborative management of semantic assets [11], appropriate tools are required to optimise the associated routines. Therefore an environment called SEHKE has been specified and its realisation is in a procurement phase. SEHKE is an Internet-based environment such that its functionality can be accessed anywhere and anytime. Moreover, SEHKE is planned to have a dedicated open API, described with a WSDL document, which allows seamless integration of the environment with other development tools and similar environments (e.g. WSMO Studio).

SEHKE differs from the majority of semantic asset creation or managed tools in the following aspects:

- True online collaboration in creation and management of assets;
- Iterative process for achieving consensus between multiple parties in creating mappings and relations between assets or modifying the latter;
- Structured versioning of semantic assets such that existing mappings can be dynamically updated at any time;
- Online validation of inserted ontologies, mappings and other assets;
- Tailored to process descriptions based on Estonian language and cultural heritage but still open to assets from other cultural spaces as well.

Moreover, creation of the semantic assets is simplified through automated detection of similar assets. The latter is supported by syntactic and semantic search algorithms and heuristics. While syntactic search is based on information retrieval algorithms, semantic search applies formal methods. Usage of similarity metrics provides technological basis for semi-automated construction of mappings based of syntactic and semantic similarities. This is essential in optimising the routines of knowledge workers while creating and managing their assets.

The mentioned functionality makes SEHKE a powerful collaborative online tool, which is intended in addition to supporting semantic interoperability of information systems, also to be applied in archiving, language technologies and other fields.

3.5. Guidelines

Department of State Information Systems, Ministry of Economic Affairs and Communications of Estonia, has released "Instructions for the Semantic Description of Databases and Operations Performed by Databases" [17] and "Methodology for the Semantic Interoperability of Databases and Operations Performed by Databases" [7] (also available in English at http://www.riso.ee/en/information-policy/interoperability).

[11] Such as ontologies, mappings between ontologies, references form data objects in information system component descriptions to concepts in ontologies, etc.

Whereas the European Semantic/Content Interoperability Strategy [18] is quite general, the "Instructions for the Semantic Description" provide more specific guidelines and rules for application owners, developers and auditors.

4. Case Study

The purpose of the case study is to analyse two aspects of web services annotation:

- To estimate the effort required to build ontologies and annotate existing web services semantically;
- To guesstimate in which extend annotation efforts can be reduced through applying automated annotation methods.

In order to answer these questions we have analyzed 24 web service descriptions consisting of 538 operations which constitutes ca 50% of functionality brokered by X-Road (see Figure 3). These 24 analyzed WSDL documents incorporate 6653 enumeration values for 110 enumerations[12]. These enumerations contain 5707 different values, which shows that overlapping of the enumerations is quite small. The latter indicates that either:

- Enumerations are reused within Web services a lot; or
- Enumerations are not reused at all, so the terminology used in enumeration values needs unification.

These 24 web service descriptions consist of ca 4000 data fields, used as inputs and outputs for web service operations. Around 3000 of them contain also human-readable documentation. For the 4000 data fields there are ca 1400 different XML Schema element names – which gives us the upper limit for the ontology size in terms of concepts one requires to semantically annotate WSDLs. In practice the number of concepts may vary between 1000 and 2000 due to homonyms, synonyms and other factors affecting their interpretation.

Based on the information presented above, the time required to semantically annotate and build models for web service operations can be estimated.

Additionally, based on the case study, one can:

- Unify/harmonise enumerations and classifiers used to encode particular data;
- Determine domains and create ontologies in bottom-up manner;
- Evaluate the quality of data models and technical descriptions of web services from the viewpoint of semantic annotation;
- Etc.

Our next effort is to analyze the quality and efficiency to use annotation heuristics to automatically add semantic annotations to WSDLs and XML Schemas. Due to the large number and variety of schemas automation is required to simplify the creation of semantic annotations.

[12] Enumerations are required to define fixed sets of values, which are used to encode certain data field values.

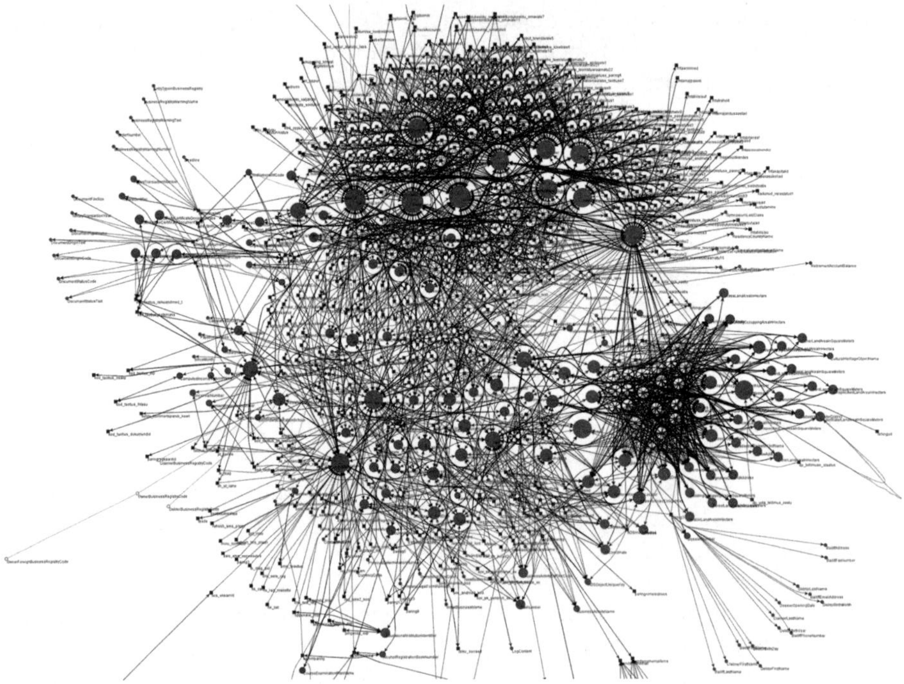

Figure 3. Automatically annotated 25% of X-Road

First experiments are depicted in Figure 3 representing semantically annotated web service operations by using annotation heuristics together with automated annotation. Altogether 270 concepts were needed to annotate ca 2200 of 4000 possible XML Schema elements (see Table 1 for more information). To compare, top 30 concepts would provide semantic annotations to ca 600 fields. These numbers indicate that the 20/80 ratio applies to semantic annotation as well – 20% of concepts would be enough for providing 80% of annotations whereas up to 80% of annotation could be provided through automated annotation methods. Our experiments indicate that building annotation heuristics takes only 5-10% of time, which is otherwise required for manual annotation.

Circles in Figure 3 represent semantically annotated data fields, which are grouped together according to their semantics, while rectangular nodes represent web service operations, which either produce or consume that data. Each circular node refers to a specific concept in an ontology, which represents particular semantics. The larger the circle node appears, the larger the number of references to a particular concept. Most important concepts are enlisted in Table 2. Please note the differences between Table 1 and Table 2 – while in Table 1 data field names are listed, in Table 2 concept labels are listed. The heuristics and annotation methods applied will be described in another paper.

Table 1. 12 most popular field names in X-Road WSDL documents.

Field name (in Estonian)	English interpretation	Occurrence
Isikukood	National identity code	141
Teade	Notification	125
Eesnimi	First name	98
Perenimi	Surname (last name)	55
Nimi	Name	51
Kood	Code	47
et_nr		44
lopp_kpv	End date	39
algus_kpv	Start date	38
Id	Identifier	37
perekonnanimi	Family name (last name)	36
Synniaeg	Birth date	35

Table 2. Most important concepts.

Concept label	Occurrence
National identity code	157
Notification	128
First name	107
Last name	97
General identifier	93
Date	89
Name	83
Address	59
Birth date	58
Application number	49
End date	30

5. Conclusions and Future Work

The main way to enhance semantic interoperability between organisations or information systems is to describe semantically the data exchanged and operations performed, i.e. to provide the terms and definitions of this data and operations by opening their meaning.

The primary task for achieving semantic interoperability between state registries in Estonia is to compile human- and machine-readable ontologies with examples for the input and output data of the system as well as a description of the operation. Such adequate description is necessary for proceeding to the next level:

- Inter-domain ontologies, multilingualism.
- Machine-processability: automatic identification, launch and composition of the operation.

Acknowledgement

This research was partially supported by the target-financed theme No. 0322709s06 of the Estonian Ministry of Education and Research and by the ERDF funded Estonian Centre of Excellence in Computer Science, EXCS.

References

[1] Semantic Interoperability Strategy/XML Clearinghouse – Interpretable exchange of data between applications, (available at http://ec.europa.eu/idabc/en/document/3875/5890)

[2] Hyvönen, E. et al (2008) Building a National Semantic Web Ontology and Ontology Service Infrastructure - The FinnONTO Approach. In Proceedings of the European Semantic Web Conference (ESWC 2008), Tenerife, Spain, (available at http://www.seco.tkk.fi/publications/2008/hyvonen-et-al-building-2008.pdf)

[3] Barzdins, J. et al (2006) Towards Semantic Latvia. In Proceedings of Communications of 7th International Baltic Conference on Databases and Information Systems. Vilnius, Lithuania, pp. 203-218, (available at http://melnais.mii.lu.lv/audris/CReady_Barzdins_TowardsSemanticLatvia.pdf)

[4] Vitvar, T. et al (2006) Infrastructure for the Semantic Pan-European E-government Services. In Proceedings of the 2006 AAAI Spring Symposium on The Semantic Web meets e-government (SWEG), (available at http://www.semantic-gov.org/index.php?name=Web_Links&req=visit&lid=4)

[5] IEEE Standard Computer Dictionary: A Compilation of IEEE Standard Computer Glossaries. Institute of Electrical and Electronics Engineers, 1990

[6] Final European Interoperability Framework version 1.0. IDABC, (available at http://ec.europa.eu/idabc/servlets/Doc?id=19529)

[7] Methodology for the Semantic Interoperability of Databases and Operations Performed by Databases. Department of State Information Systems, Ministry of Economic Affairs and Communications of Estonia, (available at http://www.riso.ee/en/files/EstonianGov_Semantic_Description-Methodology_v1.2.pdf)

[8] Kalja, A., & Vallner, U. (2002) Public e-service projects in Estonia. In Databases and information systems: Proceedings of the Fifth International Baltic Conference, Baltic DB&IS 2002. Tallinn, Estonia, pp. 143-153.

[9] Kalja, A. (2002) The X-Road Project: A project to modernize Estonia's national databases, Baltic IT&T Review, 1(24): 47-48

[10] Kalja, A. et al (2005) eGovernment in Estonia: best practices. In Technology Management: A Unifying Discipline for Melting the Boundarie, IEEE, pp. 500-506.

[11] Vallner, U. (2006) Nationwide Components of Estonia's State Information System, Baltic IT&T Review 3(42)

[12] Gruber, T.R. (1993) A Translation Approach to Portable Ontology Specifications, Knowledge Acquisition, 5: 199-220

[13] OWL Web Ontology Language. The World Wide Web Consortium, (available at http://www.w3.org/TR/2004/REC-owl-features-20040210/)

[14] Gómez-Pérez, A. M., & Fernández-López, O. Corcho (2004) *Ontological Engineering with examples from the areas of Knowledge Management, e-Commerce and the Semantic Web*. Springer, 2004

[15] Semantic Annotations for WSDL and XML Schema. World Wide Web Consortium, (available at http://www.w3.org/TR/2007/REC-sawsdl-20070828/)

[16] Ontology Definition Metamodel 1.0 beta. OMG Adopted Specification. The Object Management Group, (available at http://www.omg.org/technology/documents/modeling_spec_catalog.htm#ODM, http://www.omg.org/spec/ODM/1.0/Beta2/PDF)

[17] Instructions for the Semantic Description of Databases and Operations Performed by Databases. Version 1.1. Department of State Information Systems, Ministry of Economic Affairs and Communications of Estonia, (available at http://www.riso.ee/en/files/EstonianGov_Semantic_Description-Instructions_v1.1c.pdf)

[18] IDABC Content Interoperability Strategy. Working paper, (available at http://ec.europa.eu/idabc/servlets/Doc?id=24405)

Information Systems and AI Technologies

Databases and Information Systems V
H.-M. Haav and A. Kalja (Eds.)
IOS Press, 2009

doi:10.3233/978-1-58603-939-4-131

Spiking Neural Networks to Detect Temporal Patterns

Janis ZUTERS[1]
Department of Computing, University of Latvia, Latvia

Abstract. Spiking neural networks (SNNs) are more powerful than their non-spiking predecessors as they can encode temporal information in their signals, but they also need different and biologically more plausible rules for synaptic plasticity. In this paper, an unsupervised learning algorithm is introduced for a spiking neural network. The algorithm is based on the Hebbian rule, with the addition of the principle of adapting a layer activation level so as to guarantee frequent firings of neurons for each layer. The proposed algorithm has been illustrated with experimental results related to the detection of temporal patterns in an input stream.

Keywords. spiking neural networks, unsupervised learning, adaptive activation, temporal patterns

Introduction

A spiking neural network (SNN) is a neural model in which the communication between two neurons is performed by a "pulse code", i.e., the process of computation considers the timings of the signals (spikes) while ignoring their strength. It has been shown theoretically that a neural network which is composed of spiking neurons is able to learn a large class of target functions. The problem of learning in spiking neural networks is still a challenging issue, and this paper introduces an unsupervised learning algorithm for SNNs.

1. Neural Networks

Neural networks represent a technology that is rooted in many disciplines: neurosciences, mathematics, statistics, physics, computer sciences and engineering. A neural network is a computational model which is made up of relatively simple interconnected processing units which are put into operation through a learning process.

Neural networks are useful tools for solving many types of problems. These problems can be characterised as mapping (including pattern association and pattern classification), clustering, and constraint optimisation. There are several neural network models which are available for each type of problem [1].

[1] Corresponding Author: Janis Zuters, Department of Computing, University of Latvia, Raina bulvaris 19., LV-1050 Riga, Latvia; E-mail: janis.zuters@lu.lv

1.1. Operation of a Neural Network

A neural network is a computational system built up of a big amount of interconnected processing units called neurons, which perform certain tasks as a team. Unlike traditional computational systems, a neural network resembles a "black box" – the role of every particular neuron in solving the task cannot be elucidated.

A neuron refers to a fairly simple processing unit with several inputs and exactly one output. In terms of functionality, a neuron resembles a multi-argument mathematical function. Eq. (1) shows a typical example of operation of a neuron.

$$y_i = f_{act}\left(\sum_{j=1}^{n} w_{ij}x_j\right), \tag{1}$$

where x_j represent the inputs to the neuron i; w_{ij} represent inner parameters, or weights of the neuron i; f_{act} is some, usually nonlinear, function.

Neurons are comparatively simple computational elements, so the power of a neural network is provided by their joint activity. A neural network, like a graph, can also be defined as a tuple of the set of neurons and the set of links between neurons. However, the neurons of a network are typically grouped into layers, and the network also operates layer by layer.

1.2. The Learning Algorithm

Learning (or training, in terms of an external process) refers to establishing weights (as well as other free parameters) and doing so on the basis of training patterns which represent a certain problem.

A learning algorithm (or training algorithm) is an important issue to characterise a neural network, and every neural network model has its own learning algorithm. However, there are several basic strategies and principles to be named as common for most neural network models.

The three main learning categories are learning with a teacher (supervised learning), reinforcement learning, and unsupervised learning. "Supervised" means that for each training pattern the desired value (i.e., the right answer) is known. In unsupervised learning there is no external teacher or critic to oversee the learning process.

A typical way of performing a training process is epochwise. An epoch refers to an interval in the training process during which each of the training patterns is presented to the neural network exactly once.

2. Spiking Neural Networks

2.1. Generations of Neural Network Models

Since spiking neural networks appeared, the neural network models became ready to be classified into three generations.

The first generation of artificial neural networks consisted of McCulloch-Pitts threshold neurons [2], where a neuron sends a binary signal if the sum of its weighed incoming signals rises above a threshold value.

The second generation neurons use continuous activation functions instead of threshold functions to compute the output signals.

The neurons of network of the first two generations communicate via a "rate code", i.e., by transmitting "pure" continuous values irrespective of the timings of the signals. Work with such models is usually arranged in steps – during each step exactly one pattern is classified or recognised, and no temporal information is processed directly by the neural network.

In contrast to classical models, spiking neural networks, or the third generation neural networks, are designed to make use of the temporal dynamics of neurons. Here, communication between neurons involves a "pulse code" – the exact timing of the transmitted signal (i.e., the spike) is of key importance, but the strength of the signal is not considered. SNNs are believed to be very powerful, but their operation is more complicated and their application is not as obvious as is the case with "ordinary" neural networks. Nevertheless SNNs have been the focus of much recent research, inspired by the opportunity to exploit another resemblance to the brain and by the sense of a challenge related to an understanding of the brain's functions.

2.2. Operation of a Spiking Neuron

Each neuron in an SNN produces a train of spikes (i.e., it fires), and the operation of the neuron i is fully characterised by the set of firing times [3]:

$$F_i = \left\{ t_i^{(1)}, \ldots, t_i^{(n)} \right\}, \tag{2}$$

where $t_i^{(n)}$ is the most recent spike of neuron i.

One of the most frequently applied spiking neuron models is the integrate-and-fire model. In this model, input signals (both actual and recent) from a neuron are combined together in order to achieve enough activation for the neuron to fire.

Neuron i is said to fire if its activation state u_i reaches the threshold ϑ. At the moment when the threshold is crossed, a spike with the firing time $t_i^{(f)}$ is generated (see Eq. 3)). Thus Eq. (2) can be clarified with Eq. (3) [3]:

$$F_i = \left\{ t_i^{(f)}; 1 \leq f \leq n \right\} = \left\{ t \mid u_i(t) = \vartheta \right\}, \tag{3}$$

where the activation state u_i is given by the linear superposition of all contributions:

$$\mathrm{u}_i(t) = \eta_i(t - \hat{t_i}) + \sum_{j \in \Gamma_i} \sum_{t_j^{(f)} \in F_j} w_{ij}\, \varepsilon_{ij}(t - t_j^{(f)}), \tag{4}$$

where Γ_i is the set of presynaptic neurons to neuron i; $\hat{t_i}$ is the last spike of neuron i; the function η_i takes care of refractoriness after a spike is emitted (Eq. (5)); the kernels ε_{ij} model the neurons response to presynaptic spikes (Eq. (6)).

See Figure 1 for a graphic interpretation. Eqs. (5) and (6) have been adapted from [3], [4].

$$\eta_i(s) = \begin{cases} -\vartheta \exp(-\frac{s}{\tau}); & s > 0 \\ 0; & s \le 0 \end{cases}, \tag{5}$$

where τ is a time constant.

$$\varepsilon_{ij}(s) = \begin{cases} \exp(-\frac{s-\Delta_j^{ax}}{\tau_m}) - \exp(-\frac{s-\Delta_j^{ax}}{\tau_s}); & s-\Delta_j^{ax} > 0 \\ 0; & s-\Delta_j^{ax} \le 0 \end{cases}, \tag{6}$$

where τ_s and τ_m are time constants, and Δ_j^{ax} is the axonal transmission delay for presynaptic neuron j.

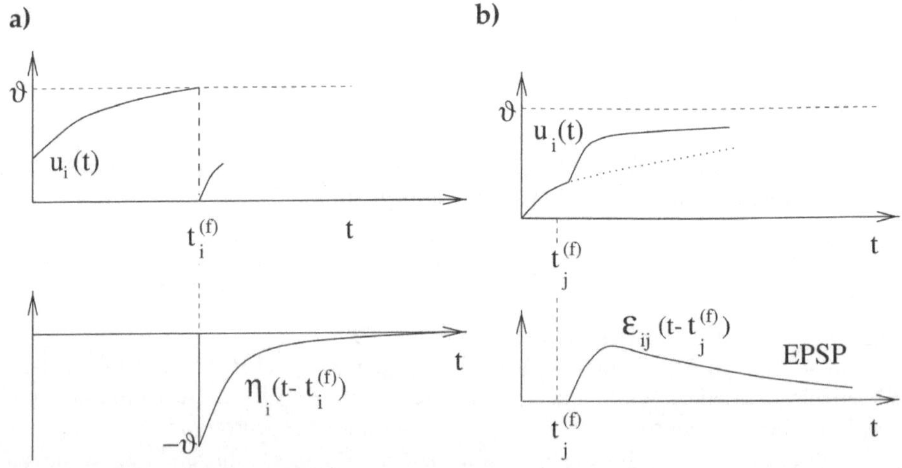

Figure 1. a) The state variable $u_i(t)$ reaches the threshold ϑ at time $t_i^{(f)}$. Immediately afterwards $u_i(t)$ is reset to zero. The reset is performed by adding a kernel $\eta_i(t-t_i^{(f)})$. The function $\eta_i(s)$ takes care of refractoriness after a spike emitted at s=0. b) The state variable $u_i(t)$ changes after a presynaptic spike has occured at $t_j^{(f)}$. The kernels ε_{ij} describes the response of u_i to a presynaptic spike at s=0. The postsynaptic potential can either be excitatory (EPSP) or inhibitory (IPSP). [3]

3. Hebbian Learning – a Learning Strategy for SNNs

Although there are several different kinds of models of SNNs, there is still the aspect of learning in relation to these. Both supervised and unsupervised learning methods are available for spiking neural networks. If supervised learning methods greatly predominate in "non-spiking" neural networks, then the situation with SNNs is quite different. Hebbian learning is one of the most popular learning strategies for SNNs.

Back in 1949, Donald Hebb proposed a precise rule which might govern the synaptic changes which underlie learning: "When an axon of cell *A* is near enough to excite a cell *B* and repeatedly or persistently takes part in firing it, some growth process or metabolic change takes place in one or both cells such that *A*'s efficiency as one of the cells firing *B*, is increased" [5].

Hebb's description states that correlations between the firings of the pre- and post-synaptic neurons drive changes in the transmission efficiency. Even though the idea of learning through correlations dates further back in the past, correlation-based learning rules are now generally called Hebbian learning. [6]

Hebb's formulation of his rule has several important features. One is causality. According to Hebb, the firing of neuron *A* must be causally related to the firing of neuron *B*, which in practice means that spikes in neuron *A* must precede spikes in neuron *B*. A simple correlation in which the order of spike times is unimportant would not satisfy Hebb's hypothesis. A second feature is the assignment of a critical role to spikes. This is explicit for the postsynaptic cell and implicit for the presynaptic cell because Hebb's discussion always considers neuronal interaction as mediated by spikes. [7]

In standard neural network theory, the Hebb rule is condensed to a formula for the change of synaptic efficacy as a function of pre- and postsynaptic firing rates. If y_j and y_i stand for pre- and postsynaptic firing rates respectively, then the change Δw_{ij} of the efficacy of a connection from j to i can be stated as follows [6]:

$$\Delta w_{ij} = c_{ij} y_i y_j + c_{ii} y_i^2 + c_{jj} y_j^2 + b_i y_i + b_j y_j + a \qquad (7)$$

The first term on the right-hand side of (7) picks up the correlations between pre- and postsynaptic activity. The next terms are useful to impose some specific requirements like a proper normalisation. So the simplest form of the Hebbian learning is described by [8]:

$$\Delta w_{ij} = c_{ij} y_i y_j \qquad (8)$$

In [6], a simple learning rule with normalization, based on (7), is shown as an example:

$$\Delta w_{ij} = \eta (y_i - y^*) y_j \qquad (9)$$

This is a special case of (7) with parameters $c_{ij}=\eta$, $b_i=0$, $b_j=-\eta y^*$, $c_{ii}=c_{jj}=a=0$. With this rule the direction of synaptic change (increase or decrease) reverses if the output rate y_i crosses the reference rate y^*. This example is just to explain the role of normalization within Hebbian based rules, and to show this to be an important part of the rule.

4. The Learning Method With Adaptive Layer Activation

In this section, a Hebbian rule-based method for learning in SNNs is proposed. The key innovations in this method are the following:

1) Adjustment of the average activation state of neurons in each layer so as to ensure a definite average rhythm of spikes within a layer;

2) Maintenance of the fixed average volume of synaptic weight in each neuron so as to avoid a situation in which weights become too "hollow" (too great in terms of absolute value).

These two ideas are described in detail in this section.

4.1. Details in the Construction and Operation of Neurons

In this subsection, a neural model is described in which the proposed learning method has been incorporated.

A feed-forward (MLP-like) network architecture is used.

The activation state u_i is computed similarly to Eq. (4) by adding the notion of **activation acceleration factor** a^{acc}:

$$u_i(t) = \eta_i(t - \hat{t_i}) + a^{acc}(t) \frac{\sum\limits_{j \in \Gamma_i} \sum\limits_{t_j^{(f)} \in F_j} w_{ij}\, \varepsilon_{ij}(t - t_j^{(f)})}{n_i}, \tag{10}$$

where n_i is the weight count of the neuron i; the activation acceleration factor a^{acc} is adjusted during learning.

The activation acceleration factor a^{acc} is introduced for each layer in order to govern the activation state u_i. Because the operation of spiking neurons is fully characterised by firings and these occur only if u_i is big enough, an adjusting mechanism is required to ensure it, and that is what the factor a^{acc} does. Because a^{acc} is in common for the entire layer of neurons, the proposed acceleration means that the firing of some neurons of the layer will be frequent while not guaranteeing the same effect for each neuron individually.

The output of the neuron (in the output layer) is defined as follows:

$$y_i(t) = \begin{cases} 1; & (t - \Delta_i^{ax}) \in F_i \\ 0; & otherwise \end{cases}, \tag{11}$$

where F_i is the spike train, generated by neuron i; Δ_i^{ax} is axonal transmission delay.

4.2. The Learning Algorithm

The proposed algorithm consists of two parts:

- Modification of synaptic weights $\mathbf{w_i}$ (Eq. (12));
- Adjustment of the activation acceleration factor a^{acc} (Eq. (13)).

4.2.1. Weight Modifications

In the proposed algorithm that is presented in Eq. (12), the synaptic weights of a neuron bear modifications only when the neuron has just fired.

The main principle of weight modification recalls the Hebbian approach – the weight value is increased proportional to how recently spikes were received from the corresponding presynaptic neuron ("recentliness" is represented by the response of the incoming neuron, and this is computed using kernel ε_{ij}).

This strategy is complemented by two additional mechanisms to normalise weight values:

- The maximum value of a weight is restricted by the constant c^{wmax};
- Hebb's rule describes the conditions under which synaptic efficacy increases but does not describe the conditions under which it decreases [7]. To determine this, the overall value of the weights of is kept at 0 (by subtracting the average weight value w_i^{avg}).

$$\Delta w_{ij} = \eta^{rate}(c^{wmax} - w_{ij}) \sum_{t_j^{(f)} \in F_j} \varepsilon_{ij}(t - t_j^{(f)}) - w_i^{avg}, \tag{12}$$

where η^{rate} is the learning rate; c^{wmax} is a constant representing maximum allowed weight value; and w_i^{avg} is the average weight value of the neuron.

4.2.2. Adjusting the Activation Acceleration Factor

Eq. (13) describes another part of the algorithm, which speaks to the adjustment of the activation acceleration factor a^{acc}. The factor a^{acc} is essential to ensure a definite rhythm of firing in a layer.

$$a^{acc}(t) = \begin{cases} a^{acc}(t-1) + c^{acc2}\left(\varepsilon^{cum}(t) - c^{\varepsilon}\right)a^{acc}(t-1); & t > 0 \\ c^{acc1}; & t = 0 \end{cases}, \tag{13}$$

where c^{acc1} and c^{acc2} are constants representing the modification style of a^{acc}; c^{ε} is a constant which represents the recommended value of the neurons' response, thus defining the direction of modification of a^{acc}; ε^{cum} is the cumulative response of all neurons in a layer in the recent period.

The main idea in adjusting the factor a^{acc} is ensuring that the cumulative responses of layers are close enough to some fixed value c^{ε} (**recommended response**).

$$\varepsilon^{cum}(t) = \begin{cases} c^{cum}\varepsilon^{avg}(t) + (1 - c^{cum})\varepsilon^{cum}(t-1); & t > 0 \\ 0; & t = 0 \end{cases} \tag{14}$$

where ε^{avg} is the average response of all neurons in a layer at time t.

$$\varepsilon^{avg}(t) = \frac{\sum_j \varepsilon_i(t)}{n} \tag{15}$$

where $\varepsilon_i(t)$ is the response of neuron i in a layer at time t (neuron i itself, not some presynaptic neuron). In terms of computation, Eq. (16) is a simplification of Eq. (6).

$$\varepsilon_i(t) = \sum_{t_i^{(f)} \in F_i} \exp(-\frac{t - t_i^{(f)}}{\tau_m}) - \exp(-\frac{t - t_i^{(f)}}{\tau_s}) \tag{16}$$

5. Experimental Work

5.1. Configuration of the Experimental Environment

The proposed learning method was tested on the detection of reiterative temporal patterns in an input stream. A trained neural network should be able to detect such patterns by giving an output of 1 after the pattern is encountered.

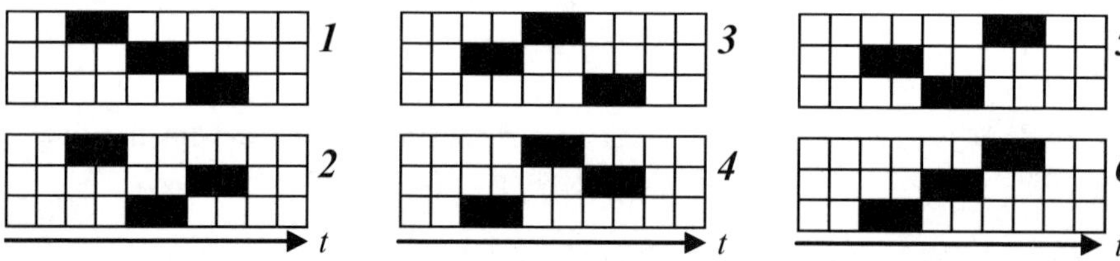

Figure 2. The 6 temporal patterns used in experiments: width=3 signals, length=10 times; black squares denote '1' or 'spike', but white squares – '0' or 'no spike'

```
Procedure run_test
Input
    ϒ – an initialised neural network
    n^(inp) – size of input of the neural network
    pattern_store – set of temporal patterns of width n^(inp)
    π^(patt), π^(1) – constants, representing probability
    n^(patt) – pattern count to be exploited
    t – time counter
    it – count of iterations to be performed
Output
    Sequence of signals generated and passed to neural network
Using
    get_random_value – generates a random value from interval 0..1
Begin
    Choose at random a subset of patterns p ⊂ pattern_store with |p| = n^(patt);
    Do it times
        If get_random_value < π^(patt) then
            Choose at random a pattern p_i ∈ p;
            For j ← 1 to length(p_i) do
                Pass p_ij to ϒ;
                run ϒ with t
        else
            For k ← 1 to n^(inp) do
                If get_random_value < π^(1) then input[k] = 1
                else input[k] = 0
            Pass input to ϒ;
            run ϒ with t
        t ← t + 1
```

Figure 3. The algorithm to generate a temporal sequence of signals to pass to a neural network

The testing environment produces three binary signals at each discrete time moment t and passes them to the input of the neural network. In general, signals are generated at random, but sometimes patterns from a predefined store are interwoven into them.

There are six possible temporal patterns in the store (Figure 2), and two are used in each test run.

Figure 3 describes the algorithm of the testing environments operation, while Figure 4 displays an excerpt from a generated sequence which uses this algorithm.

The neural networks, which were used in the experiments, operated as described above in Eqs. (3), (10), (11), (12) and (13).

Table 1 describes the architecture of neural networks, as well as the various constants which affect the operations so as to illuminate the experimental environment. The parameters of Table 1 and Table 2 were mostly obtained via optimisation in a broader experimental project which goes beyond the scope of this paper.

Table 1. Parameters of configuration of neural network.

Parameter	**Used in Eqs.**	**Value or description**
Input count $n^{(inp)}$		3
Output count $n^{(outp)}$		1
Layer topology t^{top}		feed-forward; one of {3, 5, 1}, and {3, 5, 3, 1}
Constants τ_m, τ_s, τ	(5), (6), (16)	1.5, 0.5, 2.0
Threshold ϑ	(3), (5)	1.0
Learning rate η^{rate}	(12)	0.05
Axonal delay Δ_i^{ax}	(6), (11)	chosen at random from {0, 1, 2, 3}
Constants c^{acc1}, c^{acc2}, c^{cum}	(13), (14)	10.0, 0.02, 0.1
Recommended response c^{ε}	(13)	0.05
Initial weight values w_{ij}		chosen at random from interval -0.3..+0.3
Maximum weight value c^{wmax}	(12)	1.0

5.2. Performing the Experiment

32,620 test runs were conducted during experiment in according the algorithm that is shown in Figure 4 and with the configuration parameters that are depicted in Tables 1 and 2.

Table 2. Parameters of experiments.

Parameter	**Value or description**
pattern_store	6 patterns, each pattern of size 10×3 (see Figure 5)
Probabilities $\pi^{(patt)}$, $\pi^{(1)}$	0.1, 0.2
Pattern count in one test run $n^{(patt)}$	2
count of iterations for the learning phase it^{learn}	5000
count of iterations for the recall phase it^{recall}	600

Procedure ***do_experiment***
Input
  Υ – a neural network
Output
  Result sets R^{good} and R^{bad}
Using
  run_test – generates input, passes it to a neural network, and runs the network
Begin
  Do many times
    Initialize neural network Υ according Table 1;
    Initialize environment according Table 2;
    $r \leftarrow \varnothing$; */* r represents results of one test run */*
    Call ***run_test*** with t = 0, it = it^{learn} in learning mode and record test parameters to *r*;
    $a^{acc\_max} \leftarrow$ maximum activation acceleration factor a^{acc} among layers after learning
    $a^{acc\_min} \leftarrow$ minimum activation acceleration factor a^{acc} among layers after learning
    If $a^{acc\_max} / a^{acc\_min} > 5.0$ then
      Add *r* to bad results R^{bad}
    else
      / recall mode differs from learning mode with the fact that no learning is performed */*
      Call ***run_test*** with t = it^{learn}, it = it^{recall} in recall mode, record input, output
       and test parameters to *r*;
      Add *r* to good results R^{good}

Figure 4. The algorithm to obtain experimental results

6. Results of the Experiment and Conclusions

6.1. The Collection and Assessment of the Results

Experiments were performed in accordance with the algorithm that is shown in Figure 4. Then the obtained result set R^{good} was analyzed further.

The main idea in analysing the result data was to account for output spikes which follow the patterns that are presented to the input. Thus we see whether a neural network has learned the regularities of the input.

Figure 5 provides a look at the performance of a neural network after the learning phase.

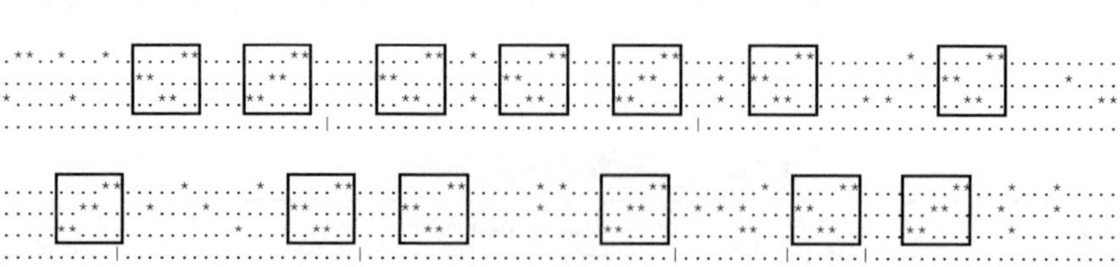

(a)

(b)

Figure 5. An example of obtained test results. Asterisks (*) represent input values of 1, dots (.) represent input and output values of 0, vertical bars (|) represent output spikes (i.e., values of 1). Actual patterns presented to input are in the frames. Two excerpts of two different tests of length of 100 are displayed. Part (a) shows that the network has learned to recognise only one of two pattern types. Part (b) shows that the network has learned to recognise both types, but with mistakes: one spike is wrong, and two of patterns have not been recognised. To better keep track of the example, consult Figure 2

The experimental results represent the percentage of "good" output spikes among all spikes.

For each pattern type in a test the "good" output spikes were accounted for with respect to six different positions, and then the maximum of the six was taken. These positions were i-3, i-2, i-1, i, i+1, and i+2, where i is the end of the pattern (the one after the last). In Figure 5a, for instance, both spikes are at the position of -1 with respect to the actual pattern (consult Figure 2 to see that each pattern starts and ends with a double 0).

For a fixed pattern p and the position pos_i^p, the spike s has been accounted for if the spike s was pos_i^p-1, pos_i^p, or pos_i^p+1. Thus, for example, both spikes (Figure 5a) were in positions -2, -1, and 0.

In that manner, a triple of numbers $<r_1, r_2, r_{total}>$ was obtained from each test: the spike count for each of two patterns, and the total spike count. The two cases of Figure 5 yield the following triples: <0, 2, 2> and <2, 2, 5>.

The quality of a neural network in each test was measured in two ways: simple $q^{(s)}$ and advanced $q^{(a)}$.

The simple way means the proportion of "good" and all spikes:

$$q^{(s)} = \frac{r_1 + r_2}{r_{total}} \tag{17}$$

where r_1, r_2 – "good" spike count for patterns 1 and 2 respectively, r_{total} is the total spike count.

For the two cases of Figure 5, this is (0+2)÷2=100% and (2+2)÷5=80%. The quality of the first case is better, because both spikes are "good".

The advanced way means taking into account the situation, asking whether **both** pattern types have been recognised correctly:

$$q^{(a)} = \frac{4 r_1 r_2}{r_{total}^2} \tag{18}$$

For the two cases of Figure 5, this is $(4{\cdot}0{\cdot}2)\div 2^2=0\%$ and $(4{\cdot}2{\cdot}2)\div 5^2=64\%$. The quality of the first case is 0, because the network was able to recognize only one of two types of patterns.

6.2. Experimental Results and Analysis

Of the 32,620 tests, 21,117 (approximately ~70%) had "good" results, i.e., they were included in the result set R^{good}, which was further analysed. A bad result means that the network has not converged during the learning.

Table 3. Experimental results overview.

Parameter	% of "good"	q^s (%)	q^a (%)
Layer topology τ^{top} = {3, 5, 3, 1}	57	70.1	33.2
Layer topology τ^{top} = {3, 5, 1}	82	60.3	24.4

Table 3 describes summarised test results in accordance with the two quality measures – $q^{(s)}$ and $q^{(a)}$. The results are grouped by layer topology. The results are to demonstrate the applicability of the proposed learning.

- The results of the experiments show good quality on measure $q^{(s)}$. This means that the obtained networks are good at detecting at least one of the hidden patterns types.
- The results in terms of the measure $q^{(a)}$ are worse. This means that the obtained networks mostly learned only one of the two pattern types.
- Networks with two hidden layers were better than those with only one, however networks with two hidden layers had lower rate of "good" results.

The parameters for neural networks used in experiments, depicted in Table 1, are optimised ones. This means that only a part of experimental results has been published here, and the total amount of performed experiments is significantly bigger.

6.3. Conclusion

Spiking neural networks are designed to make use of the temporal dynamics of neurons. SNNs are believed to be very powerful, and their principles of operation are more complicated than those of "ordinary" neural networks.

The problem of learning in spiking neural networks is still a challenging issue. This paper presents an unsupervised learning method which exploits the co-operation of neurons making use of a mechanism of adaptive layer activation. This method is suitable to train neural networks to detect regularity in a stream of data.

Although the environment of the experiments was fairly simple, the first results are to be considered as very promising and inspirational for further research.

Acknowledgements

This research was supported by the ESF
(Contract No. 2004/0001/VPD1/ESF/PIAA/04/NP/3.2.3.1/0001/0001/0063).

References

[1] Fausett, L. (1993) Fundamentals of Neural Networks. Prentice-Hall, Inc., 469 p.

[2] Maass, W. (1997) Networks of spiking neurons: the third generation of neural network models. Transactions of the Society for Computer Simulation International, 14(4): 1659-1671

[3] Gerstner, W. (1999) Spiking Neurons. In Maass, W. & Bishop, C. M. (eds) Pulsed neural networks. MIT Press, 407 p.

[4] Maass, W. (1999) Computing with Spiking Neurons. In Maass, W. & Bishop, C. M. (eds) Pulsed neural networks. MIT Press, 407 p.

[5] Hebb, D. (1949) The organization of behavior. John Wiley and Sons, New York, 335 p.

[6] Gerstner, W. et al. (1999) Hebbian Learning of Pulse Timing in the Barn Owl Auditory System. In Maass, W. & Bishop, C. M. (eds) Pulsed neural networks. MIT Press, 407 p.

[7] Roberts, P. D. & Bell, C. C. (2002) Spike timing dependent synaptic plasticity in biological systems. Biological Cybernetics, 87, pp. 392-403.

[8] Haykin, S. (1999) Neural networks: a comprehensive foundation. 2nd ed. Prentice-Hall, Inc., 842 p.

Databases and Information Systems V
H.-M. Haav and A. Kalja (Eds.)
IOS Press, 2009

doi:10.3233/978-1-58603-939-4-143

Opportunities to Improve Software Testing Processes on the Basis of Multi-Agent Modeling

Guntis ARNICANS[1] and Vineta ARNICANE
University of Latvia

Abstract. Testing is a process which can be viewed as a complex system. There are techniques for reducing the level of complexity which come from ways of establishing multi-agent systems that have been discovered in the area of artificial intellect. The idea is that testing processes should at least in part be viewed as multi-agent systems. Different paradigms for organising testing processes become possible if many primitive agents are established and if operations and tasks are broken up into primitive units. This makes it possible to use available resources more effectively. The principles which are presented in this paper can gradually develop testing processes into more effective operations. We particularly focus on the organisational aspects of the testing process.

Keywords. testing, testing process, agent-based systems, complex systems

Introduction

Testing is a fundamental component in the design and maintenance of software. 30-60% of all resources are taken up by testing [1, 2]. These resources include time, money and people and depend on the specifics of the project.

Back in 2000, the European Systems and Software Initiative study found that most software in Europe is produced by organisations whose basic area of operations is not related to IT. The researchers established that software produced by such organisations represented 70% of all produced software [3]. Because of shortages of specialists small and medium companies use their own employees as testers of software. Many of these people had good knowledge about business, but poor knowledge about IT, including skills related to software testing [4]. It must be added that the prestige of the testing profession and the wages that are paid to testers continue to prevent any major inflow of good specialists into the profession.

We believe that the roots of many problems rest in the complex nature of testing processes. This paper offers an untraditional view of how testing processes can be organised. Our aim being to indicate ways in which the complexity of testing can be reduced. We look for solutions in the theory of complex systems or in areas in which such problems are researched.

We describe the complex system of testing as a multi-agent model. These models and the architectures which are based upon them are used to design software which in a

[1] Corresponding Author: Guntis Arnicans, University of Latvia, Raina blvd. 19, Riga, Latvia, LV-1089; E-mail guntis.arnicans@lu.lv.

simplified way copies or simulates real-world objects and their behaviour [5, 6]. Models from the real world choose only that issues which is of fundamental importance in complex systems, and they represent simplification of those systems. We propose pay more attention on those organizational principles which are of key importance for establishing multi-agent models to improve testing process management. The result is, to a certain extent, a simpler model which describes the testing process. This model may help in noticing many important things which we fail to notice in everyday situations because of the complexity of the relevant system.

Chapter 1 of the paper describes the complexity of testing processes. We show that the testing process is so complex that it can be seen as a complex system. This means that techniques which simplify complex systems can be used to improve the testing process and to manage it in a better way. Chapter 2 offers a brief review of the most important concepts and modeling techniques for multi-agent systems – those which the authors believe can help in improving the testing process. Chapter 3 reviews ways of reducing the complexity of the process with the help of modeling, also looking at the most important principles that can be used in assembling a multi-agent system. Chapter 4 discusses issues concerning the need to establish a model and the opportunities which emerge in that context. The possible benefits are also considered.

1. The Complexity of Testing Processes

There are several dimensions or aspects in testing processes which have an effect on one another [2, 7-12]:

1. What is to be tested? What are the size and the complexity of the software that is to be tested? What is its level of testability? At what level will the testing occur? What is the quality of the software when it is submitted for testing? How often are new software versions submitted for testing?
2. Why is the testing being conducted? What are its goals? How is the testing to be conducted? What equipment and methods will be used? What types of mistakes the specific method will reveal and what types it will not reveal?
3. What resources are available? How much time is there? What's the budget? What's the testing environment? How much work needs to be done? What are the specifics? What are the software tools – computer equipment, databases, communications?
4. What is the software development methodology? How long will software maintenance take? During that period, is there reason to believe that there will be substantial changes in the software?
5. Who will conduct the testing? How many people will be on the team? What do they know about the software that is to be tested? What are their skills and knowledge in the area of testing? What are their motivations?

All of these are issues which affect one another. The goals of testing, the skills of those who are involved, the software that is being tested and the complexity and quality of the process – all of these will determine the testing methods that are to be used. The amount of time that is afforded for the testing and the equipment that is used, in turn, will determine the extent to which these methods will be usable.

Each of these aspects in and of itself can substantially complicate the testing process. For instance, the larger and more complex the software that is to be tested, the more complicated it is to test it.

The complexity of testing is increased even more if there is a combination of these various aspects. In practice, for instance, it often happens that those who have commissioned extensive and complicated software must conduct acceptance testing in just a few days' time. That usually means that future system users, who are not professionals in the area of testing, are the ones who are expected to do the work. Only luck will help this situation, unless there is an active, creative and professional approach on the part of those who are organising or managing the testing process. There is little time, there is a lot of work, and the responsibilities are very serious. What to do to ensure that the work makes as much sense as possible?

We believe that as the complexity of each dimension of the testing process increases, the complexity of the entire testing process increases many times over. We consider the testing process is a complex evolving social system.

2. The Framework of the Multi-Agent Model

2.1. Describing the Real World with the Multi-Agent Model

Multi-agent models as such are based on real world principles. The agent is an analogue to a human being in that it handles tasks which are entrusted to it. Agents work together, react to changes in their surrounding environment, are born, die, educate themselves, try to achieve their own goals, and try to achieve the global goals of the entire system.

Our approach is based on the assumption that lengthy research results in an identification of the most important things and principles in the real world – something which makes it possible to develop a more primitive model. The transformation scheme is from "*real world*" to "*software that is based on the model*". Our hypothesis is that it is also possible to engage in successful transformation or conformity in the opposite direction – from "model" to "real world," because the model includes the most important principles of the real world. That which is not important or that might even be hindrances in the real world is cast off.

There are many different frameworks under which the architecture and principles of multi-agent systems can be determined. We could use any framework that includes basic concepts and principles. For our proposal, we are using a framework proposed by [13, 14], because it was established on the basis of human organisational principles. Let us now turn to the most important concepts that we are using in our model. We assume that the reader is familiar with multi-agent systems and the most important concepts therein.

2.2. The Agent

Here is one definition of an agent: "An agent is an encapsulated computer system that is situated in some environment and that is capable of flexible, autonomous action in that environment in order to meet its design objectives" [13]. Each agent is limited in its capacities – what it can do, understand and learn, and how effectively can it do that. It is also limited in terms of physical capacities (what are the available resources), time-related capacities (the lifespan of the agent, the deadlines involved in the work that is done), as well as institutional limitations (what is permissible in legal, political and ethical terms).

An agent has precisely defined boundaries (its body) and contiguity (the ability to communicate with other agents). Agents are in specific environments that can be identified with sensors and changed according to the agent's views and capacities. Agents do the work that is assigned to them, seeking to achieve their own goals and those of the whole system. Agents are autonomous and can determine their own situation and their own behaviour. Agents can analyse situations and deal with problems. They can react to changes in the surrounding environment or even create the necessary environmental changes that will allow other agents to handle the tasks that have been entrusted to them. Agents are divided up into classes in accordance with their purpose.

2.3. The Task

A task represents the work that needs to be done in order to achieve global goals, as well as the goals of individual agents. Higher-level tasks are usually so complicated that even a fine specialist has problems in handling them. Here a specialist can use the divide-and-conquer principle, also known as decomposition. The task is broken up into separate parts up to the point where the different parts are quite primitive, and it is clear that the work can be done. Different links can be established between tasks and subtasks, and that will create a graph or network of dependency. Tasks can also be grouped in accordance with desirable principles so that they are easier to administer.

2.4. The Operation

Operations help to do the work that is needed. The operations are handled by agents, and they are based on the objects that are available. An object can be data, information, knowledge, tools, storage devices such as databases, or material resources. Typical activities with objects include creating, changing, destroying and consuming them.

We recommend the selection of several typical classes of operations, using standardised templates in terms of how these classes are to be put to use. Depending on the behaviour of agents that are involved in the process, operations can be active (the agent initiates the operation, makes sure that there are all necessary entrance data and resources, changes the surrounding environment, and transfers the results to other agents), or passive (the agent waits for other agents to do as much as possible - deliver entrance objects, initiate the operations, and take over the resulting objects). Let us also note that operations can be described with a precise algorithm, or they can be ones in which the agent must come up with its own innovative solution in each specific situation.

2.5. Co-Ordination and Its Mechanisms

Co-ordination can be vertical, with a leader and a subordinate, or horizontal, in which all agents have equal rights. Co-ordination can be used to achieve the global goals of the entire system or to achieve the private goals of individual agents or groups of agents. These latter goals may be undesirable in the context of the system's overall goals.

Co-ordination activities are grouped into classes. For instance, in the class called Strategy there are activities aimed at planning the full operations of the system in pursuit of the goal; in Supervise we have activities which control subordinate agents; in

Co-operate we have activities aimed at ensuring that agents which are not subordinate to one another work together in operations that are advantageous to both of them or to the system as such.

Typical mechanisms of co-ordination include direct supervision (ensuring vertical co-operation, with the leader managing the operations of the subordinate), standardisation of work (co-operation is described with precise standards or instructions as to how co-operation and joint work are to be pursued), and mutual adjustment (formal or informal communication).

2.6. The Organisational Structure and Relationships Among Its Components

In real life, systems have an organisational structure which defines the groups of elements in the system and the "legal relationship" among these groups. In companies, this involves a classical organisational structure with various jobs for employees. The jobs can be grouped into classes or roles. In AI each agent has a specific job or performs a specific role.

Sometimes it is also useful to describe informal organisational structures with different relationships among the elements and objects. Examples of these relationships include producer/consumer (one agent produces objects, the other consumes them), common limited object (agents need the same object to conduct their operations), report (one agent reports to another), conflict (one agent must report to another that a conflict has emerged), command and instruct (transfer of commands and instructions from one agent to another), and delegation (one agent delegates its rights and responsibilities to another agent).

2.7. The Capabilities of the Agent

An agent requires necessary capabilities if it is to handle the tasks that are assigned to it. For our approach, we selected a model for the description of capabilities - 5C (Five Capabilities) model [13]. There are five groups of capabilities in this model – *communication*, *competence*, *self*, *planner* and *environment.* These are the most important considerations if the agents are to be a capable as possible in handling tasks in our system.

Communication ensures co-operation between one agent and others, as well as with the surrounding environment and the maintenance of the necessary knowledge. *Competence* (knowledge and methods) ensure that the job can be done in technical terms. *Self* supports the agent's "intimate life" – the agent maintains its goals, the work that needs to be done and the opportunities that are at hand, it supervises, maintains and improves itself, and it manages its operations. *Planner* refers to the ability of the agent to decide on operating strategies, the order in which tasks are to be handled, what techniques are to be used, etc. – in other words, the agent plans its own operations. Finally, the capabilities under the heading of *environment* enable the agent to gain information about the surrounding environment, other agents, and the processes which are occurring.

3. Establishing a Model for Testing Processes

In establishing models for multi-agent systems, ideas are sought in real life. The motto for this search is this: "How can human organisational principles be used for multi-agent architectures?" We already noted that we have chosen the opposite direction: "How can the architecture of a multi-agent system and the principles whereby that architecture is developed be used in order to organise testing processes in a better way?"

In many books about testing, there is nuanced review not only of testing techniques, but also of the way in which testing processes are organised. Sadly, good books and the knowledge contained therein are not put to sufficient use. One reason is that these are thick textbooks, and people just lack the time to study them carefully. The second problem is that the reader will get confused about many issues, because he will not be able to find the most important things in the book, as it is simply too long and complicated. This is particularly evident in those cases when testing is assigned to employees for whom it is "temporary" or "forced" work and who do not have fundamental knowledge about IT.

It has also been noticed that people are often ineffective when they face complicated situations. Some people do nothing, while others actively do something inappropriate. Few people manage to move toward the stated goal. If, by contrast, the situation is a simple one, and the person understands the order of things, then he feels more comfortable and acts more effectively and with grater purpose. It is also true that people will choose the tool and method that they are familiar with.

The multi-agent model simplifies many things by making use of known techniques in order to reduce the complexity of the system. Complexity of software can be reduced with decomposition, abstraction, organization [15].

Decomposition. A large issue is divided up into smaller sub-issues. This process of division continues until such time as the sub-issues are understandable and easier to solve. The level of complexity is reduced, because each phase in the solution is understandable, the solution is more trivial, and it is easier to ensure at the necessary level of quality.

Abstraction. Technique to distinguish which issues are the most important and to hide details that are not of importance at the relevant level. The level of complexity is reduced, because the focus can be on the most important aspects of the issue.

Organisation. The components can be grouped into more universal and homogeneous components, ones that are at a higher level. There is identification of the techniques that are to be used in organising co-operation among components so as to handle a complex task. It is also possible to reduce duplication of effort in the work that is done.

In order to simplify the testing process, we propose that first the essential be separated from the non-essential. This is a process which we handle gradually. Our first step is to establish an agent-based model. Such models describe only the most important things, because it is impossible to describe everything. The establishment of the model can be an informal process – a mental model in the brain of the organiser of the testing, if there is "laziness" or an "inability" to write it down on paper or model it on a computer. Such models, however, will be too complicated for non-specialists. Moreover, they are more meant for the design of intelligent software. The second step is to look at the agent-based models and to select a few items and principles which are sufficiently simple to be understood and ensure a greater level of freedom in terms of adapting them to real life. Our practical experience shows that when this approach is understood, there can be successful use of just a few principles and that even though the model itself is basically just a vision.

Let us now look at the most important principles that can be adapted from multi-agent systems, as well as at the techniques for establishing these. We will add identifiers to the essential principles, using a different letter for each one – A (Agent), T (Task), O (Operation), C (Co-ordination), S (Structure of organisation), and F (Functioning, which refers to the agent's capabilities.

A1: The agents which will do the work are as primitive as possible. An agent is a person with his or her set of capabilities, or it is software that is needed for a specific task. Examples of such agents include handlers of test cases, evaluators of the results of a test case, the designer of test cases in accordance with criterion C1, documenters of mistakes that are identified, and the receiver of a list of all software screen forms.

A2: Agents are grouped into typical classes or groups, and relations among them or within them are defined. The subordination of agents is specified (leader/subordinate), the upper level specialisation of the agent is defined (operator, manager, planner, resource manager), the lower level specialisation is also defined (evaluator of test results, preparer of reports about errors, designer of test cases), and the participants which will handle specific tasks (regressive testing, testing of scenarios, testing of performance) are identified.

A3: Agents which exist in a single individual or computer are merged into an agency. According to the A1 principle, a person or computer can contain many primitive agents. Accordingly, the activities of the agents are limited – one agent acts under the framework of the assigned time slot. The parallel activities of several agents, however, can be simulated within the framework of a single agency.

A4: The agencies that are available to us and the agents residing therein must regularly be identified. This means that we are aware of the resources that are available to us, and we can plan specific activities – we choose the operations that can be handled with the available resources, we seek opportunities to gain a new agency with a necessary agent, or we establish a new agent in the existing agency.

A5: We determine the ability of each agency to create new agents. We must be familiar with the ability of each employee to gain new skills (i.e., create a new agent in himself). We must also be familiar with the computer and its software in terms of opportunities to use or configure these or to create opportunities for automatic adaptation of the software).

A6: Planning the effective use of the agency. Each agency has its operating costs. We use employees with a low level of qualifications to handle primitive and standardised tasks. The computer is what handles operations that are frequently repeated and can be computerised – this makes the testing automatic. Highly qualified employees must be used for non-standard and innovative operations, and they should not be assigned tasks that can actually be handled by employees who are lower on the ladder of qualifications.

T1: We divide up the tasks to get primitive sub-tasks. There must be harmony here with the A1 principle. The more primitive the tasks and the agents that handle them, the less complex the system will be. We assume that the system's "complexity of understanding" declines more rapidly than the "complexity of the quantity of components" increases, because we can make use of resources that are offered by abstraction and grouping. Here we have great opportunities for optimal operations, because major tasks can be handled by more than one.

T2: Specification of critical tasks. In evaluating risks and the interests of various stakeholders (the client, the agent doing the work, the user), we can prioritise the tasks that are necessary. We start this evaluation by the highest-level tasks. Evaluation of sub-tasks is conducted only for the critical upper tasks. This helps us to define our testing strategy, to decide whether new tasks must be created, and to come up with conditions for the establishment of a plan to perform the tasks.

T3: Defining those groups of tasks which will require a lot of time to perform. Here we determine which tasks are interdependent on the basis of various criteria that will affect the total amount of time that is needed (the tasks have to be handled in sequence, they consume one and the same resource, etc.).

T4: Determining those tasks which only a limited number of agents can handle. Usually there will be tasks which require someone with a high level of qualifications to handle them, and that means that there is a deficit of appropriate agents and agencies. Such agencies must be reserved for these critical functions, keeping them from doing other, simpler work.

O1: We divide up the operation into primitive sub-operations. As was the case with principle T1, we reduce the complexity of the overall job and make it more possible to manoeuvre with the selection of agencies for each sub-operation. It is also easier to monitor the performance of the work.

O2: We define the most important classes of operations and specify their operational algorithm. Typical solutions are identified for those operations that are more important and must be handled more open. Templates help us to describe the way in which the operation is to be conducted. Those operations that can be performed on the computer can later be programmes, and the relevant software agents can be created.

O3: Protection against deadlock. Because most agencies will be human beings who have a great deal of freedom in taking decisions, we must make sure that there are controls to ensure that the work is done. In practice, an agency can make some of his agents passive or fail to give them the time that is necessary to do the work. The result is that work on an operation can come to a halt, and that will have an effect on the behaviour of other agencies. When the agent is actually software, the work is easier to adjust and forecast.

C1: We specify the best possible co-ordination mechanism for each task. Depending on our strategy for ensuring the testing process and the agencies that are available, we define the best co-ordination mechanisms among agents and among agencies. The testing process is very flexible and dynamic. It depends on the project phase and the testing methods that are used. This means that many different versions of co-operation will be used simultaneously in the system.

C2: Promoting co-operation among agents and agencies. We set up opportunities for co-operation, show why they should be used, ensure an environment for the pursuit of global goals, and then let agencies themselves decide on co-operation as such. The goal could be to set up a self-organising system, because such a system is far more effective and viable under critical circumstances. Let's be careful, however, to make sure that the agencies do not get too carried away with private goals and ignore the system's goals.

C3: Use of existing co-operation mechanisms. The cornerstone for the testing process, at the end of the day, will involve living people, and the organisation will have specific co-operation models for specific individuals. There is no ideal co-ordination mechanism among people, because each person prefers his own desired mechanism or a combination of mechanisms. This will depend on the individual's personal characteristics, the level of the individual's maturity, and the goals which the individual sets. People don't like to accept rapid changes in their lives, and that's why we need to try to use the existing co-operation model, gradually transforming it in the desired direction.

S1: We select the best organisational structure for each class of tasks. We have an official organisational structure for our agencies, and that must be taken into account. At the same time, however, there are also informal relations among agencies. We can choose and govern both formal and informal structures. This must be in line with principle C1.

S2: We use existing organisational structures. The analogue is with principle C3.

F1: We determine the most important abilities of agents and agencies. We must know the resources that are available to us before we can plan our testing strategy and activities.

F2: We determine the most important abilities of agencies that are needed for the most critical tasks. This has to be harmonised with the results that we get when applying principles T1, T2 and T3. We can define the missing functions, which will be the difference between those functions found with principle F1 and those found with principle F2.

F3: Seeking out alternative functions. We look for ways of replacing those functions that are missing with others, perhaps looking for entirely different solutions to the problem. Testing is a process in which different methods can be used to achieve the same goal, and that also means different functions. This represents dynamic adaptation to the circumstances which prevail.

F4: Developing new functions. We look at ways of ensuring those functions which are missing and ensure that they are gradually developed. This means creating new agents by training employees, obtaining new software, or configuring existing software.

The strategy for the simplified use of the listed principles was first described in [16]. The introduction of these principles is a gradual process, making it possible to evolve toward a better operating model.

4. Development and Maintenance of the Model

The models that are described here do not tell us anything fundamentally new. The same can be found in many sources of information about testing, and it can be formulated in different ways. In practice, however, there are problems with organising effective testing processes. Our observation is that testing is often organised on the basis of a simple and understandable principle – each functional component of software is handed over to a tester, and the tester's job is to test that component. The rest depends on how capable the tester is in doing the work.

This easily understood approach, of course, has the key problem of poorly qualified testers, whose activities are usually limited to the use of simple and typical test cases. The skills of such testers are so poor and so fragmentary that planned and serious testing is simply not possible.

In practice, the key issue is whether the testing team has at least one good tester, as well as whether that tester can organise the resources that are available in pursuit of the goal that is at hand. Good specialists can plan optimal testing strategies on the basis of their own capabilities. Sadly, there is a lack of human resources for this purpose. An unqualified tester cannot be expected to handle a high-level task which he does not understand.

A solution here is to break large tasks up into primitive sub-tasks, and then to plan the handling of those tasks with the assistance of the entirely testing team. This represents fundamentally new thinking, because the delegation of tasks no longer involves large functional blocs. Instead there are small and clearly defined tasks – ones which the employee is capable of handling. The multi-agent approach makes it easier to move toward this paradigm in the organisation of testing processes.

Does a multi-agent system model need to be established in a formal sense? Sadly, the current level of development suggests that the answer is probably "no." Testing teams don't have the capacity for this – there's a lack of qualified specialists, and there is a lack of free time, too. In small projects, it is easier to maintain an informal model which is understood by a few senior employees, but is not written down on paper or modeled on a computer. In large projects, by comparison, attempts to establish and maintain a model without specialised tools will demand too much in the way of resources.

At the same time, it has to be said that it is possible to establish a formal or semi-formal model. Testing includes work done by people, but also automated computer processes. Some activities may involve pre-existing standards and procedures as to how the operations can be handled. The use of testing tools can also be described quite easily.

The multi-agent system approach has the advantage that unified principles can be used to describe the co-operation or symbiosis of people and computers in pursuit of the common goal. This makes it easier to replace computerised operations with human activity, as well as to formalise operations by describing them with algorithms which make it possible to create software-based agents.

These principles can define many sub-tasks which represent a duplication of offer. Large functional blocs, for instance, use one and the same sub-functionality, and each tester seeks to test it. Once is enough in this regard. When a test case is run for one purpose, it can also be used to test another area, but there is no common database of test cases among the testers, and there is no co-operation in the preparation or the handling of the test cases.

This also makes more evident those things that have to be taught to employees. When a large task is divided up into small and understandable sub-tasks and a simple technique for handling them is presented, it becomes far easier to discover the areas in which an employee has weak skills. That makes it clear what the employee must learn before he can be entrusted with a major task all on his own.

Our recommendation is that before delegating a task to an employee, the testing process planner and manager must establish a sub-model for handling the task, at least in their minds. In [16] is offered an example which is focused on the seemingly trivial task of "checking whether all windows in the informational system can be opened and closed". The fact is that even such a simple task can cause many problems, misunderstandings, poor performance, and inadequate reaction to results. The imagined sub-model can be written down to a certain extent on paper and submitted to the employee as a specification of what needs to be done. Even such minor improvements can substantially enhance the quality of the testing process. If the job specifications are gathered together, that makes it possible to assemble a set of fragments from the large model, and that is a good base for the development of knowledge.

5. Conclusions

Our aim in this paper was not to review a specific model for organising a testing process, and we have not done so. Techniques for establishing models can be found in the literature which describes the establishment of multi-agent systems. The thing that must be remembered, however, is that the literature mostly deals with computerised systems, while testing mostly depends on people. It's not worth rewriting the many things which multi-agent systems have adapted from the real world and which can be adapted successfully during testing processes, because those who are interested in these can find them themselves and put them to use as needed.

In this paper we have mentioned only those concepts and principles of multi-agent systems which are important for us and are based on our own experience. Other authors may have different priorities and different sets of principles. Also, we have only mentioned those principles which help to improve the management of testing processes, because we see that this makes it possible to improve testing to a substantial degree and with less effort. We are not talking about principles that can be used to ensure adequacy in testing – a minimal set of test cases that can be handled with minimal effort, one which offers precise evaluation of results and the conclusion that preventing the consequences of any potential mistakes which have not been discovered might be cheaper than the consumption of additional resources that are needed for testing.

Although we have argued in this paper that it is not really realistic to establish formal models at this time, the fact is that it is worth considering the possibility of establishing special tools and methodologies to make it easier to observe the principles of multi-agent systems in testing processes.

In conclusion, we wish to stress once again that the use of the ideas which are presented here will largely depend on the presence in a testing team of at least one specialist who truly understands multi-agent systems and has good knowledge in the area of software testing. We have seen nothing to indicate that without this, it is possible to improve testing processes in any substantial way. The key figure here is the specialist who can imagine the testing process as a set of many primitive agents which handle small tasks and all move toward the common goal, and who can establish and constantly update the specific model for the project, at least in an informal and mental manner.

Acknowledgements. This research is partly supported by European Social Fund under grant "Doctoral student research and post doctoral research support for University of Latvia".

References

[1] Paradiso, M. (2001) Software Verification & Validation Introduced. In Haug, M., Olsen, E. W., & Consolini, L. (eds) Software Quality Approaches: Testing, Verification, and Validation. Springer-Verlag, pp. 36-45.

[2] Perry, W. E. (2000) Effective Methods for Software Testing. John Wiley & Sons, 2nd ed., 832 p.

[3] Haug, M. (2001) Software Process Improvement: A European View. In Haug, M., Olsen, E. W., & Consolini, L. (eds) Software Quality Approaches: Testing, Verification, and Validation. Springer-Verlag, pp. 3-14.

[4] Arnicane, V. (2007) Use of Non-IT Testers in Software Development. In Münch, J., & Abrahamsson P. (eds) 8th International Conference on Product Focused Software Process Improvement (PROFES 2007), July 2-4, Riga, Latvia, Berlin: Springer, (LNCS), pp. 175–187.
[5] Russell, S. J., & Norvig, P. (2003) Artificial Intelligence: a Modern Approach. Pearson Education, 2nd ed., 1132 p.
[6] Boccara, N. (2004) Modeling Complex Systems. Springer-Verlag, 397 p.
[7] Craig, R. D., & Jaskiel, S. P. (2002) Systematic Software Testing. Artech House Publishers, 536 p.
[8] Lewis, W. E. (2005) Software Testing and Continuous Quality Improvement. Auerbach Publications, 2nd ed., 560 p.
[9] Veenendaal, E. (2002) The Testing Practitioner. UTN Publishers, 524 p.
[10] Black, R. (2004) Critical Testing Processes. Addison-Wesley, 608 p.
[11] Watkins, J. (2001) Testing IT: An Off-the-Shelf Software Testing Process. Cambridge University Press, 315 p.
[12] Black, R. (2002) Managing the testing process: Practical Tools and Techniques for Managing Hardware and Software Testing. Wiley Publishing, 2nd ed., 528 p.
[13] Aart, C. (2005) Organizational Principles for Multi-Agent Architectures. Birkhauser Verlag, 204 p.
[14] Jennings N. R. (2000) On agent-based software engineering, Artifical Intelligence, 117: 277-296
[15] Booch, G. (2007) Object-Oriented Analysis and Design with Applications. Addison-Wesley, 3rd ed., 720 p.
[16] Arnicane, V., & Arnicans, G. (2008) Using the Principles of an Agent-Based Modeling for the Evolution of IS Testing Involving Non-IT Testers. In Haav, H. M., & Kalja A. (eds), Proceedings of 8th International Baltic Conference on Databases and Information Systems (Baltic DB&IS 2008), June 2-5, Tallinn, Estonia, Tallinn University of Technology Press, pp. 129-140.

Databases and Information Systems V
H.-M. Haav and A. Kalja (Eds.)
IOS Press, 2009

doi:10.3233/978-1-58603-939-4-155

Approach and Technical Solutions for e-University Initiative

Inga MEDVEDIS, Laila NIEDRITE[1], Aivars NIEDRITIS, Maris TREIMANIS and Arnis VOITKANS
University of Latvia

Abstract. Nowadays to be competitive universities as well as other organizations are forced to improve effectiveness and efficiency of their services. Implementation of different e-initiatives is a typical solution to take advantage of ICT to reduce operating costs of the institution, to increase responsiveness to customers, etc. This paper describes conceptual approach and technical solutions to an e-University initiative. The proposed approach allows setting up measurable business goals, to measure business processes in context of defined goals and to search for business process improvement. In this paper also two levels of measurement of systems that support business processes are considered.

Keywords. e-university, business processes, information systems, e-learning, data warehouse, information and communication technology, measurement

Introduction

Nowadays in time of "the business revolution in the computer industry caused by the move to the internet as platform" [1], every university to be competitive has to reconsider its relationships and services and adopt information technologies to be able to offer its services through internet.

The e-University initiative at the University of Latvia, as one of the strategic priorities of the University, was defined by decision of Senate in November, 2001, and launched in April, 2002 [2]. The University of Latvia with 24 thousand students (19% of higher education market of Latvia) and two thousand faculty members and service staff is the largest university in Latvia. The development goal of the e-University initiative was to take advantage of ICT to improve, diversify and extend university's services, to be more effective and efficient, to be more attractive and competitive in a local and global market.

E-university initiatives in some extent were carried out in many (rather all) universities [3], [4]. These initiatives typically dealt with development of management information system [5 -7], portal [8], [9], ICT technical infrastructure, e-learning [10-12], but often neglected business processes: definition, setting of business goals, measurement and continual improvement (in contrary of [13], [14]). Nevertheless the needs for business process reengineering [15-17], as well as approaches to process measurement are well-known in for-profit organizations.

[1] Corresponding Author: Laila Niedrite, University of Latvia, Raina bulv. 19, LV-1586, Riga, Latvia; E-mail: Laila.Niedrite@lu.lv

We will present in this paper the measurement of information systems (IS) that are used to support the business processes. A lot of research is done to find out the most appropriate way to measure the effectiveness of information systems. The IS effectiveness could be evaluated according the product, process, and service aspect of the information system [18]. Each of these aspects could be assessed using different measures. The focus of our research is the product aspect of the information system that could be characterized among other measures also by the response time of the system and by the system usage. Many studies investigate different individual measures, for example, the usage of a system is explored in following papers [19], [20]. Not so many models are described that represent all IS effectiveness measures and their relationships. DeLone and McLean offered their later widely cited "IS success model" [21], where the term "IS success" was used instead of effectiveness. Some researchers [22] disagree with DeLone and McLean about the system use that was included as one of the six different dimensions in the model as a measure for the IS effectiveness. Despite these objections system use was repeatedly included into revised "IS success" (effectiveness) model [23]. The authors argue that the simplistic definition of the system use raises these misunderstandings. They say that "researchers must also consider the extent, nature, quality, and appropriateness of the system use".

The focus of this paper (also partly published in [2], [24-29] is on conceptual approach and technical solutions to the e-University initiative at the University of Latvia. In section 1 the approach and solutions for setting up business goals, for measuring business processes in context of defined goals and for searching a ways for business process improvement, are outlined. In section 2 the solutions are described in context of three largest subsystems: management information system, e-learning systems and data warehouse, as well as two levels of possible measurement of systems are considered. In section 3 the conclusions are given.

1. Conceptual Approach

When e-University initiative was started, the following conceptual cornerstones were accepted and approved by the key stakeholders:

1. The e-University concept. e-University is a translation of key relationships and services, as well as academic, outreach and business processes, through the use of Internet technologies [3].
2. The e-University framework. e-University framework consists of people, e-business, business processes and ICT infrastructure [4].

Relationships, services and processes mentioned in the concept of e-University occur in two key domains of activity: in studies and in science. Management of studies and science is one more domain which is especially important from the perspective of e-University initiative, but actually it is just a natural part of two other domains.

When the relationships, services and processes in these three domains are translated through the use of Internet technologies, we get three main domains of e-business activities:

1. e-Learning (including things like blended learning and social software)
2. e-Science (computationally intensive science as well as modest usage of ICT for information exchange and organization of research)
3. e-Management (usage of ICT in management)

In this article we shall discuss in detail e-Management and organizational and technical aspects of e-Learning. e-Science will not be discussed.

From the four components of the e-University framework, mentioned above, the people are clearly the most important. Nevertheless, we shall not discuss it in this article. E-business, business processes and software part of ICT infrastructure shall be discussed.

In e-University initiative we see usage of ICT as a tool for providing more effective and efficient services for people involved in educational, research and management processes. For example, we see student as a person who in order to study is willing to use services of e-learning. Furthermore, services are provided not just by a person or information system – services are provided by business processes [16], bringing together staff, students, information systems, manual procedures and regulations (Figure 1). Business process based approach not only allows achieving better results putting together all needed components. It also gives a basis for allocation of limited information system development resources to crucial tasks, which otherwise would be difficult, as University of Latvia is not fully business-driven enterprise.

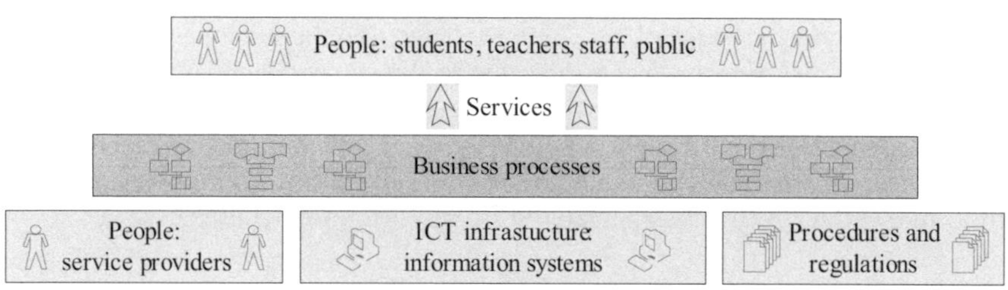

Figure 1. Business process oriented approach

2. Solutions

2.1. Business Process Reengineering

We have come to a necessity of business process reengineering (BPR), looking at the problem from viewpoint of information system development. Our situation is not easy – we have nine major information systems for different purposes, with different interfaces and heavily depending on each others data (Figure 2).

In the past development and implementation of information systems was often frustrating. Implementation was difficult, changes of requests – frequent, and resources spent for maintenance – often much larger than for development. There was also an evident lack of motivation in the use of information systems among the administrative staff.

As far as possible, a full cycle of BPR is applied to business processes:

1. Description, analysis and improvement of existing processes,
2. Implementation of improved processes,
3. Regular maintenance of improved processes – mostly based on collected effectiveness and efficiency indicators and feedback from students and staff.

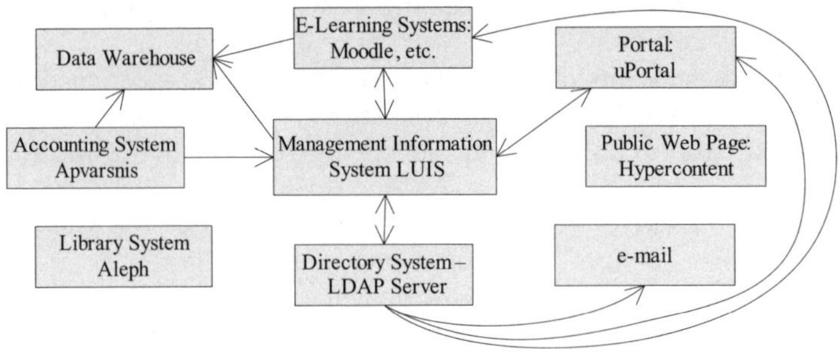

Figure 2. Major information systems and data flow

There are 250 business processes at the University of Latvia, but only small part of them has currently been improved. Business modelling tool GRADE [30], [31] is used for analysis, description and maintenance of business processes.

Before continue with detailed description of specific information systems, clarification of terms is needed. Up to here we have used the term "service" to describe an output of business process that is of value to the students and stuff. Further, when talking about specific information systems, we shall use term "services" to describe packages of functionality, provided by information systems, to implement business processes. Such terminology and methodology conforms to Service-Oriented Architecture (SOA) [32], but technically SOA interfaces are not used.

2.2. Management Information System LUIS

The main purpose of the Management Information System at the University of Latvia (LUIS) [33] is to support the administration of the study process [25]. The system consists of following subsystems: employee registration and orders, salary subsystem, student admission, student enrolment to a semester, study fees administration, course catalogue, study courses offer, student enrolment to study courses, preparation of diploma supplements and many others.

All the services provided via the business processes to the users can be divided into three groups (Figure 3): 1) core services, which support the main business functions implemented in the previously mentioned subsystems of LUIS, 2) functions for the self service needs and 3) public services.

The most important users who maintain the key information are employees. They work mostly with the core services. Every user has a limited access to the system according to the given Oracle database privileges and to their responsibilities.

Another important part of the LUIS functions is an access to the personal information for all students and staff. This is the part of LUIS provided for the self service [29]. All students and employees use accounts saved in LDAP (Lightweight Directory Access Protocol) for this purpose. LDAP account maintenance is also one of the LUIS functions.

The same LDAP account is used for access to many other systems: SSH, Network access, Moodle and Portal, where the access to all these systems is implemented from one access point.

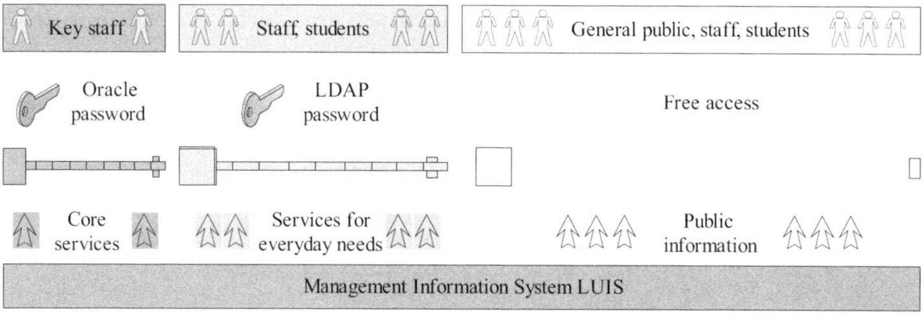

Figure 3. Three groups of services of the LUIS

The creation of LDAP accounts for all students starts when prospective students apply to the studies. They get accounts when they are registered into student admission subsystem. Usually accounts are created in LDAP once per day by executing scripts prepared by LUIS. Now we have more than 50.000 active LDAP accounts in the system. There are more than 1000 defined database users. The average number of different users that work in LUIS every day is near 500.

The third group of the LUIS services are public functions which are available to everybody without any access control. These functions are mostly informative; they publish the information about study programs, available courses and different statistics, for example, the statistics about student admission.

The LUIS is integrated with the other systems and the overall schema of all system interfaces is given in Figure 2. An example how the interface between LUIS and another systems works, in this case the e-learning system Moodle, is described later in the paper.

The LUIS system is also used by other universities in Latvia and seven of them use the same possibility for the student personal information access.

The system is developed using Oracle environment. The user interface is web-based. The Oracle database server and the Oracle HTTP Server are running on HP Server.

2.3. E-Learning Systems

E-learning systems of any university can consist of many different components and nowadays it is a field which is developing very rapidly. Constantly new technologies, new practices and new Internet services that could be used to support every aspect of e-learning at universities are emerging.

A diagram of e-learning support systems at the University of Latvia is shown in Figure 4. and it represents following components:

1. Moodle – Learning Management System (LMS) of the University of Latvia;
2. Blog system WordPress, implemented and integrated with Portal;
3. University Portal – users can login into Portal and access different services of the University, for example LMS and Blog. No further authentication is necessary since single sign-on mechanism is implemented;

4. Video Streaming consists of two parts – live streaming and on-demand streaming services. On-demand streaming service, which is the most important for e-learning needs, currently almost implemented.
5. Wiki system can be used to support knowledge aggregation for different educational projects of the University of Latvia. Currently Moodle Wiki functionality is used;
6. Social Networking Service, e-Portfolio.
7. Open Moodle is other version of LMS for purposes of different scientific and collaboration projects. Not so strictly integrated with the other University information systems and therefore more open to non-standard use.

The last three components are currently under discussion and are not implemented.

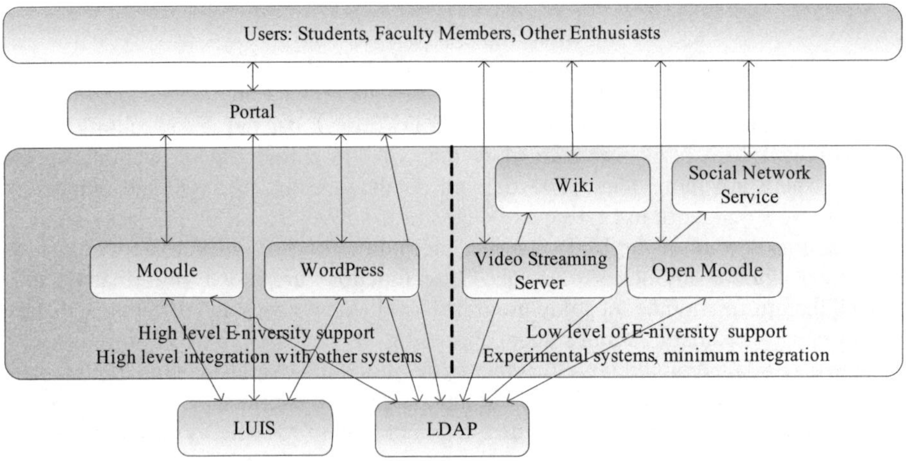

Figure 4. E-learning systems

In different periods of time two different e-learning systems were used at the University of Latvia – WebCT CE 4 from year 2002 to 2008 and Moodle [34], [35] since year 2007.

Currently Moodle 1.9 is used and is implemented using Apache web server with PHP 5 support and MySQL database. Two-server configuration is used to separate the MySQL database and the web server, both servers are running Linux.

Moodle is integrated with the other main information systems: LDAP, Portal, the Management Information System LUIS and Data Warehouse.

Users can access their e-courses in two ways – weather through portal or directly. In both ways authentication is done according to LDAP, but if users are connecting through Portal no additional authentication is required since Single Sign-On mechanism is implemented.

During user login to the Moodle automatic synchronization tasks are performed. Moodle connects directly to the Information System, synchronizes user's data (name, surname, e-mail) and checks if there are changes in the user's enrolments. These synchronization tasks are performed in real time. If the students in LUIS register or are registered to new courses, the Moodle automatically enrols students to corresponding e-courses.

Teacher enrolments in Moodle are also automatically synchronized with LUIS. If teacher is assigned to some course in the Information System, he/she automatically gets assigned to the corresponding Moodle e-course with a corresponding role.

Although it is possible by universities to use many free internet services to support e-learning (for example, social networking websites Facebook or MySpace, YouToube and Google Video for video streaming), it is a decision of the University of Latvia to implement core e-learning services like Learning Management System, blogs, video streaming locally (in IT infrastructure of the University). Implementation of these services locally has some advantages. Firstly, it is possible to offer the best bandwidth for computer classrooms in the University and country. Secondly, services implemented by University are advertisement-free and lastly the University remains in control of its services and generated content.

2.4. Process Measurement Solutions

2.4.1. Two Level Measurement of Processes

Before to start measurement activities it is necessary to decide what and how should be measured. We consider two levels of possible measurement. The first, high level measurement considers the whole systems as measurement objects, as it appears in the e-university framework. The second measurement level is the detailed measurement of the business processes. In this level the functions of a particular system that support the chosen business process are investigated and measured. The detailed measurement of particular business processes could be done using the Process measurement and monitoring system, implementation of which is described later in this section. The results and analysis of this level measurement are provided in the case studies of our approach [36].

The effectiveness and the efficiency of the Information Systems are often measured to evaluate the importance and usefulness of the investments and management activities. Therefore we suggest to evaluate the IS effectiveness in the high level measurement. The "IS success model" [21], [23] that describes different aspects of effectiveness represents 6 interrelated dimensions – system quality, information quality, service quality, system use, user satisfaction, and net benefits. Nevertheless the authors [21], [23] emphasize also that "the choice of success variables is often a function of the objective of the study, the organizational context". They also suggest to "reduce significantly the number of different measures used to measure IS success". So the choice of appropriate measures and the number of them should be justified before the measurement activities are performed.

2.4.2. The System Level Measurement of E-University Systems

When new initiatives in the e-university e.g. e-science are undertaken or the existing systems are improved or expanded it is reasonable to understand the situation with the existing information systems (IS). In this case the system level measurement is appropriate. For example, let us evaluate IS effectiveness by the means of system usage dimension. According to the schema in the Figure 2, different systems are used at the university for different purposes, but they use the same infrastructure, they are connected with many interfaces and therefore influence each other. They also have the same set of potential users.

We should measure the use of the systems so that the results are comparable to each other.

Let's see the systems that should be evaluated in more detail. The properties that influence the use of the systems and should be described for each system are as follows:

- Is the use of the system optional or mandatory
- The way of access control
- The existence of user access mechanisms that restrict the use

The management IS (LUIS) was described previously in this paper, so we can conclude that three ways are used for the access to the system – for the self service functions, for the core functions and also a public part of the LUIS exists.

The system should be used mandatory in the part of the core functions, but the functions in the self-service part of the system allow sometimes parallel way of reaching the desired goal, e.g. the students instead of usage of self service functions go to the study advisor and ask them for the assistance and the same task can be done using core functions by the study advisors. Many functions are informative in the self-service part of the system e.g. about personal information so they can be used optionally. So we can say that the use of the system in the self-service part of the system is not strictly mandatory. The public part of LUIS is optional.

There exist in the part of core functions the access control mechanisms that controls the number of functions that are allowed for each user in individual user level. In the self-service part of LUIS two user categories exist that have each own set of functions – students and employees. The restrictions in this case exist only for the allowed information for each individual user. The public part offers its functions all without any access control.

The portal has two parts – one part uses access control and the other part is public. All portal functions are optional for the authorized portal users.

The e-learning system Moodle uses also access control. If the e-course have only supplemental nature and the student will not gain the maximum possible result then the optional use is possible.

So the use of each system can be compared, because the parts or the whole systems allow some degree of free choice to use the system or not. We can measure also the part of LUIS with core functions to make decisions e.g. about further development of the system, but the results are hardly comparable with other systems because of mandatory nature of the use. The use of public parts of the systems could also be analyzed separately and compared to each other.

The focus of further described studies in this paper is on the authorized parts of the systems without the core functions of LUIS, which use different access control mechanisms with more restrictions.

The measures that could be measured are as follows:

- The number of users
- The number of potential users
- The number of sessions

The way we have collected the data for the system level measurement was simple, because all these systems have log files ore tables that collect the data about usage of each system. We need only carefully to analyze the meaning of each entry into the log file and to understand the format of the log files.

The management IS LUIS save the usage information into the database table, the chosen granularity is summary for a day because of the amount of data collected. So per year we have 50 million records collected according this granularity. The E-mail usage is recorded into the Unix log file. The Moodle usage is recorded into the Apache Web Server log file.

All these log file or table were analyzed and as a result we found out that we can collect following data in the granularity of a particular day from all systems: <user_name><activity><IP address><date><the number of performed activities>. The <user_name> means a particular authorized system user, but the <activity> is the system's function, which in the system level measurement corresponds to the login activity.

We performed the high level measurement of systems during the spring semester 2008 and the results for core systems are given in the Table 1. The measurement result that is not included into this table, because it does not change over period, is the number of potential user for each system. There are 20478 potential users for LUIS and portal that means the number of all enrolled students to the semester. There are 6861 potential users for Moodle that means the number of enrolled students to the study courses with corresponding e-courses. The first measure for each system is the number of users (the number of unique logins per month), the second measure is the percent of active users according to the all potential users, the third measure is the number of sessions per month, and the last measure is the average number of sessions per one active user.

Table 1. The system level measurement results.

	Moodle				Portal				LUIS			
Mar	4158	61%	37225	9,0	6227	30%	52329	8,4	12909	63%	77403	6,0
Apr	4090	60%	35102	8,6	5895	29%	56271	9,5	12083	59%	84300	7,0
May	5256	77%	39488	7,5	6195	30%	57845	9,3	14628	71%	121495	8,3
Jun	3150	46%	26384	8,4	5702	28%	58896	10,3	14976	73%	202448	13,5

The results of the system level measurement can be used to find out whether the strategic guidelines of the management are implemented. For example, if the portal is planned as the entry point to all systems, the measurements have to reflect this issue. If we see the results in Table 1 LUIS has users twice as much than portal. Therefore we can conclude that alternative ways are used to access the system instead of using portal. Another subject to an analysis can be the target audience of the systems. We can evaluate how many of possible users are involved and if we have possible problems with some systems. Our results showed the similar results according the involved users for two systems. They are between 60% and 70% for two systems, but half as much for the third system. The reasons of problems are then subjects of further studies and probably more detailed measurement should be performed.

2.4.3. The Implementation of Process Measurement System

The Process measurement and monitoring system (PMMS) was created as an integrated part of the Management Information System LUIS. The data warehouse is used as one of the important elements of this solution. Other important components of the PMMS are: 1) process operational monitoring component, 2) process measurement system, and 3) process execution log file. The whole process measurement and monitoring scheme is illustrated in (Figure 5).

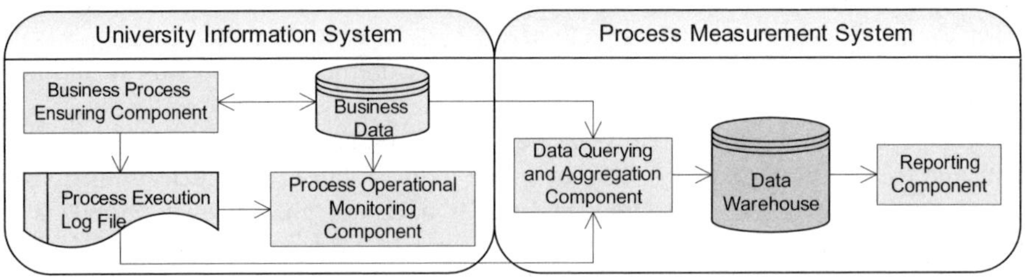

Figure 5 . Process measurement and monitoring

The Process Operational Monitoring Component creates separate reports from the log file data and from the business data from the information system. The Process Operational Monitoring Component is developed as a part of Management Information System LUIS using the same technologies.

The Process Operational Monitoring Component supports analysis of indicators about the process workflow directly from the log file during the process execution. Then Indicators are loaded into the data warehouse and used for the process measurement.

The Process Measurement System is based on the data warehouse models, which were designed according to three new methods – user-driven [25], data-driven [26] and goal-driven [27]. The measurement that can be performed by a usage of the data warehouse data can be the measurement of process execution itself or the measurement of the results of the process execution.

Process Measurement System has also an ETL (Extract, Transform, Load) part – the Data querying and aggregation component. This component integrates the log file data and the business data from operational data sources, for example the LUIS. Data is extracted from operational systems (Figure 2), transferred to the staging area and transformed according to data quality needs and data marts model requirements. Data is stored in the Oracle database server. Oracle Workflow is used for the automation of ETL processes.

Process execution log file is the last but not the least component of the PMMS. After development of the data warehouse model and its mapping with the data sources it was discovered that some data about processes is not available. In order to accumulate the data about processes that must be measured, records in a log file were created for each workflow execution.

The Reporting component is used to show results from different data marts. This component is implemented by means of Oracle Discoverer.

3. Conclusions

The integrated approach, described in the paper, has been used at the University of Latvia for 5 years and has shown a reasonable sustainability. We believe it can be used in other universities as well, as it allows definition of SMART business goals and measure progress towards accomplishment of these goals. The technical solutions are also important, but they can be changed and replaced as long as integrated approach is kept. But, above all, the key for success are people.

University is not an easiest place for business process reengineering. With its strong traditions, with academic freedom, often applied to the management issues as well, with relatively weak impact of market forces, business processes in the University of Latvia were (and probably still are) more vague than in most business entities. But, although the business process reengineering path is not easy, it is very unlikely it can be escaped.

The future activities of the e-University initiative will be also based on this integrated approach. The goal is to improve and integrate into information systems as many of core business processes as possible. It is also planned to improve the technical solutions, first of all, by developing the portal as a unified front-end for all information systems of the University of Latvia.

Acknowledgments

This research is partly supported by European Social Fund.

References

[1] O'Reily, T. (2006) Web 2.0 Compact Definition: Trying Again. O'Reily Radar, (available on http://radar.oreilly.com/2006/12/web-20-compact-definition-tryi.html)

[2] Treimanis, M., & Stonis, J. (2005) Unified Approach to Implementation of E-university Initiative. In Proceedings of 11th International Conference on Technology Supported Learning and Training, Berlin, Germany, November 29 - December 2, pp. 186 – 188.

[3] Edgar, T., & McQuesten, P. (2000) Report of the e-University Task Force, (available at http://www.utexas.edu/faculty/council/1999-2000/minutes/min032000.html)

[4] It's About People: The UBC e-Strategy Framework, (2001) (available at http://www.e-strategy.ubc.ca/__shared/assets/esc_presentation_nov011343.pdf)

[5] Mincer-Daszkiewicz, J. (2003) Deploying University Study-Oriented System at Polish Universities. In Proceedings of 9th International Conference of European University Information Systems , Amsterdam, 2-4 July, pp. 513–517.

[6] Šorm, M., & Netrefová, H. (2006) Complex University Information System at Mendel University Brno. In Lillemaa, T. (ed), Proceedings of 12th International Conference of European University Information Systems, Estonia, Tartu, pp. 94-97.

[7] Desnos, J. (2002) A National Data Warehouse Project for French Universities. In Knop, J., Schirmbacher, P., & Mahnic, V. (eds) Proceedings of the 7th international Conference of European University Information Systems on the Changing Universities - the Role of Technology, Berlin, March 28 - 30, 2001, pp. 146-152.

[8] uPortal: portal under development by institutions of higher education, (available at http://www.uportal.org)

[9] HyperContent: Content Management System, (available at http://hypercontent.sourceforge.net)

[10] Robal, T., & Kalja, A. (2005) e-EDU – An Information System for e-Learning Services. In Barzdins, J., & Caplinskas, A. (eds) Databases and Information Systems: Selected Papers from Sixth International Baltic Conference DB&IS'2004, IOS Press, pp. 288 - 298.

[11] Jasinska, M., Grad-Grudzinska, M., & Wodecki, A. (2006) Training Methodology and Organization of Virtual Campus within Traditional University: What Works, What doesn't Work? In Book of Abstracts, Online EDUCA 2006, Berlin, pp. 272-275.
[12] Granow, R. (2006) Strategic E-Learning Implementation at Lübeck University of Applied Sciences: Experiences and Roadmap. In Book of Abstracts, Online Educa 2006, Berlin, pp. 265-267.
[13] Adenso-Díaz, B., & Cantelli, A.F. (2001) Business process reengineering and university organisation: a normative approach from the Spanish case, Journal of Higher Education Policy and Management, 23(1), pp. 63-73.
[14] Balaji, M. (2004) Reengineering an Educational Institute: a Case Study in New Zealand, (available at www.crie.org.nz/research_paper/M.Balaji_WP2.pdf)
[15] Harrington, J. H., Esseling, K. C., & Van Nimwegen (1997) Business Process Improvement Workbook. McGraw-Hill, 314 p.
[16] El Sawy, O. A. (2000) Redesigning Enterprise Processes for e-Business. McGraw-Hill, 224 p.
[17] Alter, S. (1996) Information Systems: A Management perspective. The Benjamin-Cummings Publishing Company, 2nd ed., 728 p.
[18] Whyte, G., & Bytheway, A. (1996) Factors affecting information systems' success, International Journal of Service Industry Management, 7(1), pp. 74-93.
[19] Trice, A.W., & Treacy,M.E. (1988) Utilization as a dependent variable in MIS research, SIGMIS Database, 19(3-4), ACM, pp. 33-44.
[20] Cuellar, M. J., McLean, E. R., & Johnson, R. D. (2006) The measurement of information system use: preliminary considerations. In Proceedings of the 2006 ACM SIGMIS CPR Conference on Computer Personnel Research, Claremont, California, USA, April 13 - 15, pp. 164-168.
[21] DeLone, W.H., & McLean, E.R. (1992) Information Systems success: The Quest for the dependent variable, Information Systems Research, 3(1), pp. 60-95.
[22] Seddon, P. B. (1997) A Respecification and Extension of the DeLone and McLean Model of IS Success, Information Systems Research, 8(3), pp. 240-253.
[23] DeLone, W.H., & McLean, E.R. (2002) Information Systems Success Revisited. In Proceedings of the Hawaii International Conference on System Sciences (HICSS-35'02), Hawaii, USA, pp. 238–249.
[24] Voitkans, A., Solodovnikova, D., & Treimanis, M. (2006) Assessing E-learning at the University of Latvia. Book of Abstracts, Online EDUCA 2006, Berlin, pp. 159–163.
[25] Benefelds, J., & Niedrite, L. (2004) Comparison of Approaches in Data Warehouse Development in Financial Services and Higher Education. In Seruca, I. et.al. (eds), Proceedings of International Conference on Enterprise Information Systems, Vol.1, Porto, April 14 - 17, pp. 552-557.
[26] Solodovnikova, D., & Niedrite, L. (2005) Using Data Warehouse Resources for Assessment of E-Learning Influence on University Processes. In Eder, J. et.al. (eds.), Communications of the Ninth East-European Conference on Advances in Databases and Information Systems, Tallinn, Estonia, September 12-15, 2005, pp. 233-248.
[27] Niedrite, L., Solodovnikova, D., Treimanis, M., & Niedritis, A. (2007) The Development Method for Process-Oriented Data Warehouse. In Mastorakis, N.E. (ed), WSEAS Transactions on Computer Research, 2(2) , pp. 183-190.
[28] Stonis, J., Niedrite, L., & Niedritis, A. (2001) The influence of the Information System on administrative processes at the University of Latvia. In Knop, J., Schirmbacher, P. & Mahnic, V. (eds) Proceedings of the 7th international Conference of European University Information Systems on the Changing Universities - the Role of Technology, Berlin, March 28 - 30, pp. 119-126.
[29] Niedritis, A., Bumanis, A., & Niedrite, L. (2007) Student and Employee Self Information/Registration Services. In Proceedings of the International Conference of European University Information Systems EUNIS 2007, Grenoble.
[30] Kalnins, A., Barzdins, J., Podnieks, K., Zarins, A. et al. (1996) Business Modelling Language GRAPES-BM and Related CASE Tools. In Proceedings of International Conference Baltic DB&IS'96, Institute of Cybernetics, Tallinn, pp. 3-16.
[31] Advanced Business and System Modeling Tools, (available at www.gradetools.com)
[32] Erl, T. (2005) Service-Oriented Architecture: Concepts, Technology, and Design. Prentice Hall, 792p.
[33] Management Information System of University of Latvia (available at www.luis.lv)
[34] Moodle, a Free, Open Source Course Management System for Online Learning, (available at www.moodle.org)
[35] E-learning System Moodle at University of Latvia, (available at www.estudijas.lu.lv)
[36] Medvedis, I., Niedrite, L., Niedritis, A., Treimanis, M., & Voitkans, A. (2008) In Haav, H.M., & Kalja, A. (eds) e-University Initiative: Approach, Solutions and Case Studies. In Proceedings of the 8th International Baltic Conference on Databases and Information Systems, June 2-5, Tallinn, Estonia, pp. 141-152.

Component-Based Systems Development

Databases and Information Systems V
H.-M. Haav and A. Kalja (Eds.)
IOS Press, 2009

doi:10.3233/978-1-58603-939-4-169

Environment Testing Enabled Software – a Step Towards Execution Context Awareness

Krišs RAUHVARGERS[1] and Janis BICEVSKIS
University of Latvia, Department of Computer Science

Abstract. The paper addresses a problem in software operation that maintenance tasks may lead to software failures. A model for automated checking of software execution environment is proposed. The provided solution is to develop a "profile" for each deployable item which contains information about software requirements regarding its execution. The profile document is added to software deliverables together with a set of tools capable of validating the adequacy of the execution environment according to the document. Regular checks of execution environment may be performed during system operation. The paper discusses first practical results of the proposed approach.

Keywords. maintenance, autonomic systems, environment testing, smart technology

Introduction

Availability of relatively cheap but yet powerful computer hardware systems has strong correlation with the complexity of nowadays' software systems. Ability to perform extensive computational processing combined with computer networking capabilities leads to increase of customer expectations. This includes both expectations on the functional scope of software systems and the user experience when using the software.

The growth of software complexity has some consequences on development and maintenance of such software – the systems become more complex to maintain and to develop. To accelerate development tasks, different technologies and frameworks are established and introduced to the developers. Such frameworks allow the developers to concentrate more on implementation of business requirements rather than background services which are invisible to the user. For instance, Java's EJB containers or Microsoft's COM+ provide transaction services, persistence solutions and other features which would otherwise require much development effort. Many other services do not have "brand names" and are included in the operating system or execution framework. For example, networking support is typically available as an operating system service, and more advanced networking technologies such as .NET Remoting and CORBA are supported by execution frameworks.

Building software systems which rely on the services provided by different frameworks eases the development processes, but apparently requires more

[1] Corresponding Author: Krišs Rauhvargers, University of Latvia, Raiņa blvd. 19, Riga, Latvia; E-mail: kriss.rauhvargers@lais.lv

maintenance effort. Each technology used yields more and more configuration settings to take care of. For instance, when a component is designed to employ services of COM+, a single configuration menu “checkbox” changes whether the component is instantiated in a server or in a client process. However, such a small nuance seriously affects the way the software system works. Hence, maintaining systems of non-trivial size requires in-depth knowledge of system architecture and the technologies employed by the system. Knowledge of working configurations of different systems owned by an organization becomes a valuable asset of the company.

Sound considerations on the need for improvement of maintenance are provided in [1], which states “When you examine data on the root cause of computer system outages, you find that about 40 percent are caused by operator error, and the reason is not because operators are not well-trained or do not have the right capabilities. Rather, it is because the complexities of today’s computer systems are too difficult to understand, and IT operators and managers are under pressure to make decisions about problems in seconds.”

In this paper we present a research in the field of software-driven validation of surrounding environment. For instance, in the COM+ example given above, the component may not be designed to support both configuration types (instantiation in the client or in the server process) and hence may lead to system failure if the setting is wrong.

A software system having the ability to self-check the environmental conditions is anticipated to be much easier to maintain. The question is – how would the system make distinction between “good” and “bad” configurations? We propose a methodology which employs configuration descriptors for validating the environment. Such a descriptor contains a list of known good configuration settings, named execution requirements. Each requirement is a verifiable statement about the configuration of execution environment, for instance, ”the COM+ component can only run in client process”, “the locale in the system must be set to ‘lv-LV(1062)’”. The main advantage of using such requirement descriptors is the ability to expand the list of requirements during system life-cycle, not only in the design and development phase. This is significant, since a lot of expectations (implicit requirements) of environmental configuration can be inherited from the design model or components used by the system.

The remainder of the paper is organized as follows – the next chapter analyzes work in related fields. Chapter 2 describes the methodology proposal in more detail and validates the methodology against related work. The last chapter shows an implementation example of the methodology and discusses the lessons learned.

1. Related Work

1.1. Smart Technology Compatible Software

The research presented in this paper belongs to the *smart technology compatible software* (STSW) initiative that is established by Z. Bičevska and J. Bičevskis and which is described in more detail in [2]. The main principles introduced by the technology are self testing (internal [3] and external environment), data quality control, automatic version updating [4], monitoring (performance, security, availability).

The present paper is a study of self testing of external environment in terms of STSW. We further analyze the requirement stated in [2]: “the software should be able to analyze versions and configurations of the operating systems and the data base management systems in accordance with the requirements of the application”. We do not restrict the scope of analysis to versions of operating system and data bases, but rather define a framework for describing any kind of programmatically verifiable requirements.

1.2. Autonomic Systems

A trend for better maintainable software was raised from the industry and was accepted by the researchers during late 1990ies. Different names were given to technologies aimed to supporting the required level of maintainability – “autonomic computing” by IBM, “trustworthy computing” by Microsoft, “adaptive enterprise” by HP. The latter two have nowadays blurred and do not have a precise meaning, however, the autonomic computing initiative by IBM is has survived and keeps its track. The success can be explained by the fact that the ideology of autonomic computing was envisioned in a document by IBM [5] named “Autonomic Computing Manifesto” and later explained in detail by scientists [1, 6, 7], most of whom were affiliated to the IBM company. The manifesto declares a structured vision of autonomic computing, as seen by IBM and sets the long-term goals of the enhancement initiative.

The term “autonomic system” and other terms used in the manifesto resemble the autonomic nervous systems of human beings and hence are easier to understand using analogies.

The manifesto rather defines properties of software systems that can be called “autonomic” than stating how to make such systems; in fact, it leaves much space for setting more detailed requirements. The original manifesto defines eight key elements of an autonomic system, which are later summarized in other sources as four self-* properties of autonomic software [1]:

- *Self – configuring* defines the ability of the system to adapt to dynamically changing environments. This involves both hardware and software environments. *Hot-swapping* and *plug-and-play* technologies are good examples of self-configuring hardware.
- *Self – healing* is a set of features that allow the system to recover as quickly as possible after a system failure or crash. This includes self-diagnosis, detection of failed elements, and replacement of failed elements. The goal of self-healing is “maximizing the reliability and availability design of each hardware and software product toward continuous availability” ([1]).
- *Self – optimizing* is used for monitoring and automatically tuning resources used by the system. This includes workload management, resource allocation, and other features that allow maximizing outcomes of system performance and minimizing the required resources.
- *Self – protecting* defines the ability of systems to defend themselves, i.e., to anticipate, detect and identify threats, and to use adequate protective measures.

On the top of providing the self-* properties as directions for research, the autonomic computing initiative suggests using five maturity levels for evaluating the level of systems “autonomism”. The names of maturity levels are somewhat similar to levels of CMMI (R) model. The defined levels of maturity are [8]: *Basic level* (maintenance tasks performed by IT professionals), *Managed level* (tools are used for gathering information from the systems. Analysis is performed by IT professionals), *Predictive level* (Individual components monitor themselves and offer advices), *Adaptive level* (Components may analyze the results group wise, human intervention is minimised), *Autonomic level* (human operators define business policies, components fine-tune themselves to adapt to the policies).

The initiative of IBM has been criticized [9] for several reasons: lack of precise definitions, naive vision of the number of "closed control loops" required for a true autonomic system, underestimation of inter-component bonds.

1.3. Built-In Tests

The idea of self-testing enabled software is borrowed from hardware systems which can successfully perform self-tests at startup or at run-time. For instance, RAM memory which checks all the memory cells before performing the actual duties of storing data. However, software systems may need more flexibility and the conditions may change dynamically. This has lead to the idea of testing only the things which are absolutely necessary and algorithmically verifiable.

At a first glance, the test-driven development [10], which is built on top of built-in testing approach, seems to be a good solution for the research problem. Though unit testing technique has a great effect at improving software quality and results at integration testing, trying to use the unit tests for validating the surrounding environment would be a misuse of the particular technology. This is because unit testing is designed to focus on testing a single unit. According to the guidelines, a unit test shouldn't pass the boundaries of the unit to be tested. To overcome the need for "outside world" reactions during tests, the unit testing model proposes the use of mock objects and fake objects [11]. Both kinds of objects are used to simulate the interface of external units required by the unit under test. The use of such substitute code indicates that unit testing may not be useful for integration between components, and, moreover, integration between the system and the surrounding environment.

Another significant application of built-in test approach is the concept of software component with built-in tests as defined in [12]. A built-in test (BIT) is a set of code functions that can be used to validate, if the component is working "as designed". The idea is somewhat similar to automated unit tests as described above, but the test sets are not divided into fixtures and are used for "unit testing" at a component level.

Authors suggest that a software component should contain one or more BITs that can be executed; and implement some specific interface to be called when the system is run at maintenance mode. Here, the authors define a concept of "maintenance mode" of a system, which is proposed as a special mode of system execution when built-in tests can be activated but the business functionality of the system is not used.

The idea of using in-built testing routines of software components is derived even further in [13] where the authors state that using such tests can be useful for validation of the environment. Authors note that every component implements its fixed interface which other components may rely on. This can be called a „contract" between components. Authors of the paper suggest that BITs are used for testing, whether the component is capable of serving the defined interfaces, i.e. if contracts are not violated.

1.4. Software Deployment Descriptor

The field of requirements descriptions is not widely researched at the moment of writing. A W3C member submission named "The Installable Unit Deployment Descriptor, IUDD [14]" (later expanded to Software Deployment Descriptor, SDD) is one of the options. The language is used by the Autonomic Solution Management Framework [15] for describing different aspects of software systems architecture such as structure, installation actions, disposal actions et cetera. The language is XML-based and its structure is defined in multiple XML schemas.

Part of the IUDD specification addresses the requirements and checks to be performed during system life cycle. Predefined checks are included in the specification and custom checks are permitted. However, IUDD (and later SDD) introduces technical restrictions, which may appear limiting when more complex data structures need to be passed to the validation routine.

2. The Proposed Methodology

Methodology proposed in this paper is based on describing knowledge about the software system execution requirements outside the executable code, as some sort of meta-data about the system. Before delivering the software product, the meta-data from different modules or components is gathered into a single requirement document. Hereinafter we propose naming such document a software execution requirement profile or simply a profile document. The profile document is used for testing the execution environment in later life cycle phases.

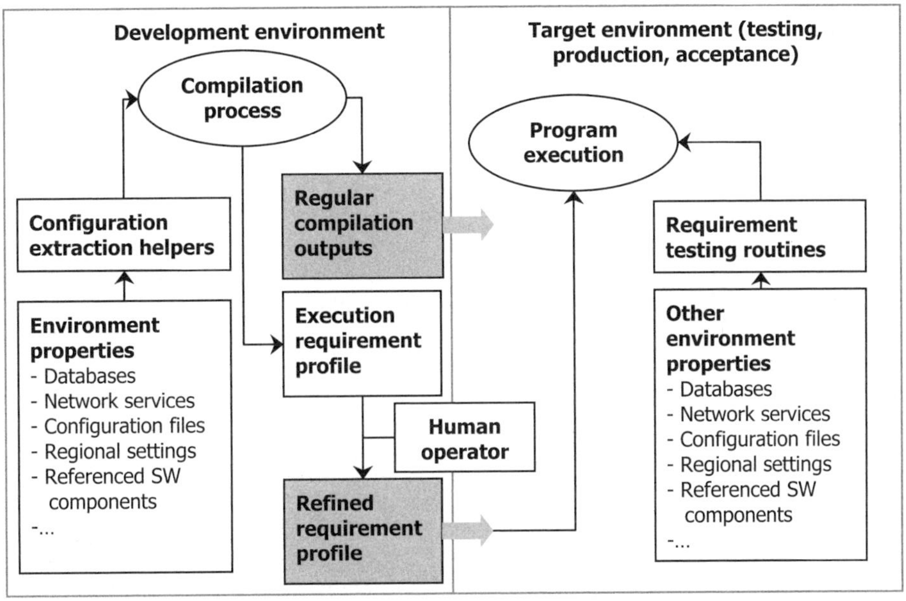

Figure 1. The use of software profile document in software life-cycle

A software requirements profile document contains listings of both the internal links between software components and dependencies on external services, facilities and interfaces. Using appropriate tools, the profile document can be employed for different purposes throughout the life-time of the system. The present paper describes the usage of software profile document as the core of execution environment validation, but other uses may exist. A summary of the proposed use of the methodology is shown in Figure 1.

The following model is offered:

- Dependencies or "bonds" of the program code with the execution environment are registered development. It can be speculated that the developer of a code unit knows most part of the explicit environmental dependencies built into the unit. Technically, specific syntax of code comments or declarative attributes such as provided in .NET [16] can be used for encoding the knowledge in a standard way.
- Upon finishing development of a particular software item, i.e. during code compilation, a document summarizing execution requirements for the particular deliverable is generated. The profile document is combined of known requirements of all code units it consists of. Specific tools can be used to extract the dependency information automatically or manual code reviews can be done. If specific tools are used for profile generation, a review performed by a human operator might be reasonable.
- The software item is delivered into another execution environment together with its profile document
- Conformance of the execution environment is validated using data from the profile document. Here, another set of tools is used for performing automated environment validations. We propose using a name "environment validation module" or EVM for the tools. Each EVM is "responsible" for validation of some requirement. For instance, an EVM can be constructed that responds to a requirement "short date format requirement (requires a specific setting)". Such EVM then has to be able to perform automatic validation of the setting.
- At least two different kinds of environment validation can be implemented according to the methodology – the initial and thorough environmental tests that are performed during the installation of software; and regular, daily checks, performed on a regular basis, for instance, every time the program is launched.

The solution is designed to be applied to internally stable [2] systems. That is, the system under test has already passed the integration tests in the development environment and is known to be working under particular circumstances.

One of the most significant uses of software profile is the area of distributed systems which are far more sensitive to changes in the execution environment's configuration than similar monolithic systems. Practice shows that in the case of failure of a distributed system it is not always easy to detect which component has failed and what configuration changes in the execution environment have caused the failure.

2.1. Implementation Architecture of Runtime Validation Framework

As recommended by [12, 13], runtime validation should not interrupt the regular work of the system under test. Our model is designed to separate not only the regular and maintenance modes, but also the executable code used in regular mode from that used for maintenance.

The software profile approach is different from a typical BIT architecture, since the tests are actually not embedded into the system. To enable a component for self-testing of the execution environment, only functionality for loading the software profile validation runtime („loaders") have to be encoded into the system.

When software is run in the maintenance mode, the loader functions are used for loading the validation runtime core module and handing the execution control to it. As the core module is loaded, it looks for requirements description document of the system under test and analyzes the description. (See Figure 2)

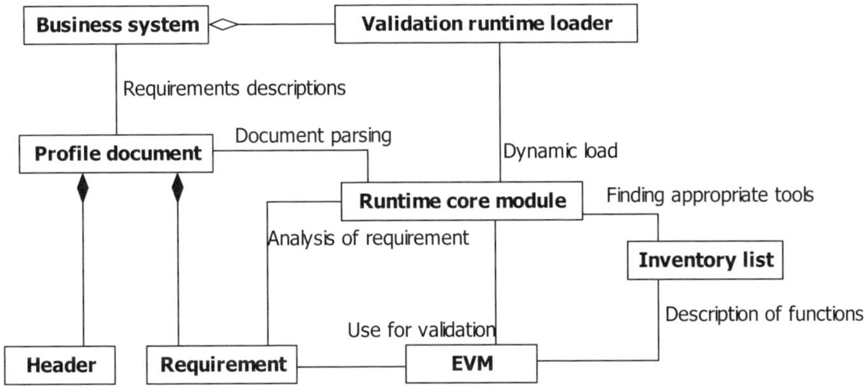

Figure 2. Most significant artifacts in runtime validation framework

The runtime core module uses an "inventory list" to map requirements to actual checks to be performed. Checks are performed by "EVMs" – external validation modules. An EVM is a small functional component that encapsulates technical logic for validating one or a few execution requirements. It looks for evidences at the particular requirement to be satisfied and reports its results. Multiple EVMs can be used to validate a single requirement.

Hence, the model relies strongly on the dynamic loading feature of the execution environment, which is first employed to load the validation runtime core module and later, to load the specific validation tools. The effect can be achieved easily in today's execution frameworks - using the reflection and dynamic load feature of .Net framework, using the ClassLoader interface of Java, even easier in scripting languages such as PHP or Python.

2.2. Validation of the Proposed Methodology

The model proposed in this paper is a synthesis of different methods described in chapter "Related Work", combining the applicable parts of each methodology.

When compared to built-in tests, our methodology has the advantage of test algorithms not being encoded in the system itself. This allows changing the environment tests if needed or adding extra tests for the same requirement without rewriting and re-compiling the executable code. The software profile methodology can be considered an extension of built-in test, since it shares several concepts (maintenance mode, some code embedded into the system), but the tests are outside of the system. Our approach can even be applied in a manner similar to unit testing.

The research described in the present paper has been criticized for escaping attention on several technologies which have similar use: installation package creation tools as Macrovision InstallShield or Nullsoft NSIS, installation configuration scripts such as Autoconf, deployment validation capabilities of Windows Installer. These tools are used for software installations and validation of the environment during installation, whereas our methodology aims to bring environmental tests into whole software life cycle. This is achieved through performing the tests at the beginning of every regular execution of the business program. Similarly to built-in testing technique, the validation algorithm of installation managers is built into the installer; hence it only allows performing tests that are known during preparation of the installation. In contrast, our model allows supplementing the list of requirements whenever it is needed.

The IBM's Solution Deployment Descriptor provides a language for installation descriptions, thus enabling the installation frameworks to use a common syntax for their results. The SDD approach rises from the autonomic software ideology. Its main contribution to the ideology is the structured information about deployment which it adds to the program code. The SDD allows creation of really complex descriptions of how the software system is constructed and how it should be maintained. However, since the language focuses on deployment, it cannot be directly used for execution environment validation. A simple mechanism for describing installation requirements is built into the descriptor syntax, but it is unsatisfactory for our purposes. Many concepts such as "describe WHAT, do not describe HOW" [17] are shared between the SDD and software profile approach, but the outcomes are different. An in-depth comparison of the two methodologies is a question of further research.

3. Lessons Learned from the First Implementation

The methodology proposed in this paper has been initially implemented at the Bank of Latvia, the Latvian Central Bank.

For fulfilling its duties, the Bank needs many information systems that help automating the work. To achieve the best adjustment to the business processes, most part of software is developed in-house. This allows for cross-system integration, hence avoiding data and functionality duplication. The number of simultaneously performing systems hosted has nowadays grown quite large thus requesting appropriate hardware infrastructure solutions for operating the software. According to empirical observations, the human effort for maintaining the systems has grown disproportionally when compared to growth of number of systems. It can be explained by the fact that modern software development technologies are applied to new software, but the existing systems remain the same. Hence, the skills needed for maintaining the myriad of systems include technologies and development approaches that have been used during the previous decade.

Recognizing the need for improvement in software maintenance, the Bank has naturally evolved in the direction of autonomic systems as described in [5]. The changes also include evolution to service-centric applications. In this architecture the main processes are performed on the server, but client applications are only used for monitoring the status and communicating the business decisions to the server. The server components are typically hosted in a service or “daemon” process which controls the state of the system. Such service processes may run for months and serve many business operation cycles accompanied by respective client component sessions.

It was realized that it is not easy to notice a failure of such long-running background process if the failure happens after a successful start-up of the process. On the other hand, it was realized that failures happen when maintenance tasks such as hardware migrations or operating system updates have recently been carried out.

Repair time is considered the most significant measure upon a system failure. However, it was not always easy to spot the setting that caused the failure and hence the repair times may be quite long.

Such observations lead to a wish to perform some kind of validation when launching the service process. Several typical reasons of failures were identified. These included wrong regional settings, wrong security configuration, missing configuration files; the latter reason being a bootstrapping issue, since the path of error log file is found in the configuration file.

The service applications were updated to perform a simple validation before launch and, if some settings did not match the requirement, the service was not launched at all. Such approach corresponds to a built in-test as described in chapter 1.3, but in at maintenance mode the component rather tests external environment than itself.

It was soon realized that such validation can help avoiding the most typical faults, but more uncommon failures were not found automatically. When manual work is used to locate the cause of a failure, the most likely symptoms are also the first ones in the check-list, hence these would be found out quite early. This meant that now the simple cases (for instance, the wrong setting of decimal separator) were resolved quickly, but complex failures would take hours to resolve.

This constituted the idea of attaching a text document to each system, which contains failure symptoms and causes. The idea later evolved to creation of an execution profile that references an enterprise-wide library of maintenance tests.

A pilot project for environment testing framework was carried out. The main goals of the project were to allow attaching a computer-readable execution requirement descriptor to the executables and automatically validating the environment using the descriptor.

A very simple XML- based language was designed for the pilot purpose. Each requirements descriptor consisted of a header part which described the artifact to which the descriptor applies and a list of requirements.

For instance, a valid profile document is shown in the following code listing.

```
<SWProfile >
  <subject type="assembly" fullname=
          "TestApp, Version=1.0.0.0,
              Culture=neutral, PublicKeyToken=28f514e8eeca027c" />
  <requirements>
    <localeDependency localeName="lv-LV" shortDatePattern="dd.MM.yyyy" />
    <assemblyDependency
       fullname="Microsoft.Office.Interop.Excel,
                  Version=11.0.0.0, Culture=neutral,
                  PublicKeyToken=71e9bce111e9429c" />
  </requirements>
</SWProfile>
```

The execution profile above describes the application “TestApp” and states requirements for specific values of regional settings and for a specific library – Microsoft Excel interoperability suite – for normal functioning.

The general architecture of the validation framework corresponds to the description in Figure 2. To make the *validation runtime* available to any system requiring it, the *loader* functionality was included in an in-house developed common code library that was referenced by nearly every business component.

Hence, to use the validation services, only a few extra lines of code are required (and, of course, the requirements document had to be created and the required *EVMs* had to be available)

```
With New EnvironmentValidator()
     'any output goes to the console screen
    .TextListener = AddressOf Console.WriteLine
     'halt if the tests have failed
     If Not .DoTests() Then Application.Exit()
End With
```

A simple *runtime core module* was developed (approx. 2000 lines of code) which provided the following services:

- finding “responsible” *EVM*s using a predefined “inventory list” (in the pilot implementation – another file which contains a listing of all available EVMs)
- loading the libraries containing the *EVM*

A common base class was developed for all *EVMs* (approx. 1000 lines of code). The base class provides basic services such as converting serialized XML data into properties accessible from object-oriented code. Hence, to create a simple EVM, one has to create a code class that inherits from *BaseEVM* class and override the *DoTest* method where the actual test is performed; for instance, the present regional settings are compared to the ones listed in the execution profile.

At the time of writing there are no statistical results yet of the effect achieved in the pilot project. However, it is clear that applying the methodology to development of business systems does not require too much additional effort. Compared to the situation before the pilot project, the development is even relieved, since one does not have to state all the execution requirements during development and encode the test routines into the system.

4. Conclusion

The introduction of software execution requirements profile is a step towards context awareness. Adaptation of the methodology is truly flexible and depends on the needs of the interested party. The profile document can be created manually or created automatically by extracting the requirements from program code (if such automated tools are available). One may build smart EVMs which carefully access the environment in read-only mode, or the same validation can be done through “trial-and-error” methods. The implementation of the methodology may be incremental, by first adapting only some notions, e.g., defining the language for describing the requirements and later implementing the automatic validation.

The initial efforts in implementing the proposed methodology show good results and thus results indicate that the approach is suitable for practical use.

5. Acknowledgements

The research is supported by the European Social Fund (ESF).

References

[1] Ganek, A. G., & Corbi, T. A. (2003) The dawning of the autonomic computing era, IBM Systems Journal, 42(1): 5-18

[2] Bičevska, Z., & Bičevskis, J. (2007) Smart Technologies in Software Life Cycle. In Münch, J., Abrahamsson, P. (eds.), Proceedings of Product-Focused Software Process Improvement. 8th International Conference, PROFES 2007, July 2-4, Riga, Latvia, pp. 262 - 272.

[3] Bičevska, Z., & Bičevskis, J. (2008) Self-testing: A New Testing Approach. In Haav, H.-M., Kalja, A. (eds.) Proceedings of the Eighth International Baltic Conference Baltic DB&IS 2008, June 2-5, Tallinn, Estonia, pp. 179 - 189.

[4] Bičevska, Z., & Bičevskis, J. (2008) Application of Smart Technologies in Software Development: Automated Version Updating. Scientific papers, University of Latvia, (vol. 733), Riga., pp. 24 - 37.

[5] Horn, P. (2001) Autonomic computing: IBM's perspective on the state of information technology. Presented at AGENDA 2001, Scotsdale, AR, (available at http://www.research.ibm.com/autonomic)

[6] Sterritt, R., & Bustard, D. (2003) Towards an autonomic computing environment. In Marík, V., Retschitzegger, W., & Stepánková, O. (Eds.) Proceedings of 14th International Workshop on Database and Expert Systems Applications, Prague, Czech Republic, pp. 694 - 698.

[7] Lightstone, S. (2007) Foundations of Autonomic Computing Development. In Proceedings of the Fourth IEEE international Workshop on Engineering of Autonomic and Autonomous Systems, March 26 – 29, Tucson, USA, pp. 163 – 171.

[8] Nami, M. R., & Bertels, K. (2007) A Survey of Autonomic Computing Systems. In Proceedings of the Third International Conference on Autonomic and Autonomous Systems IEEE Computer Society. Washington, DC, USA, pp. 26 - 31

[9] Herrmann, K., Muhl, G., & Geihs, K. (2005) Self management: the solution to complexity or just another problem?, Distributed Systems Online, IEEE, 6 (1) (available at http://dx.doi.org/10.1109/MDSO.2005.3)

[10] Janzen, D., & Saiedian H. (2005) Test-Driven Development: Concepts, Taxonomy, and Future Direction. IEEE Computer, 38 (9): 43 - 50

[11] Kim, T., Park, C., & Wu, C (2006) Mock Object Models for Test Driven Development. In Proceedings of the Fourth International Conference on Software Engineering Research, Management and Applications, pp. 221 - 228.

[12] Wang, Y., King, G. & Wickburg, H. (1999) A Method for Built-in Tests in Component-based Software Maintenance. In Proceedings of the Third European Conference on Software Maintenance and Reengineering, pp. 186 - 189.

[13] Barbier, F., & Belloir, N. (2003) Component Behavior Prediction and Monitoring through Built-In Test. In 10th IEEE International Conference and Workshop on the Engineering of Computer-Based Systems (ECBS'03), pp.17 - 22.

[14] Draper, C., George, R., & Vitaletti, M. (2004) Installable unit deployment descriptor for autonomic solution management. In proceedings of 15th International Workshop on Database and Expert Systems Applications, Proceedings, pp. 742 - 746.

[15] Vitaletti, M. (Ed.) (2004) Installable Unit Deployment Descriptor Specification, Version 1.0., W3C Member Submission, (available at at http://www.w3.org/Submission/InstallableUnit-DD/).

[16] Newkirk, J., & Vorontsov, A. A. (2002) How .NET's Custom Attributes Affect Design, IEEE Software, 19(5): 18-20

[17] McCarthy, J., & Miller, B. A. (2008) Solution Deployment Descriptor (SDD), Part 1: An emerging standard for deployment artifacts (available at http://www.ibm.com/developerworks/autonomic/library/ac-artifacts)

Databases and Information Systems V
H.-M. Haav and A. Kalja (Eds.)
IOS Press, 2009

doi:10.3233/978-1-58603-939-4-180

Audit Log Unification and Review with Log Management Information Bases

Wai Man TO[a], Theo TRYFONAS[b, 1] and Dave W. FARTHING[c]
[a]*Serious Fraud Office, UK*
[b]*University of Bristol, UK*
[c]*University of Glamorgan, UK*

Abstract. Computer auditing involves the manual collection and review of independent log files that may be completely different in format and contents, yet they may be conceptually related as they could be part of the picture for an incident. The aim of this paper is to investigate the feasibility of heterogeneous log integration via the use of Log Management Information Bases, i.e. metadata descriptions of each proprietary log that would allow for log 'unification' in a standardised language such as XML, and their subsequent correlation into a software module that could be either an independent application or an add-on module of generalised audit software.

Keywords. audit log processing, network security auditing

Introduction

Information systems auditing includes tasks such as logical and physical access control reviews, environmental and physical inspections, data integrity verification, compliance checks etc. A specialist who audits a system needs to manually export, import and format various pieces of electronic audit evidence in the form of documentation, configuration settings, design and in particular, log dumps from various monitoring applications or operating systems. Further to their identification and extraction from the original source, such proprietary logs have to be edited and formatted appropriately in order to be used within general purpose applications, including spreadsheet applications or general auditing software (GAS), so they can be analysed. This is a challenging and effort-intensive operation conducted via the use of proprietary scripts or other conversion and cleansing utilities.

A possible approach to reduce the complexity of this task would be to impose the use of a standardised log format industry-wide, where the field names within it and its structure are fixed. In this case GAS could directly import log dumps from various tools or operating systems logs, as the log format is known. However, getting the industry as a whole to agree on a standardized format for recording system-related information is difficult and, despite the fact that log information is somewhat similar across platforms and devices, there may still be a tremendous variation in the format, locations of storage etc.

---

[1] Corresponding Author: Faculty of Engineering, University of Bristol, BS8 1TR, Bristol, UK; Email t.tryfonas@bristol.ac.uk.

The aim of this paper is to review the feasibility of an alternative approach by designing and implementing a log information base, where each individual proprietary log is described in terms of a standardised format. GAS and vendor products can indirectly exchange information via this, as an aid to standardise automated audit log analysis. The paper then is structured as follows: section 1 provides the background of audit work on computer networks and the role of various proprietary logs; in section 2 we discuss the technologies that may provide for log standardisation; section three proposes a design for a log information base and its specification; finally section four discusses further work.

1. Information Systems Security Auditing

Information systems (IS) auditing has become more important since events of corruption have had a global impact, e.g. the Enron scandal [1]. Such incidents have moved IT governance up the agenda of corporations and governments, as most of them occurred in large multinational organizations and the effects have been felt throughout the world. The Sarbanes-Oxley Act 2002 [2], introduced to mitigate such risks in the future, moved up issues of compliance and tightened auditing regulations that had an impact on information systems.

Weber [3] defines computer auditing as the process of collecting and evaluating evidence to determine whether a computer system safeguards assets, maintains data integrity, achieves organizational goals effectively and consumes resources efficiently. It can be broken down to physical and environmental, system administration, application software, network security, business continuity and data integrity reviews [4]. ISACA's *IS Standards, Guidelines and Procedures for Auditing Control Professionals* [5] outlines IS auditing standards in detail, but we only focus on the computer network security aspects; particularly within the categories of *"intrusion detection, firewalls, and security assessment – penetration and vulnerability testing"*.

The US General Accounting Office has identified that the information systems audit usually requires at least four types of specialists [6]; specialists involved are *network, Windows, UNIX and mainframe* analysts. A more generalist professional may conduct the overall audit, focused on more traditional audit tasks, whilst computer network auditing is conducted by specialists and may cover various operating systems and equipment. The audit data may be of different format for each operating system, test application, and appliance (e.g. router). Indeed, as an information system could be a collection of interdependent systems (individual workstations, servers, routers, firewalls etc.) several tools may be needed to test specific aspects of the system. The log files generated by these systems may be in various formats, and general auditing software should be used to adjust and edit them, so they are workable through a more standardised format, e.g. in a spreadsheet. Usually this log processing and transformation is done manually and is a time consuming and effort intensive task.

Figure 1 shows a typical workflow of an IS audit for an enterprise system with the following components of networks, Windows, UNIX and mainframe systems. As one tool cannot audit the whole information system, the IS auditor requires to use a library of tools to tackle each aspect of the IS audit procedures. That collection of tools usually includes a number of log parsers, but they are normally limited to the particular file formats they understand. Log parsers are programs that are specially designed to import a log file in its native form, then reformat the information in a way that is easily understood by the analyst. The IT specialists have also to use tools like penetration testing and vulnerability assessment applications and manually collect logs.

With regard to the frequency of occurrence of computer audit work, this could be a regular inspection performed at pre-specified periods, for example an annual external IS audit or quarterly internal IS audit. Alternatively it could be part of a continuous auditing process, where a system is continuously monitored as a result of the capabilities offered by information technology and process automation [5].

2. On the Feasibility of Audit Log Standardisation

Examples of audit log parses include Auditware's Unix Security Auditor and Microsoft's Log Parser. Those tools are usually constrained to process only the log formats they understand. In a complex enterprise system as discussed above, a single log parser may not be able to process certain types of logs and a number of different tools may need to be used. Use of log parsers requires manual intervention at each step of the audit process, the general flow diagram of which can be shown in Figure 2. Log parsers do not automate the log collection and do not usually have the ability to integrate with general auditing software, although some commercial products do so (e.g. the Unix Security Auditor integrates with IDEA).

To conduct integrated log analysis we first need to understand what events are logged and how the information is stored across various systems to facilitate handling of multiple log formats. A possible route to automation of importing logs and analysis is through the use of a standard log format, which would be used by all software, hardware, and systems developers. Part of the existing research in techniques that cross reference different logs to allow analysis and correlation of event information is based on standardizing and normalizing log information. This also enables the automation of importing and processing of logs using general auditing software. Generating scripts with GAS tools is simplified and scripts can be applied to all of the logs collected within the enterprise system. The general workflow when using a standard log format is shown in Figure 3.

Another possible route to automate heterogeneous log processing is through a common information data interchange standard, which allows for vendors to use proprietary formats within their own products and would provide the auditor with a tool to bring to a unified format all collected logs. The automation of log collection and processing could then be achieved by a software module compliant with that standard. The software module would use a file to abstract information from the native log, which is saved locally, and then manipulate the source information to a plain format that a general auditing software can use to analyse further. The general workflow when using a log information base is shown in Figure 4.

2.1. Proposals for Standardizing and Normalizing Log Formats

Bishop [7] proposed a standard log format, where the # was used as field separator in the log. The log started with #S# and ended with #E#. The original log had values and had no field name information, therefore Bishop proposed that the field name and value to be included in the field information. Those were separated by an "=" symbol. Bishop also proposed that the standard should be portable, flexible and extensible. This was possible due to this format did not have fixed names of fields or the number of fields in the log format. The main assumption here is that the log files will always be in ASCII format. In reality, the range of log formats found in operating systems such as variants of Windows and UNIX, mainframes, embedded systems and bespoke software is as complex as the many versions of systems. Some vendors follow their own specifications, whilst others conform to de facto standards such as *syslog*. The information could exist in ASCII format, while other vendors may utilise binary forms.

Although Bishop proposed to standardize the format, he did not formalised the structure of the fields, exactly because log formats used by various platforms and applications vary so much. Therefore information from the logs could not be shared or analysed, due to the field names and structures of the various log formats are not following the same naming convention and field structure order; therefore analysing log file by cross referencing logs is not possible. Also a question is raised about what information should be logged.

Chen et al. [8] proposed normalizing audit data in XML-format, so it would be possible to use binary and ASCII files to extract information and then transfer the information into a database; therefore the data can be shared and analysed. They too highlighted that there was no international naming convention for field names. Chen et al. also needed to find a way for their solution to have data portability across various platforms and XML was chosen to allow data transfer portability across multiple platforms. They proposed that the format of the log file should have descriptive and header information at the beginning of the file, and then two XML components.

The order of the XML components is important to allow the log format to work: first exists the XML component that contains the field format structure, followed by a second XML component, which had log data. The field format structure variables proposed by Chen are, Field DataField, Description, Format, Name, and Type. The log data variables are Field Description, Format, Name, Type, and Value (the 'Value' is the data from the original log file).

The data conversion to XML format was done manually; therefore their process was not automated, so errors could be introduced during this process. An issue that was highlighted was that binary files had too much information for example *user-id, group-id, IP address*, *host-id,* etc. [8]. With the use of all the binary file information this can generate logs with large number of fields, and questions on how to use this information effectively. Therefore there is a need to be selective on the information that is needed to be extracted when using binary files, as information overload is possible if all fields were used in the log. Also they demonstrated that with their XML-Format it was possible to share information and analyse log information from various platforms or applications. Therefore an IDS log, port scanning log, and a web server log could be compared to see if any suspicious activity is happening from a specific IP address. A possible example of what can be achieved if logs can be cross referenced through a database is the detection system enumeration using several IP address, or system enumeration over long period using single IP address.

An area of research that emerged as of requiring further consideration was on logs cross-reference, so security alerts could be raised through the analysis of the log information. Combining the merits of the two ideas we will subsequently produce a XML logging format that is feasible to implement, so sharing log information could be possible across various vendor products. A XML based format could be used either as an exported data 'shaper', or as a native format for storing logs. We will further elaborate on this and amend it with design principles found in other fields where cross-reference of logged information is significant.

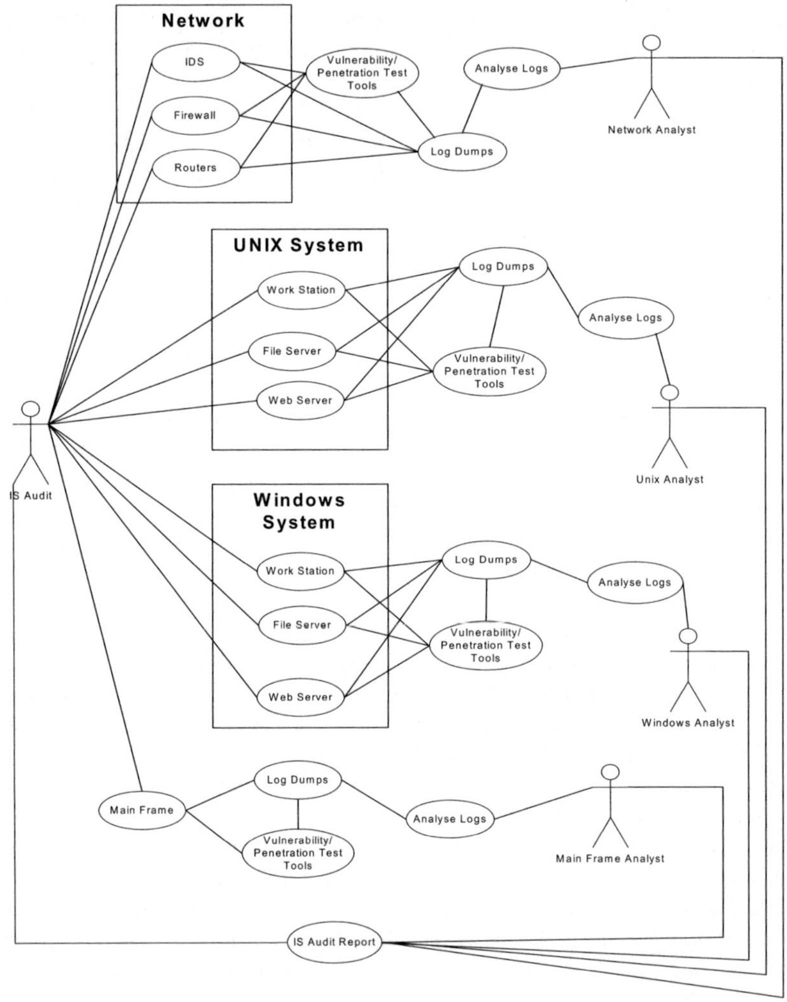

Figure 1. Audit of computer network systems as a use-case specification

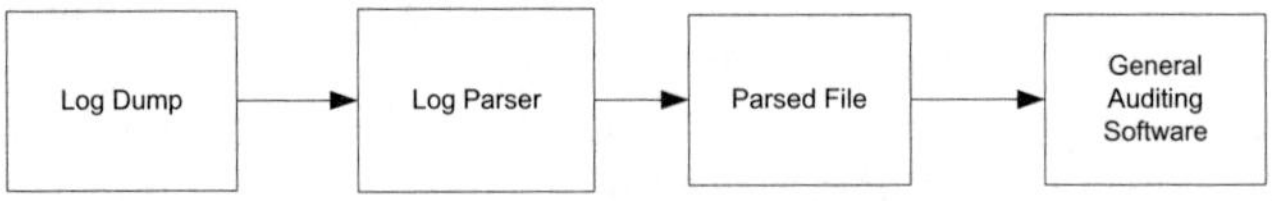

Figure 2. Log parsing work flow

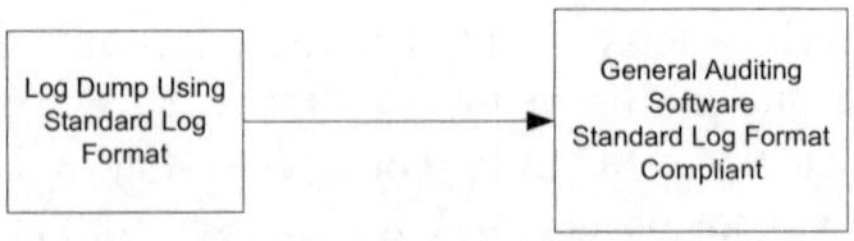

Figure 3. Standard log format work flow

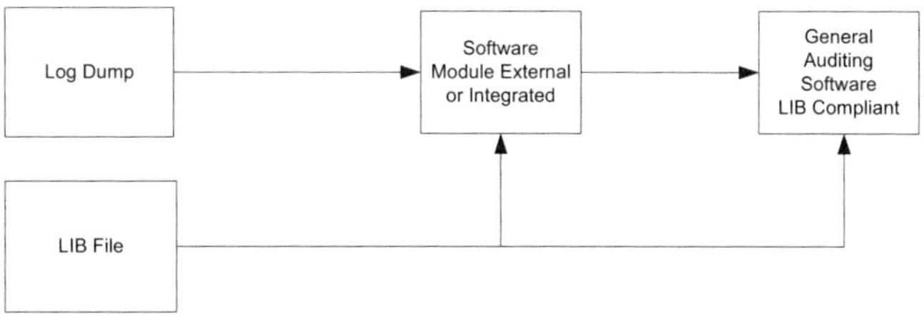

Figure 4. Log information base work flow

An area of research that emerged as of requiring further consideration was on ways to cross reference the logs, so security alerts could be raised through the analysis of the log information. Combining the merits of the two ideas we will subsequently produce a XML logging format that is feasible to implement, so sharing log information could be possible across various vendor products. A XML based format could be used either as an exported data 'shaper', or as a native format for storing logs. We will further elaborate on this and amend it with design principles found in other fields where cross-reference of logged information is significant.

2.2. Design Principles of Cross-Referenced Information Bases

The Common Information Model (CIM) standard was created by the distributed management task force (DMTF) [9], so that vendors of various platforms have a standard that can be used to exchange management information over a network. The CIM model is orientated to information used to manage information about computer systems and network appliances. The vendors select modules from the CIM standard schema, so when designing the platform it will be able to exchange management information with CIM compliant software or appliance.

The CIM schema for CIM_Systems [10] has a logging component to allow for sharing of log information from the CIM standard. The CIM logging information model is structured into three components. The first is the Object Name, similar to a label for a category. The second component named class is a compulsory component and specifies the order of the information and its format. The third component is optional and can hold more detailed information such as parameter types, operating functions of the parameters etc.; it specifies the format of the parameters.

The CIM standard's objective [10] is to create a model to allow management data to be exchanged between various platforms in an enterprise system, but does not address standardisation of log file formats nor it provides a solution to extract log information in a way that will help the IS auditor. The CIM standard allows log files to be written as a bespoke design, but data to be exchanged across the enterprise system. CIM does not standardise the log file layout.

Design principles of the Management Information Base (MIB) standard are also of interest, as it illustrates that it is possible to manage a system (software or appliance), gather and share information from various vendors over a network using Simple Network Management Protocol (SNMP). When a vendor creates a SNMP compliant product, they must have an associated SNMP agent to allow data to be transmitted or controlled via this. The SNMP compatible management software is vendor neutral and can be designed by third party software developers who understand the SNMP protocol and the structure of the MIB [11]. Also SNMP is part of the Internet protocol suite [12] [13] and therefore the management information is transmitted within the managed

TCP/IP network itself. RFC 1213 [14] describes the structure and definitions in the MIB standard so that exchange of network management information between various applications and appliances using the SNMP protocol is possible.

The MIB file contains the objects that are managed by the management system [15]. The objects are information and variables that are required by the management system, so that it can manage, monitor or gather information about that system. The MIB file is used by an SNMP agent and the management software. The SNMP agent uses the MIB file to send SNMP information on the state of a system, to control specific system functions, gather or send information. The management software uses the MIB file to see which SNMP information it can gather, and what product functions it can control using the SNMP protocol.

The structure of the MIB objects is a hierarchal tree. A typical MIB object has an object identification number, and then 5 fields where information can inserted into the MIB object, therefore information can be also extracted from the MIB object. The MIB object manager is able to handle many MIB objects. The following Request For Comments (RFC) documents RFC1213 and RFC1155 provide further detailed information on the MIB standard and structures. An example of SNMP management software is HP Openview [16].

Finally, elements of the architecture of Electronic Data Interchange (EDI) are also of interest, because they demonstrate that it is possible to exchange information between different organisations electronically and transfer the data into a database directly using third party software. Different formats of business documents like *invoices, orders, and order confirmations* exist from organisation to organisation [17], however EDI allows for the transparent standardisation and transfer directly to database without human intervention, of information of various formats. The EDI standard has changed over the years to accommodate the different types of forms/documents that have arisen; this illustrates the scalability and flexibility of the EDI standard over the years since its inception [17].

3. The Log Management Information Base Approach

The main concept of a Log Management Information Base (LMIB) is that every event log could be described in an associated file containing the formatting and type definitions of the log, in metadata descriptions based on a standardised data description language, such as ASN.1, used in network MIBs. If that information is available it will be subsequently feasible to create an application or module able to analyse log files that have been previously brought into a 'canonical' format, following a common information data interchange standard for log files.

Based on the principles discussed earlier, a LMIB could be a possible solution to the automation of processing of disparate security logs during the course of a systems audit. Vendors of applications, operating systems or appliances may have their own way to represent their logs but they can also use a standard export formatting (in effect an XML wrapping) to enable third party software applications to understand a native log dump. Alternatively, if the vendor does not accommodate that, the LMIB module could provide the definitions needed to transform the acquired log information into the 'canonical' format and import it for further analysis.

Our common log information interchange standard will be modelled around the MIB standard, because it is an example that allows multiple vendors to exchange information via a MIB file. This has allowed software vendors to write software that uses the MIB file information, so it can manipulate the raw information from various vendor products; therefore present the information in a preferred format and have possibility of analysis of the information. An important feature in the development of the LMIB proposed standard is that it is transparent across all platforms and is not bound to specific vendors of appliances or software. MIB objects exist in a hierarchal tree structure. As mentioned earlier, a MIB object has an object identification number, and then it has 5 fields where information can be inserted into and extracted from. The MIB object manager is able to handle multiple MIB objects [15].

The proposed application fits into the audit process as illustrated in Figure 5. The assumptions are object categories are representative of the information gathered in an IS audit. Another assumption is that the developed LMIB schema is available to software developers so they can use it to develop software to allow data manipulation (export) in appropriate XML output.

Therefore from the class and object type information a software developer can develop software similar to log parser, to manipulate and format the information that is compatible with general auditing software. Therefore log dumps can be automated, imported, and formatted without human intervention. The log management information base standard will allow log formats from various vendors to easily describe the log file structure, so importing and reformatting of the log dumps to a format that general auditing software can be automated using a combination of software module, native log dump, and LMIB file.

Some of the header variables types that will be used are based on Bishop's work [7]. A sample description from the data dictionary for the LMIB standard is shown in Table 1. To derive the object data model that will allow us to define the LMIB structure and develop the XML 'wrappers', we cross-correlated the standard information that can be found in different logs via the use of field name specification aggregation tables, as shown in Table 2. In essence, the LMIB file is used to describe the log format, and what fields are used (Figure 6).

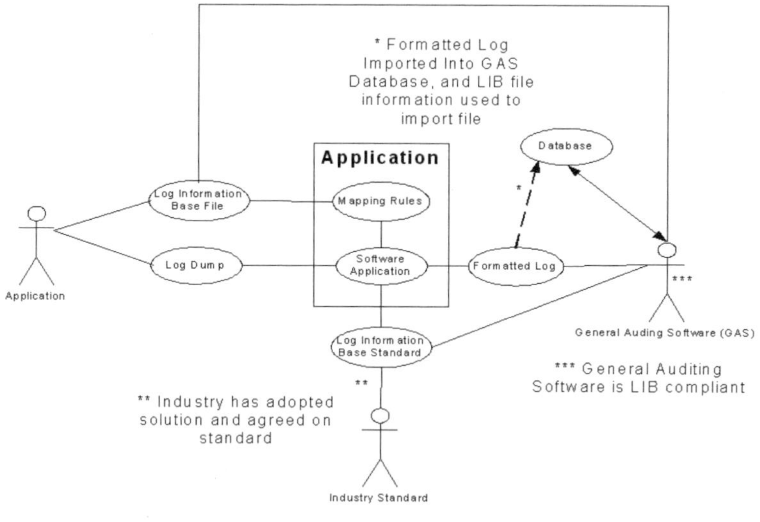

Figure 5. Log information workflow diagram

Use of the LMIB file will allow the software module to transpose incompatible field names, date and time formats from the native file to the preferred format. The LMIB file aggregates the variables it requires from the common information data interchange LMIB standard to create a LMIB file that describes how the log is formatted. Therefore the Log Management Information Base is an object naming schema for all possible log field names in a log file; also the LMIB holds information on the design of the log file format, so that program modules can automatically import log dumps and manipulate the data, from the LMIB file supplied by the vendor. The LMIB file is used to describe the log format, and what fields are used. The complete LMIB data model is illustrated in Figure 7. The complete data dictionary for the LMIB proposed standard and further information on the full Field Name Specification Aggregation Tables can be obtained from [18].

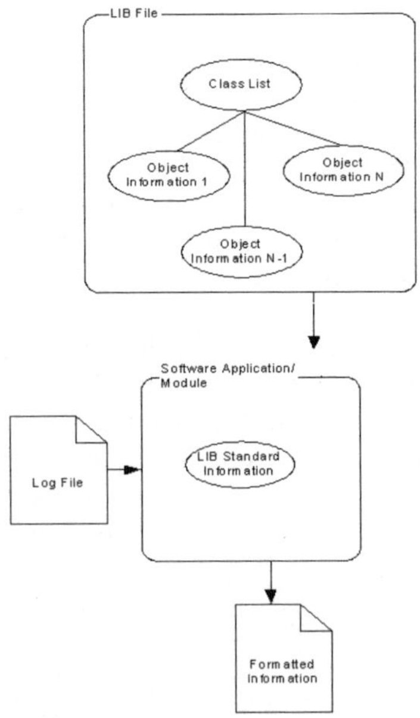

Figure 6. Implementing the LMIB standard

Table 1. Data dictionary header variable types.

Header	::= Header information on file format;
Date & Time	::= Date and time formats;
Names and ID	::= Name formats for users and hosts;
Address and Port	::= Port, IP and MAC address formats;
IP Protocol & Packet	::= IP Protocol / Packet information variables;
TCP	::= TCP information variables;
ICMP	::= ICMP information variables;
Web Server	::= Web server information variables;
Message	::= Message information variables;
Files	::= File attribute variables;

Systems	::= Windows, UNIX and Mainframe logging vars;
Misc	::= Variables that do not fit into a category;
Reserved 1	::= Reserved for future use;
Reserved 2	::= Reserved for future use;
Reserved 3	::= Reserved for future use;
Reserved 4	::= Reserved for future use;

Vendor Name	::= $^{1}\{\text{Alphanumeric}\}^{256}$;
Vendor Code	::= $^{3}\{\text{Digit}\}^{3}$"."$^{3}\{\text{Digit}\}^{3}$;
Log Description	::= $^{1}\{\text{Alphanumeric}\}^{256}$;
Version Number	::= $^{1}\{\text{Alphanumeric}\}^{256}$;
Start Log Character(s) Code	::= $^{1}\{\text{Alphanumeric}\}^{4}$;
End Log Character(s) Code	::= $^{1}\{\text{Alphanumeric}\}^{4}$;

Table 2. Sample of field name specification aggregation table.

Field Name/System or Application	**Firewall**	**IDS**	**Port Scan**	**Event Log**	**Syslog**	**IIS Web Server**	**Apache Web Svr**	**OpenVMS**
Month/Day	x						x	
Time (hh:mm:ss)	x		x	x	X	x	x	
Firewall Name	x							
Packet-Log	x							
Packet-Direction	x							
Interface Name	x							
Protocol	x	x					x	
Source Address	x	x						
Source Port	x							
Destination Address	x	x						
Destination Port	x	x						
Packet Length	x							
TCP-Flag-S	x							
Flag-I	x							
TCP-Flag-F	x							
TTL	x	x						
Rule Number	x							
Time Stamp		x						
Ethernet Source		x						
Ethenet Destination		x						
TCP Flags		x						
TCP Sequence		x						
TCP Acknowledge		x						
ICMP Type		x						
ICMP Code		x						
ICMP Sequence		x						
Year/Month/Date			X		x			
IP Address			X					
Host			X					
Port			X					
IP Protocol			X					
Service			X					
State			X					
Date/Month/Year				x		x		

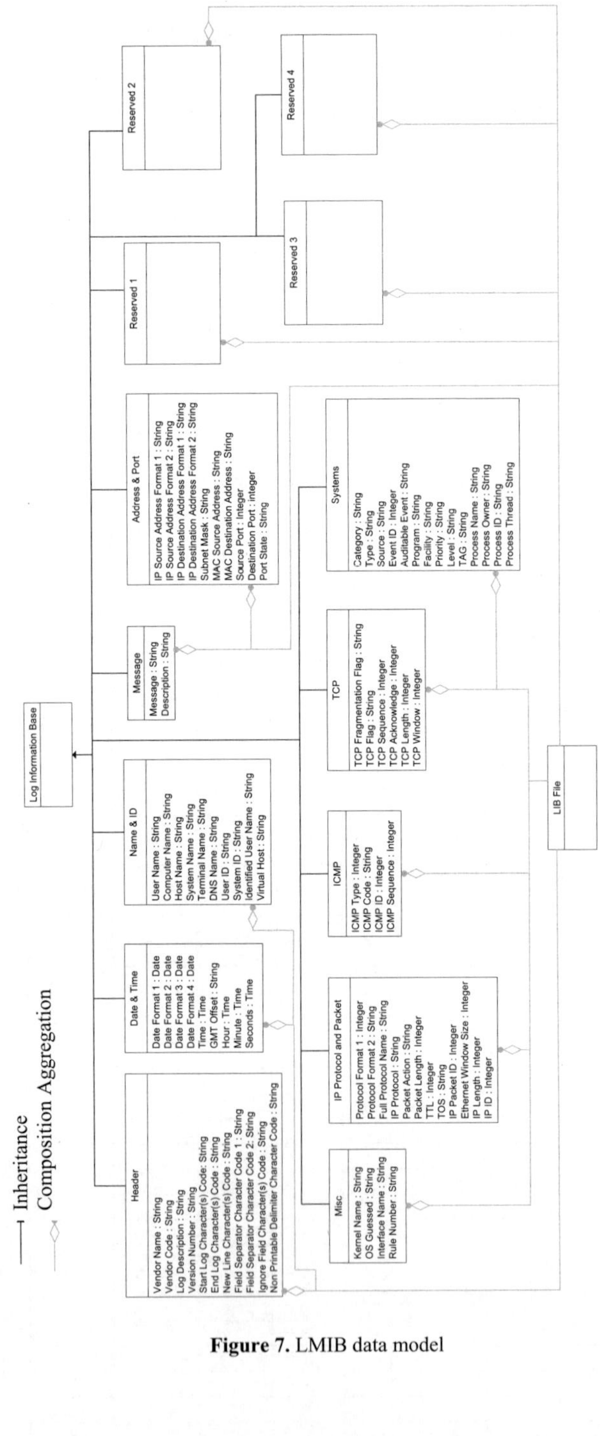

Figure 7. LMIB data model

4. Summary and Further Work

The Log Management Information Base is an object naming schema for all possible log field names in the log file; also the LMIB holds information on the design of the log file format so a program module can automatically import the log dump and manipulate the data, from the LMIB file supplied by the vendor. LMIB is a common information data interchange standard for log files that could form the basis for an industry standard to describe the log file and log structure; it was created using a platform independent language; and GAS can understand how to use the LMIB, so it can manipulate logs.

The standardisation of field names and their data format is an aspect that needs to be further addressed, so that LMIBs are standardised and exchanged. The further work on the project work so proposed solutions can be refined by enlarging the scope of the data used to include log formats from bespoke software or products, and to include field names from application logs used in IS auditing.

References

[1] BBC (2002) Enron scandal at-a-glance. (available at http://news.bbc.co.uk/1/hi/business/1780075.stm)
[2] FindLaw.com (2003) Sarbanes-Oxley Act 2002. US Government. (available at http://news.findlaw.com/hdocs/docs/gwbush/sarbanesoxley072302.pdf)
[3] Weber, R. (1988) EDP Auditing – Conceptual Foundations and Practice, 2nd Edition, McGraw-Hill.
[4] Sayana, S.A. (2002) IT Audit Basics: The IS Audit Process, Information Systems Control Journal, Volume 1.
[5] ISACA (2005) IS Standards Guidelines and Procedures for Auditing Control Professionals. (available at http://www.isaca.org/Template.cfm?Section=Home&Template=/ContentManagement/ContentDisplay.cfm&ContentID=15262)
[6] US GAO (2001) Management Planning Guide for Information Systems Security Auditing. (available at http://www.gao.gov/special.pubs/mgmtpln.pdf)
[7] Bishop, M. (1995) A Standard Audit Log Format, University of California. (available at http://www.mirrors.wiretapped.net/security/development/secure-programming/bishop-1995-a-standard-audit-trail-format.pdf)
[8] Chen et al. (2004) Normalising Security Audit Data in XML-format, Lulea University of Technology. (available at http://epubl.luth.se/1402-1536/2004/13/LTU-TR-0413-SE.pdf)
[9] DTMF (2005) About the DTMF. (available at http://www.dmtf.org/about)
[10] DTMF (2005) CIM_System. (available at http://www.dmtf.org/standards/cim/cim_schema_v29/CIM_System.pdf)
[11] Linktionary.com (2005) MIB (Management Information Base). (available at http://www.linktionary.com/m/mib.html)
[12] Wikipedia (2005) Simple Network Management Protocol. (available at http://en.wikipedia.org/wiki/Simple_network_management_protocol)
[13] Webopedia (2005) Transmission Control Protocol/Internet Protocol.(available at http://www.webopedia.com/TERM/T/TCP_IP.html)
[14] RFC 1213 (1991) Management Information Base for Network Management of TCP/IP-based internets: MIB-II. (available at http://www.faqs.org/rfcs/rfc1213.html)
[15] TCPIPGuide.com (2004) TCP/IP MIB Objects, Object Characteristics and Object Types. (available at http://www.tcpipguide.com/free/t_TCPIPMIBObjectsObjectCharacteristicsandObjectTypes.htm)
[16] HP (2004) HP OpenView Network Node Manager Advance Edition 7.5 Software: data sheet. (available at http://www.managementsoftware.hp.com/products/nnm/ds/nnm_ae_ds.pdf)
[17] UN (2005) Part 4 United Nations Rules for Electronic Data Interchange for Administration, Commerce and Transport. (available at http://www.unece.org/trade/untdid/texts/d422_d.htm)
[18] To, W. M. (2006) Automation of an Audit Log Analysis via a Standard Log Format or Log Information Base within the Scope of Computer/Network Security Audits, Unpublished MSc thesis, University of Glamorgan.

Databases and Information Systems V
H.-M. Haav and A. Kalja (Eds.)
IOS Press, 2009

doi:10.3233/978-1-58603-939-4-192

Applying Self-Testing: Advantages and Limitations

Zane BICEVSKA and Janis BICEVSKIS[1]
University of Latvia, Riga, Latvia

Abstract. The paper is dedicated to principles of smart technologies as well as advantages and restrictions for usage of them. Self-testing as a feature of smart technologies is analyzed more closely. Self-testing is carried out using complete test cases and a built-in test execution mechanism (self-testing mode). The self-testing feature enables testing of software during the whole life cycle and especially in the maintenance phase since this feature operates in both testing and productive environments. The paper also contains an experience-based report about economical aspects of usage of smart technologies and especially self-testing.

Keywords. smart technologies, maintenance, testing, self-testing

Introduction

Every successful software solution has been used and improved for significantly longer time period that it was created for. Successfully developed system might be used for many years simultaneously modified, improved with new functions permanently satisfying occurring client needs. Thus every time changes occur in software or operational environment issue of testing software's correctness becomes crucial.

Therefore, to ensure software reliability in long-term the system already in its early development phases should comprise not only client defined functionality but also additional mechanisms to support usage, maintenance and further development of software.

The smart technology is based on the idea about "smart" software that like living beings is able to "self-management". It means the software should be able to handle unpredictable events in unknown environments. A smart technology conform software should be able to react on internal (related to internal structure and functioning of the system) and external (originated outside of the system) events adequately.

Smart technology oriented approach [1] implies that the core functionality of software solution should be enhanced with several additional features supporting the usage, maintenance and further development of software. These additional features, like scaffolding in the construction process of a building, are created in the process of software design and implementing. But unlike the building process the "scaffolding" of

[1] Corresponding Author: Janis Bicevskis, University of Latvia, Raina blvd. 19, Riga, Latvia; E-mail: Janis.Bicevskis@lu.lv.

an information system is never taken down, it stays in the information system for its whole life time.

The typical components of smart technologies are following:

- Business model is incorporated into software
- Version management – automatic updating of versions from the central server, including the adequate conversion of data structures and data
- License management – automatic control of licence conditions, updating of standard and specific software according to them
- Context help – integrated functionality of context sensitive help system
- Environment testing - ability to analyse the external environment (for example, options of operating system and data base management system) and to adapt itself to the specific environment
- Self-testing - ability to check the internal integrity by automatic execution of test cases in the productive environment and to inform users and developers about detected inconsistencies
- Load testing - ability to provide monitoring of performance and load balancing
- Availability testing – monitoring of system availability using agent technologies; ability to inform remote about the status of the software and additional components needed for a correct functioning
- Security testing - monitoring of system security using agent technologies
- Data quality monitoring - ability to check the completeness and integrity of data accumulated in the database

Smart technologies are based on similar or even partially overlapping ideas with autonomous systems [2, 3, 4, 5] and their features - self–configuring, self–healing, self–optimizing, self–protecting software. Self-adaptive software researchers are focusing on software ability to adapt itself to implementation environment and external conditions thus allowing even code translation to the targeted environment and defining rules for software reaction on external events. This report sets different targets: troubleshooting SW exploitation failures by applying automatic indication of possible failures and reporting them to staff. Implementation of this approach is more beneficial and convenient to use in practice.

Detailed analysis of features of smart technologies can serve as a subject of separate research papers. This paper discusses only one of the smart technology features – self-testing.

1. Self-Testing

1.1. Motivation for Usage

The conventional life-cycle models of software development [6] view testing from two aspects:

- Software testing done by developers who have good knowledge of software architecture, so called „the white box approach"
- Functional software testing against the requirements done by independent experts, so called „the black box approach"

The white box approach considers software developers as the experts having the best knowledge of the system from internal point of view, Therefore they are the most appropriate experts to verify if software testing procedure based on certain testing criteria (coverage, modules, interfaces etc.) has included all appropriate software components [7].

Software requirements (if they are documented) contain the general information on the software, and thus can be used to verify its operational correctness without any particular knowledge and penetration into the system's architecture. The functional testing is done based on the "black box approach". This approach involves independent testing experts, for software developers are believed to be very uncritical towards their own products and unable to ensure high level testing.

The above mentioned conventional testing approach works exceptionally well for development of new products, when it is crucial to present the best possible quality software with a high operational probability complying with the requirements (usually at the start of software usage). In cases when a software system is already in-use and due to software change requests an updated version is required, the modern literature suggests regress testing.

However, this approach is successful only if the software developer can act as a "ruler" over the production environment including standard product versions and other customized applications running on those resources. In such case the developers and testing experts can be assured that operational effectiveness of the software in the production environment will be the same as during the testing phase.

Nevertheless the modern reality is much more complex. As to the real systems the focus shifts from a number of separate systems each aimed at ensuring a particular business requirement, to the heterogeneous combination of information systems. Due to the rush and uncoordinated development of sophisticated components, conflicts can arose among different components of information systems and unexpected infrastructural effects can appear, etc.

In order to reduce risks, we propose to develop software based on smart technology principles [8], providing self-testing features both in testing and production environments.

1.2. Components of Self-Testing

The concept of self-testing in common with other principles of smart technologies is based on the idea that software like living being is able to react on previously unpredictable events in unknown environments. It is very important not only to determine the environmental parameters [9], but also to adapt itself to the modified environment.

In the hardware industry it is a usual feature that equipment tests itself as soon as it is switched on; in the software industry this approach has been mostly seen as innovation. In the case of software solutions conformable to smart technologies, the self-testing means the ability of software to run automatically in the production environment a predefined set of test cases to check self status.

Functionality of self-testing contains two basic components:

1. Test cases of critical functionality and benchmark values (data component)
2. Built-in mechanism providing automatic running of test cases (software component)

The critical functionality is a set of system functions which are essential for using the system. It is impossible to use the system if these features do not function. The critical functionality covers all basic functional requirements of a system – for instance, calculation algorithms, workflows etc. - but usually does not include non-functional requirements like performance, navigation and others. To implement self-testing functionality the developers should prepare functional test cases covering all critical system's functions (complete set of test cases) and save them into the database/file system.

In addition to that an automatic test running and comparing of results with benchmark values should be implemented. As it will be shown in the next chapters, the implementation of self-testing is related to incorporation (at least partially) of testing support tools into the IT solution.

The most important feature of self-testing is an ability to test the software in the production environment during almost every moment of the system's functioning without any impact on system's usability.

The key feature that separates the self-testing from the conventional testing is running of self-testing in the production environment, including an access to the real database. It means there should be guaranteed that the content of production database has not been changed by the self-testing mechanism; it uses production data in the read-only mode. Every self-testing session includes regress testing according to the gathered and stored test cases.

In the case the system has been changed the test cases are also customized accordingly to ensure full coverage of the critical functionality. The self-testing feature which is run regularly ensures a high quality of software.

There should be emphasized that self-testing does not replace the traditional testing and its techniques, it just supplements them. As every functional software feature, the self-testing should not only be implemented, but also should be appropriate tested. The self-testing feature puts an additional mechanism for quality control on the IT solution: The ability to perform the test cases in the production environment and to compare the acquired results with benchmark values.

The idea of self-testing has been developed for long years, beginning with the old paper in the mainframe era [10] up to the built-in-test ideas for component-based software [11]. The main innovation in this paper in distinction to the above mentioned papers, is the proposed way of implementation of the self-testing feature, emphasizing the similarity of the self-testing feature with the features of testing tools.

2. Implementation of Self-Testing

2.1. Self-Testing and Testing Support Tools

In order to implement self-testing feature, software should include some options of conventional testing tools such as test accumulation, test replay, benchmarking of test results and other. The main restriction of the test support tools is that they can be used only in the test environment. They can not be used in production environment since it is hardly possible to perform an appropriate testing without making records on the database, and that is not acceptable in production environment. This becomes especially important in situations when crucial operational parameters such as classifiers, configuration data etc. are held in the database. Due to this the testing environment and production environment may differ significantly and, therefore, problems occurred in production environment are hardly to reproduce in test environment.

The solution to these problems should include either creation of test environment on user computers that is technically time consuming and expensive due to licensing, or transferring of production environment to the test environment in order to reproduce and investigate the problems detected in production environment. Resolving detected production problems gets even more complicated in cases when software developers have delivered their product, thus accomplishing the contract task, but the maintenance is carried out by different company.

2.2. Implementation of Self-Testing Components

The self-testing offers a different approach. The self-testing feature is incorporated into the software functionality already during the implementation phase, and it is usable during the whole software life cycle – from the implementation till the maintenance. Moreover, the software containing the self-testing feature can be tested in both testing and production environments.

The self-testing mechanism should be built-in into the software that should be tested using the self-testing mode. To obtain the self-testing functionality the following components should be prepared:

- Functional test cases covering all critical system's functions (complete set of test cases)
- Software modules for the automatic test case execution and results comparison with the benchmark values

The self-testing must be safe executable in the production environment, i.e. the test cases and operations with them may not impact the production database.

There are some suggestions for implementing of the software modules for the automatic test case execution and results comparison with the benchmark values discussed in the following chapters.

2.2.1. Management of Execution Modes

As the system can be used in both production and testing modes, it can be useful to introduce two global parameters (for example, mode and info) that determine the actual mode of software execution and the volume of test's execution results.

There should be at least three modes in the software execution: production, self-testing, test-create (mode = {production, self-test, create-test}). By default the software is used in the production mode. The authorized users can switch the mode to self-testing. Additionally for creating test cases and benchmark values the create-test mode can be used.

The second parameter (info = {high, middle, low}) is independent from the first one, and it defines the volume of information to be written into log files for analysis of correctness of software functioning.

2.2.2. Mode Production

No testing activities are performed in this mode. Yet the architecture of the system anticipates that read/write operations (reading of information from screen forms and data base tables) and control flow changing operations (menu and buttons) are implemented in separate modules. It will help to modify the read/write operations for their usage in the test mode.

It is advisable to implement and set up a special variable indicating that no system accidents are recognized in this mode. Otherwise a warning message with additional information is sent to the responsible staff to inform it about an accident.

2.2.3. Mode Self-test

An automated testing of the software is performed in this mode. The reading operations are modified replacing input of data from the production database with input of data from the database/file (from test_Base). Also the results of system's execution are not written into production database but into the test database/file (into result_Base). After the execution the real results (stored in result_Base) are compared with the benchmark values that are accumulated in the create test mode and are stored in the test database/file (in etalon_Base). If there is discrepancy between the benchmark values and real values, the appropriate messages are sent to the responsible staff.

The way to handle replacing of read/write operations is specific for different information systems, and the implementation of the mode takes additional development resources.

2.2.4. Mode Create-test

An automatic test accumulation is performed in this mode to make the test cases usable for the self-testing mode. The system registers all read/write and control flow change operations and stores them into the test database/file (test_Base). Also the results of system's execution are not written into production database but into the test database/file (into result_Base).

The way to handle the accumulation of operations and the volume to be stored is specific for different information systems. This mode is not compulsory; the tests can be stored into the test database/files in some other way. But it is very advisable to implement it to achieve a high level of self-testing automation.

This mode could also be used for registration of discovered errors (into test_Base) and reporting of them in form of incident reports to the maintenance staff.

2.2.5. Parameter Info

The software is run in the mode chosen by the user. The trace of activities and results are saved into the log file according to the value of parameter info. The gathered information can be used for analysis of reasons of discovered problems. Most of programming environments offer the possibility to trace the values of variables and activities of execution. But in self-testing case the volume of gathered test information can be managed in the production environment.

It is useful to implement the function for automated execution of all self-tests in one session. It can be achieved by a special self-testing control table (test_Plan) containing the names of test cases to be run in the self-test mode. The driver of self-testing will be able to run all test cases included in the control table ensuring the possibility of selective self-testing.

3. Statistics

In order to evaluate advantages and limits for applying of smart technologies, we will analyse statistics from a project of a governmental importance – the State Revenue Service (SRS) portal development and maintenance project. The main characteristics of this development project are the following:

- A well-developed specification since the public procurement procedure requires precise and detailed specification. Besides, SRS already had an older portal version in use, which should be replaced by a newer portal version. The older portal version contributed to the precise formulations of requests for the new version of the portal
- Experienced and competent team of developers. The team had an excellent experience in development of several governmental portals

The statistical data on portal development and maintenance was registered from 1st quarter 2005 until 3rd quarter 2008. The acceptance testing was carried out by the customer in 1st and 2nd quarters 2005. The portal was put into operation in 2nd quarter 2005. All testing and productive events, further called problem notifications, were registered by an automated problem notifications' registration system. Therefore, the given statistic reflects the customer's opinion on the project and does not cover developers' internal communication. Moreover, only officially registered problem notifications (any other communication on software errors was not accepted) were included into statistics, therefore the presented statistical data should be regarded as full and complete.

Totally 234 problem notifications were received (see Table 1.). These problem notifications relatively can be divided into 5 groups:

1. Errors (totally 55). The problem notifications in this group were clearly classified as portal's operational inadequacy with regard to the specified requests
2. Misinterpreted requests (32). The developer had developed software adequate to his/her interpretation of the specified requests. However during the acceptance testing the client reveals inadequacies and the developer must acknowledge his/her misinterpretation of the requests
3. Loose requests (25). The problem notification has been received; however its cause can not be classified as programmer's error due to loosely formulated request
4. Changed requests (83). As a result of acceptance testing and/or due to productive usage of the portal the system requests are changed
5. New requests (39). The client makes new requests that were unknown to developers in the beginning phase of the project

The statistical analysis disproves the widely spread statement that programming errors make out the greatest part of all problems within an IT project. The statistics shows: Only 23% from all received problem notifications are real programming errors! Especially interesting is a problem notification split by time, showing operative elimination of programming errors due to developer's internal project work organization. The project manager spent a significant effort specifying tasks for each programmer and controlling work results by careful testing. Testing within the project team took approx. 40% of resources. The self-testing was not applied in this project, however if it had been applied, the automated portal testing would have enabled to save up to 25% of project resources. If developers were involved in self-testing it would enable detecting and eliminating a significant number of programming errors even before the acceptance testing, where totally 55 errors were detected.

Table 1. Problem notifications (by group and time).

Quarter, Year	Errors	Misinterpreted requests	Loose requests	Changed requests	New requests	Total
I - 2005.	36	9	0	12	3	60
II - 2005	11	9	0	17	0	37
III - 2005	0	0	0	3	0	3
IV - 2005	5	0	0	4	0	9
I - 2006	2	4	0	0	0	6
II - 2006	1	0	0	2	0	3
III - 2006	0	0	0	0	1	1
IV - 2006	0	4	4	3	21	32
I – 2007	0	3	7	4	8	22
II – 2007	0	0	1	7	1	9
III – 2007	0	2	2	3	1	8
IV – 2007	0	0	2	9	0	11
I – 2008	0	0	2	5	4	11
II – 2008	0	1	4	11	0	16
III – 2008	0	0	3	3	0	6
Total	55	32	25	83	39	234
%	23%	14%	11%	35%	17%	

Obviously by executing self-testing it would not be possible to reduce the number of problem notifications caused by misinterpreted (14%) and loose requests (11%). Similarly, it would not be possible to reduce the number of changed and new requests by carrying out self-testing procedure. However, it is statistically proven that implemented portal changes should be regarded as necessary and preferable part of portal development. Since changed requests made up 35% of total number of problem notifications, self-testing would have significantly reduced efforts on regression testing carried out before installation of each new software version (more than 40 times during the total period of 4 years of portal development and maintenance).

The following conclusions can be drawn from the statistical analysis:

- In projects, where software development and maintenance last over a period of several years, changed requests and newly defined requests have greater significance than elimination of programmers' errors.

- Self-testing may play significant supportive role in detecting of programming errors during software development phase and regression testing during software maintenance phase.
- Self-testing may significantly facilitate software acceptance testing done by the customer since developer has been able to reduce number of programming errors during software development and maintenance phases. However the developer will not be able to reduce number of changed and new requests.

4. Economic Aspects of Applying Smart Technologies

As above mentioned an incorporation of smart technologies into information systems involves extra resources. Hence the consequent question is about economic justification: In what cases and under what conditions is implementation of smart technologies not only useful for IT professionals but also gives return on investment.

According to theories of information asymmetry [12], well-known in science of economics and especially in the contract theory, business partners make their decisions in the market on the base of incomplete information. It means the decisions in transactions are made where one party has more or better information than the other. This creates an imbalance of power in transactions which can sometimes cause the transactions to go awry. Therefore the topic of the better informed and the most interested party that could be a motive power for implementation of smart technologies is essential.

In general there could be two kinds of drivers for usage of smart technologies possible:

- A customer, being well-informed about problems related to software maintenance, requires the implementation of smart technologies as a part of contract in the very beginning of software development or as a part of modernization in the maintenance phase
- A supplier, based on long-term agreements or hoping for resource savings in the future, incorporates components of smart technologies into software products at his/her own risk

The assumption - the applying of smart technologies could be required by customer - should be verified by analyzing of tenders and their results. As costs and requirements of information systems is a business secret in general, the only reliable source of information about software procurements is public tenders. The Public procurement law that regulates public procurement in the Republic of Latvia prescribes the tenders' documentation is overall accessible and detailed results of public tenders are accessible for those who have taken part in it.

The authors analyzed a documentation of public IT tenders accumulated within last 5 years by an active local supplier of IT services. The goal of an investigation was to detect the amount of tenders anticipating system requirements to build up or to incorporate smart technologies into information systems.

There could be recognized that customers most frequently require non-functional features concerning security and stability, like availability testing, load testing or security testing. De facto never are required features concerning aspects of software maintenance like environment testing or self-testing. In several cases requirements for incorporate business model, data quality monitoring and version management are included.

The results of the investigation shows the typical local customer in Latvian does not recognize the advantages of smart technologies and hence does not include the appropriate requirements into public tenders' documentation.

It means, the main or even the only driver for usage of smart technologies is a supplier him-/herself. As a rational party the supplier is interested to invest, if the probability to earn an extra profit is high enough.

There are two different strategies common in practice:

- The development or incorporation of smart technologies is included into cost-calculation for implementation of functionality required explicitly by the customer (the customer pays for smart technology features at the same time as for development of base functionality)
- The development or incorporation of smart technologies is performed on the own risk, i.e., return on investments is planned in the future as a part of maintenance service or change requests (the customer pays for smart technologies indirect, in form of heightened service costs)

In the first case the customer (mostly being uninformed about it) buys a better product for higher price. The investment is made by the customer and the supplier as a know-how owner obtains advantages for the further maintenance phase. Identifying of break–even point is irrelevant in this case, as the effort of supplier is already compensated in a hidden form.

On the other hand, if investments were made by the supplier on his/her own initiative (and it's quite often in the public procurement), criteria for determining of the break-even point are very important. The authors have indentified the following essential criteria for suppliers to be interested to invest in implementing of smart technologies:

- There are long-term maintenance agreements between supplier and customer
- The software is running in geographically distant places
- The software is running in different (non-homogenous) environments
- High level support (for example first level support via helpdesk) is needed for end-users

5. Conclusions

The self-testing takes different place in the software life cycle compared to the testing in the traditional software life cycle models (for example in "V" model). Software developers (programmers) themselves are responsible for the complete software testing by implementing the self-testing feature in the architecture of the system. This includes the following steps:

- A complete set of test cases should be prepared either by the client or developers for the complete testing of the system
- The appropriate self-testing procedures should be developed
- The source code written by developers should be tested by the developers in the automated self-testing mode without any support of external testing tools

Incontestably, integration of the above mentioned features into software requires additional efforts; however theses efforts would bring positive results: reduced number of errors detected during acceptance testing and automated regression testing. The real project statistics provide a credible basis for the following conclusions:

1. The self-testing - one of the smart technology components – provides significant economy of resources by supporting systematic testing within development group
2. The resources planned for acceptance testing can be significantly reduced by execution of qualitative testing within the development group having full attention on detecting inadequate interpretations of system's requirements during development and maintenance phases
3. As shown by the statistical analysis the software used over the long period of time becomes a target of permanent improvements and additional requests. The regression testing that should be carried out several times repeatedly can be replaced by automated self-testing mechanisms
4. The clients seldom require ensuring smart technology features, including self-testing. Although the clients approve opportunities provided by the smart technologies, usually, they are not willing to provide additional financial means to ensure them
5. The risks of implementation of smart technologies pay-off in cases of long-term cooperation between the developer and the customer or in cases of standardized software products

References

[1] Bičevska, Z., & Bičevskis, J. (2007) Smart Technologies in Software Life Cycle. In Münch, J. & Abrahamsson, P. (eds.) Product-Focused Software Process Improvement, 8th International Conference PROFES 2007, July 2-4, Riga, Latvia, Berlin: Springer, (LNCS), pp. 262 - 272.

[2] Horn P. (2001) Autonomic computing: IBM's perspective on the state of information technology. Presented at AGENDA 2001, Scotsdale, AR. (available at http://www.research.ibm.com/autonomic/)

[3] Ganek, A. G., & Corbi, T. A. (2003) The dawning of the autonomic computing era, IBM Systems Journal, 42(1): 5-18

[4] Sterritt, R., & Bustard, D. (2003) Towards an autonomic computing environment. In Proceedings of the 14th International Workshop on Database and Expert Systems Applications, pp. 694 - 698.

[5] Lightstone, S. (2007) Foundations of Autonomic Computing Development. In Proceedings of the Fourth IEEE international Workshop on Engineering of Autonomic and Autonomous Systems, March 26 – 29, pp. 163 – 171.

[6] Pressman, R. S. (2005) Software Engineering: A Practitioner's Approach. McGrawHill, 6th ed.

[7] Beizer, B. (1995) Black-Box Testing Techniques for Functional Testing of Software and Systems. John Wiley & Sons

[8] Bičevska, Z., & Bičevskis, J. (2008) Self-testing: A New Testing Approach. In Proceedings of the 8th International Baltic Conference on Databases and Information Systems (Baltic DB&IS 2008), June 2-5, Tallinn, Estonia, pp. 179 - 189.

[9] Rauhvargers, K., & Bicevskis, J. (2008) Automating the Software Environment Testing Process. In Proceedings of the 8th International Baltic Conference on Databases and Information Systems (Baltic DB&IS 2008), June 2-5, Tallinn, Estonia, pp. 155-166.

[10] Бичевский, Я., & Борзов, Ю. (1982) Приоритеты в отладке больших программных систем, Программирование, №3.

[11] Chengying, M., Yansheng, L., & Jinlong Z. (2007) Regression testing for component-based software via built-in test design. In Proceedings of the ACM symposium on Applied computing, March 11 – 15, Seoul, Korea, pp. 1416 – 1421.

[12] Macho-Stadler, I., & Perez-Castrillo, J. (2001) An Introduction to the Economics of Information. Incentives and Contract. Oxford University Press, 2nd ed.

Information Systems Integration

Databases and Information Systems V
H.-M. Haav and A. Kalja (Eds.)
IOS Press, 2009

doi:10.3233/978-1-58603-939-4-205

Analysis of Open Source Software Evolution Using Evolution Curve Method

Robertas DAMAŠEVIČIUS[1]
Software Engineering Department, Kaunas University of Technology

Abstract. Design and evolution of modern information systems is influenced by many factors: technical, organizational, social, and psychological. This is especially true for open source software systems (OSSS), when many developers from different backgrounds interact, share their ideas and contribute towards the development and improvement of a software product. The evolution of an OSSS is a continuous process of source code development, adaptation, improvement and maintenance. Studying changes to the various characteristics of source code can help us understand the evolution of a software system. In this paper, the software evolution process is analyzed using a proposed Evolution curve (E-curve) method, which is based on information theoretic metrics of source code. The method allows identifying major evolution stages and transition points of an analyzed software system. The application of the E-curves is demonstrated for the eMule system.

Keywords. software evolution, open source software, software metrics

Introduction

Software development is not purely a technical task, but also a social process embedded within organizational and social structures [1, 2]. These structures influence and govern work behaviour and final work products of programmers such as source code and documentation. This is especially true for open source software systems (OSSS), when many programmers from different backgrounds interact, share their ideas and contribute towards the development and improvement of a software product.

Software is not written, but rather it is being evolved by people (developers, maintainers, etc.). Software evolution is a continuing process that concerns how a software system evolves over time with respect to some essential software properties. It encompasses software development activities, such as modification, adaptation or maintenance, which occur after the delivery of the first operational release to the users. It has been reported that costs devoted to system maintenance and evolution now account for more than 90% of total software costs [3].

During the lifetime of a large software system usually many versions are produced. Analyzing changes to various characteristics of source code of these versions and other release information can reveal trends and anomalies in the software development process. The empirical study of software evolution is important because it can help to identify major factors influencing software change, predict possible evolution trends,

[1] Corresponding Author: Robertas Damaševičius, Kaunas University of Technology, Studentų 50-415, LT-51368, Kaunas, Lithuania; E-mail: robertas.damasevicius@ktu.lt.

develop credible methods to measure, observe, model and analyze software evolution process [4], and it ultimately leads to a more holistic understanding of software.

Several papers have studied the evolution of software across several versions of the same system [5-9]. As a software system evolves, new code fragments are added, some parts are deleted, modified or remain unchanged, therefore, overall evolution is difficult to measure using common software source code metrics such as the number of functions, files or lines of code. Common software metrics can be helpful to estimate software "size" or amount of work done. They also are used as an aid in judging the quality and reliability of software development. However, they usually focus on a software system as a final product and do not show how software evolves.

For software evolution research, specific evolution metrics can be used, e.g., SDI metric [10] measures the system-level design changes and combines four types of changes in an object-oriented system — the percentage of classes whose names have changed, percentage of added classes, percentage of deleted classes, and percentage of classes whose inheritance hierarchy have changed. L–metric [11] is based on Shannon entropy. It measures how much information exists in the development process. AICC-metric [12] and G-metric [13] are used for estimating system complexity. Hassan and Holt [14] apply the ideas of the information theory and entropy to measure the amount of uncertainty/chaos/randomness in the software development process.

One of the major difficulties of software evolution analysis is huge amount of data that have to be analyzed. Hundreds of versions of thousands of files are common in a single software project. Understanding of this data can be eased using software *evolution visualization* techniques [15].

We propose a novel software evolution analysis and visualization method, called *Evolution curve* (E-curve), which allows identifying major stages and transition points in the evolution of a software system. The structure of the paper is as follows. Section 1 discusses factors and forces that influence software evolution. Section 2 describes the transition-based model of software evolution. Section 3 presents the information theory approach to software evolution measurement. Section 4 describes the proposed E-curve method. Section 5 presents a case study. Finally, Section 6 presents conclusions.

1. Factors and Forces of Software Evolution

Open-source software systems (OSSS) refer to software systems that are free to use and whose source code is freely accessible to anyone. In comparison to the traditional IS, the OSSS are mostly developed based on a less strict control and management model [16]. Usually an OSSS is started by a single developer, who wants to solve his or her own particular problem and makes the solution available to others for free. Because it is free, it often attracts many users, some of whom may become co-developers by extending or improving the initial system. The evolution of an OSSS begins in response to the needs of users and is carried out by contributing co-developers [17]. Spontaneous collaboration is promoted and backed by a decentralized developer community using the internet-based development systems such as SourceForge.

Some reasons for software evolution are the addition of new functionality, modification of existing functionality, corrective and preventive maintenance, software reengineering using newer technology, architectural transformation, code refactoring, and code rewriting for optimization. The OSSS evolution process is governed by some basic evolutionary mechanisms that also apply to the natural world such as competition against similar OSSS or natural selection, during which some systems thrive and others die off. Basically, there are two groups of these mechanisms [18]: *variation-increasing* (such as versioning) and *variation-decreasing* (such as selection).

Variation is a process that creates configurations (or versions) of a system that are different from the previous ones. For example, standardization as a business policy decreases variation, whereas product family-based model of software development increases variation. Variation can be either *sequential,* when a system passes through a variety of subsequent versions, or *parallel*, when a system is being diversified into different versions, whichfurther may evolve independently from each other. Variation may be driven by psychological, intellectual, social and cultural, economic and business factors, which may act in any direction.

Software variation is decreased by selection. Selection is the elimination or reduction of the variety of configurations produced by variation. Selection of software is performed by its users, who may select a system based on a number and quality of provided services, ease of use, absence of serious bugs, visual appeal of an interface, or their personal preferences. The system, which loses its users, also inevitably will lose its developers, will stop evolving and, finally, will vanish. In fact, when there many similar OSSS, which offer similar services as, e.g., in P2P, audio/video player or text editing domains, these systems compete for users and developers similarly to biological species competing for resources such as food, water, territory, or sunlight. Since only a limited amount of resources (users, developers) are available, such competition usually leads to the dominance of a software system best suited for survival. As a result, several less successful software systems, which are less suited to compete, may either adapt (e.g., specialize for certain niche applications with a small but constant number of devoted users and less stringent competition) or die out.

To better explain forces and factors that affect software evolution, Lehman [19] has formulated 8 laws of software evolution, of which the first two laws are most important:

1. *Law of Continuing Change:* A system undergoes continuing changes until it is judged more cost effective to freeze and recreate it.
2. *Law of Increasing Complexity:* The complexity of a system increases with time, unless specific work is executed to maintain or reduce it.

Basically, these laws claim that software evolution is inevitable as new requirements constantly emerge and that there are limits to software usability and maintainability introduced by software aging and growth of its complexity. Lehman's laws have been empirically proved by studying projects developed in traditional industrial software development environments [20]. E.g., it has been established that most large software systems grow at an inverse square rate [19]. A statistical study [21] proposed the equation $S_i = S_{i-1} + \frac{E}{S_{i-1}^{\ 2}}$, where S_i is the number of source modules of the i-th release of a system, and E is a parameter. An explanation that is given for this equation states that for a system of size n (modules), the maximal number of possible interconnections is $n \cdot (n - 1)$. As the system grows, the introduction of new modules will impact a growing number of the existing ones and more effort will be required.

However, the study of Linux kernel [22] has discovered an apparent contradiction with Lehman's laws and with the statistical evidence from [21]. The study claims that Linux kernel exhibits a super-linear growth rate with most of the growth appearing due to new functionality and added hardware support, rather than to bug fixing.

2. Transition-based Model of Software Evolution

One of the aims of software evolution research is to establish the presence of stages in software evolution and to determine what exactly triggers them. Software evolution is commonly characterized as a slow process of incremental change. However, software systems also exhibit characteristics of sudden change during their evolution [23]. In many systems different software evolution phases often overlap themselves. The breakpoints (or junction points) between different phases are called punctuations or *transitions* [24]. These transitions separate two periods of stability (or equilibrium) in the evolution process. Transitions occur because as a system evolves, its structure must be regularly adapted to the changing requirements and environments. Within equilibrium periods, a system's architecture stays relatively stable, and it remains capable of accommodating forecasted changes in requirements. Changes are small and incremental, and they rarely violate the principles imposed by the architecture. However, the architecture may exhibit symptoms of gradual decay, erosion or drift [25], which are normally caused by the accumulating effects of maintenance activities, such as bug fixes and feature modifications. The system architecture needs to be evolved to counter such erosion. This can occur through gradual software changes such as corrections and code cleanups, or by sudden qualitative change which occurs in a short time.

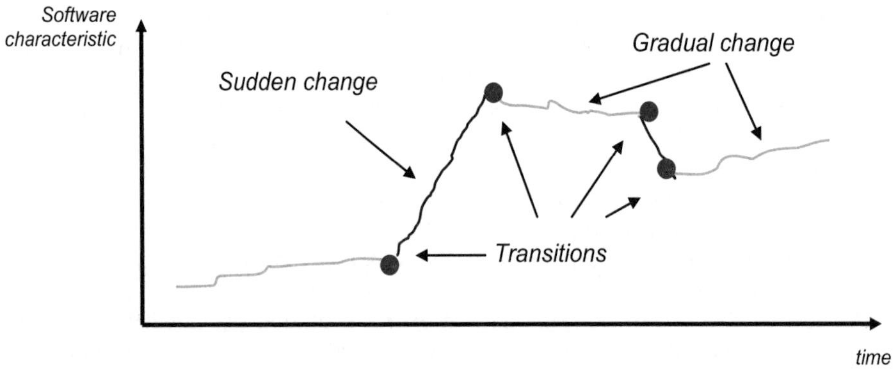

Figure 1. Types of changes in transition based model of software evolution

The view adopted in this paper considers software evolution as a transition-based process (see Figure 1), which consists of:

1) *gradual change*: a slow process of incremental change caused by accumulating maintenance steps or gradual decay, during which a system's architecture stays relatively stable;

2) *sudden change*: significant changes in the evolving system or in the process by which it is evolved, which occurs in a short time; and

3) *transitions*: breakpoints between stages, which represent significant changes in the evolving system or in the process by which it is evolved, and separate two stages in the evolution process.

3. Information Theory Approach to Software Evolution Measurement

3.1. Shannon Entropy

If a discrete information source (e.g., program source code) is treated as a Markov process, Shannon entropy *H* [26] can be used to measure how much information is generated by such process. The information source generates a series of symbols x_i belonging to an alphabet with size *N*. If symbols x_i are generated according to a known probability distribution $p(x_i)$, the entropy function *H* of a sequence *X* can be defined:

$$H(X) = -\sum_{i=1}^{n} p(x_i) \cdot \log_2 p(x_i) \tag{1}$$

Shannon entropy is a measure of the uncertainty associated with a random variable. If the message sequence (source code, in this case) consists of a series of symbols, the quantity of information reaches a maximum, when the sequence satisfies the statistical criterion that all possible subsequences should appear with roughly equal probability.

The higher the entropy of the system, the more complex the system's code becomes over time. Low entropy points to the existence of some repeated patterns of source code (e.g., code clones or snippets). Such repetitions may point to reuse of existing code by copying and pasting and indicate the need for code maintenance.

3.2. Kolmogorov Complexity

Kolmogorov Complexity [27] measures the 'complexity' (i.e., information content) of an object by the length of the smallest program that generates it. Generally, we have a domain object *x* and a description system (e.g., programming language) φ that maps from a description *w* (i.e., a program) to this object. Kolmogorov Complexity $K_\varphi(x)$ of an object *x* in the description system φ is the length of the shortest program in the description system φ capable of producing *x* on a universal computer:

$$K_\varphi(x) = \min_w \{\|w\| : \varphi_w = x\} \tag{2}$$

Kolmogorov Complexity $K_\varphi(x)$ is the minimal quantity of information required to generate *x* by an algorithm, and is the ultimate lower bound of information content. Unfortunately, it cannot be computed in the general case and must be approximated. Usually, compression algorithms are used to give an upper bound to Kolmogorov Complexity. Suppose that we have a compression algorithm C_i. Then, a shortest compression of *w* in the description system φ will give the upper bound to information content in *x*:

$$K_\varphi(x) \le C(x) := \min_i \{\|C_i\|, \phi_{C_i} = x\} \tag{3}$$

4. Evolution Curve Method for Software Evolution Visualization

The addition of new features to a software system leads to the change of basic characteristics (complexity/entropy) of the system. These characteristics are related to the Lehman's Second Law [19], which suggests the need for maintenance activities to reduce complexity that increases as new features are added to the system. We use the change of software size and complexity as a means to determine different stages of evolution of a software system. Here we propose a novel software evolution visualization method, called *Evolution curve* (E-curve). This method is inspired by Z-curve [28] and DNA walk [29] methods used in analysing complex genetic sequences.

The E-curve is composed of a series of nodes $E_i = (x_i, y_i)$, whose coordinates are x_i and y_i (i=1,2,...,N), where N is the number of versions of the analyzed software system. The nodes E_i are connected sequentially with straight lines. The coordinates x_i and y_i are calculated iteratively as follows:

$$x_i = \begin{cases} x_{i-1}+1, & if \quad K_i > K_{i-1} \\ x_{i-1}, & if \quad K_i = K_{i-1} \\ x_{i-1}-1 & if \quad K_i < K_{i-1} \end{cases} \tag{4}$$

where K_i is the Kolmogorov Complexity of the i-th version of a software system;

$$y_i = \begin{cases} y_{i-1}+1, & if \quad H_i > H_{i-1} \\ y_{i-1}, & if \quad H_i = H_{i-1} \\ y_{i-1}-1 & if \quad H_i < H_{i-1} \end{cases} \tag{5}$$

where H_i is the Shannon entropy of the i-th version of a system; $x_0 = 0$, $y_0 = 0$.

The two components of the E-curve, x_i (relative information content) and y_i (relative complexity), represent two independent (orthogonal) characteristics of software evolution of the studied system:

- the x-component of a E-curve x_i represents the amount of information contained in a software system and is an estimation of software size;
- the y-component of a E-curve y_i represents the information entropy of a software system and is an estimation of software complexity.

Based on the behaviour of the E-curve, we can identify 4 major stages of software evolution process (Figure 2):

- *Software Growth*, when $K_i > K_{i-1}$ and $H_i > H_{i-1}$. It is characterized by increase both in actual information content of a system (software size) and its complexity.
- *Software Maintenance*, when $K_i > K_{i-1}$ and $H_i < H_{i-1}$. It is characterized by increase in information content of a system and decrease of its complexity. In other words, software becomes simpler often at a cost of its size.
- *Software Improvement*, when $K_i < K_{i-1}$ and $H_i > H_{i-1}$. It is characterized by decrease in information content of a system and increase in its complexity, i.e., software becomes more complex and generic.

- *Software Shrink*, when $K_i < K_{i-1}$ and $H_i < H_{i-1}$. It is characterized by decrease both in information content of a system and its complexity. In other words, the functionality of a system is reduced. Sustainable software shrink is rarely observed in successful software projects.

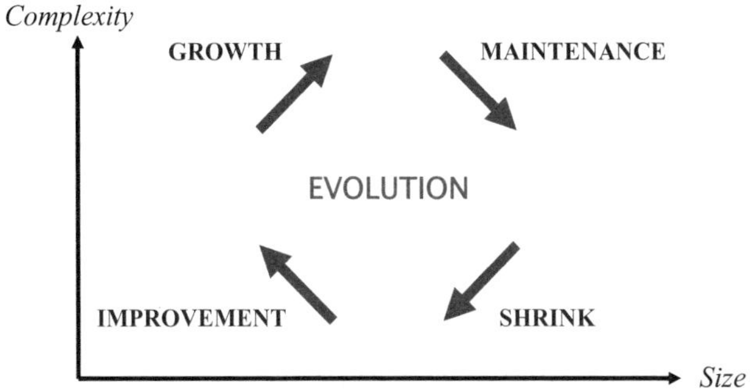

Figure 2. Software evolution stages

The trends in the behaviour of the E-curve also can be used identify the initial development status of the analyzed software system: actively developed systems show long upward trends, while mature systems show long downward trends, which correspond to software maintenance and improvement.

5. Case Study: eMule

eMule [30] is one of the biggest P2P file sharing clients around the world. eMule is free software, released under the GNU General Public License. eMule is coded in Microsoft Visual C++ using Microsoft Foundation Classes. The source code of eMule was first released at version 0.02 and published on SourceForge on July 6, 2002. The latest release, 047c, contains 222,680 lines of code. This system is actively developed by 5 developers. Current development status is "Production/Stable".

For analysis, 68 versions of eMule source code were used starting from release no. 002 to release no. 047c, which span a period of over 4 years. Source code files of each version were concatenated and then analyzed using Shannon entropy and Kolmogorov Complexity metrics. For estimation of Kolmogorov Complexity, *zzip* compression tool was used, which implements Burrows-Wheeler transform (BWT) algorithm.

Shannon entropy graph (see Figure 3) shows how source code entropy has been changing across different program versions. Entropy increase represents source code complexity growth and vice versa. The plot shows that major changes have occurred in version no. 10 (015a), where entropy has increased significantly, and version no. 14 (018a), where entropy has decreased. A major trend that could be noticed is that source code complexity was growing until its maximum value at version no. 43 (030a), where it stabilized and later decreased slightly. Thus the system has reached its complexity limits and later major development effort is directed and maintaining and improving source code rather than including support of major new features.

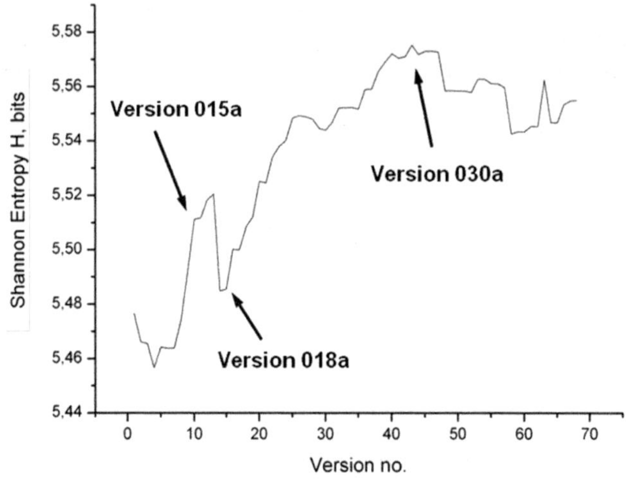

Figure 3. Shannon entropy of eMule system versions

In Figure 4 we can see, how information content measured using Kolmogorov complexity grows depending upon version no. This dependability can be fitted to a 2-nd degree polynomial. We can see that growth is fairly smooth without large deviations and we basically cannot identify any meaningful evolution stages from this graph. However, we still can use this graph to forecast the size of the future system versions.

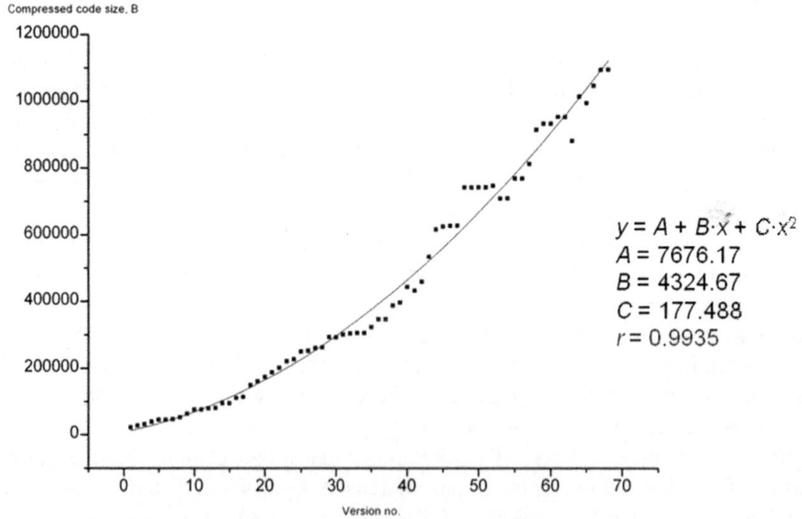

Figure 4. Size of eMule system versions

Also we have noticed that Kolmogorov's complexity K correlates nicely with McCabe's Cyclomatic Complexity MVG [31] (Figure 5). Both metrics measure the complexity of a program. Cyclomatic complexity measures the number of linearly independent paths through a program's source code, and is a metric of *structural* complexity of a program. And Kolmogorov complexity measures the length of the shortest description required to generate a program, and is a metric of *informational* complexity of a system. Such correlation means that both complexities computed using different methods indeed carry important information on the complexity of a program.

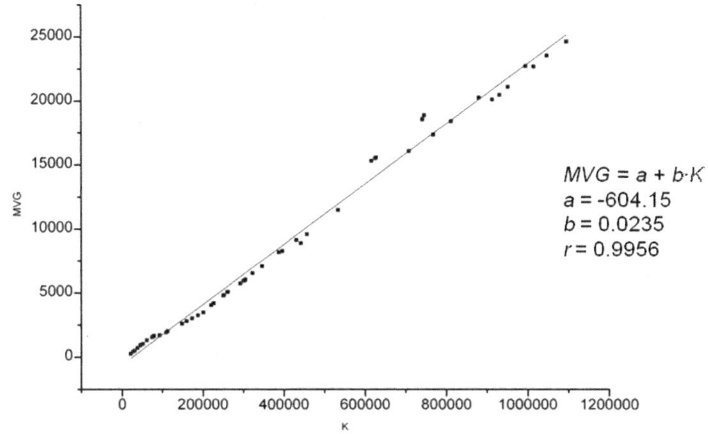

Figure 5. Size of eMule system versions

Finally, Figure 6 shows the E-curve constructed for the eMule software system. From the E-curve graph, we can identify 5 major successive stages in eMule evolution: 1) a growth stage until release no. 023b, 2) a rather short maintenance stage until release no. 025b, 3) a second growth stage until release no. 030e, 4) a second maintenance stage until release no. 044b, followed by 5) a short improvement stage.

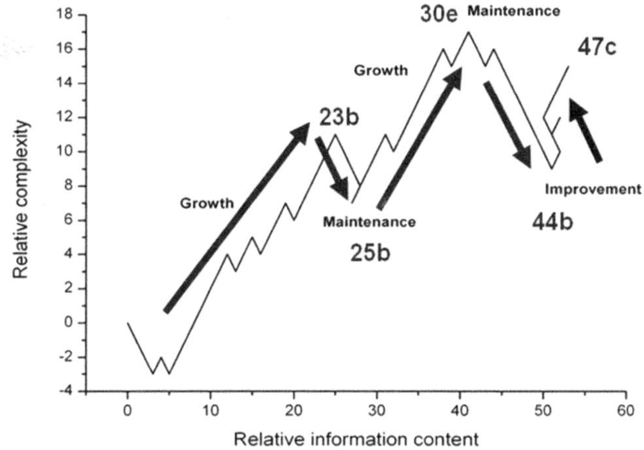

Figure 6. Evolution curve of eMule system

The characteristics of major transition points in the eMule evolution process are summarized in Table 1.

Table 1. Characteristics of eMule system evolution transition points.

Ver. no.	Rel. no.	Source code size, B	Inf. content, B	Shannon entropy, b	E-curve node coordinates		Comments
					x_i	y_i	
1	0.02	130,092	21,545	5.4767	0	0	First release
26	0.23b	1,564,188	251,688	5.5493	25	11	End of 1-st growth stage
30	0.25b	1,815,160	292,587	5.5439	27	7	End of 1-st maintenance stage
47	0.30e	4,049,007	627,521	5.5728	42	16	End of 2-nd growth stage
58	0.44b	5,943,455	913,924	5.5426	51	9	End of 2-nd maintenance stage
68	0.47c	7,258,205	1,095,248	5.5549	53	15	Latest release

Does the E-curve for the eMule system have anything to do with reality? From Figure 6 and Table 1 we can see that one of the most significant transitions in the eMule evolution happened on or after version 0.30e. The eMule's changelog (see Figure 7) can provide some explanation to this event. The eMule system is based on the Kad network. The Kad network is a peer-to-peer (P2P) network which implements the Kademlia P2P overlay protocol. The person who developed the Kad code and also was one of the authors of Kademlia has left the project. It appears that the code he left was functional, but untested. So, the remaining developers of eMule have concentrated on bug fixing and code maintenance rather than on development of new features.

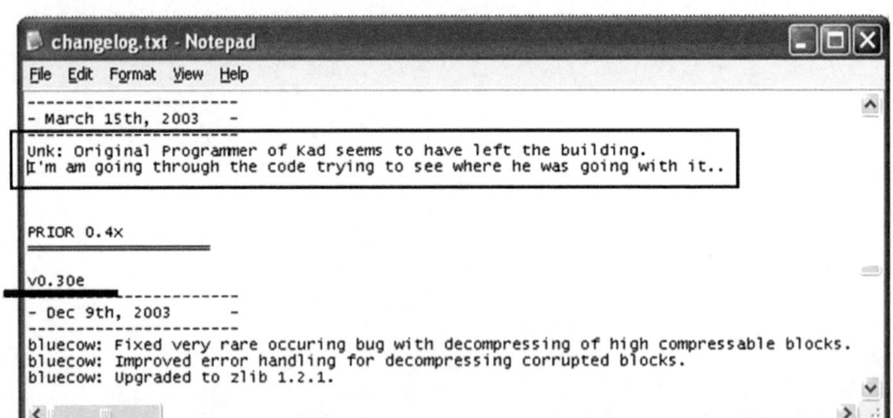

Figure 7. Snapshot of eMule's changelog

6. Conclusion

Our case study shows that evolution process of open-source software can be coarsely divided into four stages: 1) software growth, where the size and complexity of developed software is increasing, 2) software maintenance, where the aim of the developer is to contain complexity and fix software bugs, 3) software improvement, where the aim is to contain software system size at a cost of increasing complexity, and 4) software shrink, when both software size and its complexity is trimmed.

These software evolution stages can repeat several times during the software system's life cycle, or even overlap themselves. The need for such repeating stages can be justified by the Lehman's Second Evolution Law, which claims that every growth of a large software system must be followed by necessary maintenance actions to reduce the growth of source code complexity.

We can identify these software evolution stages using the proposed Evolution curve (E-curve) method, which can visualize software evolution process based on the Kolmogorov Complexity and Shannon entropy characteristics of software source code. The E-curve also can identify the initial development status of the analyzed software system: actively developed systems show long growth trends, while mature systems show maintenance and improvement trends.

Furthermore, the E-curve method is independent from the implementation language of the analyzed software system, because both metrics, Shannon entropy and Kolmogorov complexity, are computed on plain source code files with no regard to the syntax or semantics of the particular programming language.

Future work will focus on the extension of the E-curve method with other entropy measures such as block entropy and Rényi entropies, which could allow to reveal more interesting evolution events and transition points hidden in software source code.

References

[1] Hales, D., & Douce, C. (2002) Modelling Software Organisations, In Kuljis, J., Baldwin, L., & R. Scoble (eds), Proc. of Annual Workshop on Psychology of Programming (PPIG 2002), June 18-21, Brunel University, UK, pp. 140–149.

[2] Damaševičius, R. (2007) Analysis of Software Design Artifacts for Socio-Technical Aspects. INFOCOMP Journal of Computer Science 6(4): 7–16.

[3] Erlikh, L. (2002) Leveraging legacy system dollars for e-business. IEEE IT Pro, May/June 2000, 17–23.

[4] Li, W., & Talburt, J. (1998) Empirically Analyzing Object-Oriented Software Evolution. Journal of Object-Oriented Programming, 11 (5): 15-19.

[5] Kemerer, C.F., & Slaughter, S. (1999) An Empirical Approach to Studying Software Evolution. IEEE Transactions on Software Engineering, 25(4): 493-509.

[6] Girard, J.-F., Verlage, M., & Ganesan, D. (2004) Monitoring the Evolution of an OO System with Metrics: An Experience from the Stock Market Software Domain. IEEE Int. Conf. on Software Maintenance (ICSM 2004), September 11-17, Chicago, IL, USA, pp. 360–367.

[7] Kothari, J., Denton, T., Shokoufandeh, A., Mancoridis, S., & Hassan, A.E. (2006) Studying the Evolution of Software Systems Using Change Clusters. Proc. of Int. Conf. on Program Comprehension (ICPC 2006), June 14-16, Athens, Greece, pp, 46–55.

[8] Robles, G., González-Barahona, J.M., Michlmayr, M., & Amor. J.J. (2006) Mining large software compilations over time: another perspective of software evolution. Proc. of Int. Workshop on Mining Software Repositories (MSR 2006), May 22-23, Shanghai, China, pp. 3–9.

[9] Capiluppi, A., & Ramil, J.F. (2004) Studying the evolution of open source systems at different levels of granularity: two case studies. Proc. of 7th Int. Workshop on Principles of Software Evolution (IWPSE 2004), September 6-7, Kyoto, Japan, pp. 113–118.

[10] Li, W., Etzkorn, L., Davis, C., & Talburt, J. (2000) An empirical study of object-oriented system evolution. Information and Software Technology Journal, 42 (6): 373 – 381.
[11] Chapin, N. (2002) Entropy-Metric for Systems with COTS Software. Proc. of the Eight IEEE Symposium on Software Metrics (METRICS 2002), June 4-7, Ottawa, Canada, pp. 173–181.
[12] Harrison, W. (1992) An entropy–based measure of software complexity. IEEE Trans. on Software Engineering 18(11): 1025–1029.
[13] Abd-El-Hafiz, S.K. (2001) Entropies as measures of software information. Proc. of IEEE Int. Conf. on Software Maintenance (ICSM 2001), November 6-10, Florence, Italy, pp. 110–117.
[14] Hassan, A.E., & Holt, R.C. (2003). Studying the Chaos of Code Development. Proc. of Working Conf. on Reverse Engineering (WCRE 2003), November 13-16, Victoria, BC, Canada, pp. 123–133.
[15] Diehl, S. (2007) Software Visualization: Visualizing the Structure, Behaviour, and Evolution of Software. Springer.
[16] Raymond, E.S. (1999) The Cathedral and the Bazaar: Musings on Linux and Open Source by an Accidental Revolutionary. O'Reilly and Associates.
[17] O'Reilly, T. (1999) Lessons from Open-Source Software Development. Communications of the ACM, 42(4): 33-37.
[18] Heylighen, F. (1992) Principles of Systems and Cybernetics: an evolutionary perspective. In Trappl, R. (ed), Cybernetics and Systems '92, p. 3-10. World Science, Singapore.
[19] Lehman, M.M., Ramil, J.F., Wernick, P., Perry, D.E., & Turski, W.M. (1997) Metrics and Laws of Software Evolution - The Nineties View. IEEE METRICS 1997, p. 20.
[20] Scacchi, W.(2006) Understanding Open Source Software Evolution. In Madhavji, N.H., Lehman, M.M., Ramil, J.F., & Perry, D. (eds), Software Evolution and Feedback, John Wiley and Sons, New York.
[21] Turski, W.M. (1996). Reference model for smooth growth of software systems. IEEE Trans. on Software Engineering 22(8): 599–600.
[22] Godfrey, M., & Tu, Q. (2000) Evolution in Open Source Software: A Case Study. Proc. of Int. Conf. on Software Maintenance (ICSM 2000), October 11-14, San Jose, CA, USA, pp. 131–142.
[23] Aoyama, M. (2001) Continuous and discontinuous software evolution: Aspects of software evolution across multiple produce lines. Proc. of Int. Workshop on Principles of Software Evolution, September 10-11, Vienna, Austria, pp. 87–90.
[24] Anton, A., & Potts, C. (2001) Functional Paleontology: System Evolution as the User Sees It. Proc. of 23rd Int. Conf. on Software Engineering (ICSE), Toronto, Canada, May 12-19, pp. 421–430.
[25] Perry, D.E., & Wolf, A.L. (1992) Foundations for the study of software architecture. ACM Software Engineering Notes, 17(4): 40–52.
[26] Shannon, C.E., & Weaver, W. (1963) The Mathematical Theory of Communication. University of Illinois Press.
[27] Li, M., & Vitanyi, P. (1997) An Introduction to Kolmogorov Complexity and Its Applications, 2nd Edition, Springer Verlag.
[28] Zhang, R., & Zhang, C.T. (1994) Z Curves, an Intuitive Tool for Visualizing and Analyzing DNA sequences. J. Biomol. Struc. Dynamics, 11: 767–782.
[29] Paxia, S., Rudra, A., Zhou, Y., & Mishra, B. (2002) A Random Walk down the Genomes: DNA Evolution in VALIS. IEEE Computer, 35(7): 73-79.
[30] eMule. (available at http://sourceforge.net/projects/emule/)
[31] McCabe, T.J., & Watson, A.H. (1994) Software Complexity. Crosstalk, Journal of Defense Software Engineering, 7(12): 5-9.

Databases and Information Systems V
H.-M. Haav and A. Kalja (Eds.)
IOS Press, 2009

doi:10.3233/978-1-58603-939-4-217

A New XML Schema Matching Approach Using Prüfer Sequences

Alsayed ALGERGAWY [1], Eike SCHALLEHN and Gunter SAAKE
Department of Computer Science, Otto-von-Guericke University, 39106 Magdeburg, Germany

Abstract. Motivated by the fact that the most prominent feature in an XML schema is its hierarchical structure, we propose a new structure matching approach for XML schema matching. Our approach is based on the node context, which is reflected by its ancestor and its descendants including both the immediate children and the leaves of subtrees rooted at the element. To this end and to quickly extract context information of the element, we present XML schemas as sequences of labels and numbers by Prüfer's method that constructs a one-to-one correspondence between schema trees and sequences. We benefit from label sequences to determine terminological semantic similarities between two schema concepts. We then develop a novel structural algorithm which is based on number sequences and is used to prune many false positive candidates. Finally, we combine two similarity measures to obtain the total similarity between schema' elements. Our experimental results demonstrate the performance benefits of our proposed approach.

Keywords. schema matching, Prüfer sequence, node context, structural matching

Introduction

The extensible markup language XML emerged as a standard for information representation and exchange on the Web. As a result, efforts to develop good information integration technology for the growing number of XML data sources become essential. Identifying semantic correspondences among heterogeneous data sources is the biggest obstacle for developing such the integrated schema. The process of identifying these correspondences is called *schema matching*.

Existing schema matching systems such as Cupid [1], COMA/COMA++ [2,3], LSD [4], BTreeMatch [5], and S-Match [6] rely heavily on either rule-based approaches or learner-based approaches. In the rule-based systems, schemas to be matched are represented as schema trees or schema graphs which in turn requires traversing these trees (or graphs) many times. On the other hand, learning-based systems need much pre-effort to train their learners. As a consequence, especially in large number and large-scale schemas and dynamic environments, matching performance declines radically.

Motivated by the above challenges and by the fact that the most prominent feature for an XML schema is its hierarchical structure, in this paper, we propose a novel approach

[1]Corresponding Author: Department of Computer Science, Otto-von-Guericke University, 39106 Magdeburg, Germany; E-mail: alshahat@iti.cs.uni-magdeburg.de

for matching XML schemas. The proposed approach is a sequence-based, wherein we propose a new tree encoding method that is based on Prüfer Sequences. We transform schemas to be matched into sequences of labels and numbers. The first, *label sequence*, is exploited by a linguistic matcher to determine terminological similarities between schemas elements. The second, *number sequence*, is used to compute structural similarities and prunes false positive candidates.

By representing schema trees as Prüfer Sequences we need to traverse these trees only once to construct these sequences. Prüfer Sequences construct a one-to-one correspondence between schema trees and sequences. Then, we develop a novel structural matching algorithm which captures semantic information existing in label sequences and structural information embedded in number sequences.

To summarize, the main contributions of our approach are: we develop an effective/efficient sequence-based approach to automatically determine the similarity between two schemas' elements, we introduce a new structural matching algorithm based on Prüfer Sequences, and we have developed several experiments to show the effectiveness/efficiency of our approach.

1. Background and Motivations

An XML schema is a set of schema components. In general, there are 13 kinds of components in all, falling into three categories. In this paper, we consider only the first two categories, the *primary components* and the *secondary components*, while the other category, helper components such as wildcard and attribute uses are left for ongoing work.

XML schemas can be modeled as rooted, ordered, labeled trees $T = (N, E, Lab)$ where N is a set of nodes, E is a set of edges, and Lab is a set of node labels. Each component is represented as a node in the tree. We categorize nodes into *atomic nodes*, which have no outgoing edges and represent leaf nodes and *complex nodes*, which are the internal nodes in the schema tree. Edges are used to represent relationships between two components.

Recently, much research effort has been focused on matching XML schemas. Identifying semantic correspondences between schema components is one of the core operations in XML database integration, in E-business, in the Semantic Web,etc. Consequently, many schema matching systems have been developed. Some of them are rule-based systems and the other are learning-based systems.

Rule-based Systems: Most of these systems start with transforming schemas into schema trees such as Cupid [1] and BtreeMatch [5] or schema graphs such as COMA/COMA++ [2,3], SF [7], and S-Match [6]. Then they apply corresponding matching algorithms on schema tress/graphs. Most of them are hybrid approaches which utilize both linguistic and structural matching. To enhance linguistic matchers, these systems employe auxiliary information systems such as WordNet [7] or external dictionaries [2,3,1] which impacts matching performance. In their structural matchers, they need to traverse schema tress/graphs many times which also impact matching performance. Moreover matching quality of most of these systems typically decreases for large-scale schemas. Our propose system is also a schema-based approach. However, each schema tree is represented using two sequences which capture both tree semantic information and tree structure. This leads to a space efficient representation and an efficient time response when compared to the state-of-the-art systems.

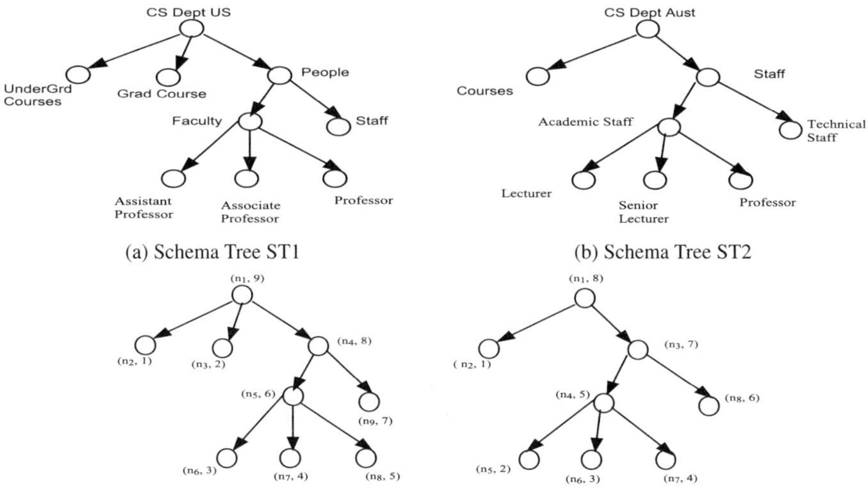

(c) Corresponding OIDs and post-order numbers

Figure 1. Computer science department schemas

Learning-based Systems: These systems utilize both schema-based and instance-based information. They depend largely on previous phases such as the training phase using unsupervised learning in SemInt [8], using machine learning in LSD [4], or using neural network-based partial least squares in [9]. The advantage of these approaches is that it can empirically learn the similarities among data based on their instance values. The disadvantage of using learner-based approaches is that instance data is generally available in very vast quantity. Hence, the computational cost is very expensive, which affects on schema matching performance

Motivations: To the best of our knowledge no work for matching XML schemas which is based on *Prüer Sequences* exists. Most of existing matching systems rely heavily on matching schema trees/graphs. In addition, these systems perform poorly when dealing with large-scale schemas. These shortcomings have motivated us to develop an XML schema matching system based on Prüfer Sequences, called *XPrüM.*

1.1. A Schema Matching Example

To describe the operation of our approach, we use the example found in [10]. It describes two XML schemas, shown in Figure 1(a and b), that represent organization in universities from different countries and have been widely used in the literature. The task is to discover semantic correspondences between two schemas' elements [2].

2. The Proposed System

In this section, we shall describe the core parts of the XML matching system. As shown in Figure 2, it has two main phases: *schema preparation* and *schema matching*. First,

[2]in this paper, we consider only element level mappings

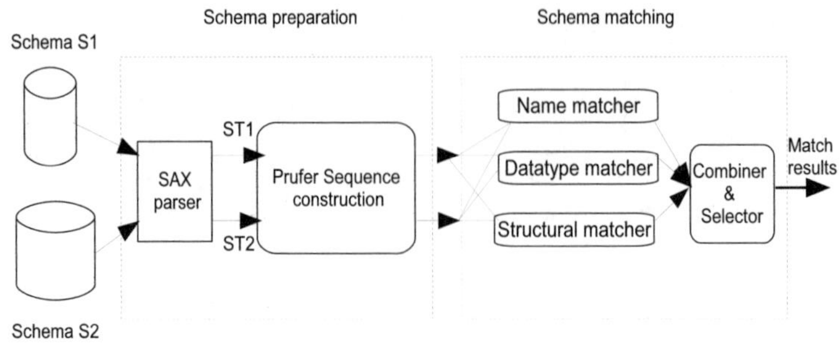

Figure 2. Matching process phases

schemas are parsed using a SAX parser [3] and represented internally as schema trees. Then, using the Prüfer sequence method, we extract both label sequences and number sequences. The schema matching part discovers the set of matches between two schemas employing both sequences.

2.1. Prüfer Sequences Construction

We now describe the tree sequence representation method, which provides a bijection between ordered, labeled trees and sequences. This representation is inspired from classical *Prüfer sequences* [11] and particularly from what is called *Consolidated Prüfer Sequence CPS* proposed in [12].

CPS of a schema tree ST consists of two sequences, Number Prüfer Sequence *NPS* and Label Prüfer Sequence *LPS*. They are constructed by doing a *post-order traversal* that tags each node in the tree with a unique traversal number. NPS is then constructed iteratively by removing the node with the smallest traversal number and appending its parent node number to the already structured partial sequence. LPS is constructed similarly but by taken the node labels of deleted nodes instead of their parent node numbers. Both NPS and LPS convey completely different but complementary information—NPS that is constructed from unique post-order traversal numbers gives wealthy tree structure information and LPS gives the labels for tree nodes. CPS representation thus provides a bijection between ordered, labeled trees and sequences. Therefore, CPS = (NPS, LPS) uniquely represents a rooted, ordered, labeled tree, where each entry in the CPS corresponds to an edge in the schema tree. For more details see [12].

Example 1: Consider schema trees *ST1* and *ST2* shown in Figure 1 (c), each node is associated with its *OID* and its post order number. Table 1 illustrates CPS for ST1 and ST2. For example, CPS of ST1 can be written as the NPS(ST1)= 9 9 6 6 6 8 8 9 -, and the LPS(ST1).name= *UnderGrad Courses, Grad Courses, Assistant Professor, Associate Professor, Professor, Faculty, Staff, People, CS Dept US.*

2.2. Schema Matching

Schema matching algorithms operate on the sequential representation of two schema trees *ST1* and *ST2* and discover semantic correspondences between them. Generally

[3]http://www.saxproject.org

Table 1. Schema tree nodes properties.

Schema Tree ST1				Schema Tree ST2			
NPS	*LPS*			*NPS*	*LPS*		
	OID	*name*	*type/data type*		*OID*	*name*	*type/data type*
9	n_2	UnderGrad Courses	element/string	8	n_2	Courses	element/string
9	n_3	Grad Courses	element/string	5	n_5	Lecturer	element/string
6	n_6	Assistant Professor	element/string	5	n_6	Senior Lecturer	element/string
6	n_7	Associate Professor	element/string	5	n_7	Professor	element/string
6	n_8	Professor	element/string	7	n_4	Academic Staff	element/-
8	n_5	faculty	element/-	7	n_8	Technical Staff	element/string
8	n_9	Staff	element/string	8	n_3	Staff	element/-
9	n_4	People	element/-	-	n_1	CS Dept Aust	element/-
-	n_1	CS Dept US	element/-				

speaking, the process of schema matching is performed, as shown in Figure 2, in two steps—*element matchers* and *combiner & selector.*

First, a degree of similarity is computed automatically for all element pairs using the element matcher phase. Recent empirical analysis shows that there is no single dominant element matcher that performs best, regardless of the data model and application domain [13]. As a result, we should exploit different kinds of element matchers. In our approach, we make use of *name matcher*; to exploit element' names, *datatype matcher*; to exploit element' types/datatypes, and *structural matcher*; to exploit element' structural contexts. After a degree of similarity is computed, how to combine different similarities from different element matchers and select top-K mappings are addressed in the second step.

In the following section, we shall describe *element matcher* algorithms. Without loss of generality, let the number of nodes in *ST1* and *ST2* are *n* and *m*, respectively.

3. Element Matcher Algorithms

To identify semantic correspondences between two schema trees, it is necessary to compute the similarity between their elements. We make use of three basic schema-based matchers (1) linguistic matching, (2) datatype compatibility, and (3) structural matching.

3.1. Linguistic Matching

The aim of this phase is to obtain an initial matching between two schema trees based on the similarity of their names. For the sake of simplicity and towards building more efficient framework, we do not make use of any external dictionary or ontology. To compute linguistic similarity between two elements'names s_1 and s_2, we use the following three similarity measures. The first one is $sim_{edit}(s_1, s_2) = \frac{max(|s_1|,|s_2|) - editDistance(s_1,s_2)}{max(|s_1|,|s_2|)}$ where *editDistance(*s_1*,* s_2*)* is the minimum number of character insertion and deletion operations needed to transform one string to the other. The second similarity measure is based on the number of different trigrams in the two strings: $sim_{tri}(s_1, s_2) = \frac{2\times|tri(s_1)\bigcap tri(s_2)|}{|tri(s_1)|+|tri(s_2)|}$ where *tri(*s_1*)* is the set of trigrams in s_1. The third similarity measure is based on Jaro-Winkler distance. The Jaro-Winkler distance metric is designed and best suited for short strings such as person names. The Jaro similarity measure is given by

$sim_{jaro}(s_1, s_2) = \frac{1}{3} \times (\frac{m}{|s_1|} + \frac{m}{|s_2|} - \frac{m-t}{m})$ where *m* is the number of matching characters and *t* is the number of transpositions.

The linguistic matching between two schema tree nodes is computed as the combination (weighted sum) of the above three similarity values.

3.2. Datatype Compatibility

We propose the use of datatype compatibility to improve linguistic similarity between the two schema trees' nodes especially atomic nodes. To this end, we make use of built-in XML datatypes hierarchy [4] in order to compute datatype compatibility coefficients. Based on XML schema datatype hierarchy, we build a datatype compatibility table as the one used in [1].

After computing datatype compatibility coefficients we can adjust linguistic similarity values. The result of the above process is an adjusted linguistic similarity matrix. To simplify the problem, in the proposed solution we do not consider datatype, defined by user.

3.3. Structural Matching

The matching algorithms described above consider only the label information and ignore the structural information. There can be multiple match candidates which differ in structure but have the same label. The structural matching algorithm prunes these false positive candidates by considering the structural information represented in the *NPS* sequence.

Our structural matcher is motivated by the fact that the most prominent feature in an XML schema is its hierarchical structure. This matcher is based on the node context, which is reflected by its ancestors and its descendants. The descendants of an element include both its immediate children and the leaves of the subtrees rooted at the element. The immediate children reflect its basic structure, while the leaves reflect the element's content. In this paper, as in [14,15], we consider only three kinds of node contexts depending on its position in the schema tree:

- *The child context* of a node n_i is defined as the set of its immediate children nodes including attributes and subelements. The child context of an atomic node is an empty set.
- *The leaf context* of a node n_i is defined as the set of leaf nodes of subtrees rooted at node n_i.
- *The ancestor context* of a node n_i is defined as the path extending from the root node to the node n_i. The ancestor of the root node is an empty path.

The context of a node is the combination of its *ancestor context*, its *child context*, and its *leaf context*. Two nodes are structurally similar if they have similar contexts. To measure the structural similarity between two nodes, we compute respectively the similarity of their child, ancestor, leaf contexts. Before we delve into the details of how to measure the structural similarity, we shall build a connection between the node context and the *NPS* sequence. To build such a connection , we first illustrate the structural features behind the *NPS* sequence. These features are:

[4] http://www.w3.org/TR/2001/REC-xmlschema-2-20010502/

The child context: The representation of a schema tree as Prüfer sequence facilitates the determination of structural properties of the schema tree. Each entry in the *CPS* presents an edge from the parent node *NPS* to its immediate child node *LPS*. Therefor, we could easily obtain the number of immediate children of a non-leaf node from the *NPS* sequence by counting its post-order traversal number in the sequence, and also we could identify these children. For example, in *Example 1, ST1*, the post-order number of node n_1 is 9. This number repeats three times. This means that it has three immediate children n_2, n_3, n_4.

The leaf context: First we notice that nodes whose post-order numbers do not appear in the *NPS* sequence are atomic nodes. From this notice and from the child context we could recursively obtain the leaf context for a certain node. For example, in *Example 1, ST1*, nodes n_2, n_3, n_6, n_7, n_8, n_9 are leaf nodes. Node n_5 has three children n_6, n_7, n_8, which are leaves. Then they are the leaf context set of node n_5.

The ancestor context: For a non-atomic node, we obtain the ancestor context by scanning the *NPS* sequence from left to right and identifying the numbers which are greater than post-order number of the node until the first occurrence of the root node. While scanning from left to right, we ignore nodes whose post-order numbers are less than post-order numbers of already scanned nodes. For a leaf node, the ancestor context is the ancestor context of its parent union the parent itself. For example, in *Example 1, ST1*, the ancestor context of node n_5 (non-atomic node) is the path n_1/n_4. While the ancestor context of node n_6 (atomic node) is the path $n_1/n_4/n_5$.

3.3.1. Structural Context Similarity Algorithm

Structural node context defined above relies on the notion of path and set. In order to compare two ancestor contexts, we essentially compare their corresponding paths. On the other hand, in order to compare two child contexts and/or leaf contexts, we need to compare their corresponding sets.

Although path comparison has been widely used, however they rely on strong matching following the two crisp constraints: node constraint and edge constraint. Under such constraints paths that are semantically similar may be considered as unmatched or paths that are not semantically similar may be considered as matched. Hence, these constraints should be soft or relaxed. Several works in query answering have proposed relaxation issues to approximate answering of queries [16]. Examples of such relaxation are allowing matching paths even when nodes are not embedded in a same manner or in the same order and allowing two elements within each path to be matched even if they are not identical but their linguistic similarity exceeds a fixed threshold [15]. In the following we describe how to compute three structural context measures:

Child Context Algorithm: To obtain the child context similarity between two nodes, we compare the two child context sets for the two nodes. To this end, see *Algorithm 1*, we first extract the child context set for each node from *NPS* and *LPS* sequences. Second, we get the linguistic similarity between each pair of children in the two sets. Third, we select the matching pairs with maximum similarity values. And finally, we take the average of best similarity values.

Algorithm 1 Child Context Algorithm: $child\_context(n_{ST1}, n_{ST2})$

```
Require: n_ST1 & n_ST1
Ensure: a child context similarity child_sim
  if n_ST1 or s_ST2 is atomic then
    return 0;
  else
    sum ← 0; max ← 0;
    child_set1 ← extractChildNode(n_ST1);
    child_set2 ← extractChildNode(n_ST2);
    while n_i in child_set1 do
      while n_j in child_set2 do
        sim ← linguistic(n_i, n_j);
        if sim > max then
          max ← sim;
        end if
      end while
      sum ← sum + max;
    end while
    return average(sum);
  end if
```

Leaf Context Algorithm: Before we delve into details of computing leaf context similarity, we shall first introduce the notion of *gap* between two tree nodes.

Definition 1. The gap between two nodes n_1 and n_2 is defined as the difference between the postorder numbers of the nodes n_1 and n_2.

To compute the leaf context similarity between two nodes, we compare their leaf context sets. To this end, first, we extract the leaf context set for each node. Second, we determine the gap between each node and its leaf context set. We call this vector the gap vector. Third, we apply the cosine measure between two vectors (see *Algorithm 2)*.

Example 2. For the two schema trees shown in *Example 1*. The leaf context set of n_1 of *ST1* leaf_set (n_1(9))={n_2*(1)*, n_3*(2)*, n_6*(3)*, n_7*(4)*, n_8*(5)*, n_9(7)} and the leaf context set of n_1 of *ST2* leaf_set (n_1(8))={n_2*(1)*, n_5*(2)*, n_6*(3)*, n_7*(4)*, n_8*(5)*}. The gap vector of (n_{1ST1}) is *gapvec*(n_{1ST1})={8,7,2,6,4,5} and the gap vector of (n_{1ST2}) is *gapvec*(n_{1ST2})={7,6,5,4,2}. The cosine measure CM of the two vectors gives *CM*(v_1,v_2)*=0.9*. Then the leaf context similarity between nodes n_{1ST1} and n_{1ST2} is 0.9. Similarly, leaf context similarity between n_{5ST1} and n_{4ST2} is 1.0 and n_{4ST1} and n_{3ST2} is 1.0

Ancestor Context Similarity: The ancestor context similarity captures the similarity between two nodes based on their ancestor contexts. As mentioned before, the ancestor context for a given node n_i is the path from the root to n_i. To compute the ancestor similarity between two nodes n_1 and n_2, first we extract each ancestor context from the *NPS* sequence, say path P_1 for n_1 and path P_2 for n_2. Second, we compare two paths. To compare two paths, we use three of four scores established in [17] and reused in [15]. The scores are:

- *LCS*(P_1,P_2): We use this score to ensure that path P_1 includes most of the nodes of P_2 in the right order. To this end, we use a classical dynamic programming

Algorithm 2 Leaf Context Algorithm: $leaf\_context(n_{ST1}, n_{ST2})$

Require: n_{ST1} & n_{ST1}
Ensure: a leaf context similarity $leaf\_sim$
  if n_{ST1} or s_{ST2} is atomic **then**
    $return$ 0;
  else
    $v_1 \leftarrow nodegapvector(n_{ST1});$
    $v_2 \leftarrow nodegapvector(n_{ST2});$
    $return\ CM(v_1, v_2);$
  end if

algorithm in order to compute the Longest Common Subsequence LCS. Then we normalize this score in [0,1] by the length of path P_1. The normalized score is given by: $LCS_n(P_1, P_2) = |LCS(P_1, P_2)|/|P_1|$

- *GAPS(P_1,P_2)*: We use this measure to ensure that the occurrences of the P_1 nodes in P_2 are close to each other. We propose to use another version of the LCS algorithm in order to capture the LCS alignment with minimum gaps. In addition we propose to normalize it by the length of the common subsequence added to the gaps value so as to ensure that the total score will be inferior to 1 as follows: $GAPS(P_1, P_2) = \frac{gaps}{gaps+LSC(P_1,P_2)}$
- *LD(P_1,P_2)*: Finally, in order to give higher values to source paths whose lengths is similar to target paths, we compute the length difference *ld* between P_2 and *LCS(P_1,P_2)* normalized by the length of P_2. Thus the final factor that evaluates the length difference can be computed as: $LD(P_1, P_2) = \frac{|P_2|-LCS(P_1,P_2)}{|P_2|}$

These scores are then combined to compute the similarity between two paths P_1 and P_2 *psim* as follows:

$$psim(P_1, P_2) = LCS_n(P_1, P_2) - \gamma GAPS(P_1, P_2) - \delta LD(P_1, P_2) \quad (1)$$

where γ and δ are positive parameters ranging from 0 to 1 that represent the comparative importance of each factor.

3.3.2. Putting It All Together

Our complete structural matching algorithm is shown in *Algorithm 3*. The algorithm accepts *CPS(NPS, LPS)* for each schema tree and the linguistic similarity matrix as inputs and produces a structural similarity matrix. For each node pairs, context similarity is computed using child context, ancestor context and leaf context. The three context values are then combined.

4. Experimental Evaluation

To implement the solution we have installed above algorithms using Java platform. We ran all our experiments on 2.4GHz Pentium IV processor with 2GB RAM running Windows XP. We shall describe the data sets used through evaluation, our experimental results, and a comparison with other matching systems.

Algorithm 3 Structural Matching Algorithm

Require: $CPS_{ST1}(NPS, LPS)\&CPS_{ST2}(NPS, LPS)\&lsim$
Ensure: $Structural\ similarity\ matrix\ ssim$
$ssim[][] \leftarrow 0;$
for i = 1 to n **do**
  for j = 1 to m **do**
    $sim_1 \leftarrow child\_context(n_i, n_j);$
    $sim_2 \leftarrow leaf\_context(n_i, n_j);$
    $sim_3 \leftarrow ancestor\_context(n_i, n_j);$
    $ssim[i][j] \leftarrow combine_{str}(sim_1, sim_2, sim_3);$
  end for
end for

Table 2. Data set details.

	Financial	*DBLP*	*TPC_H*
No. nodes(S_1/ S_2)	14/14	69/20	43/17
Avg No. nodes	14	40	30
Max. depth (S_1/ S_2)	3/6	4/6	3/6

4.1. Data Sets

We experimented with the data sets shown in Table 2. These data sets were obtained from[5]. We choose these data sets since they capture different characteristics in the numbers of nodes (schema size), their depth (the number of nodes nesting) and represent different application domains. Table 2 provides additional information such as the maximum depth, the number of elements.

4.2. Experimental Results

The proposed system considers both performance aspects —matching effectiveness and matching efficiency. Along this light of thinking, we have carried out two sets of experiments. The first set demonstrates the effectiveness of the matching system. The second set of experiments investigates the system efficiency.

To measure the effectiveness of matching result, we use the same measures used in the literatures including *precision, recall* and *F-measure*. On the other hand, we use the response time as a function of the number of schemas and the number of nodes to measure matching efficiency.

Matching Quality: The data set illustrated in Table 2 is introduced to the matching system two schemas at a time. Element matchers discover candidate matchings that exceed a predefined threshold. Then these candidate are ranked for each element up to the top-3 ranking (if found). Then matching quality measures are computed. The matching quality of the COMA++ and Similarity Flooding SF systems are also evaluated and compared with our system. Results are summarized in Figure 3, which illustrates that COMA++ and SF have higher precision but our system has higher recall and F-measure.

[5]http://www.cs.toronto.edu/db/clio/testSchemas.html

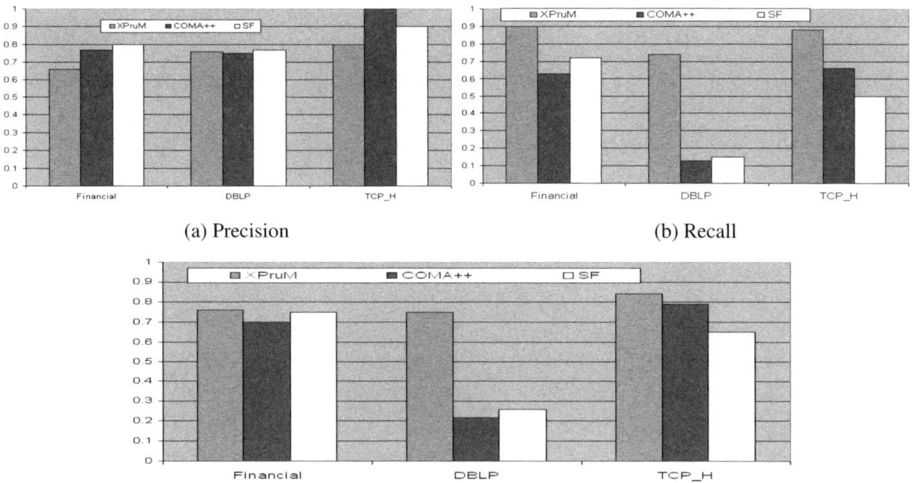

(a) Precision

(b) Recall

(c) F-measure

Figure 3. Matching quality measures for XPrüM (the proposed system), COMA++ and SF systems

Matching Efficiency: We measure the time response of the matching system as a function of the number of schemas or the number of nodes. To this end, we use another data set to reflect matching efficiency and two sets of experiments have been conducted. The first with schemas whose sizes are less than *10KB* is used to measure matching efficiency as a function of the number of schemas. While the second with schemas whose sizes are greater than *10KB* are used to measure matching efficiency as a function of the number of nodes. For the first set, we found that our proposed system needs 0.3 second to identify correspondences among 45 schemas from the *university domain*[6], while it takes 1.6 second to match 560 schemas of the *XCBL domain*[7]. For the second set, the proposed system takes a longer time to discover semantic correspondences between schemas. It takes 27 seconds to identify correspondences between 4000 schemas from the *OAGI domain*[8] containing 36,000 nodes. These results show that our system has the ability to discover correspondences among large set of schemas and among large number of nodes.

5. Summary and Future Work

In this paper we have proposed and implemented an XML matching system, a hybrid matching algorithm to automatically discover semantic correspondences between XML schema'elements. It starts with transforming schemas into schema trees and then constructs a consolidated Prüfer sequence *CPS* for each schema tree. *CPS* consists of *NPS* which represents structural information of the schema tree and *LPS* which captures semantic information of the schema tree. Experimental results have shown that our proposed system is a highly scalable with respect to large-scale schemas. Moreover, it could

[6]http://www.cs.toronto.edu/db/clio/testSchemas.html

[7]http://www.xcbl.com

[8]http://www.oagi.org

preserve matching quality beside its scalability. The approach has other features including it is independent on data mode and the application domain, it does not use any external dictionary.

What has been done is considered a step towards building a complete framework. In our future work, we should improve and suggest matching algorithms for atomic elements. In this paper, we consider only one-to-one matchings, other types of matching such as complex matchings should be considered.

References

[1] Madhavan, J., Bernstein, P. A. & Rahm, E. (2001) Generic Schema Matching with Cupid. In VLDB2001, Proceedings of 27th International Conference on Very Large Data Bases, Roma, Italy, pp. 49-58.

[2] Do, H.H. & Rahm, E. (2002) COMA- A System for Flexible Combination of Schema Matching Approaches. In VLDB2002, Proceedings of 28th International Conference on Very Large Data Bases, Hong Kong, China, pp.610-621.

[3] Do, H.H. & Rahm, E. (2007) Matching Large Schemas: Approaches and Evaluation, Information Systems, 32(6): 857-885

[4] Doan, A., Domingos, P., & Halevy, A. (2001) Reconciling Schemas of Disparate Data Sources: A Machine-Learning Approach, In ACM SIGMOD 2001, Santa Barbara, California, USA, pp. 509-520.

[5] Duchateau, F., Bellahsene, Z., & Roche, M. (2007) An Indexing Structure for Automatic Schema Matching. In ICDE Workshops 2007 Proceeding, Istanbul, Turkey, pp. 485-491.

[6] Giunchiglia,F., Yatskevich, M., & Shvaiko, P. (2007) Semantic Matching: Algorithms and Implementation, Journal on Data Semantics, 9:1-38

[7] Melnik, S., Garcia-Molina, H., & Rahm, E. (2002) Similarity Flooding: A Versatile Graph Matching Algorithm and Its Application to Schema Matching. In ICDE'02, Proceedings of the 18th International Conference on Data Engineering, San Jose, California, USA, pp. 63-74.

[8] Li, W. & Clifton, C. (2000) SEMINT: A Tool for Identifying Attribute Correspondences in Heterogeneous Databases using Neural Networks, DKE, 33(1):49-84

[9] Jeong, B., Lee, D., Cho, H., & Lee, J. (2008) A Novel Method for Measuring Semantic Similarity for XML Schema Matching, Expert Systems with Applications, 34(3):1651-1658

[10] Doan, A., Madhavan, J., Domingos, P. & Halevy, A. Ontology matching: A machine learning approach. Handbook on Ontologies, pp. 385-404

[11] Prüfer, H. (1918) Neuer Beweis eines Satzes uber Permutationen, Archiv für Mathematik und Physik, 27: 142-144

[12] Tatikonda, S., Parthasarathy, S., & Goyder, M. (2007) LCS-TRIM: Dynamic Programming Meets XML Indexing and Querying. In VLDB2007, Proceedings of 28th International Conference on Very Large Data Bases, Vienna, Austria, pp. 63-74.

[13] Domshlak, C., Gal, A., & Roitman, H. (2007) Rank Aggregation for Automatic Schema Matching, IEEE on KDE, 19(4):538-553

[14] Lee, M. L., Yang, L. H., Hsu, W., & Yang, X. (2002) XClust: Clustering XML Schemas for Effective Integration. CIKM'02, Proceedings of the 2002 ACM CIKM International Conference on Information and Knowledge Management, McLean, VA, USA, pp. 63-74.

[15] Boukottaya, A. & Vanoirbeek, C. (2005) Schema MAtching For Transforming Structured Documents. DocEng'05, Proceedings of the 2005 ACM Symposium on Document Engineering, Bristol, UK, pp. 101-110.

[16] Amer-Yahia, S., Cho, S., & Srivastava, D. (2002) Tree Pattern Relaxation. EDBT'02, 8th International Conference on Extending Database Technology, Prague, Czech Republic, pp. 496-513.

[17] Carmel, D., Efraty, N., Landau, G. M., Maarek, Y. S., & Mass, Y. (2002) An Extension of the Vector Space Model for Querying XML Documents via XML Fragments, SIGIR Forum, 36(2)

Databases and Information Systems V
H.-M. Haav and A. Kalja (Eds.)
IOS Press, 2009

doi:10.3233/978-1-58603-939-4-229

Integration of MDA Framework into the Model of Traditional Software Development

Oksana NIKIFOROVA [a], Vladimirs NIKULSINS [a,1] and Uldis SUKOVSKIS [b]
[a] *Riga Technical University, Institute of Applied Computer Systems*
[b] *Riga Information Technology Institute*

Abstract. OMG initiative, The Model Driven Architecture (MDA), shifts the focus of software development from writing code to building models. MDA is a model-oriented software development paradigm, which can be applied to any software development methodology. MDA gives no guidelines in terms of the processes such as activities and phases, roles and responsibilities which are involved in the software development process. When an organization considers applying MDA-based software development process, it will face the lack of methodological guidelines. The aim of this paper is to integrate MDA framework into the model of traditional software development.

Keywords. model driven architecture, software development lifecycle, software development process, heavyweight methodologies

Introduction

Both business and software systems become more complex. With environment undergoing frequent changes, businesses are challenged to adapt via business process enhancement and corresponding software systems improvement. Using any new technology involves a lot of activities that need to be done again and again. Systems are rarely based on one technology and often systems have to communicate with other systems [1].

Code and documentation are still separated from each other. When quick changes to the software system are applied, it is typical that documentation is not updated. Through the time documentation can become useless.

According to [2] the main problems of the traditional software development are:

- The productivity problem (developers often consider code is to be productive, writing models and documentation are not)
- The portability problem (frequent technology update or change)
- The interoperability problem (the complexity of the communication between systems)
- The maintenance and documentation problem (documentation has no influence on code and vice versa)

[1] Corresponding author: Vladimirs Nikulsins, Riga Technical University, Meza 1/3, LV-1048 Riga, Latvia; E-mail: ranva@inbox.lv

Various approaches, methodologies, techniques and tools supporting the development of software systems exist and evolve, becoming more and more complex. They don't affect the underlying software development principle: working code will always be the ultimate goal of software development.

A promising approach to resolve these problems is the Model Driven Architecture (MDA), a framework for software development defined by the Object Management Group (OMG) [2], [3]. Key to MDA is the importance of models in the software development process. Within MDA the software development process is driven by the activity of modelling the software system. Through the various automated and semi-automated transformation models are being transformed into the working code.

Since MDA does not prescribe a development methodology, each MDA-based development project has to define its own methodology or apply existing ones. MDA gives no guidelines in terms of the processes such as activities and phases, roles and responsibilities that are involved in the development software development. Furthermore, the MDA technologies are not explicitly related to identifiable activities within software development processes, as these technologies are being developed to be generally applicable in combination with development processes that may already be anchored in organisations [4]. Hence, there is a potential research opportunity in applying MDA to the traditional software development.

The goal of the paper is to integrate general framework of the model driven development into the model of traditional software development process. The guidelines on the life cycle modifications of some popular heavyweight methodologies are provided.

General methodological approaches to software development are briefly described in Section 1. Section 2 gives a short overview of MDA. More information about this architecture can be found in [3]. Overview of the current status of the research field is outlined in Section 3. Section 4 provides guidelines and comments on how to map software development activities within MDA and integrate MDA into the software development life cycle. Followed by this section, Section 5 describes conclusions and future work plans.

1. General Methodological Approaches to Software Development

The essential criteria of success in software development lie in the selection and utilization of efficient software development approach. Nowadays almost every software development project is being managed based on some software development methodology. Methodologies specify artifacts, provide formal guidelines and instructions on how to organize and manage software development process. Software development methodologies are especially valuable for large systems development like enterprise systems development.

Software development approaches could be classified into the heavyweight and lightweight (or agile) methodologies. The selection of the methodology depends on the size of software development team, the problem complexity and client's needs. The more complex and versatile the problem being solved, the more strict software development process needs to be used.

Heavyweight software development methodologies are based on a sequential series of steps, starting from requirements gathering and resulting in system deployment. At the same time, modern heavyweight methodologies are flexible in some matters, therefore they could adapt properly to the changing environment. For large decentralized projects heavyweight and strict process should be applied.

The lightweight methodologies are much less document oriented. Lightweight methodologies tend to be code oriented, and the produced high-quality source code serves as documentation. Lightweight methodologies generally propose continuous delivery of small functionality, which can be immediately tested. Small frequent cycles used in lightweight methodologies provide more opportunities for customers to review the project definition, and if needed, adapt to the new business requirements.

General software development process is based on iterative waterfall model. The following software development life cycle phases could be found in one or another form both in lightweight and heavyweight approaches [2], [5]:

- Conceptualization and requirements gathering
- Analysis and functional description
- Design
- Coding
- Testing
- Deployment

In addition to the life cycle phases, methodologies provide guidelines on how to manage the whole development process, and how the process infrastructure elements should be maintained.

There are various software development methodologies available on the market, both customized and commercial off-the-shelf methodologies. Choosing the wrong methodology could be critical for the overall project success. The recent survey shows that the most common heavyweight methodologies used in practice in the Latvian software development industry are based on Rational Unified Process (RUP) and Microsoft Solutions Framework (MSF) [6]. Hence, activities and appropriate development phases stated in this paper, form a part of the software development life cycle, and will be mostly applicable for these methodologies, but not limited to.

2. Essence of Process in Model Driven Software Development

Problem in software development begins starting from requirement elicitation within the initial development phase. Requirements are being formalized and documented using some kind of notation. Then, based on these requirements the detailed software design takes place. When software developers begin implementation, they can incorrectly interpret the requirements, which can lead to the incorrect producing of code. The requirements can be changed in almost any of software development phase also. Often the code is being updated directly, without modifying the design. In such cases the link between the documentation and implemented changes will be eliminated. Furthermore, if the designed system is complex and consists of many interrelated systems and modules, then it complicates the whole development cycle.

Even if software is implemented and already established in production environment, it remains valuable for limited amount of time. When the maintenance of software product starts exceeding the price needed for the new software development and deployment, the migration to the new system is being initiated.

Model driven software development process helps in removing this gap.

The OMG's Model Driven Architecture initiative (started in 2001) shifts the focus of software development from writing code to modeling [3]. The design becomes a part of implemented solution, which is expressed in models. Any changes in design will immediately affect the models itself. MDA, by explicitly incorporating models at multiple levels of abstraction, enables developers to view complex systems from different viewpoints. It allows integrating modelling with other development activities.

MDA makes a sharp distinction between a model of the business (the computation-independent model, or CIM), the business model in a specific technology context (PIM), and a model that is tied to the business and uses platform-specific code (PSM).

The MDA software development life cycle therefore includes a four-step process [7], [8]:

- Capturing of the requirements in a Computation Independent Model (CIM), which shows the business model of the system and is usually made by a business analyst.
- Creation of a Platform Independent Model (PIM) which is a model of the system functions, usually made by an architect.
- Transformation of the PIM to one or more Platform Specific Models (PSMs), which tailors the PIM implementation, adding platform-specific rules and code that the transformation has not provided.
- Transformation the PSM to code and deployment of the system in a specific environment.

The MDA software development process is being driven by modeling activity. The important aspect of modeling and usage of the modeling artifacts is tools availability and definitions of unambiguous transformations. Tools, which are being used for modelling, should be coupled together, thus supporting PIM development, transformations from PIM to PSM, from PSM to code or code deployment within the production environment. There is still a lack of tools, which fully supports the whole model driven development process. Such problems are out of scope of this paper.

3. Using MDA to Customize a Solution Framework

Modern heavyweight software development methodologies (like Rational Unified Process and Microsoft Solutions Framework) are quite general and can be applied to various software development projects. From the other side, MDA also does not prescribe a specific development methodology to be used. Organizations that use internal software development methodology may utilize their own development experience in this area and apply MDA to the already established process [1].

3.1. Existing Researches

There are various researches available on the software development process usage tied with MDA. However, only few of them provide particular guidelines and recommendations on how to map MDA to the typical software development methodology which is being used in practice. OMG proposes that MDA is not limited to be used in any software development project. Case study analysis can enrich the establishment of a methodological base.

One of the results of such researches is a MASTER project (Model-driven Architecture inSTrumentation, Enhancement and Refinement) deliverable called Process Model to Engineer and Manage the MDA Approach [9]. The main part of that report describes a standard software process (SSP) for software development following a model-driven and system family engineering approach. Such SSP should be instantiated to each specific project through a derivation mechanism which is also explained. The process model described is based on SPEM (Software Process Engineering Metamodel), a metamodel and a UML profile dedicated to software process modelling. It is useful for modelling a family of related software processes using UML notation. Importance of process improvement initiatives is also covered, making the methodology compliant with CMM requirements.

Integrated software development methodology, which was applied to the telecommunication domain, was proposed in the MODA-TEL project [10]. Through the assigning appropriate methods to the software development processes like Rational Unified Process (RUP), V-model or CMM, MDA-supported methodology will be devised [11]. However, complete and consistent software process based on MDA is beyond the scope of the MODA-TEL project.

Similar to MASTER project, the phases and activities in the development process, as well as the roles and products of each activity in accordance with the Software Process Engineering Metamodel (SPEM) were identified and proposed in the new methodology [4]. However, this methodology is designed for distributed applications development only.

By analyzing case studies it is possible to get an overview on how to fit MDA into the software development process when the web services based solution is being implemented [12]. The overview of the main aspects covers process roles, artefacts and deliverables, tools (by providing an example of using Codagen tool) and separation of life cycle phases within the RUP software development process. In that way collaboration between all the interveners of the development cycle is achieved and visualized. It is possible to extend and implement this approach to other software development projects as well.

4. Mapping of MDA Models into the Software Development Process

The activity of developing models as main artifacts replaces traditional views in software development, which emphasizes writing code as main functionality deliverable. According to SPEM extensions, each software development process can be described using the following interrelated elements [13]:

- Basic Elements
- Dependencies
- Process Structure
- Process Components
- Process Lifecycle

Software Process Engineering Metamodel can be useful when the software development process needs to be formalized. Therewith, it is a deliverable of OMG, and uses UML as a notation, which is consistent with MDA concepts.

4.1. Software Development Activities and Their Accordance with MDA

The essence of MDA is knowledge formalization within the different models, which can be later transformed into the executable code. Such process consists from a concrete set of activities. According to the [14], it is essential to review MDA process from activities and their interrelationships point of view. The examination of these activities, which are applied to the simple hypothetic system using single source model and single target implementation model, takes place initially. Further, the simplified system description is enriched by adding concepts for MDA iterative development and models transformations into various platforms.

MDA activities could be divided into the following activity groups: the first one includes formalization of the knowledge domain. Later this knowledge is being used in the models implementation. Hence, the development of model takes place within first activity group. The mapping of formalized knowledge into the target platform (which will define the final system) takes place within the second activity group.

The development process is managed iteratively. Therefore, both activity groups are performed incrementally, and even if the iteration was not successful, it is possible to go back. When both source and target models (including the mapping functions) are well tested, the integration test is performed.

Knowledge formalization can be divided into four activities:

- Elicit requirements within the domain of interest
- Abstracting knowledge
- Express formal concepts within the model
- Test the model

For eliciting requirements the use cases or user stories can be used. Requirements can be expressed in use case diagrams, some formalized document or simple text. Requirements should be grouped together and abstracted within the concept group. When the analysts choose proper abstract group, they should also choose modelling language and metamodel. The next step is creating a model for these abstractions. The model defines and describes abstracted concepts, as well as formalizes knowledge.

As soon as the model was created, it should be also verified in order to check if it complies with the user requirements. One of the possible testing methods is the model review. However, such manual model verification can leave some errors unexposed. The problem is in different model perception, especially if general metamodel is being used. The alternative testing approach is the model execution using test cases (when initial conditions defined). Model gets stimulus, which raises model output and changes system condition. These test cases can be derived in one or another form from use cases or user stories.

The mapping process can be categorized into four basic activities [14], [15]:

- Specifying mapping functions
- Marking models
- Verifying mappings
- Transformations of models

When specifying mapping functions, source model and target model should be already created. Target model consist from formalized knowledge about structure and behaviour of target platform. The linking problem between these models is being solved by specifying mapping functions.

As soon as goal of mapping function is identified, the facilitator of mapping function should answer to the following two questions:

- Is it possible to use MDA concepts for specifying mapping function by getting model specification and using mapping functions, thereupon transforming the model into executable code?
- Which are the mapping output optimization criteria for the target model (e.g., simplicity of mapping or efficiency)

Mapping functions are being used in the following way: each source model element is being marked in order to define specific mapping function. If the input consist from source model and the target model is defined and enriched with partial mapping, such models should be mapped.

Though, it is highly advisable to use metamodels as activities inputs instead of models. The mapping rules should consist of at least one mapping rule. They are applied to target model from source model. In exceptional cases it is possible to perform incomplete mapping. For example, if it is identified that the target model (not the metamodel) will never perform some kind of functionality. In such case it is needed to define such exception as a rule for all other models which could be developed. The goal is to restrict the models from mapping errors. The second goal is to verify if the mapping rules are selected unambiguously. If the mapping rule retrieval is not unambiguous, then it should be marked in the source model.

Marking process is finished when the mapping function is created for each element of source metamodel, and each element of source model is marked with unambiguously defined rule. When the knowledge about system is formalized into the model and is marked with mapping functions, it is needed to ascertain that the result of such mapping is valid.

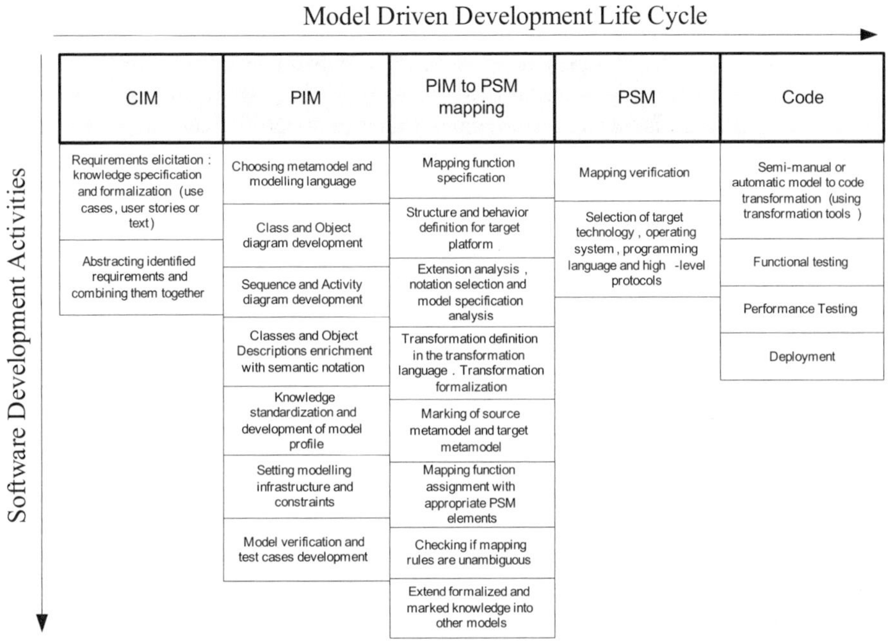

Figure 1. Software development activities mapping into the Model Driven Development life cycle

Since the model is successfully verified, the transformation is being initialized from PSM to another PSM (or code). Model verification should be performed each time the process is being initiated. It allows identifying errors and getting rid of them in the later stages.

If the requirements are changed, then the changes should be performed in the model level. The knowledge formalization always should happen within the models, regardless of chosen platform. This process is performed iteratively.

Listed MDA activities are grouped and organized according to the Model Driven Development life cycle (shown in Figure 1). It consists of static MDA concepts starting from CIM, moving forward to PIM, PSM and finally, executable code. Activities, which belong to the mapping process between PIM and PSM, are relocated in separate category.

This mapping does not provide strict sequence of activities being executed. Though, it allows getting structural overview of the universal activities, which should be executed in almost every software development project. Listed activities are not limited to concrete methodology (both heavyweight and lightweight).

If the model driven approach is being adapted within some software development methodology, these processes can be mapped to that methodology and utilized as a reference to the activities within the already established software development process.

4.2. Integrating MDA into the Software Development Life Cycle

There is no specific model driven based software development life cycle defined by OMG. It is proposed, that important aspect of MDA is its ability to be used within any of software development processes. However, when MDA is being applied in practice, it is essential to integrate model driven development activities into the established methodological software development life cycle.

Heavyweight methodologies require more formalism adapting MDA within its software life cycle. The alignment of CIM, PIM, PSM and code related development is depicted in Figure 2. Software development activities should be allocated through this mapping diagram based on Figure 1. Additional phase called "PIM to PSM mapping", which can be found in Figure 1 is not defined here. Appropriate activities should be distributed between PIM and PSM phases, depending on their action belonging either to the source or target model. According to the Section 1, it is beneficial to integrate MDA to the methodologies, most widely used in practice. Rational Unified Process (RUP) and Microsoft Solutions Framework (MSF) are picked up in relation to this need.

MSF and RUP phase mappings to the MDA life cycle defines approximate boundaries of each phase between traditional software development (vertical) and model driven software development (horizontal). Software development life cycle integration with MDA is described in relation to MSF methodology. Similar activities, described below, are applied to other methodologies as well, e.g., RUP [1].

At the Envision phase, requirements specification with well-defined terminology should be elicited (probably, resulting in ontology) [11], [16], [17]. Structuring of captured information should be performed. This formal structured information and the terms of the ontology could later be used to refine the requirements into design-oriented models. Later, models should point back into the requirements for traceability and test specification formalisms (validating a resulting system against the requirements). The formalized outcome is CIM model. Preparations for PIM development starts at the beginning of Envision phase as well. Metamodel development is being initiated.

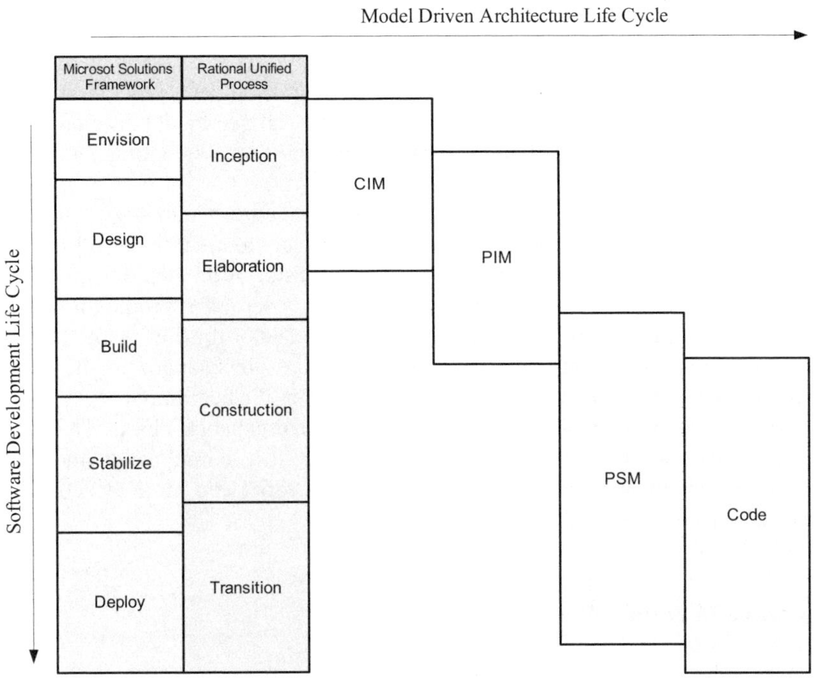

Figure 2. Software development life cycle relations to MDA life cycle

MSF standard deliverable Risk Assessment Document should be enriched with MDA related information (transformation tools availability, metamodels facilities evaluation, mapping complexity assessment and etc.). Vision/scope Document should be enriched with Project Structure Document and conceptual model.

MDA modeling activities will affect the MSF Plan phase to a great extent, where the design of PIMs and initial planning of PSMs should be clearly identified. The metamodels or profiles of the domain analyzed should be extracted first and then models based on these models can be used to formally describe the system. This is an incremental activity - each new instance of a metamodel could bring up some improvements for the metamodel. Additional constraints in the models should be defined with Object Constraint Language (OCL). Functional specification semantics, which is the standard MSF deliverable, should be captured in the models as well.

At the Build phase, development or improvement of model transformation algorithms or code generators activities should be performed. Both PIM and PSM models should be marked, and mappings rules should be defined. Additional complex business rules and transaction methods, where a further structure could not be abstracted from the use cases should be implemented. MSF Build phase deliverables – source code and executables, are replaced with marked PIM and PSM models. Test specifications and test cases are defined both for models and for the final solution resulted in code. Once the models are marked, it is possible to make automated (or semi-automated) PIM to PSM transformation and PSM to code (or PSM to PSM transformation as well). The transformation process should occur at the end of Build phase, resulting in an additional deliverable – executable model.

PSM covers the most part of stabilize phase. Stabilize phase allows to test models conformance with test cases, which were created in the previous Build phase. As [16] outlines, one of the famous slogans of extreme programming- "tests first" – can be translated in the MDA world to "verify first". The development process itself is iterative, so if any inconsistence found in the target model, source model or appropriate mapping functions should be modified. The transformation process continues until the bug convergence is reached.

During the Deploy phase, the team deploys the core technology and site components, stabilizes the deployment, transitions the project to operations and support, and obtains final customer approval of the project. The result of the deployment phase is a working system, which is implemented in code and is set up in production. Most deployment information is based on some sort of metamodels or profiles (some PSMs). In case requirements for the system are revised or there are changes in the target architecture, the software development life cycle starts from the beginning.

The most impressive benefits are acquired in the maintenance phase. The more dynamic and structured the architected system is, the less complicated and time consuming development phases are necessary and the cheaper and more effective the maintenance phase will be.

5. Conclusions and Future Work

This paper provides guidelines and instructions on MDA framework integration into the model of traditional software development. Software development activities from popular heavyweight methodologies like RUP and MSF are analysed taking into account the aspects of their usage within the model driven development. Analyzing existing research in this area, a lack of well formalized knowledge was identified. There are various case studies and MDA process specifications available. However, they are not general ones and are limited to specific domain (e.g., distributed applications).

Future research in this area can possibly lead to universal methodology development, which could be applied both to the heavyweight and agile methodologies. It is planned to proof the outcome of such MDA-based methodology in practice within one of the Latvian software development companies' environment. A special attention should be given to the transition of the software development process from the traditional form into model-driven.

Acknowledgements

This work has been partly supported by the European Social Fund within the National Programme „Support for the carrying out doctoral study program's and post-doctoral researches" project „Support for the development of doctoral studies at Riga Technical University".

References

[1] Nikulsins, V., Nikiforova, O. & Sukovskis, U. (2008) Mapping of MDA Models into the Software Development Process, Databases and Information Systems, Haav, H.-M. & Kalja, A. (Eds.), Proceedings of the Eighth International Baltic Conference (Baltic DB&IS 2008), Tallinn University of Technology Press, June 2-5, Tallinn, Estonia, pp. 217-226.
[2] Kleppe, A., Warmer, J. & Bast, W. (2003) MDA Explained: The Model Driven Architecture: Practice and Promise. Addison Wesley.
[3] OMG Model Driven Architecture (available at:http://www.omg.org/mda)
[4] Gavras, A., Belaunde, M., Pires, L.F. & Almeida, J.P. Towards an MDA-based development methodology for distributed applications
[5] Kruchten, P. (2000) The Rational Unified Process. An Introduction, Second Edition, Addison Wesley.
[6] Nikulsins, V,. Nikiforova, O. & Sukovskis, U. (2006) Analysis of Activities Covered by Software Engineering Discipline, Databases and Information Systems, Vasilecas, O., Eder, J. & Caplinskas, A. (Eds.), Seventh International Baltic Conference on Databases and Information Systems, Communications, Materials of Doctoral Consortium, VGTU Press „Technika", Vilnius, Lithuania, pp. 130-138.
[7] Meservy, T. & Fenstermacher, K. D. (2005) Transforming Software Development: An MDA Road Map. University of Arizona.
[8] Kontio, M. (2005) Architectural manifesto: MDA for the enterprise. An architect's approach to more productive development. IBM.
[9] European Software Institute (2003) Process Model to Engineer and Manage the MDA: Model-driven Architecture inSTrumentation, Enhancement and Refinement Approach (available at http://modeldrivenarchitecture.esi.es/pdf/Deliverable-D32.zip)
[10] Belaunde, M. (2002) Initial identification of issues for further research. Deliverable 2.2. MODA-TEL. Interactive Objects Software GmbH (available at http://www.modatel.org/~Modatel/pub/deliverables/D2.2-final.pdf
[11] Steinhau, R. (2002) Model Driven Architecture Definition and Methodology. Deliverable 3.1. MODA-TEL. Interactive Objects Software GmbH, (available at: http://www.modatel.org/public/deliverables/D3.1.htm)
[12] Bertrand, D. (2003) Model-Driven Architecture Case Study: Model-Driven Architecture with Codagen. (available at http://www.omg.org/news/meetings/workshops/MDA_Wksp_Manual/06-1_Bertrand_Brassard.pdf)
[13] OMG (2005) Software Process Engineering Metamodel Specification (SPEM), Version 1.1, OMG specification (available at http://www.omg.org/docs/formal/05-01-06.pdf)
[14] Mellor, S.J., Scott, K., Uhl, A. & Weise, D. (2004) MDA Distilled: Principles of Model-Driven Architecture. Addison Wesley.
[15] Meservy,T. & Fenstermacher, K. D. (2005) Transforming Software Development: An MDA Road Map.
[16] Steinhau, R. (2003) Guidelines for the Application of MDA and the Technologies covered by it. Deliverable 3.2. MODA-TEL. Interactive Objects Software GmbH (available at: http://www.modatel.org/~Modatel/pub/deliverables/D3.2-final.pdf)
[17] Microsoft (2002) Microsoft Solutions Framework: MSF Process Model v. 3.1. White Paper

Business Information Systems

Databases and Information Systems V
H.-M. Haav and A. Kalja (Eds.)
IOS Press, 2009

doi:10.3233/978-1-58603-939-4-243

Agile Software System Development and Customisation Using Business Rules

Aidas SMAIZYS[1] and Olegas VASILECAS
Klaipeda University

Abstract. Flexible customization and adaptation of the software before deployment into the information systems of separate organizations challenge large requirement conformity, project and specification management, design and architecture complexity, code integration, compatibility and interoperability issues, frequently causing the need of reengineering through the entire all the system development lifecycle. In this paper, we focus on these criteria and propose the use of decision tables as alternative business logic visualization formalism, used for business rule representation, which leads building a model of business logic and implementing it using software configuration parameters stored in the database and automatically generated methods of business objects implemented into the classes of business logic tier of n-Tier architecture.

Keywords. business rules, decision tables, configuration management

Introduction

Even if organisations are acting according to the same legal regulations their business models are not the same and their business processes are functioning according to the slightly different logics. As the result it leads problems and limitations of software system (SS) functionality, compatibility and interoperability. Because of rapidly changing business environment and evolving business user needs, the scope of customisations and SS versions is growing rapidly. Subversion management systems are helping a lot for managing changes and providing version control. However, further implementation of new functionality is going to be consuming too many resources and is impossible without total reengineering.

Software system developers face software customisation problems and challenges quick software system adaptation to the special customer needs and business logic of different organisations. It is especially relevant topic, when deploying same software systems into the large amount of slightly different information systems (IS) of separate organizations.

In this paper we discuss the use of decision tables (DT) as alternative business logic visualisation formalism used for business rule representation. We propose solution of the SS parameterisation tasks by automatically building SS configuration parameter set and executable components of n-Tier architecture according to the set of rules in DTs, previously captured by a business domain analyst. This leads to the need of persistent control and synchronisation of DTs rule model and SS after appearing

[1] Corresponding Author: Aidas Smaizys, Klaipeda University, Herkaus Manto str. 84, LT-92294 Klaipeda, Lithuania; E-mail: smaizys@ik.ku.lt.

changes in business environment. The paper proposes a method for such change management and automated way of configuration implementation into the final software system code using metamodel based transformations.

The paper is organised as follows. In section 1 we briefly elaborate the topic of business logic separation from the SS code and discuss usage of decision tables for solution of SS parameterisation problems. Section 2 discusses basic concepts of customisable SS development and introduces a method, based on n-Tier architecture and decision table transformation into the database model and software system components using metamodel transformations. Section 3 illustrates how decision tables can be applied for automated configuration implementation, based on our research and experimental implementation of security control system. Section 4 discusses automation of data model modification and adaptation to the changes of business logics. Section 5 concludes the paper.

1. Related Work

Business systems are functioning according to business rules in a specific business domain. Due to the dynamics of its nature, business environment is changing frequently according to internal and external influences such as changes in law, new competition etc. [1]. Although Business rules (BR) of particular problem domain are similar in several organizations but they are never applied in the same way, even they depend on the same legal regulations. A decision in business is a choice about a "course of action". A course of action may include many individual actions and a decision may be characterized on a continuum from unstructured to structured [2].

The complexity of slightly different business rule application on every specific business system cause to choose from several alternative options:

- Splitting the source code line into the alternative paths, implementing specific business requirements by redesigning models through all the entire layers (business system, information system and software system layer) and producing separate executable code;
- Design and implementation of modular software system architecture and customization of the separate modules according to the customers needs;
- Implementation of all the possible variations of the same business rule application into the software code and activation using specific parameter values for every particular implementation;
- Change of business system according to constrains caused by particular implementation of business rules hard coded into the software system.
- Every solution proposed has its own specific limitations. Separate code lines result in dramatic usage of resources to manage the changes and are rarely used in practice, unless it is planned to split and develop separate software because of different target market segments, pricing policy etc.

Modular architecture allows separation of core functionality and creation of separate modules prepared for customization according to the customer needs, but it causes integration problems after core modules are renewed. Such upgrades often result in unacceptable risk, especially in case of business critical applications.

The solution based on configuration parameters requires redesign of software system code for every implementation of every different aspect of business rule implementation according to the specific customer needs and redesign of the configuration parameter storage or at least a change of configuration values. In large systems such configuration parameter set can grow dramatically and cause large configurations and complicated management. Usually it is very difficult to follow the meaning of every parameter and prevent duplication or contradicting settings that result in unpredictable behaviour of the system.

The accommodation of business system according to the proposed software system of information system is the easiest way for developer, but the least acceptable for business people, because of unpredictable influence of such modification for business system efficiency, competitiveness and etc. This way is applied very rarely and only partly in changing business processes that are most critical for implementation.

Similar engineering problems usually are solved using adaptable design [3], quality function deployment (QFD) [4, 5] and logical project design according to the Logical framework approach (LFA) [6]. The concept of adaptable system design is not new. Various related approaches have been described as table-driven, data-driven, rules-based, parameter-driven, dynamic, configurable, component-based, plug-and-play and expert systems. Depending on definition of a rule, all of these could be classified generally as rules based systems [3]. The formation of reengineering strategies based on QFD covers business reengineering of the first three steps to determine functional objectives of business process reengineering and tackle external customer requirements and internal problems in an integrative way.

Rules can be graphically represented in multiple ways for usability purposes. Two structures are primarily used: decision trees and decision tables. A decision table defines a process as an ordered set of conditions and their related actions. Tabular approaches to problem solving were developed in the 1960's by General Electric and other organizations. Official decision table components and terminology were standardized by the cooperative efforts of a number of organizations, including the Conference on Data Systems Languages (CODASYL) in 1962. The basic format of decision tables remains largely unchanged today [3].

The constructed decision tables allow asking targeted questions by neglecting the irrelevant inputs during decision process [7]. Hence rule engines do not really care about the rule representation since either structure is compiled into similar executable rule statements. Such executable statements are produced from DTs using set of knowledge representation CODASYL languages as COBOL [8, 3], PROLOGA [7], etc. We appreciate its power; however they are difficult to understand for business people. Hence these languages are used in most DT design tools for rule manipulation. In some cases decision tables are designed to be converted into executable software code, often based on optimal test sequences [9].

According to [10, 11] business rules are involved in capturing requirements and creating business or information system model and stored in graphical specifications. However, the main reason why business patterns or models are not reused without further manual interpretation is because the computation of a floating decimal number remained in gross-to-net pay obviously did not remain the same even in two installations in the same city. That means - design process does not eliminate or control further manual transformation of the requirements and the final result usually depends on the developer. Thereby by implementing the requirement in development process the relations to the business rules are lost. The other problem is that the meaning of the Business rule embedded in a graphical model can change already in design process by adding new business rules and storing them by adding new components and relations to the model. Such changes can result in contradictions and incompleteness of business rule set.

The decision table formalism is not an isolated technique and shows a lot of interfaces to other representation formalisms such as code, trees, rules, etc. Making good use of these connections, however, is only possible through flexible computer support. Therefore a variety of bridges have been built between the decision table workbench and other representations, resulting in a large application domain for decision table modelling [8].

Decision tables are also context free. Unlike decision trees, no prior path must be completed for the table to arrive at a decision. Only input values for the necessary parameters along the axes are required. Decision tables are best used for a consistent, but limited, set of parameters, where potentially a large number of possible values persist for those parameters. That is the main reason why we have selected DTs as the best solution for software configuration embedded business rules used for process logic modifications according to the business object condition represented by values of selected business object attributes. However a table with many different parameters quickly becomes complex which diminishes its usefulness as a simplification concept.

Whatever DTs is the technique used to visualize business rules (Decision table or tree viewer), it is necessary to have a language which makes it possible to specify the syntax and the semantics of the rules. [8, 12] We disagree with such a point of view in the Decision table usage. We think that in some cases it's a perfect solution for BR specification interface design.

Business analysts or domain experts need to develop clear, precise and complete business rules that represent real life business process logics and these processes need to be logically robust as a software implementation. On the other hand the programmers use the same business rules, interpreted as software system functional requirements that are later translated into a programming language that becomes part of the application. Software development involving code writing covers every possible combination of circumstances – user input, database transaction, or any other event – that the program will encounter. When the programmer or analyst overlooks a possible combination of inputs or events, the program will do things in an unpredictable way and produce unexpected results. Even worse are the errors, made by programmers who do not fully understand the interaction between different options and their combinations. The automated implementation of the DTs represented rules into the software system code would allow error prone solution of all the possible problems like omitted, duplicated, or contradictioning conditions and inadequate implementation.

There are two main views in dynamic business rule driven software system design. One of them is to design predefined executable processes and execute them by using rules in software system, where processes and execution rules are derived from business rules using transformations [13]. The other is discussed in our papers [14], where business rules and facts describing current business system state are loaded into inference engine of the software system and transformed into software system executable data analysis process according to the results of logical derivations.

The authors in [15] say that „model translations can be specified in a truly generic way: the source and the target metamodels are parameters of the entire procedure and specify the operation of model translation as a special diagram operation well known in category theory under the name of pull-back. At the heart of the approach is a mapping between the two metamodels, which governs the entire translation procedure". We support this point of view and use similar approach for BR transformation, however we use XML based transformations as described in [14].

2. Decision Table Based Method for Formal Business Rule Representation and Automated Implementation

The main problems, implementing changes of business logic, are related to the changes in rule structures, attribute values and rule precedence. Traditional software engineering in such cases requires redesign of data, object and process models and further review of all the entire SS code, where changing business logics have already been implemented. To avoid such problems, we focus on few concepts, changing traditional view of software engineering process:

- Separation of business logics from SS code;
- Automated implementation and synchronisation of business logics in SS components of n-Tier architecture and database.
- Automated implementation and change of rule attribute values in SS configuration parameters stored in the database.
- Automated implementation and change of rule structures in database logical model.
- Automated decision execution process implementation in business logic tier of n-Tier architecture for use in different SS systems of information system.

The Method for implementation of business logics into the software system configuration is based on business system rule management, proposed in this paper and meets criteria described before. The method schema (Figure 1) was developed according to the framework presented in [16], where we have proposed the general structure of models and requirements for business rule based information system modelling.

As the first step, according to the method, business rules are captured in business system usually interviewing business people, analyzing business processes, studying documentation and legal regulations. Captured informal business rules are placed into repository and represented in a form of decision tables for later representation of configuration rules. One part of a Decision table (DTs) contains conditions that can be linked to create a rule, and the other part contains actions that are related to the rules. Once the rules are defined in DTs tool, it is needed to perform automated analysis, addition of missing rules, and to remove these that are redundant or contradictory.

Later the decision tables are directly implemented into the software system database, using metamodel based transformations and automated logical data model generator, and prepared for further transformation into the information system rules. Information system rules are implemented according to the architectural context into the software system components of information system (business object classes) in business logic tier of n-Tier architecture.

After deployment of the rules into the database, logical data model is to be reverse engineered, using special design tool, back into the software system model and later used for building business layer of software system model. This allows automated access and manipulation from information or business system model, implementing business objects automatically into the separate software system module later on.

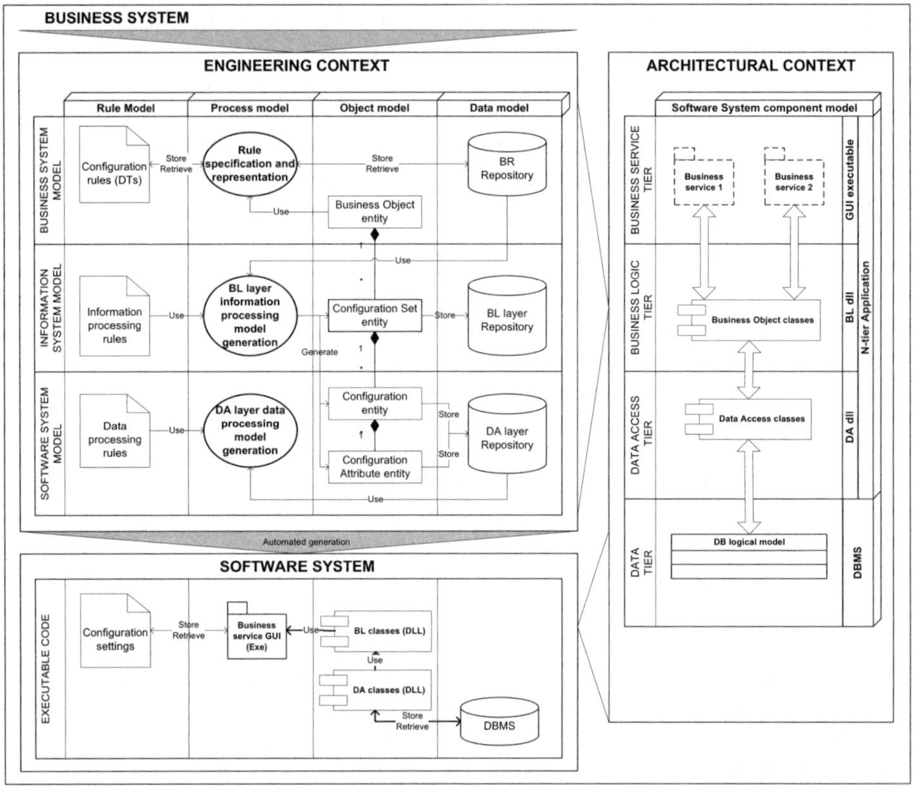

Figure 1. Agile method for automated business rule based configuration implementation

Summarising the method, shortly presented in this section, it is possible to group into the set of three main consequent tasks: DT based BR representation, metamodel based transformation of DTs into the configuration tables of software system database and automated software system code generation of components represented by n-Tier architecture as described in next subsections.

2.1. Decision Table Based Business Rule Representation

Business analysts often use decision tables to represent a particular set of requirements, so replicating that the structure in the rule engine reuses a familiar concept. Decision tables can quickly highlight where an outcome or decision is missing. Each decision table should only make one particular type of determination. Also, not all parameters have valid decision outcomes in all the cases.

Rule set based on MOF/UML metamodel can be represented as decision table (Figure 2), that captures business rules used to represent business process model, which logics depend on the configuration parameters stored into final software system. A decision table rule set consists of subjects, properties and variables, which are represented by subject atoms and property atoms. Furthermore a rule set consists of an ordered composition of condition labels. These condition labels group the conditions of the rule set in sets of exhaustive and mutually exclusive conditions.

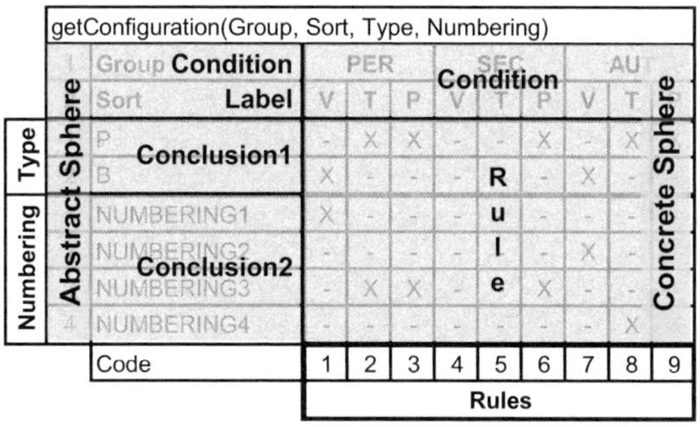

Figure 2. Main DTs metamodel nodes for rule representation

Each condition is a logical formula that refers to the domain atoms and variables of the rule set. The actual rules of the rule set are an ordered conjunction of conditions, such that a rule contains at most one condition of each condition label. Notice that not every conjunction of conditions is necessarily meaningful. In other words, it might be the case that a specific condition is only meaningful in combination with other specific conditions. In addition to conditions, a rule refers to one or more conclusions.

The selection of numbering and type of the pass can be processed according to the group and sort of the pass according to the set of rules used for security system Pass issue process logic representation in form of DT (Figure 2). As we can see from example, DTs based configuration management not only provides better understanding of the logics, but should also allow addition of the attributes for condition labels and conclusions. This is important for later generation of the configuration data tables and filling them with configuration values, after the logics represented by the rules has changed.

The next section presents how DTs rules are stored using metamodel and used for later transformation into the Entity-Relationship (ER) model.

2.2. Metamodel Based Transformations

For further business logic implementation into the configuration of software system, we have used slightly modified MOF/UML DTs metamodel presented in [12] and created similar ER metamodel. Such metamodels were used for specification of the transformations needed to produce ER model from DTs created as described in the previous section. The models represented in typed graphs were transformed into XSD schemas and mapped according to the method described in [17]. All the mapping functions were collected into XSLT transformation schema and the transformation executed using XML parser (Figure 3).

As a result of the presented transformations the ER model was produced. Such ER model was used for creation of the database and filling it with data entered in DTs. For this purpose we use SQL data description language (DDL) and generate CREATE TABLE, JOIN and INSERT clauses.

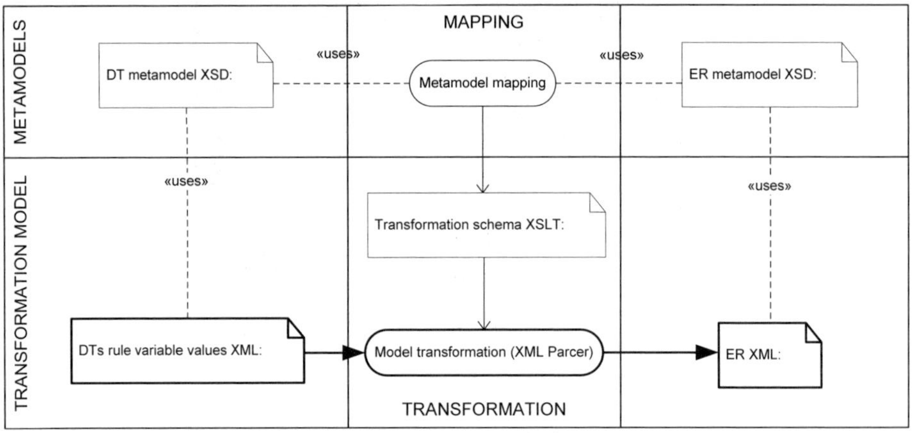

Figure 3. DTs Transformation into the ER using metamodels

Execution of these instructions in DBMS allows creation or modification of database schema according to the ER model and fills configuration tables with data from DT's. The generated database is used for business object processing automation presented in the next section.

2.3. Automated Software System Code Generation

As the result from previous sections we have business process logics represented as DTs, data model in ER and data values filled into the database. This allows generation of IS process code in the SS according to the Information processing rules (Figure 1). The proposed method allows generation of business object processing interface in business service tier and supporting classes in business logic (BL) tier used for automation of the collection and entity operations like save, get, delete, filter etc. The access to the database is performed through generated DAO classes in data access (DA) tier according to the data processing rules stored in predefined template.

Summarising the proposed method of automated software configuration implementation, the main advantages of the method proposed are following: it allows changes of process logics by changing configuration values directly in the software system and is limited only by data model implemented into the database, if such modifications are needed all the automated reengineering process starting from the changes of DTs rules can be processed, continuing adding new conditions and conclusions and finishing with execution of automated transformations. The n-Tier architecture allows compatibility of the old business service tier applications with newly extended lower tier classes, with exception of newly implemented logics. Anyway in case of large count of installations the rules of specific software installation are stored in the configuration table of the database. So, it allows easy and less complicated upgrade of the software used in production already.

3. Experimental Evaluation of the Method

The proposed method was applied for development of the automated security system used for transport and visitor control and access log data exchange system. According to the method proposed, we have collected informal business rules used for access restrictions and regulations and transformed them into the formal decision rules of information system layer creating decision table. Such rules represented in DT were dedicated for decision processing of numbering and type of the pass selection according to the group and sort of the pass. Then DT was transformed into the logical data model, represented by ER diagram and implemented directly into the software system database for use in the automated software system code generation, producing separate parts of the software system code.

Such approach of software engineering allowed automated implementation of the business system logics into the software system by automatically building decision model acting according to the parameters filled into the previously built database used as configuration storage.

Further, we give an example of automatically generated software system code used to get right numbering scheme for the “Pass”, depending on the Group, Type and Sort values according to the configuration values delivered as Configuration object entity. The automatically generated method getConfiguration (Figure 4) is stored in business logic (BL) tier and uses method getConfigurationEntity of ConfigurationEntity class, which uses generated DAO classes from data access (DA) tier to get the data from the database (line 27). In the same way software system code for creation and edition of the “PassEdit” object was generated, providing input selection of the Group and Sort combo boxes in the form etc.

```
    'Generated Software system Business logic tier code using ER model
021 Imports DA.DaoClasses
022 Namespace BL.EntityClasses
023     Public Class ConfigurationEntity
            ...
024         Public Shared Function getConfiguration _
025                 (ByVal Group As String, ByVal Sort As String, _
026                  ByRef Type As String, ByRef Numbering As String) As Boolean
027             Dim Configuration As ConfigurationEntity = GetConfigurationEntity(Group, Sort)
028             If IsNothing(Configuration) Then Return False
029             Type = Configuration.Type
030             Sort = Configuration.Sort
031             Return True
032         End Function
033     End Class
034 End Namespace
```

Figure 4. DTs Transformation into the ER Using Metamodels

Decision tables are well understood by system engineers, but difficult to read for business users. Therefore, we have designed transformations used to extract the business rules implemented into Software system Configuration according to the currently entered configuration parameter values and represent them in a plain text. Similarly the decision tables were transformed into the Horn clauses and used as the logical control code uploaded into the security system controllers.

4. Discussion

Discussing the proposed method we are always getting question about how to manage changes if we have production database already. We agree that there are some limitations for modification of existing data model, but according to the method proposed we allow change of existing and addition of new rules, conditions and conclusions (actions), propagating it directly into the data model of database management system and running new iteration in automated way according to the method proposed. It is required automated refresh of logical model in business layer, which is updated directly from modified data model in automated way and automated generation (refresh) of the code in business logic tier according to the n-Tier architecture. Business rules represented in decision tables are already tested for completeness. It allows deploying them directly into the database of working software system together with new version of executable software code. Such way of business logic implementation allows agile and flexible improvement of software system and implementation of new business logic and rules without splitting source code for each new customer.

The only existing limitation that we experience assuring compliance of already existing business data records to the new business rules is that we not deal in automated way with existing attributes and relations of business entities to the entities engaged in the configuration part of the software representing business rules. We do not allow automated way of deleting relations in data model yet. However we allow automated addition of new relations and their management directly in the model of business logic tier of n-Tier architecture components for automated generation of business logic components and implementation or modification of such relations without direct implementation into the data model of existing database. Such approach allows keeping consistency of previously entered business data records in the database and providing new business logic for newly created records. Such problems usually can be solved by additional modification of existing business data too, but we expect solving it in individual way or leaving already existing business data as is, because at that time when such data were created it was consistent and in compliance with temporary business rules.

5. Conclusions

In this paper, we have set out concepts for easy and flexible customization, change and configuration management of software systems of information systems and proposed a method which uses business rule model stored in decision tables to represent the semantics of domain specific, business object attribute value dependent process logics and allows automated implementation of them into the configuration of the N-tier architecture based software system and process code.

The proposed method of automated software configuration implementation allows changes of process logic by changing configuration values directly in the software system and is limited only by data model implemented into the database, because if such modifications will be needed it should be produced all the automated reengineering process starting from the changes of DTs rules adding new conditions and conclusions and finishing with application of automated transformations.

All the limitations of the DTs belong to the proposed method too and should be solved using other engineering methods.

To this end we have constructed a generic set of metamodels and transformations in XML that are the basis of method proposed in this paper and used for engineering process automation based on metamodel transformation. We have shown how to automate business object configuration based decision processes using methods of classes stored in the business logic tier. Such business logic tier classes provide a chance of operation with business objects, their properties and methods without any thinking about data model implemented in the database or using any Horn clauses. They are replaced by the data selection operations implemented in the data access tier and made accessible as public methods for upper level services. The latter indicates how to embed business logic in a service oriented, event-driven N-tier architectural framework.

At the present we are continuing our research in the following directions. First of all, we are working on information processing rule templates for the validation of business object entities and their attributes in the software system business logic and service tier. In addition we envision extension of the presented method, metamodels, transformations and templates to allow automated incorporation of business rules used for validation into the generated software code.

Acknowledgments

The work is supported by Lithuanian State Science and Studies Foundation according to High Technology Development Program Project "Business Rules Solutions for Information Systems Development (VeTIS)" Reg. No. B-07042.

References

[1] Barbara von Hale (2001) Business Rules Applied: Building Better Systems Using the Business Rules Approach. John Wiley & Sons, Inc., New York.

[2] Simon, H. A. (1977) The new science of management decision, Prentice Hall PTR.

[3] Cunneyworth, W. (1994) Table Driven Design – A Development Strategy for Minimal Maintenance Information Systems, Data Kinetics Ltd.

[4] Zhou, Y., & Chen, B. (2003) The Methodology for Business Process Optimized Design. In Proceedings of Industrial Electronics Society IECON '03. The 29th Annual Conference of the IEEE, vol. 2, pp. 1819-1824.

[5] Zultner, & Richard, E. (1992) Quality Function Deployment (QFD) for Software. In Shulmeyerr G.G. & McManus J. I. (eds) Total Quality Management for Software, New York: Van Nostrand Reinhold.

[6] Gasper, D. (1999) Problems in the Logical Framework Approach and the Challenges for Project Cycle Management, The Courier, vol. 173. Brussels: European Commission, pp. 75-77.

[7] Baesens, B., Mues, C., Setiono, R., De Backer, M., & Vanthienen, J. (2003) Building Intelligent Credit Scoring Systems using Decision Tables, Enterprise Information Systems V, Kluwer, pp 131-135.

[8] Vanthienen, J. (2001) Ruling the Business: About Business Rules and Decision tables. Vandenbulcke J., Snoeck, M. (eds): New Directions in Software Engineering, Leuven University Press, Leuven, pp. 103–120.

[9] Vanthienen, J., & Dries, E. (1994) Illustration of a Decision Table Tool for Specifying and Implementing Knowledge Based Systems. International Journal on Artificial Intelligence Tools, 3(2): 267-288

[10] Kilov, H., & Simmonds, I. (1996) Business Patterns: Reusable Abstract Constructs for Business Specification. In Humphreys, P., et. Al (eds) Implementing Systems for Supporting Management Decisions: Concepts, methods and experiences, Chapman and Hall, pp. 225-248.

[11] Orriens, B., & Yang, J. (2003) Model Driven Service Composition. In Proceedings of the First International Conference on Service Oriented Computing, December 15-18, Trento, Italy.
[12] Goedertier, S., & Vanthienen, J. (2005) Rule-based Business Process Modeling and Execution. Proceedings of the International IEEE EDOC Workshop on Vocabularies, Ontologies and Rules for The Enterprise (VORTE 2005), pp. 67-74.
[13] Orriens, B., Yang, J., & Papazoglou, M. P. (2003) A Framework for Business Rule Driven Service Composition. Proceedings of the Fourth International Workshop on Conceptual Modeling Approaches for e-Business Dealing with Business Volatility, October 13-16, Chicago, United States, Lecture Notes on Computer Science, Springer-Verlag, Berlin, Germany.
[14] Vasilecas, O., & Smaizys, A. (2006) Business Rule Based Data Analysis for Decision Support and Automation, International Conference on Computer Systems and Technologies - CompSysTech'06, pp. II.9-1-II.9-6.
[15] Diskin, Z., & Dingel, J. (2006) A Metamodel Independent Framework for Model Transformation: Towards Generic Model Management Patterns in Reverse Engineering. In Proceedings of the 3rd International Workshop on Metamodels, Schemas, Grammas and Ontologies for reverse engineering (ATEM-2006), pp. 55-66.
[16] Vasilecas, O., & Smaizys, A. (2007) The Framework for Business Rule Based Software Modeling: an Approach for Data Analysis Models Integration. Databases and Information Systems IV, vol. 155 Frontiers in Art, IOS Press, Amsterdam.
[17] Vasilecas, O., & Smaizys, A. (2005) Business Rule Specification and Transformation for Rule Based Data Analysis. Proceedings of 19th International Conference on Systems for Automation of Engineering and Research (SAER 2005), Sofia: CAD Research and Development Centre "Progress", pp. 35-40.

Databases and Information Systems V
H.-M. Haav and A. Kalja (Eds.)
IOS Press, 2009

doi:10.3233/978-1-58603-939-4-255

Business Rule Management in Enterprise Resource Planning Systems

Vladimir AVDEJENKOV[1], Olegas VASILECAS and Aidas SMAIZYS
Vilnius Gediminas Technical University

Abstract. Nowadays Enterprise Resource Planning (ERP) systems are not only supplying information for all departments within an enterprise to support decisions, but also are used together with other software systems to automate business processes. Business processes are running according to the business rules. However business processes are changing rapidly and especially because of changes in business logics and sequentially changes in rules system. To implement such changes into the business system, all software systems of information system (IS), which are supporting business, should be readjusted to be in alignment with business. Separation and centralisation of business logics represented by business rules from the code of software system of IS is one of the ways to solve the problem. The paper analyses problems and available solutions of integration tasks to allow ERP system the collaboration with other software systems of IS. The main contribution of the paper is a business rule management system based method for solution of such a problems by providing of the separated component of shared business logics for all software systems of IS that are servicing the business system.

Keywords. business rules, business rules management systems, ERP systems, integration

Introduction

Nowadays growing popularity of information systems, new technologies and tools like business intelligence (BI), online processing and analytics (OLAP) make available integration of enterprise resource planning (ERP) system as a new opportunity. Emerging use of service oriented architecture (SOA) in ERP systems challenges integration tasks concentrating on business value, thus not only ensuring comprehensive information delivery and analysis delivering unstructured and structured information but also embedding data and data processing capabilities from different software systems to enable intelligent business services across all the information systems in the enterprise used for implementation and optimization of business-related processes in the enterprise. The real value of information systems is not in applications and amount of transactions performed or data processed and stored, but in value and quality of services provided for business users. This is especially important when implementing new automated decisions based on business logic across all enterprise systems. However, business logic (BL) used in business processes is distributed through different software systems of information systems and usually

[1] Corresponding Author: Vladimir Avdejenkov, Vilnius Gediminas Technical University, Sauletekio al. 11, LT-10223 Vilnius, Lithuania; E-mail: vladimir@isl.vgtu.lt.

differs depending on technology used for each particular software system. This leads to the problems dealing with inadequate automated decision processing and implementation of changes into different software systems of an information system. The implementation of such changes into a different system is a long and resource consuming process. Business rule separation from the code and use of business rule management systems (BRMS) for this purpose is the way to simplify and reduce the costs of system integration, support and adjustment [1].

This paper defines problems and solutions of ERP system integration with other software systems of an information system. Centralised use and separation of business logics represented by business rules from the software system of information system code is one of the ways to solve this problem offered in the paper.

The paper is organised as follows. In section 1, we briefly elaborate the topic of business logic separation from the software system code and discuss software system integration problems. Section 2 discusses basic concepts of software system integration, provides a framework for software system integration and introduces framework based method for ERP system integration. Section 3 illustrates how the proposed method can be used for system integration based on our research and experimental implementation of "Scala" ERP system. Section 4 concludes the paper.

1. Related Work

In the end of the 1960's, a new idea to create a integrated data model within a single organization was developed. Further evolution of ERP systems closely followed the spectacular developments in the field of computer hardware and software systems. [2] Most organizations designed, developed and implemented centralized computing systems, mostly automating their inventory control systems using inventory control packages (IC). Material requirements planning (MRP) systems based on BOM (Bill Of Material) were developed in the 1970s which involved mainly planning the product or parts requirements according to the master production schedule. Following this route new software systems called manufacturing resources planning (MRP II) were introduced in the 1980s with an emphasis on optimizing manufacturing processes by synchronizing the materials with production requirements. MRP II included areas such as shop floor and distribution management, project management, finance, human resource and engineering. This way, in the beginning of the ninth decade, the term of Enterprise Resource Planning (ERP) system [3] emerged as a successor of Management Information Systems (MIS) and Expert Systems with the power of enterprise-wide inter-functional coordination and integration. Based on the technological foundations of MRP and MRP II in the 1990s, ERP vendors added more modules and functions as "add-ons" to the core modules giving birth to the "extended ERPs." These ERP extensions include advanced planning and scheduling (APS), e-business solutions such as customer relationship management (CRM) and supply chain management (SCM) [2].

Currently, the definition of Enterprise Resource Planning encompasses a wider scope of tasks than when it had just emerged.

Usually ERP solutions addresses some senior management and all middle management processing: customer information, sales targets, quotas and sales order management, supply chain business partners and vendor selection, purchases, production planning and control, quality assurance, facilities scheduling, inventory control and warehousing, human resources management, cost accounting, efficiency and return on investment calculations. Top management support and general accounting are not directly addressed in this list. General accounting, however, has been a part of an ERP system, as is the case with SAP's R/2 and R/3. In fact, R/2 was started as a general accounting package. Therefore, ERP can be historically linked to the development of software for accounting purposes. [4].

The modules of ERP system are integrated and are using a unified database. The most popular business management systems are SAP, Oracle Applications, Navision, Epicor, Scala, Axapta, Microsoft Dynamics, etc [5].

Even having wide range of functionality no separate ERP system can support all services across the enterprise [6]. Most ERP systems have components allowing some functionality of customer relationship management (CRM) or supply chain management (SCM) systems [5]. However ERP systems are usually installed locally and not connected to the external environment of the enterprise, e.g. organisations with multiple sites or wide range of suppliers require Internet-oriented ERP support and usually are implementing internet based customer relationship, client handling and supply chain solutions so that data and processes of the enterprise can be integrated into a unified aggregate. [4] The level of integration differs depending on technology used. Business logics in these systems can be changed by either system parameterisation or changing the code and creating additional applications.

1.1. ERP Integration Problems and Solutions

ERP is based on the creation of a seamless data repository. This depository stores all the business, financial, production, human resources management information which occurred as the result of the company activity. Any piece of information possessed by the company becomes accessible to all authorized employees at any time. The concept of ERP became very popular in the production sector, because resource planning allowed reducing the time of production, the amount of stock in the warehouse, to improve customer relations, and to curtail the administrative apparatus at the same time. The ERP standard allows a merge of all enterprise resources into a single integrated system. Then integration of external applications like mass-customization production systems was started, providing real-time information combined with an effective dynamical scheduling [7]. However such integration was performed almost at data integration (DI) level only and business processes with supporting logics were left without decent attention. Modern ERP system evolution lead concentration on business services and as the result implementation of service oriented architecture (SOA) emerged. Future growth and success of ERP adoption and development will depend on the ERP system's capability of extending to Customer Relationship Management (CRM), Supply Chain Management (SCM) and other extended modules, and integration with the Internet-enabled applications [2].

Three main advantages of business-oriented systems are distinguished as system agility, reducing the costs, and system transparency [8]. The agility of an information system means that applications can adapt quickly in case of changes the business policy. In businesses where the market or other external factors force to change the business policy, one of the goals is zero latency between the confirmation and implementation of a new policy. When organizations ensure zero latency their competitive ability increases. In order to ensure zero latency between the confirmation of a policy and the implementation of rules, a modelling tool for business rules management system and business rules must be employed, and it should be available for business analysts to use. When business analysts are able to set the rules, zero latency can be announced as achieved.

Use of business rules management can reduce costs of change the business processes significantly, to compare with the use of common programming. Such a tendency can be noticed in terms of the time needed to implement the policy: business rules technologies require fewer human resources and therefore less time for the policy to be implemented. Research shows that IT departments using business rules technologies managed to save 5 to 40% of budget dedicated to application logic and infrastructure changes.

Ensuring system transparency is another important task for ERP and integrated systems. In cases when business policy is realized using business rules technologies, it is easier for business analysts and other business people to understand the existent, currently installed business policy. When business policy is realized in monolithic applications using 'C', 'Java' etc. programming languages, it is difficult for business people to control this process and ensure transparency needed.

Due to the fact that ERP systems usually encompass either all or nearly all enterprise business processes, installation of suchlike system requires much time (up to a couple of years), and the maintenance takes decades. The peculiarities of ERP systems cause a problem: ERP systems are not always able to satisfy the business needs; the contemporary business is changing rapidly, and new business demands emerge. This leads to the need of integration with other systems and implementation of changes across all software systems of information system in the enterprise.

There is a couple of ways to adjust ERP systems to the business needs; among them, modification of system parameters and changes to the system code.

The first method allows limited changes to system functionality; we can only change the system default functionality of the system. In this case, changes can only be made if functionality was provided while the system was being created. If the functionality we need was not provided, this method will not help to reach the goals. As we see, this method does not always let to tackle the tasks the business might demand.

Changes to system code are, on one hand, expensive, and on the other hand, not always possible. This method may be used in cases when an ERP system is created on demand and if it is adjusted to the needs of a particular customer. In such case, the customer and the system provider have the source code, and programmers can change it for develop additional or change existing system functionality.

In case if an ERP system is not created by a particular order, but is purchased „as is", there is a possibility to adjust the system using special adjustment tools, if such are provided by ERP system vendor. For example, programming language ABAP (Advanced Business Application Programming) is denoted for programming in SAP environment, and VBA (Visual Basic for Application) is used for programming in both Scala and Navision ERP systems. Such programming tools are commonly licensed and sold separately from ERP systems.

The use of business rules in ERP systems would allow a quick adaptability of these systems to the business needs and prepare them for integration with other systems. The use of business rules is not intended for all ERP systems. Further in this paper, we discuss possibilities to use business rules for solution to ERP integration tasks where such a possibility is not originally intended.

1.2. Using of Business Rules Management Systems for Business Logic Representation

Nowadays, talking about information systems, more and more attention is paid to the using business rules in information systems [9], [10, [11]. Business rules are the inseparable part of business; they describe the workings of business and delineate business processes which take place inside and outside an organisation. Business rules are formulated by business or state holders; normally the language used in this context is informal. The main principle for using business rules in information systems is that the business rules should be separated as independent component like DBMS from information system. On that score, if business logic changes, usually only business rules need to be changed, and the code of the information system itself is stationary. This allows reducing costs in system installation and support.

With the view to facilitate the employment of business rules (designing, editing, managing, etc.), so called business rules management systems are used (e.g. Business Rules Engine-BRE). The essence of suchlike systems is that rules are separated from applications and databases (this separation could be either logical or physical). Rules are designed separately and stored in rules repositories. During the course of running an application, rules are called out from the rules repository. If new rules are created or the existent ones are modified, all changes are made in the rules repository. The use of such systems reduces the time needed to create an application and significantly curtails support and improvement costs. Rules may be changed not only by programmers, but also by other business participants.

Business rule management systems are used to make the process of creation, modification and implementation of rules faster and more effective. Such systems are using complex algorithms to optimize computer resources when implementing business rules. During the process of integrating a business rules management system into a business system, every rule is entered as an independent statement describing a certain aspect of business, and in such a case business rules are functioning as autonomous units in this way are separated from the main application logic. The transparency of business rules, reduced costs and high system agility are the three main advantages, in comparison with information systems without business rules management systems integration.

Next section presents basic concepts of Enterprise Resource Planning and Business Rules Management Systems system integration, provides a framework for software system integration and introduces proposed method for future ERP and BRMS systems integration.

2. Business Rule Management and ERP System Integration

There are a couple of methods used to integrate business rules into information systems [12], [13], [14]. It can be either an application server implementing business rules, or the business rules management system itself, which is controlling and implementing business policy defined by business rules.

One of the ways to realize business rules in information systems are the active database management systems [15], [16], [17]. Active database triggers are using the ECA rules model and are consisting of three parts: an event, a condition and an action, abbreviated as ECA. An event marks the moment when the rule comes into effect, a condition is committed when the rule begins to operate, and an action is performed when an event comes into effect and the condition is correct. If a set event takes place, a condition is checked: this could be either a check of installed or deleted data, or a check of data in other charts, etc. Depending on the results of condition checking, it could be any kind of SQL language command: a reject of a transaction, changes to the data either in the base table or any other tables, a sending of messages, etc.

We suggest to use one business rule based meta-rules system for entire enterprise with an integrated business rule repository database, inference engine (IE) and interfaces to external users, software subsystems and design subsystem as it is presented in Figure 1. Business rule based meta-rules concentration in one BRMS and rule exchange interfaces support intelligent interaction between different subsystems in enterprise. Also, because of flexible XML language used for business rule formalization, it allows introducing an open organisation structure with a new intelligent functionality [18].

The business rules in BRMS are the intelligence resource of the meta-system. It provides a resources for meta-system to carry out smart resolution tasks in the inference engine. It usually consists of a compiler and a BR representation (structured frame knowledge) facility. The compiler converts external knowledge representation, obtained through meta-system interfaces into internal formal representation forms available for storing in BR repository database and for processing in inference mechanism. Such a business rule based meta-knowledge base system creates an open organization structure and allows new intelligent functionality to enter the meta-knowledge and use it in all subsystems with corresponding rule exchange interfaces to engage more duties in decision-making.

Inference engine carries out various actions based on the reasoning results that are transferring data between any two subsystems or new designed business rules or sorting new rules and data entered by users directly from business system into BR repository database. After being processed into the inference mechanism, the rule sets represented in XML are stored in repository for further transformation in all subsystems.

The interface to the external systems builds the communication between users, internal BRMS system components and external software systems (subsystems). The emerging agent software can be used for automatic BR discovery as well. The interface plays a key role in an open structured BRMS software system: codify human expertise into the computer system such that it can adopt the most creative intelligence and knowledge in decision making, transform formally represented business rules into human language for review and edit by users, communicate with other external intelligent software system agents for more complicated tasks. The interface can use DML and DDL interfaces of DBMS to transform business rules to Data Manipulations Language (DML) and Data Definition Language (DDL) instructions.

According to the framework in Figure 1, BRMS in this context allows not only integration of new services and business logics into the existing applications at the physical layer but also allows indirect integration between applications through BRMS or DBMS, too. According to the framework, the integration possibilities are limited only by architecture of the application and functionality of external communication interfaces of DBMS and applications. DBMS usually include at least two interfaces for message exchange in Data manipulation and description languages, represented as DML and DDL interfaces in the framework.

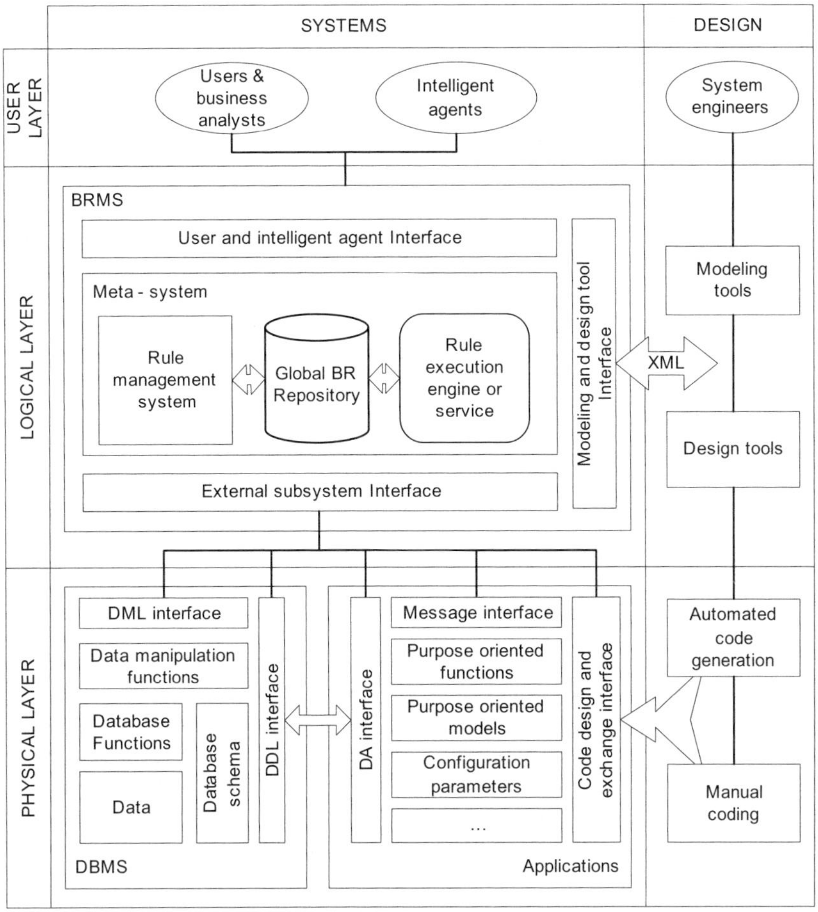

Figure 1. The Framework of integrated intelligent system using business rule management system

As we see, the employment of triggers can ensure wide functionality of a business management system [3]. As an example, the study [15] analyses a solution to the debtor management task using triggers. Debtor management is marginally automated in business management systems, moreover, conditions and business policy regarding it may change rapidly, therefore the employment of rules at this point would ensure all benefits of business rules management (business rules could be changed quickly, debtor management would be transparent, maintenance costs would be reduced). In the study, it is suggested to design the rules using UML diagrams. The rules designed are transformed into DBMS triggers and integrated into a business rules management system.

Despite of advantages and an example of a successful realization, modelling of business rules using UML diagrams is not perfect enough. In order for it to be used more widely, it must be formalized additionally, considering the requirements of DBMS triggers. Also, some other advantages already existing in business rules management systems are missing (e.g. user interfaces, rules depository, versions control, etc.).

Still, the very method of business rules integration into business management systems (with the help of DBMS triggers) is worth attention. The main advantages of this method are these: business rules are separated from program system code, they can be easily and quickly changed, they can be used in different systems; moreover, this method does not require additional programming equipment (an application server, etc.). In certain cases, this is even the only method to modify the functionality of a business management system.

The analysis of business rules management systems QuickRules, Oracle Business Rules, Versta, Ilog Rules and Open Rules under different aspects [20], [21], [22], [23] showed that the method of integration of rules into information systems using triggers is not offered in those systems. This is because usually business rules management systems are oriented towards the newly created systems. When creating a system, other ways to realize business rules are anticipated (e.g. application servers, objects, plug-ins, etc.). Additionally, an analysis of business rules management systems was performed, considering the potential to be connected to BRMS rules depository for the further use of rules.

Considering this, a method was offered to model business rules using a business rules management system, also using a written system extension to analyze business rules created and transform them into DBMS triggers. This way, the advantages of using business rules management systems will be ensured by integrating business rules into an enterprise resource planning system.

The business rules management system chosen for an experiment is OpenRules. It is an open source system with the interfaces for creating rules and is easily comprehensible not only for technical specialists, but also for the business people. In order to have a possibility to describe triggers with the help of OpenRules, a new keyword “TriggerEvent” was entered into the OpenRules system. The created extension analyses the described business rules, generates the SQL trigger code, and installs triggers into a database management system as displayed in Figure 2 and described in next section.

3. Experimental Validation Using BRMS and DBMS Triggers

In order to test the method of implementation of business rules into ERP systems, we have chosen “Scala” as a business management system and debtor management as a business scope of an enterprise resource planning system. Moreover, the chosen system is linked to our subject scope. The choice of an enterprise resource planning system was determined by the fact that this system allows to perform real trials and to obtain tangible results which can be assessed. Also, this enterprise resource planning system is well-known worldwide. Its clients are based in 140 countries, with the number of clients exceeding 20 thousand. ERP system “Scala” uses Microsoft SQL Server 2005 or Microsoft SQL Server 2000 DBMS.

The problem area chosen for this paper is debtor management in a trade company. Debts and credits are among the most important components of the company property, as they require additional costs, human resources and time in order to be managed qualitatively and effectively. Debts and credits are the main indicator of the company balance. Financial situation of the company is affected both by the balance of debts and credits, and the turnover period of those.

This choice was determined by the importance of automated debtor management to the majority of companies, and, on the other hand, ERP systems do not always properly automate this process. In the chosen ERP system "Scala", debtor management is not properly automated either.

With the help of the business rules management system OpenRules, the following debtor management rules were created:

- Block the delivery of goods to the customer, if his credit limit is exceeded after the trading operation.
- Block the delivery of goods to the customer, if his payment is 3 or more days late.
- Allow the customer to make the purchase, if his payment is not 3 or more days late.
- Send a reminder e-mail to the customer and the sales manager working with the customer, if the delivery is blocked.
- Send a reminder e-mail to the customer and the sales manager working with the customer, if the delivery is unblocked.

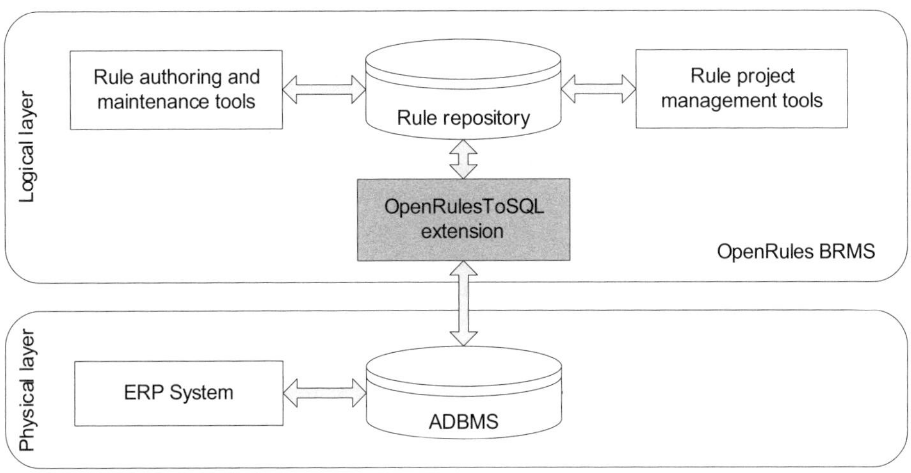

Figure 2. The scheme of business rule integration into the ERP system using OpenRules BRMS and OpenRulesToSQL extension

We have applied our experiment to ERP system "Scala" in a trade and production company. Companies yearly turnover amount is 40 mil. Eur. The number of debtor's are about 300, and amount debts are approximately 6 mil. Eur.

System databases, schema of ERP system databases, connection parameters and other service information are described in parameters of OpenRules business rules. The business rules in OpenRules BRMS described using ECA model. In order to encode ECA type rules (for later transformation into ADBMS triggers) we have extended OpenRules notation by an additional keyword TriggerEvent, followed by keywords BEFORE or AFTER, describing the time when the rule is coming into effect, then followed by keywords INSERT, DELETE or UPDATE describing the event for the business rule to react. After the event description, it is denoted which ERP object the business rule is attributed to.

Next row in the table includes a link into the OpenRules decision table describing conditions to be checked and actions to be taken as subject to the result of condition check. Both, the link to the decision table and the decision table, match the ordinary OpenRules notation. Decision tables include links to the methods that are implemented in trigger actions depending on the results of conditions later on.

With the help of OpenRulesToSQL extension, SQL triggers were generated and installed into a active database management system (Figure 2). After the installation of triggers, the correctness of operations in the ERP system was verified. Then, after the system check, ERP and CRM system was launched in a usual mode, with the integrated business rules. Business rules are separated from the ERP; rules parameters, such as deviations from the credit limit overdrafts or the allowed extension of a payment deadline may be changed by business people as well.

In two months after implementation of debtor management business rules, the situation with debtors in the company tested has improved: debt turnover decreased from 70 till 60 days, debts decreased by 15% and bad debts decreased by 25%. Moreover, the work with debtors in the entire company has become easier. Salesmen and business managers now are informed about changes to the debtor situation on time. Debtor control requires less time, and salesmen can dedicate more time for their direct responsibilities.

4. Conclusions

The presented study determined that one of the methods for business rule implementation can be created using database management system triggers operating according to ECA business rules. Analysis shows that this method is suitable not only for Enterprise Resource Management systems (ERP) integration, but also for ERP systems integration with other systems used by enterprises (e.g. CRM). Modification of business logic as well as integration of such systems is complex enough, especially if systems are standardized and offer low possibilities for integration and expanding of functionality. Usually these processes require a lot of time and resources.

The use of already existent business rule management systems is suggested for creation and management of business rules. For the integration of those rules into the Enterprise Resources Management a business rules management system extension is proposed. This extension is connected to the rules repository of a business rules management system, analyzes rules and transforms them into the triggers of database management systems. These triggers implemented to DBMS, which are used for regular transaction processing for ERP system. This way, integration between BRMS and ERP systems is insured.

The proposed method of integration of rules allows the supervisors of Enterprise Resource Planning system to apply business rules and modify business logics of their systems elaborating business processes. The method presented is suitable for the insufficiently transparent systems which were not anticipated for use of business rules. Additionally, the employment of a business rule system allows a centralized creation and management of business rules together with the transparency of rules and system agility. In future, created rules may be used for modification of an enterprise resource management system.

Acknowledgments

The work is supported by Lithuanian State Science and Studies Foundation according to High Technology Development Program Project "Business Rules Solutions for Information Systems Development (VeTIS)" Reg. No. B-07042

References

[1] Morgan T. (2002) Business Rules and Information Systems. Addison Wesley, 384 p.
[2] Hossain L., Patrick J. D., & Rashid M. (2002) Enterprise Resource Planning: Global Opportunities and Challenges. IGI Global, 308 p.
[3] Light, B., Holland, C., Kelly, S. & Wills, K. (2000) Best of Breed IT Strategy: an alternative to enterprise resource planning systems. In Proceedings of the 8th European Conference on Information Systems, 2000, Vienna, Austria, 1, pp.652-659.
[4] Chorafas D.N. (2001) Integrating ERP, CRM, Supply Chain Management, and Smart Materials. Auerbach Publications; 1 edition, 408p.
[5] Shanks G., Seddon P.B. & Willcocks G. (2003) Second-wave Enterprise Resource Planning Systems : Implementing for Effectiveness. Cambridge University Press, 468p.
[6] Curtis G., & Cobham D. (2005) Business Information Systems: Analysis, Design and Practice. Pearson Publications Company, 5th edition, 686p.
[7] Penya Y. K., Bratoukhine A., & Sauter T. (2002) ERP Integration into Generic Plant Automation Model. In the Workshop on Information Systems for Mass Customization, ISMC'2002, Sept., Málaga, Spain, pp. 137-148.
[8] von Halle., B. (2001) Business Rules Applied: Building Better Systems Using the Business Rules Approach. John Wiley & Sons, Inc., 464p.
[9] Avdejenkov V., & Vasilecas O. (2004) Business rules systems modelling with UML and rules enforcing in active relational databases. Lithuanian mathematical collection. Vilnius, MII, t. 44, TEV, pp. 383-387.
[10] Ross R. G. (2003) Principles of the Business Rule Approach. Addison-Wesley Professional, 400p.
[11] Valatkaite I., & Vasilecas O. (2005) On Business Rules Automation: the BR-centric IS Development Framework. In Eder, J. et al. (Eds.): ADBIS 2005, LNCS 3631, Springer-Verlag, pp. 350–365.
[12] Cibrán M. A., D'Hondt M. & Jonckers V. (2006) Mapping High-Level Business Rules to and Through Aspects, in: L'Objet, April–September, 12(2–3): 63–88
[13] Grosof B. N. (2001) Standardizing XML Rules: Preliminary Outline of Invited Talk International Joint Conference on Artificial Intelligence (IJCAI-01) (available at: http://xml.coverpages.org/IJCAI-grosof20010518.pdf)
[14] Hall C., & Harmon P. (2006) The 2006 BP Trends Report on Business Rules Products, Business Process Trends. (available at: http://www.bptrends.com/reports_toc_03.cfm)
[15] V. Avdejenkov, & O. Vasilecas. (2007) Business Rules Applying to Credit Management. In Khaled Elleithy (ed.) Advances and Innovations in Systems, Computing Sciences and Software Engineering. Springer, pp. 481-484.
[16] Valatkaite I., & Vasilecas O. (2002) Deriving active database triggers from business rules model with conceptual graphs. Lithuanian mathematical collection, Vilnius, MII, t. 42, pp. 289 - 293.
[17] Vasilecas O., & Lebedys E. (2006) Moving business rules from system models to business rules repository. INFOCOMP, V5, No 2, pp. 11 - 17.

[18] Vasilecas O., & Smaizys A. (2005) Business rule based knowledge base integrated intelligent system framework. Information Sciences 2005, Vol. 34, . Vilnius University Press, pp. 195 - 200.

[19] Badwy M., & Richta K. (2002) Deriving triggers from UML/OCL specification. Advances in Methodologies, Components and Management. Kluwer Academic Plenum Publishers, pp. 271 - 280

[20] Business Rules Management System ILOG Rules. (available at: http://www.ilog.co.uk/products/rules/)

[21] Business Rules Management System QuickRules (available at: http://www.yasutech.com)

[22] Open Rules - Open Source Business Rules Management System (available a: http://openrules.com)

[23] Business Rules Management System Versata; Versta, Inc. (available at: http://www.versata.com)

Databases and Information Systems V
H.-M. Haav and A. Kalja (Eds.)
IOS Press, 2009

doi:10.3233/978-1-58603-939-4-267

Service Oriented Architecture Application for Latvian Public Sector E-service Development

Pavel SEMENCHUK [a, 1], Yuri KORNIENKO [b] and Vita NARNICKA [c]
[a] *Applied Computer Science Department, Riga Technical University*
[b] *Modeling and Simulation Department, Riga Technical University*
[c] *Secretariat of Special Assignments Minister for Electronic Government Affairs*

Abstract. At present time, a few integration and e-service development projects were started in Latvia. One of them is Integrated State Information System (ISIS, Latvian abbreviation IVIS), which was started in January, 2006. Customer and provider of this project is the Secretariat of Special Assignments Minister for Electronic Government Affairs (SSAMEGA)). This project solution forms the infrastructure for e-service development. The infrastructure is already accessible for e-service designers and developers since the middle of 2007. There are 12 e-services, which were developed using ISIS infrastructure, already accessible for Latvian inhabitants on Latvian government e-service portal (www.latvija.lv). It is planned to release else 18 new e-services till the end of 2008. ISIS is based on Service Oriented Architecture (SOA) principles and includes many individual innovations and modern solutions. The paper describes development architecture and innovations, which are used in ISIS solution and in the current government projects.

Keywords. e-government, e-service, SOA, URN

Introduction

Electronic service development and state electronic government implementation is one of priorities almost in all the most developed countries of the European Union and the world, Latvia included. It is very important that e-government and integration process would occur not chaotically, but unitarily. Preceding decade could be considered as time, when primary data registers were created. The new decade, evidently, will be oriented on these registers integration, offered services electronization and their accessibility for inhabitants. All developed countries of the world are going this way now.

Before ISIS system creation the world and another Baltic state experience was taken into account. Major part of attention was fixed on Estonian X-Road [1] system. ISIS was created on X-Road successfully usage principle: defined centralized data exchange point, standardized data exchange formats and protocols. The main difference is that ISIS tries to use already existing state registers and information systems data

[1] Corresponding Author: Pavel Semenchuk, Riga Technical University, Meza 1/3, LV-1048 Riga, Latvia; E-mail: Pavels.Semencuks@abcsoftware.lv.

exchange infrastructure, if it exists. At the moment X-Road integrates 150 data bases and information systems and is used widely, but ISIS usage at the moment is only for e-services functionality providing. Lithuanian integration project (e-Gate) [2] goes similarly as ISIS project. It was started in 2004. In 2008 is planned, that two pilot e-services will be created for e-Gate project.

In ISIS system some original solutions are included and used. Using this system and its infrastructure couple projects were developed. ISIS solution and one project are discussed and presented further in this paper.

1. Principles of ISIS Creation

The time, when in the integration process was applied principle 'each system is to be integrated with each other system' had gone, and today this approach is not acceptable, because it's a technological deadlock. Information is stored in data bases, which number continues uninterruptedly grow. Data base realization technologies are different; therefore, if there are not used technologic platforms independent integration methods, technologic compatibility problems often appear. Communication infrastructure, which is used for information exchange, is in different technical condition and does not guarantee uninterrupted connection. The integration software should be able to process situations, when communication channels become very slow or inaccessible. This situation determines the choice, offering a definite technologic solution, which is based on the following principles:

- Integration technologic standard should be prevalent, i.e. independent of different software technologies.
- Integration standard should be based on the best world-scale experience and correspond to standard, which is accepted and developed by international level IT companies at present time.
- Integration software should be scalable: have possibility to increase its performance without complex reprogramming work, in fact, decreasing "down-time" to minimum, because the infrastructure of this software will be the basis for the e-service implementation, and in the future is planned, that service electronization and use intensity will grow.
- Integration software should have guaranteed development perspectives by the producer.
- As the integration software will simultaneously be the environment, in which e-services will be developed, there should be a possibility to modify e-service or to make it from the beginning, putting in as less programming work as possible.

ISIS solution includes best practices of similar e-government integration approaches which are, for example, in Denmark [3], UK [4], New Zealand [5], Hong Kong [6], Estonian [1] and elsewhere. ISIS solution contains some original ideas:

- The use of Service Oriented Architecture (SOA).
- Identification standard.
- The use of unified standards for e-service development and integration projects at the state level.

- Centralized use of XML schemas, Information System (IS) services, e-services and public services catalogue.
- And others.

2. Description of the Solution

ISIS ensures a possibility mutually integrate state and municipal information systems, which now or in the future will be providers or recipients of various e-services including numerous portals, from which e-services will be accessible for inhabitants. Not only state or municipal institutions will take part in the development of the e-services, but also commercial institutions, for example, banks, which will be necessary to involve for paid e-services realization.

ISIS solution is based on the following principles:

- The use of Service Oriented Architecture (SOA).
- The solution technologically supports the integration with numerous e-service providers.
- Identification standard, which provides world scale unique number assignment.
- The use of state level unified standards for e-service and integration projects development e-service – XML schemas development standards [7], IS service development standards [8], e-service development standards [9], SOA standards.
- Four centralized catalogues development – XML schemas catalogue, IS service catalogue, e-service catalogue, and public services catalogue.
- Common use e-services and IS services are technologically accessible from many access points – state and municipal portals, institution home pages, etc.
- Use of e-service envelope, when implementing asynchronous e-service.
- Safe mailboxes providing for office workers and inhabitants with possibility perform tasks, which are provided by e-service during implementation process
- Data Distribution Network (DDN) – a secure communication channel between government information systems, suitable for large amount of data asynchronous transmission.

ISIS solution conceptual description is shown on the Figure 1. Registers are related to integration software. For each data object, which is required for e-service realization, is necessary to work out XML schemas set. This process is regulated by the corresponding standards and guidelines and is used for XML schema basic objects and types description. Data call from the corresponding register is performed by Web services help (in ISIS context these are named as IS services). During IS services calls occurs metadata sending, which describes the call. With the metadata register provider will receive the information, which is necessary for him to fill in his system's audit notes about a specific request. IS service development and using also is regulated by a corresponding standard. IS services are divided into two groups: Business IS services (includes some specific business activities, for example, get inhabitant's first name and last name by the personal code) and Integration IS services (includes some other Business IS service calls and e-service business logic). Implementation of Integration IS services usually is provided by the BizTalk server – one of the basic e-service infrastructure parts.

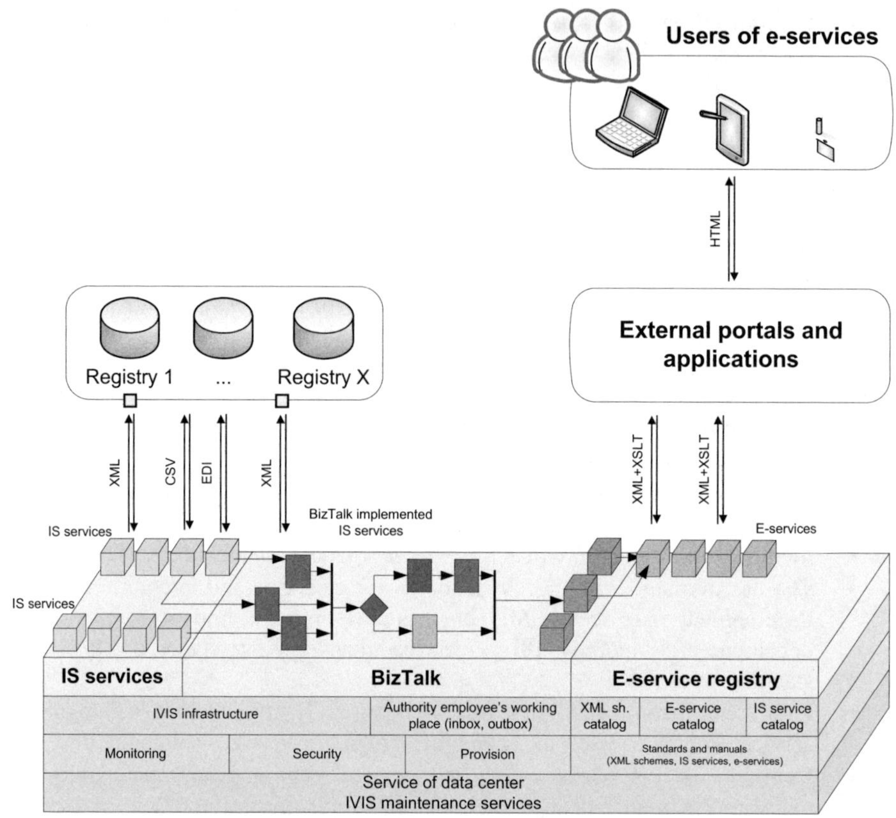

Figure 1. Logical schema of solution basic elements

Further in the paper is given a description of conceptual designing, basic elements upgrades and innovations, which are used in ISIS realization.

2.1. ISIS System Conceptual Model

E-services implementation platform form several components (see Figure 2):

- External portals and applications, which form:
  - o E-services presentation layer.
  - o External services and business logic libraries.
- ISIS infrastructure, which form;
  - o Request service.
  - o ISIS infrastructure help IS services.
  - o Integration IS services.
  - o Orchestration IS services.
  - o Business IS services.
- Authentication and authorization information providers: ISIS users and user group management module (UUGMM), state portal inhabitant accounts, JSC Latvia Post secure digital sign.
- ISIS applications.
- State and municipality IS.

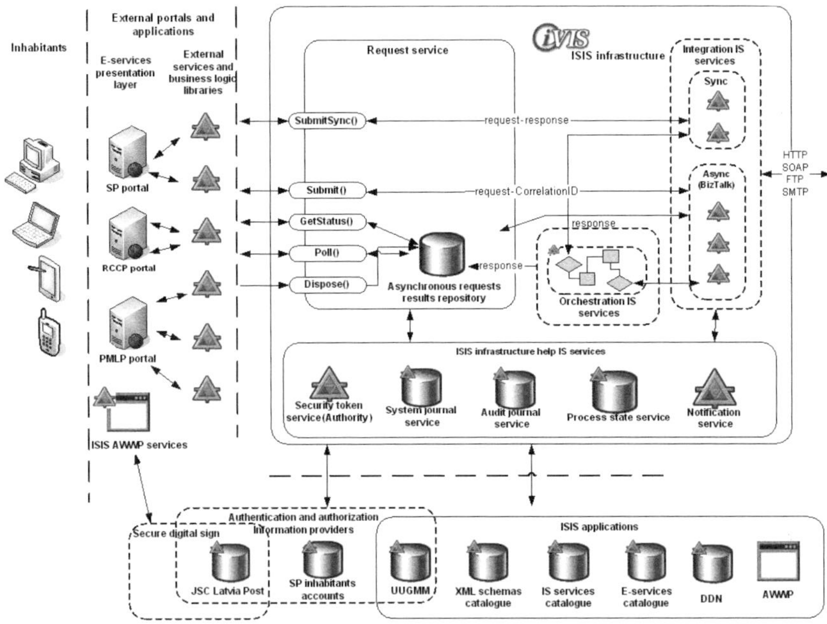

Figure 2. ISIS system conceptual model

2.1.1. External Portals and Applications

External portals and applications are: Latvian state portal (SP), Riga City Council portal (RCCP), Data Distribution Network (DDN) and others. Latvian state portal provides for inhabitants special user accounts, which, using ISIS services and ISIS authority worker work place (AWWP) application, provide interface to text messages, work tasks, status information of specific e-service instance in implementation context.

2.1.2. ISIS Infrastructure

ISIS infrastructure is software, which for external portals and applications provides e-service implementation environment and access point to service, state and municipality IS services. ISIS creation primary goal is to realize environment, where it will be possible quickly and with less of programming work create e-services.

2.1.2.1. Request Service

ISIS Request service is unified interface to another IS services and components. Request service is accessible as XML Web service. It provides according methods for synchronous (SubmitSync) and asynchronous (Submit) requests, sending to these methods request (IVISRequest) in envelope form [10].

2.1.2.2. Integration IS Services

Standardized information system approach kind, which provides external interface to information resources (state and municipality IS). Previously created IS services and integration tools are offered to developers for repeated use. That eases composed IS services development using BPEL as a base. ISIS integration IS service usually consists of two parts: server side and client side. Server side – IS service realization on institution side (realization kind selection is in institution competence; preferable (but not obligate) interface describing desideratum standard is WSDL); client side – standardized IS service interface realization on ISIS infrastructure side (provides necessary audit and control). By this way became possible to use already existed organization exchange environment and security facilities and not necessary to build up a brand new interface. There are two kinds of IS services:

- Synchronous IS services.
- Asynchronous IS services (usually are implemented by BizTalk).

2.1.2.3. Orchestration IS Services

Orchestration IS service coordinates implementation, which defines business process – e-service or composed IS service. Activities, which systems execute, are realized in coordinated form accordingly to process models. Orchestration IS service realize process firing accordingly to business events (business IS service calling counting), sends messages between processes, gets status information about activities and, if needed, requests human involvement. Usually this is implemented by BizTalk and is asynchronous.

2.1.2.4. Business IS services

Business IS services make activities only with business transactions, which are related to specific life situation or checking and are widely used to all e-services. Business IS services is possible to call only within ISIS infrastructure.

2.1.2.5. ISIS Infrastructure Help IS Services

ISIS infrastructure help IS services:

- Security token service (STS). Security token service is used by all centralized external and internal applications, services and portals and is based on WSE 2.0 [11]. In the future it is planned to use WSE 3.0 [11] for this task
- System journal service. This service is used by ISIS applications and IS services to register system errors.
- Audit journal service. Internal service, which is used by ISIS applications and IS services to register the information about system user activities.
- Process state service. Internal service, which is used by ISIS request service to register milestone execution, which is reached by e-service.
- Notification service. It is used to send messages to inhabitants.

2.2. ISIS Identification Standard

By analogy with e-GIF, AGLS, and other e-government initiatives about metadata standards [12], Dublin Core (DC) elements set [13] was used. Additionally, XML schema was provided for checking metadata elements [14].

The second part of standard provides identification system implementation, which is based on IETF RFC2141 [15]. Analyzing existent possibilities for resource identification, unique identifier delivery schema was created accordingly to URN principles, which are regulated by IETF RFC4617 [16]. ISIS assigned identifier (by URN syntax it is called as number) is written as follows:

URN:IVIS:100001:DOC-RCM-META

ISIS system's unique identifier inherited all of URN standard's advantages, among them:

- Structured formation. The identifier has a definite structure (XML schema form as well) and its automated control is possible.
- Readability. The identifier is understandable and usually includes for persons understandable directions to it originate resource.
- Uniqueness. The unique identifier is used for information unit unequivocal identification (XML schemas, documents and standards, ISIS IS services, e-services and e-service instances).
- Stability. ISIS identifier remains unchangeable from the moment of its creation up to the moment when it is deleted. It is possible to delete ISIS code, if it is useless (nobody uses it or will not use).

URN identifier extension infrastructure has not yet been created on a world scale. Global URN identifier extension system will be a two-stage process. There will be a global identification register created ("identifier space"), which will be able to find national, international or any other server, which contains information about registered URN and is responsible for information with a definite NID (URN schema). To such server will be redirected query to get identifier extension.

Dublin Core metadata elements set [13] is widely used in ISIS. Its primary use is to describe context of XML schemas, IS services etc. Besides of that, there are two important tasks, where these metadata is used:

- XML schemas search and hierarchical structure browsing mechanisms.
- ISIS URN resolution.

2.2.1. XML Schemas Search and Hierarchical Structure Browsing Mechanisms

XML schemas count in XML schemas catalogue is running to grow, that's why XML schema search mechanism was created. There are two ways of quick XML schemas search:

- Comprehensive search type. This kind of XML schema search allows find XML schemas by any typed text, which was entered for searching.
- Advanced search type. Each XML schema, which is registered in ISIS system, has metadata section, which describes this XML schema and which consists of elements set. This elements set is defined by DC standard [13]. This kind of XML schema search allows find XML schemas by these metadata section elements.

XML schemas metadata section is primary devised to software developers. It describes XML schema context in user understandable language.

For XML schemas developers more important to know XML schema's structure, that's why XML schema hierarchical structure browsing mechanism was created. This mechanism retrieves from XML schema:

- Other XML schemas hierarchies (import) list, which are used in XML schema.
- These XML schemas hierarchies (include) list, which are used in XML schema.
- XML schema elements list, complex types list, simple types list etc. Each XML schema element, complex type, simple type is described accordingly to W3C standard [17].

2.2.2. ISIS URN Resolution

There are a lot of functions, which are executed using ISIS URN, in ISIS system. By ISIS URN is possible to get information about ISIS entity (XML schema, IS service, e-service etc.) to which this URN belongs. This information is metadata about specific ISIS entity. Metadata is based on DC elements set [13].

At present time only one authority (SSAMEGA) issue such kind of URN to ISIS entities. In the future it is planned, that any authority will be able to issue ISIS URN according to agreement. This leads to the situation, where all important state entities will have globally unique identifier at state level – ISIS URN. All inhabitants will be able to get information about entities (resources), which provides specific authority. For this purpose it is planned to create ISIS URN resolution service.

ISIS URN resolution form several components (see Figure 3):

- External portal and application. Web application for users. This application organize ISIS URN input and by this URN metadata output.
- Business logic library. Specially created library, which by ISIS URN determines, which authority IS Service to call. Authority IS service returns metadata about identified entity with ISIS URN.
- Authorities IS services. Specially created services for retrieving metadata about entity by ISIS URN.
- Authority data bases. Repositories with data (metadata) about authority entities.

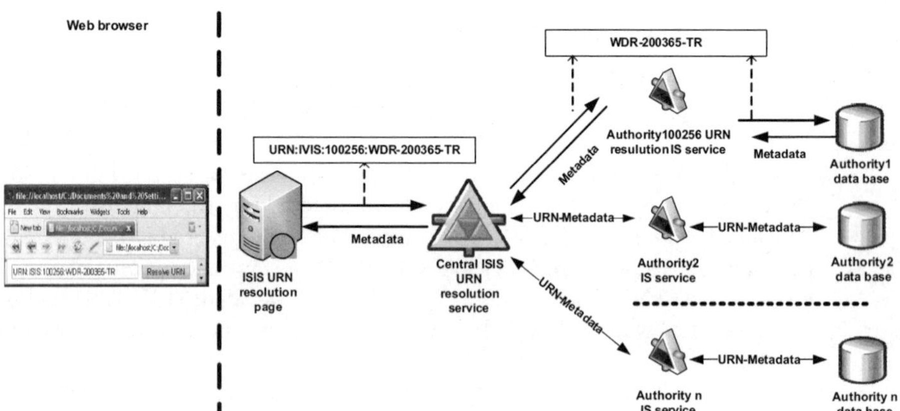

Figure 3. ISIS URN resolution

2.2.3. Data Distribution Network

DDN is subproject of ISIS infrastructure development. It forms virtual environment, where authorities can regulate automatic communications between theirs IS. IS of authorities (which are registered in ISIS system) can exchange with messages. These messages are in XML format, which is previously defined. Communication appears using virtual channels.

2.2.3.1. Motivation

There is a serious problem in Latvia (as in other world states): actual data inclusion in any specific place (registry or information system) bothers this data access and usage – communication channels are impacted.

In the world this problem solve with data replication:

- Data is copied outside of data repositories;
- Copy is synchronized with original: if data is actualized in original place, then this data automatically actualized also in all other copies.

Data replication is realized in the different ways, using different tools, guidelines and approaches. There is no unified standard in the world, how to realize it.

To realize each data replication as the individual solution is not possible, because it doesn't comply with ISIS strategy and not also accepted because of:

- Bothers these varied replications management and administration;
- IT integration enterprises are too expensive.

DDN realize centralized solution for providing of varied data replications.

2.2.3.2. Description of the Solution

DDN logic is presented below (see Figure 4).

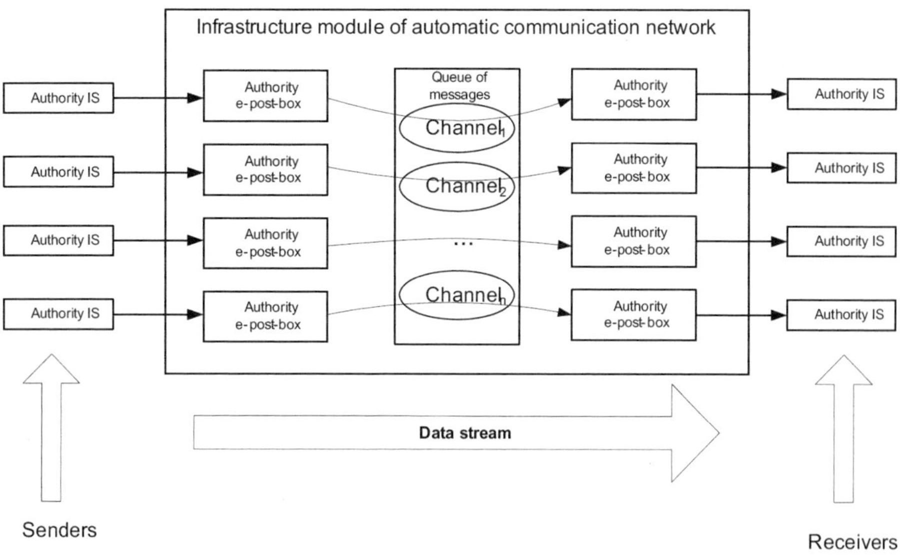

Figure 4. DDN logic

Each channel has one owner and 0 to N subscribers. Owner – authority, which created the channel. Subscribers – authorities, which owner connected to channel. There are two directions for each channel messages stream:

- Main direction, where primary messages are sent;
- Feedback direction (for error messages).

There are two types of the channels:

- Data Distribution Channel (DDC) (see Figure 5), where the main direction is from owners to subscribers. Owner send primary message to the channel (not to concrete addressee, but to the channel). Subscribers get these messages to their e-post-boxes. If subscribers need to provide a feedback (to announce about the error), then they can to send answers on received messages. This way owner gets answers.

- Data Collection Channel (DCC) (see Figure 6), where the main direction is from subscribers. Subscriber sends the primary message to the channel. Owner gets the distributed message to his e-post-box. If owner wants to provide a feedback (to announce about the error), then he sends an answer on received message. Subscriber gets this message.

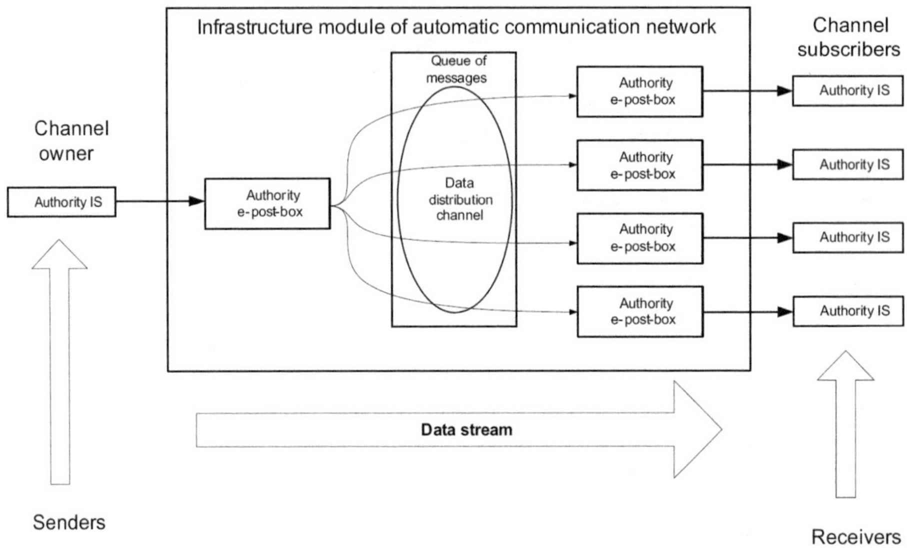

Figure 5. DDC and its context

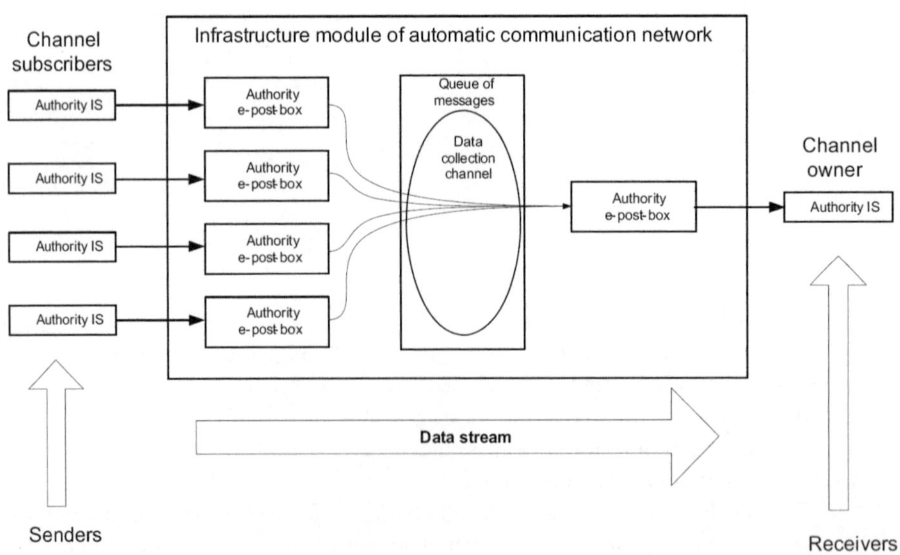

Figure 6. DCC and its context

Authorities can create their own channels or to subscribe to already existing channels (get role of subscriber). For each channel owner selects the message type, which will be send via the channel. There is the e-post-box created for each authority. E-post-boxes working principles are similar to those, which use popular e-mail systems. Difference is in user class. These e-post-boxes are mostly devised for information systems and for automatic communications, not for people. Information systems are the main users of e-post-boxes, which get or send messages using Web services of post-boxes. Role of human working with DDN e-post-box is quite administrative.

3. Conclusion

The aim of e-service infrastructure creation is to implement an environment, in which it would be possible quickly and with minimal amount of programming work to implement e-services.

The created infrastructure of e-services provides:

- Increased quality and accessibility of state and municipal services (increased convenience and time economy for clients).
- Increased efficiency and examination of state and municipal institution activities (rational use of state and municipal funds).
- Ensured, advantageous and convenient service delivery procedure for clients.
- Ensured service accessibility, using various service delivery channels, which are appropriate for each client, such as ports, customer care centres, telephones, Internet, etc.

E-service infrastructure implementation prognosticates positive results, such as:

- Possibility to decrease total state and municipal expenses in IT sphere by implementing centralized services and solutions.
- Possibility to increase new projects integrity and compatibility by implementing centralized infrastructure.
- Possibility to improve management and coordination of national IT system development.
- Possibility to provide individual services independent development by implementing common standards.

During e-service infrastructure designing, various problems and risks in its development and implementation should be taken into account. It may be concluded unequivocal, that at the moment there are no technical or technological problems; however there are administrative or procedural type problems, which are typical for all solution implementation at the State level.

References

[1] X-Road regulations, (available at http://ftp.ria.ee/pub/x-tee/doc/X-Road_regulations.pdf)
[2] Internal portal "e-Gate of the Government", (available at http://64.233.183.104/search?q=cache:S0cP9_ONKhwJ:www.ivpk.lt/en/report/report.pdf%20e-GATE&hl=en&ct=clnk&cd=2&gl=lt#27)
[3] InfoStructureBase, (available at http://isb.oio.dk/info/)
[4] Information on policies and standards for e-government, (available at http://www.govtalk.gov.uk/)
[5] E-government in New Zealand, (available at http://www.e.govt.nz/)
[6] Office of the Government Chief Information Officer, (available at http://www.ogcio.gov.hk/eng/infra/eif.htm)

[7] XML shēmu izstrādes vadlīnijas v1.0, (available at https://ivis.eps.gov.lv/IVISPortal/files/folders/vadlinijas/entry8.aspx)
[8] IS servisu izstrādes standarts v1.0, (available at https://ivis.eps.gov.lv/IVISPortal/files/folders/standarti/entry10.aspx)
[9] E-pakalpojumu standarts v1.0, (available at https://ivis.eps.gov.lv/IVISPortal/files/folders/standarti/entry41.aspx)
[10] IVISRequest XML shēma, (available at https://ivis.eps.gov.lv/epak/xsdk.WebSite/v1-7/?PagestatusID=XSDView&URN=URN:IVIS:100001:XSD-IVIS-IVISRequest-v1-0)
[11] Web Services Enhancements (WSE), (available at http://msdn2.microsoft.com/en-us/webservices/aa740663.aspx)
[12] Metadatu un e-pakalpojumu identifikācijas standarts v1.0, (available at https://ivis.eps.gov.lv/IVISPortal/files/folders/standarti/entry38.aspx)
[13] Dublin Core Metadata Initiative, (available at http://dublincore.org/)
[14] IVIS Metadatu standarta XML shēma, (available at https://ivis.eps.gov.lv/epak/xsdk.WebSite/v1-7/?PagestatusID=XSDView&URN=URN:IVIS:100001:XSD-IVIS-Metadata-v1-0)
[15] Moats R., URN syntax, (available at http://tools.ietf.org/html/rfc2141)
[16] Kornijenko J. A Uniform Resource Name (URN) Formal Namespace for the Latvian National Government Integration Project, (available at http://www.ietf.org/rfc/rfc4617.txt)
[17] W3C. World Wide Web Consortium, (available at http://www.w3.org/)

Data and Knowledge Management

Databases and Information Systems V
H.-M. Haav and A. Kalja (Eds.)
IOS Press, 2009

doi:10.3233/978-1-58603-939-4-281

Query Classification in Content-Based Image Retrieval

Ilya MARKOV [a,1] and Natalia VASSILIEVA [b]
[a] *Department of Computer Science, Saint-Petersburg State University*
[b] *HP Labs, Saint-Petersburg*

Abstract. Image retrieval by using content analysis is known as a difficult task. In our previous studies [1] and [2] mixed-metrics were proposed in order to combine color and texture metrics for image retrieval task. It was shown that it is always possible to mark out the best mixed-metrics for every group of similar images and improve retrieval effectiveness. In order to get the proper mixed-metrics a particular query-image should be classified to one of the predefined groups of perceptually similar images and this should be done in the real-time mode while processing the query and retrieving the result. In our previous work [3] the highly specialized classification method was proposed to solve this task. In the current study Naive Bayes and SVM classifiers are discussed and applied to the mixed-metrics approach to image retrieval. Classification result for these classifiers in comparison with the classifier, proposed in [3], are presented.

Keywords. content-based image retrieval, image classification

Introduction

Content-based image retrieval is a way of searching in image collections when no additional information about images is given. Every image in a collection is represented by one or several feature vectors. These feature vectors are numerical descriptors of image content. Feature vectors are built upon the information extracted from pixel values. Usually one feature vector represents one of the low-level image features (color, texture, shape). At a query time feature vectors are extracted from a query-image and compared against existing vectors of images stored in an image collection.

Common approach is to match vectors describing different low-level features independently. All vectors of an image collection describing the same feature form multidimensional vector space (feature space). To measure image similarity one should define metrics for every feature space. The main assumption here is that two images are similar to each other if and only if corresponding vectors are similar too in accordance with the metrics specified.

Many researchers showed that it is necessary to combine various features for effective image retrieval. Merging results obtained for the same query by using different metrics in different feature spaces is known as a challenging task.

[1]Corresponding Author: Ilya Markov, Saint-Petersburg State University, Universitetsky 28, 198504 Saint-Petersburg, Russia; E-mail: ilya.markov@gmail.com.

Color and texture are the common features which are used for searching in natural images. In [1] we proposed a technique to combine color and texture metrics taking into account a particular query-image. Weighed linear combination of color and texture metrics (mixed-metrics) is considered as a fusion function. Our approach is based on the hypothesis, proposed and proved in [1], that there are optimal weights to combine color and texture metrics for every query-image and these weights are unique for a given query. By using these optimal weights one can improve retrieval results. We showed that it is always possible to mark out the best mixed-metrics for every group of similar images (and thus for every query-image). In [2] it was shown that mixed-metrics based approach outperforms widely used CombMNZ data fusion method in some cases, and has close results in the others.

It was stated that in order to perform a search over an image collection by using mixed-metrics one should prepare training set which represents the collection well. The training set should be somehow divided into groups of similar images and best mixed-metrics for every group should be calculated. To perform a search itself, one should classify a query-image as belonging to one of the groups. After that a search can be performed by using mixed-metrics of the group which the query-image is classified to.

The approach described above improves retrieval efficiency only if classification task is solved. A simple and highly specialized solution for that task in the described context was proposed in our previous work [3]. According to that approach every group of perceptually similar images is represented with a set of "centers" or centroids. A query-image classification is performed based on the distances between its feature vectors and groups' centroids. The better centroids represent the groups the more precise classification and retrieval are.

In this study we solve the same classification task by using Naive Bayes and SVM classifiers, which was chosen for their known classification performances in pattern recognition and CBIR context. Their applicability to the query image classification task is discussed and comparative classification results are given.

1. Related Works

Grouping images into semantic classes by using low-level visual features is an important task. Many researchers claim that solving this problem can not only significantly improve image retrieval results ([4], [5], [6]), but could also allow using more convenient query forms instead of query-by-example ([7], [8]).

The first researchers who followed the idea of general image classification proposed the usage of binary classifier to decide whether an image belongs to a certain semantic class or not. These studies include techniques that can decide whether an image is indoor/outdoor ([6], [9]) or city/landscape ([10]). Vailaya et al. [10] stated that multiple two-class classifications may be more feasible than multi-class classifications. The usage of weighted k-NN classifier is typical for these binary classification tasks.

The same authors summarized binary classifiers in [4], proposing binary hierarchy of vacation images, where the first level of the hierarchy is indoor/outdoor images, the second is city/landscape and other levels are related to the specific classes of natural scenes. Bayesian classifier is used to assign an image to its best related group for each level of the binary hierarchy.

Application of a Bayesian frameworks in CBIR is also discussed in [11], [12] and [13]. Cox et al. [11] developed the Bayesian image retrieval system, called PicHunter, which is a simple instance of a general Bayesian framework.

The usage of SVM classifiers in CBIR is widely discussed during past 10 years ([14], [15], [16], [17]). Chang et al. [14] summarized the problems, which arise when applying SVM techniques to the visual information retrieval. The first one is "scarcity of training data", when a number of training instances is less than a dimension of a feature space. The second problem is "imbalance of training classes", when a number of negative training instances is much greater then a number of positive ones. These problems make class prediction unreliable. Several SVM modifications are proposed to deal with stated challenges. Application of Kernel functions is discussed in [15], [16] and [17]. [14] proposes active learning, recursive subspace co-training and adaptive dimensionality reduction techniques.

2. Task Definition

In [1] we proposed a technique to combine image similarity measures which takes into account a particular query-image. We introduced mixed-metrics obtained from color and texture metrics (C and T respectively) by using their weighted linear combination $a \cdot C + (1 - a) \cdot T$, where a is a varying coefficient which depends on a query-image. We stated and proved the hypothesis that optimal value of a is the same for similar query-images.

It was shown that in order to perform searches over an image collection by using mixed-metrics, training set, which represents the collection well, should be prepared. The training set should be somehow divided into groups of similar images and optimal mixed-metrics coefficient a should be calculated for every group by using the algorithm proposed in [1].

To perform a search with a particular query-image, optimal coefficient a should be found for the given query. Thereto the query-image has to be classified to only one of the groups of similar images defined on the previous step. The classification is performed in the real-time during retrieval process, therefore it should be as fast as possible and simple enough involving just a few computations. Thus we have two important requirements for the classification algorithm to be used:

- an object should be classified to exactly one of the groups;
- computational complexity of the prediction stage should be low.

3. Classification Algorithms

The goal of classification is to take an input vector x and to assign it to one of K discrete classes C_k where $k = 1, ..., K$ [18]. In the most common scenario classes are disjoint, so that each input is assigned to one and only one class. Binary classification can be considered as a special case of multi-class problem when the number of classes $K = 2$. Well-known classification methods including decision trees, Bayesian networks, support vector machines and neural networks were initially devised for the binary case. Although many binary classifiers can be naturally extended to multi-class domain by using winner-take-all strategy [19], this can be computationally heavy when the number of classes is big. When it is not possible to directly extend a binary method to a multi-class modification or the resultant method is computationally complex, multi-class classifiers are often built based on a set of binary classifiers by using one-versus-the-rest, one-versus-one or error-correcting-output-coding strategy.

3.1. Centroid-Based Classifier

In [3] we proposed a simple and highly specialized solution for the classification task, described in section 2, which satisfies all the stated requirements. According to that approach every group of perceptually similar images is represented with a set of centroids. One centroid is built for every feature. In our case color and texture features are combined, therefore two centroids have to be built for every group: one representing "central" color of the group and other representing "central" texture.

According to the "best image in the group" centroid building method, proposed in [3], color/texture group's centroid should be an image, belonging to the group, having the highest precision when performing a search by using color/texture metrics with that image as a query. Building algorithm is the following: for every image in the group a search by using color/texture metrics should be performed and retrieval precision should be calculated. Images from the same group as the query-image are treated as relevant, while others are not. Image with the highest precision is treated as a color/texture centroid of the group.

At a search-time the distances between query-image and groups' centroids are calculated. The query is classified to the group with the nearest set of centroids. Therefore the computational complexity of the proposed classification algorithm is equaled to the number of groups multiplied by the number of features (one centroid per feature) because the query is compared to the groups' centroids only.

3.2. Naive Bayes Classifier

Naive Bayes is a simple probabilistic learning algorithm based on applying Bayes' theorem with the following "Naive" assumption: distributions of input features are assumed to be independent. This assumption is rarely true in the real-world applications, but in spite of this Naive Bayes classifier performs surprisingly well in many complex classification tasks.

In order to perform multi-class classification of an input, Naive Bayes algorithm computes a posterior probability that the input belongs to a class for every class in the system. The result of the classification is the class with the highest posterior probability.

An advantage of the Naive Bayes classifier is that it requires a small amount of training data to estimate the parameters necessary for classification. Its disadvantage in the CBIR area is that Bayesian probability model operates with discrete features. Therefore image features should be discretized first before using Naive Bayes classifier, which is not a trivial task.

3.3. SVM Classifier

Support vector machines are a set of supervised learning methods used for classification and regression. The goal of SVM classifier is to find the best hyperplane separating classes. The best hyperplane has the maximum distances to the nearest data points from the classes to be separated.

Initial SVM method is linear and assumes that points from different classes are linearly separable. Several extensions to the initial case were proposed including soft margin extension to deal with noisy data sets and non-linear SVM classifier (also known as Kernel Machine) to deal with non-linear spaces such as image feature vector spaces.

Although Kernel Machines method is known to be a very powerful non-linear classifier, it has several disadvantages. It is computationally demanding to train and, what is more crucial in our case, to run. Sensitivity to noisy data is among other known disadvantages, which is also critical for the task, described in section 2.

4. Experiments and Result Analysis

We use experimental image database from [2] which consists of 650 images from Corel Photo Set collection. It is divided into 9 groups based on images content by 2 experts. Resultant groups are: City, Clouds, Coasts, Buildings, Fields, Lakes, People, Rocks and Trees. This set of images can be considered as a training set for some larger collection.

For every image in the database color and texture features are extracted and for every pair of images color and texture distances are computed. Metrics values are normalized according to the following rule:

$$metrics_{result}(image) = (metrics(image) - Average)/Deviation. \qquad (1)$$

Therefore color and texture metrics values distributions have the same $Average$ and $Deviation$.

We reuse classification results for centroid-based classifier from [3], where every image is classified to exactly one of the groups. On the contrary, only binary versions of Naive Bayes and SVM classifiers are used because of their simplicity in comparison with multi-class modifications. Therefore they perform as many classifications as many groups we have. However the binary case still shows the main trends of using such classifiers in the area of content-based image retrieval.

We use Peltarion Synapse framework [20] to get the results for Naive Bayes and SVM classifiers. Synapse utilizes Kernel Adatron SVM modification because it is reasonably fast in comparison to other SVM models.

Comparative classification results are shown in Table 1. Naive Bayes and SVM classifiers are run with the color information only because of the dimensionality problem, which is discussed below in this section.

It can be seen, that Naive Bayes classifier tends to reject most of the images, which results in the high false negatives rate. It means that Naive Bayes classifier can simply reject an image from the right group. Exceptions are "Clouds" and "Rocks", where false negatives rate is low. It is very natural, that clouds can be easily separated by color from all other groups, therefore all the classifiers perform good on this class with low both false positives and false negatives rates.

Vise versa, SVM classifier accepts most of the images and has low precision of positives and high false positives rates in most cases. It means that SVM classifier can easily misclassify an image and put it to the wrong group. Therefore we cannot trust the classification results obtained by using SVM classifier too.

Table 1. Classification results for Centroid-Based, Naive Bayes and SVM classifiers (%).

Group	Precision of positives			Precision of negatives		
	Centroids	Bayes	SVM	Centroids	Bayes	SVM
City	19	100	6	92	28	75
Clouds	86	96	95	97	93	99
Coasts	44	89	21	95	25	76
Buildings	71	98	37	87	31	71
Fields	66	94	40	92	25	74
Lakes	56	81	28	91	23	76
People	35	100	18	99	43	76
Rocks	28	100	43	100	87	98
Trees	78	94	51	94	37	49

Group	False positives			False negatives		
	Centroids	Bayes	SVM	Centroids	Bayes	SVM
City	81	0	94	8	72	25
Clouds	14	4	5	3	7	1
Coasts	56	11	79	5	75	24
Buildings	29	2	63	13	69	29
Fields	34	6	60	8	75	26
Lakes	44	19	72	9	77	24
People	65	0	82	1	57	24
Rocks	72	0	57	0	13	2
Trees	22	6	49	6	63	51

Table 2. Classification results of using color, texture and both features with Naive Bayes classifier (%).

Group	Precision of positives			Precision of negatives		
	Color	Texture	Both	Color	Texture	Both
City	100	4	4	28	99	99
Clouds	96	0	0	93	100	100
Coasts	89	2	1	25	99	99
Buildings	98	2	2	31	100	100
Fields	94	2	2	25	99	99
Lakes	81	6	8	23	97	97
People	100	0	0	43	100	100
Rocks	100	0	0	87	100	100
Trees	94	13	11	37	97	97

Centroid-based classification results lay between those borderline cases described above having acceptably high precision of positives in most cases, but high false positives rate in some of them.

All the classifiers face the "imbalance of training classes" problem here. The training set consists of 650 images divided into 9 groups, therefore the number of positive instances for each group is 8 times less on the average than the number of negative ones.

The results shown in Table 1 are obtained by using color information only for Naive Bayes and SVM classifiers. Comparative results of using color, texture and both features together are shown in Table 2 and Table 3.

Table 3. Classification results of using color, texture and both features with SVM classifier (%).

Group	Precision of positives			Precision of negatives		
	Color	Texture	Both	Color	Texture	Both
City	6	19	19	75	87	87
Clouds	95	22	22	99	87	87
Coasts	21	22	22	87	87	87
Buildings	37	22	22	71	86	86
Fields	40	47	47	74	86	86
Lakes	28	35	35	76	85	85
People	18	0	0	76	88	88
Rocks	43	10	10	98	87	87
Trees	51	20	20	49	87	87

The "scarcity of training data" problem is seen here. Color feature is represented with 45-dimension vector which is much less than the size of the training set (650 images). Therefore both classifiers show acceptable results when using color feature only. Texture has 714 dimensions which is greater than 650. Therefore both Naive Bayes and SVM classifiers cannot separate groups from each other, showing nearly constant precision across all the groups when using texture or both features together. To use texture feature with these classifiers the dimension should be decreased, which takes additional resources and does not feet the requirement that computational complexity of the prediction stage of a classifier should be low.

For centroid-based classifier dimensionality problem is hidden inside the metrics calculation and affects only metrics evaluation time, therefore proposed classifier does not depend on the feature space dimension at all.

5. Conclusion

In this study we addressed query image classification problem applied to the mixed-metrics approach developed in [1]. It was shown that Naive Bayes and SVM classifiers cannot be directly applied to solve the classification task described in 2, while centroid-based classifier, proposed in [3], suit that task well, being very simple and still showing acceptably good classification results in comparison with Naive Bayes and SVM classifiers.

Acknowledgments

This work was partially supported by RFBR (grant 07-07-00268a).

References

[1] Markov, I., Vassilieva, N., & Yaremchuk, A. (2007) Image retrieval. Optimal weights for color and texture features combining based on query object (In Russian). In Proceedings of 9th Russian Scientific Conference on Digital Libraries (RCDL 2007), October 16–18, Pereyaslavl-Zalessky, Russia, pp. 195–200.

[2] Markov, I., & Vassilieva, N. (2008) Image retrieval. Color and texture combining based on query-image. In Proceedings of International Conference on Image and Signal Processing (ICISP 2008), July 1–3, Cherbourg-Octeville, France, pp. 430–438.

[3] Markov, I., & Vassilieva, N. (2008) Building Up Low-Level Centroids for Groups of Perceptually Similar Images. In Proceedings of 8th International Baltic Conference on Databases and Information Systems (Baltic DB&IS 2008), June 2–5, Tallinn, Estonia, pp. 341–348.

[4] Vailaya, A., Figueiredo, M.A.T., Jain, A.K., & Zhang, H.-J. (2001) Image classification for content-based indexing, IEEE Transactions on Image Processing, 10(1): 117–130

[5] Kaick, O., & Mori, G. (2006) Automatic Classification of Outdoor Images by Region Matching. In Proceedings of 3rd Canadian Conference on Computer and Robot Vision (CRV 2006), June 7–9, Quebec, Canada.

[6] Serrano, N., Savakis, A., & Luo, L. (2002) A computationally efficient approach to indoor/outdoor scene classification. In Proceedings of 16th International Conference on Pattern Recognition (ICPR 2002), August 11–15, Quebec, Canada, pp. 146–149.

[7] Vassilieva, N., & Novikov, B. (2004) A Similarity Retrieval Algorithm for Natural Images. In Proceedings of 6th International Baltic Conference on Databases and Information Systems (Baltic DB&IS 2004), June 6–9, Riga, Latvia.

[8] Vassilieva, N., & Novikov, B. (2005) Establishing a correspondence between low-level features and semantics of fixed images (In Russian). In Proceedings of 7th Russian Scientific Conference on Digital Libraries (RCDL 2005), October 4–6, Yaroslavl, Russia, pp. 236–240.

[9] Szummer, M., & Picard, R.W. (1998) Indoor-outdoor image classification. In Proceedings of IEEE International Workshop on Content-Based Access of Image and Video Database (CAIVD 1998), January 3, Bombay, India, pp. 42–51.

[10] Vailaya, A., Jain, A.K., & Zhang, H.-J. (1998) On Image Classification: City Images vs. Landscapes, Pattern Recognition, 31(12): 1921–1935

[11] Cox, I.J., Miller, M.L., Minka, T.P., Papathomas, T.V., & Yianilos, P.N. (2000) The bayesian image retrieval system, PicHunter: Theory, implementation and psychophysical experiments, IEEE Transactions on Image Processing, 9(1): 20–37

[12] Heller, K.A., & Ghahramani, Z. (2006) A Simple Bayesian Framework for Content-Based Image Retrieval. In Proceedings of IEEE Computer Society Conference on Computer Vision and Pattern Recognition (CVPR 2006), June 17–22, New York, USA, pp. 2110–2117.

[13] Vasconcelos, N., & Lippman, A. (1998) A bayesian framework for content-based indexing and retrieval. In Proceedings of Conference on Data Compression Conference (DCC 1998), March 30–April 1, Snowbird, USA.

[14] Chang, E., Li, B.T., Wu, G., & Goh, K.S. (2003) Statistical learning for effective visual information retrieval. In Proceedings of IEEE International Conference on Image Processing (ICIP 2003), September 14–18, Barcelona, Spain, pp. 609–612.

[15] Chapelle, O., Haffner, P., & Vapnik, V. (1999) SVMs for histogram based image classification, IEEE Transactions on Neural Networks, 10: 1055–1064

[16] Chen, Y., Zhou, X.S., & Huang, T.S. (2001) One-class SVM for learning in image retrieval. In Proceedings of IEEE International Conference on Image Processing (ICIP 2001), October 7–10, Thessaloniki, Greece, pp. 34–37.

[17] Gosselin, P.H., & Cord, M. (2004) A Comparison of Active Classification Methods for Content-Based Image Retrieval. In Proceedings of 1st International Workshop on Computer Vision meets Databases (CVDB 2004), June 13, Paris, France.

[18] Bishop C.M. (2006) Pattern Recognition and Machine Learning (Information Science and Statistics). Springer Science and Business Media.

[19] Aiolli, F., & Sperduti, A. (2005) Multiclass Classification with Multi-Prototype Support Vector Machines, Journal of Machine Learning Research, 6: 817–850

[20] Peltarion Synapse documentation, (available at http://www.peltarion.com/WebDoc)

Databases and Information Systems V
H.-M. Haav and A. Kalja (Eds.)
IOS Press, 2009

doi:10.3233/978-1-58603-939-4-289

A Comparison of the Universal and the Regular Database Design

Erki EESSAAR [1] and Marek SOOBIK
Department of Informatics, Tallinn University of Technology

Abstract. It is tempting to design a database according to very abstracts concepts in order to cope with changing requirements. The generic design, which is called "universal database design", allows us to record all possible facts in terms of object types, objects, attributes, attribute values, and relationships. Arguably this kind of design simplifies the recording of new kinds of facts. However, the design has many associated problems. In this paper, we introduce a framework for evaluating database designs. We present the analysis of some of the advantages and disadvantages of the use of the universal design by using the framework.

Keywords. database design, data management, universal design, SQL

Introduction

Two important properties of the system development methodologies of the *Internet time* are constant time pressure to the developers and vague requirements that often change [1]. One tempting solution for dealing with changing requirements to databases seems to be the use of a highly generic database design that has different names and variations: "Universal Data Model" [2], "The entity-attribute-value representation with classes and relationships (EAV/CR)" [3], "Generic data model" [4], and "vertical design" [5]. However, ease of evolution is not the only aspect that we must consider in case of selecting a suitable database design. In addition, if we consider ease of evolution, then we must also consider how we can enforce integrity constraints.

The *goal* of the paper is to introduce a framework for evaluating database designs and analyse *some* of the advantages and disadvantages of the use of the *universal design*. This analysis is based on the *experiments* and the results of a literature review. Existing studies consider only *few* disadvantages and provide few experimental results. In this paper, we extend the work that was started in [6]. We use the concepts of SQL [7] because existing literature about the universal design uses these concepts.

The rest of the paper is organized as follows. Firstly, we explain the principles of the universal design. Secondly, we introduce a framework for evaluating database designs. Thirdly, we analyze some advantages and disadvantages of the use of this design. Finally, we draw conclusions and point to the future work.

[1] Corresponding Author: Erki Eessaar, Tallinn University of Technology, Raja 15, 12618 Tallinn, Estonia; E-mail: eessaar@staff.ttu.ee.

1. The Universal Design

The part a) of Figure 1 is pictorial representation of the universal design. The part b) of Figure 1 presents an example of the *regular design*. It is also possible to use a combination of these designs. The conceptual data model, which illustrates the regular design, is a fragment of the model that is presented in the specification of the Transaction Processing Performance Council (TPC) benchmark C (TPC-C) [8].

The specification of the universal design uses the modeling principle, according to which a model should be explicitly divided into operational and knowledge levels [9]. "The knowledge level objects define legal configuration of operational level objects."[9] Data about an object system is recorded at the operational level in terms of the objects, their attributes, and relationships. Entity type *Attribute_value* has a set of attributes. The specification of each attribute in this set has the general form: *<<data_type_name>>_value data_type_name*. These attributes allow us to record values that have different types. The amount of these attributes and their data types depend on a database system (DBMS) where this database is created. Data at the knowledge level determines the legal values that can be associated with an object at the operational level. The knowledge level contains data about object types and their attributes. Next, we list some of the *variations* of the universal design.

- The word "object" can be replaced with the words "entity" or "thing".
- Hay [2] proposes a many-to-many relationship between *Attribute* and *Entity_type* and specifies it by using entity type *Attribute_assignment*.
- *Attribute* or *Attribute_assignment* could have associated entity type *Legal_value* that allows us to specify the legal values of the attributes [2].
- *Attribute* could have an attribute or even associated entity type *Format* in order to permit recording of a format for the values of an attribute [2].
- Each supported data type should have exactly one corresponding table for recording attribute values with this type according to the EAV/CR approach [3]. This is different from the design a) in Figure 1. There is one generic entity type *Attribute_value* that has an attribute for each supported data type.
- Karanikolas et al. [10] propose *Frame DataBase model*. It is a variation of the universal model. For instance, it provides support to multilinguality of data in a database and allows designers to use subfields.

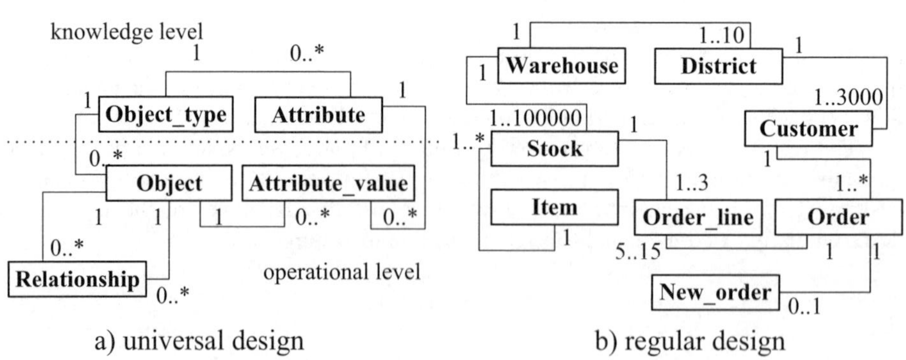

Figure 1. Examples of the database designs

At first glance, the universal design seems like an easy way to achieve quick success. However, it also has many serious problems. Some authors have pointed to the problems with query complexity [4, 11] and query speed [4, 5]. These are not the only problems. It seems that there is a lack of *consensus* about this design and no *comprehensive* discussion of its shortcomings. Developers have tried to use it repeatedly in order to achieve maximum *flexibility*.

Systems that use some form of the universal design have to manage large amounts of data. Some bioinformatics systems use a database that is designed according to EAV/CR approach: (a) Subsystem of system net-TRIAL that helps to manage procedures and laboratory results of the clinical trials [12]; (b) SenseLab database for recording neuroscience data [13]; (c) System PhD for web-based management of phenotype data [14]; (d) Qure Data Management platform [15]. System GenMapper that helps scientists to integrate heterogeneous molecular-biological annotation data [11] uses database that is designed according to *Generic Annotation Model* that is a variation of the universal data model. It contains the source level (knowledge level) and the object level (operational level).

Jäger et al. [15] claim that Qure Data Management platform, the database of which is created based on the EAV/CR approach, can be used with small variations in order to perform computer-aided personal interviewing, self-administered interviewing, or telephone interviewing. Some *software engineering systems* also use the universal design. Bernstein et al. [16] describe the Microsoft repository that uses a SQL-based relational DBMS in order to provide persistent storage for the different software tools. This database contains generic tables *Object* and *Relationship* among others. Habela [17] proposes a flattened metamodel that resembles the universal data model. Habela [17] envisages that the schema of a metadata database could be designed based on this metamodel. Bednárek et al. [18] describe the data integration system DataPile that records data in a repository that follows the rules of the universal design.

2. The Method

The framework for evaluating software systems [19] proposes the use of three dimensions that correspond to three types of interested parties – software producers, operators, and users. Each dimension has a set of associated factors. We have to evaluate a software system in terms of each factor.

Which dimensions and factors we could use in case of evaluating database designs? ANSI/SPARC architecture of database systems specifies three levels of a database system and a database – internal level, conceptual level, and external level [20]. These levels are concerned with data storage inside a system, representation of the information content of the database, and individual user perceptions of the data, respectively [20]. We propose to use corresponding dimensions in an evaluation framework of database designs. For each dimension, we have to evaluate a database design in terms of different factors. For each factor, we can use zero or more software measures. Next, we list *some* possible factors together with short descriptions.

External level.

- Updatable views – how easy is to implement views through which we can update data in a database?

- User interface design – how easy is to design user interface of an application that uses a database?
- Access control – how easy is to give to a user rights to use data in a database?

Conceptual level.

- Database schema evolution – how easy is to make changes in a database schema?
- Expressiveness of a database schema – how easy is to understand the meaning of data in a database by studying the schema of the database?
- Missing data – how easy is to represent missing data in a database?
- Integrity constraints – how easy is to implement integrity constraints in a database?
- Compensating actions – how easy is to implement a compensating action that a DBMS should perform in case of violation of an integrity constraint?
- Default values – how easy is to implement default value of an attribute?
- Query complexity – how easy is to construct queries based on a database?
- Dependencies between database objects – how easy it is to implement the checking of dependencies between different database objects?

Internal level.

- Size of data – how much storage space is needed in order to record all the data in a database?
- Performance of database operations – what is the performance of database operations that are performed in a database?
- Concurrency control – how easy is to implement concurrency control?

The more we could use system-defined features of a DBMS the better because it improves *productivity* of developers. If we want to evaluate a database design *d*, then we have to create a database that is designed according to *d*. We decided to perform experiments based on databases that are created based on the specification of the TPC-C [8]. Why we decided to use this kind of simulation domain? Firstly, it is specified in a well-known benchmark and has therefore probably been carefully evaluated. Secondly, the specification provides requirements to the test data. Thirdly, the specification is available to public and therefore it is easier to repeat the experiments. Fourthly, it is in our view reasonably complex in terms of the amount of tables, data types, and integrity constraints. Finally, it is quite *generic* and represents "any industry which must manage, sell, or distribute a product or service" [8].

We used the database system (DBMS) PostgreSQL v8.1 [21]. The DBMS was installed in the server with the Intel Xeon CPU 2.40GHz processor (with Hyper-Threading technology) and 1 GB RAM.

We created tables based on the specifications in Figure 1. We assume that each entity type in the conceptual data model (see Figure 1) has a corresponding base table (table for short) in a SQL database that is created based on this model. The names of the tables are the same as the names of the entity types. For each table of the regular design the set of columns and their data types match with those presented in the TPC-C. Both sets of tables must contain data about the same objects and relationships.

For generating data, we created in a database user-defined functions that use system-defined generators of random values. The data was generated based on the requirements to the test data that is specified in the TPC-C. We generated data for the tables of the regular design (in the round brackets is the amount of rows): *Warehouse* (2), *District* (20), *Customer* (60000), *Item* (10000), *Stock* (20000), *Order* (60000), *Order_line* (599394), and *New_order* (18000). The amount of rows corresponds mostly to the requirements of the TPC-C. The only difference is that tables *Item* and *Stock* contain 10 times less rows than is advised in the benchmark specification, due to restrictions to storage space.

We loaded all the data from these tables to the tables of the universal design (in the round brackets is the amount of rows): *Object* (767416), *Relationship* (1376808), and *Attribute_value* (4657166). Tables *Object_type* (8) and *Attribute* (63), which are at the knowledge level, were populated based on the specification of the regular design.

3. The Analysis

In this paper, we do not analyse the universal design in terms of all the factors (see Section 2) due to space restrictions.

Firstly, we evaluated the designs that are specified in Figure 1 by using some *database design measures* (metrics). Piattini et al. [22] write: "the number of foreign keys in a relational database schema is a solid indicator of its complexity". The number of foreign keys is 6 and 8 in case of the universal design and the regular design, respectively. It shows that the *complexity* of the universal design is somewhat smaller compared to the complexity of the regular design. Piattini et al. [23] write: "the table size metric (TS) is a good indicator for the maintainability of a table". In our case all the columns of the tables are "simple columns" and hence the table size is the amount of columns in a table. The median TS is 3 in case of the universal design and 9.5 in case of the regular design. According to this measure the *maintainability* of the tables of the universal design is better compared to the tables of the regular design. Unfortunately, as we see in the next sections, these measures do not take into account all the factors of database design.

3.1. Database Schema Evolution

It is possible to make some extensions in a database without executing Data Definition Language (DDL) statements in case of the universal design. Instead, a user has to modify data at the knowledge level and the system has to execute Data Manipulation Language (DML) statements. Wang et al. [5] claim that it is possible to define new attributes (data elements) "without the additional programming". These changes do not require corresponding changes in the user interface of an application, if there is one to one mapping between the columns in the tables and fields in the forms. Still, experts (and not end users) must perform extension of the database because "incorrect metadata will yield a malfunctioning application." [13] Question remains – why is this approach better compared to the generation and execution of DDL statements by a system based on the instructions of a user?

However, a database that is created according to the universal design may still need schema changes in the future because of the data types that are usable in a DBMS. Each data type could have a corresponding column in table *Attribute_value* or even a separate table in case of the EAV/CR approach. The set of predefined data types in a DBMS may change from release to release. Some of these changes are caused by the changes in standards. For example, SQL:1999 introduced the predefined type BOOLEAN [24]. SQL:2003 deleted the data types BIT and BIT VARYING [7]. DBMSs, which follow the prescriptions of SQL:2003, provide data type constructors and allow database designers to create user-defined types. Therefore, a large amount of data types could be used in a database. If new requirements stress the need for having an attribute with a data type that has no corresponding column in table *Attribute_value* or no corresponding separate table, then the database structure has to be changed. It seems reasonable to use the most popular predefined data types at the beginning and gradually add support to the data types. The result of the application of this kind of design could be the use of the limited amount of simple data types (for example, VARCHAR and INTEGER) as column types [25]. For example, the median of the amount of data types in case of the examples in [3, 11, 14, 17, 18] is 4. This, on the other hand, limits and complicates operations with the data values. An application that uses this database must perform type conversions.

All the data values that otherwise would be part of different tables are now in table *Attribute_value*. A DBMS usually locks a table exclusively in case of changing its structure. If someone changes the structure of *Attribute_value*, then it locks a very large portion of a database. Therefore, all the schema changes have to be done at the times, when the use of the *entire database* is as minimal as possible. Corruption of a database table or its indexes has far greater consequences compared to the regular design.

3.2. Expressiveness of a Database Schema

The *external predicate* of a table is an *informal* construct that specifies what the data in the table means to a user [20]. The *parameters* of the predicate correspond to the columns. We write the parameters in *italics*. External predicates of tables do not give any information about the object system, the data of which is recorded in a database in case of the universal design. For example, table *Attribute_value* could have the external predicate Eq. (1). The exact predicate depends on the used types.

> The object *object_id* with the type *object_type_id* has an associated value of the attribute *attribute_id,* which is either an integer value *int_value*, or string value with the length between 0 and 2 characters *string_value_2*. (1)

We need a special tool in order to present database conceptual schema based on the data at the knowledge level.

3.3. Query Complexity

A query for finding all the data about an object has to access only one table (*Attribute_value*) in case of the universal design. If the attributes of an object type change, then the query does not need reprogramming [25]. If an object has attributes with the different types, then more than one table has to be accessed in case of the EAV/CR approach. In this case the query may need reprogramming.

Next, we present an informal specification of four queries. *(Q1)*: Find the amount of customers whose last name starts with the letter "B". Table 1 presents the SQL code of this query in case of the different designs. *(Q2)*: Find the amount of customers whose last name starts with the letter "B" and who live in the state of Nebraska. *(Q3)*: Find the amount of customers whose last name starts with the letter "B", who live in the state of Vermont, and who belong to a district, the location of which is also Vermont. *(Q4)*: Find the amount of order lines where the price of the associated item is bigger than 99.

We selected the queries based on their complexity. *Q1* and *Q2* use data about one type of objects. *Q3* and *Q4* use data about two and three types of objects, respectively. In case of the regular design, the restriction condition of *Q1* is a simple predicate that involves no connectives and the restriction condition of *Q2* is a compound predicate that involves one connective.

Intuitively, we see that the SQL code is more complex in case of the universal design (see Table 1). How can we show it formally? Piattini and Martinez [26] propose and evaluate three measures for measuring maintainability of SQL code. They perform experiments and correlation analysis. According to the analysis the NT measure (number of tables referred in the SELECT statement) and the NN measure (number of "SELECT" in the SELECT statement) have strong significant relationships with the variable that represents time of maintenance. In Table 2, we present the measurement results of NN and NT measures in case of the four queries (*Q1–Q4*).

The bigger the value is, the more maintenance problems the corresponding query has. Based on Table 2 we can conclude that the required time of maintenance of the queries that are used in order to resolve *the presented problems* is bigger in case of the universal design than in case of the regular design.

If we increase the amount of entity types, the corresponding data of which we want to ask with a query, then the value of the NT measure increase in case of the regular design. In case of the universal design the maximum value of the NT measure is quite small (5 according to Figure 1) and doesn't change if we add or remove entity types, the data of which we want to record in a database. However, if the complexity of queries grows, then the value of NN measure may increase because we may need to ask data repeatedly from the same table. However, a problem with the NN measure is that often it is possible to create more than one query in order to solve the same problem in SQL. Some of the queries may use a join operator instead of a subquery. In this case the value of the NN measure might be small although the query is quite complex.

How could we take into account join operations during the evaluation of SQL code? There exist proposals to use graph structures [27] in order to present and evaluate database schemas and queries. Tow [28] proposes a method of tuning SQL queries, a step of which is the creation of a *query diagram*. It is a directed graph that represents a query. In this graph the nodes are *table aliases* and arcs represent *join* and *semijoin operations*. We can use the measures of complexity of a graph [29] in order to measure the complexity of a query. We constructed the query diagrams and in case of each diagram counted the amount of nodes (N) and the amount of arcs (A). From the set of complexity measures that are introduced by Latva-Koivisto [29] we calculated the *Coefficient of Network Complexity*: CNC=(A*A)/N (see Table 3). The bigger the value is the more complex is the graph (query). It is possible to use other complexity measures as well.

Based on Table 3, we can conclude that the resolution of *the presented problems* requires more complex queries in case of the universal design than in case of the regular design. It is possible to simplify the query-writing task by creating operators [11] or viewed tables. However, after performing the view resolution, a DBMS still has to execute a complex query even in case of the simple problems.

Table 1. An example of queries in case of different database designs.

Universal design	Regular design
SELECT Count(*) AS amt FROM Attribute_value AS AV INNER JOIN (Attribute AS A INNER JOIN Object_type AS OT ON A.object_type_id = OT.object_type_id) ON (AV.object_type_id = A.object_type_id) AND (AV.attribute_id = A.attribute_id) WHERE OT.name = 'CUSTOMER' AND A.name = 'C_LAST' AND AV.text_value LIKE 'B%';	SELECT Count(*) AS amt FROM Customer WHERE c_last LIKE 'B%';

Table 2. Maintainability of queries.

	Universal design		Regular design	
Query ID	NT	NN	NT	NN
Q1	3	1	1	1
Q2	3	2	1	1
Q3	4	4	2	1
Q4	5	5	3	3

Table 3. Complexity of queries.

	Universal design			Regular design		
Query ID	N	A	CNC	N	A	CNC
Q1	3	2	1.33	1	0	0.00
Q2	6	5	4.17	1	0	0.00
Q3	10	9	8.10	2	1	0.50
Q4	9	8	7.11	3	2	1.33

Chen et al. [3] propose to use combinations of simpler queries and temporary tables in order to speed up the queries. In this case, a user of a database looses an advantage of a DBMS according to which a user can make a (complex) query and a DBMS decides how to execute it. In this case, a query designer has to describe a *procedure* how to retrieve the desired results.

3.4. Integrity Constraints

Next, we present an informal specification of four constraints. *(C1)*: The combination of the district name and the name of the city of the district must be unique in case of each district. *(C2)*: the credit status of each customer must be either GC or BC. *(C3)*: Each warehouse must have a name. *(C4)*: Each warehouse can have at most 10 associated districts. We selected the constraints because they represent different types of constraints. In case of the regular design we can enforce *C1*, *C2*, and *C3* by using a UNIQUE, a table CHECK, and a NOT NULL constraint, respectively. We have to use triggers in order to enforce *C4* in case of the regular design. On the other hand, we have to enforce all these constraints by using triggers in case of the universal design. If data changes at the knowledge level, then triggers have to be created/altered/dropped as well. This means that the system has to generate and execute DDL statements after all.

How could we evaluate and compare the complexity of implementations of integrity constraints in case of different database designs? Diaz et al. [30] propose three measures for measuring triggering-interaction complexity on active databases based on triggering-graphs. On the other hand, it is possible to implement some of the integrity constraints by using *declarative* statements. Therefore, in this case we cannot use these measures in order to compare the database designs.

We decided to count the physical lines of source code in order to compare the implementations of integrity constraints (*C1–C4*) in case of the different designs. We had to create 11 SQL statements in case of the universal design. We had to create 7 SQL statements in case of the regular design. The trigger procedures were created by using PL/pgSQL language. The result of measurement of physical lines of code depends on formatting of statements. We wrote each statement for creating a declarative constraint by using one line. We used *pg_dump*, which is a PostgreSQL client application, in order to get formatted SQL commands for creating triggers and trigger procedures. We used the program LocMetrics [31] in order to count the physical lines of executable code (SLOC-P). We didn't count the blank lines and the lines that contain only comments. The value of SLOC-P was 40 in case of the regular design. The value of SLOC-P was 164 in case of the universal design. We can conclude that enforcement of the *presented* constraints requires more effort in case of the universal design than in case of the regular design.

Trigger procedures contain SQL queries that we could model as graphs (see Section 3.3). Papastefanatos et al. [27] propose to model relational tables, views, database constraints, and SQL queries uniformly as a graph. We can use complexity measures of graphs in order to evaluate the complexity of implementations of integrity constraints. We constructed a query graph for each implementation of a constraint and calculated *Coefficient of Network Complexity*: CNC=(A*A)/N (see Table 4). As you can see, the complexity is generally bigger in case of the universal design.

How did we create the graphs? If a constraint was implemented by using a set of trigger procedures, then we created a separate query graph based on each SELECT and LOCK statement that was used in the procedures. LOCK statement allows us to lock a table. We created the graph of the entire constraint by merging all the query graphs without performing any duplicate elimination. In case of each constraint, which was enforced by using a declarative statement, we created a graph where N=1 and A=0, because each constraint declaration refers only to one table.

Table 4. Complexity of constraints.

	Universal design			Regular design		
Constraint ID	N	A	CNC	N	A	CNC
C1	6	5	4.17	1	0	0.00
C2	2	1	0.50	1	0	0.00
C3	7	1	0.14	1	0	0.00
C4	5	0	0.00	2	0	0.00

3.5. Size of Data

Chen et al. [3] write: "The EAV/CR representation consumed approximately four times the storage of our conventional schema." Conventional schema is created according to the regular design.

Our findings support this conclusion. We analyzed the tables that are specified in Section 2 (see Table 5). PostgreSQL provides the system-defined functions *pg_relation_size* that can be used in order to find the disk space (in bytes) used by a table [21]. PostgreSQL provides the system-defined function *pg_total_relation_size* that can be used in order to find the total size of a table together with its associated indexes and toasted data (in bytes) [21]. Before calculating the size of tables we collected statistics and reclaimed storage that was occupied by deleted rows.

The only indexes that the tables had during the calculation of data size were the B-tree indexes that were created automatically due to the primary key constraints. Each table had the primary key. The primary keys of the tables of the regular design are specified in the document of TPC-C [8]. In average, both the tables of the universal design and the regular design had 2.4 columns in a primary key. Each index contains the values of indexed columns. Therefore, due to large indexes, the difference between the *sum of table size* and the *sum of total table size* is relatively big.

Data in the row "Sum of table size" is calculated by summarizing the sizes of tables that are found by using *pg_relation_size.* The sum of sizes of tables of the universal design is approximately 4.8 times bigger than the sum of sizes of tables of the regular design. Data in the row "Sum of total table size" is calculated by summarizing the sizes of tables that are found by using *pg_total_relation_size.* The sum of total sizes of tables of the universal design is approximately 6 times bigger than the sum of total sizes of tables of the regular design.

"It is true that EAV/CR is more space-efficient for sparse data." [3] Our test data is not *sparse*. Only 2.4 percent of columns of the tables of the regular design (Figure 1, part b) are optional (permit NULLs).

3.6. Performance of Database Operations

Next, we present the results of measurements of *the performance* of database operations in case of the different designs. We performed five times each query (Q1-Q4) that was specified in Section 3.3. In addition, we measured the performance of a transaction (RW): Create a new order where the amount of order lines is between 5 and 15. The amount of order lines is randomly selected.

Each time we measured the time (in milliseconds) that a DBMS needed in order to perform the operation and present the results. For each operation, we calculated the *average* time in millisecond (see Table 6) based on these five measurements.

Table 5. The size of tables that are created according to the different designs.

	Universal design	Regular design
Sum of table size (in bytes)	687415296	144728064
Sum of total table size (in bytes)	1083359232	180404224

Table 6. Performance test results.

Operation ID	Universal design (ms)	Regular design (ms)
Q1	877.700	259.213
Q2	1865.397	260.305
Q3	654.364	26.252
Q4	599.413	1581.838
Q4 *	599.413	396.471
RW	327.591	207.682

In case of *Q4* the performance was firstly better in case of the universal design. However, the performance of the same operation was better in case of the regular design (*Q4**) after we created a composite index that covers the columns *ol_i_id* and *ol_supply_w_id* of table *Order_line*.

4. Conclusions

In this paper, we introduced a framework for evaluating database designs and used it in order to analyse the universal and the regular design. Some studies suggest that it is easy to extend a database, which is created based on the universal design. However, we found that it is quite difficult to extend this kind of database in terms of the use of data types and integrity constraints. In addition, experiments showed us that the use of the universal design causes problems in terms of query complexity, data size, and performance. Whether or not to use the universal design depends on the importance of the different database design factors in a particular project. The results also illustrate the need to create new database design measures. For instance, existing measures do not consider all the types of integrity constraints.

The future work must include more experiments based on databases from different domains. There is a need to investigate alternative database designs that can be used in order to cope with changing requirements. We have to improve and evaluate the evaluation framework of database designs. We could use the Analytical Hierarchy Process (AHP) in order to select the most suitable database design from a set of designs. In this case database designs are alternatives. Dimensions and factors of the evaluation framework are criteria, based on which we have to select the most suitable alternative. AHP allows us to determine the relative importance of each criterion.

References

[1] Baskerville, R., & Pries-Heje, J. (2001) Racing the e-bomb: how the Internet is redefining information system development methodology. In Proceedings of the IFIP TC8/WG8.2 Working Conference on Realigning Research and Practice in Information System Development, pp. 49-68.

[2] Hay, D.C. (1996) Data model patterns: conventions of thought. Dorset House Pub, 1996, 268 p.

[3] Chen, R.S., Nadkarni, P., Marenco, L., Levin, F., Erdos, J., & Miller, P.L. (2000) Exploring Performance Issues for a Clinical Database Organized Using an Entity-Attribute-Value Representation, Journal Of The American Medical Informatics Association, 7: 475-487

[4] Kyte, T. (2003) Effective Oracle by Design. McGraw-Hill Osborne Media, 2003, 688 p.
[5] Wang, S.A., Yang, F., Huey, C, Pecjak, F., Upender, B., Frazin, A., Lingam, R., Chintala, S., Wang, G., Kellog, M., Martino, R.L, & Johnson, C.A. (2004) Performance of using Oracle XMLDB in the evaluation of CDISC ODM for a clinical study informatics system. In Kawada, S. (ed), Proceedings of the 17th IEEE Symposium on Computer-Based Medical Systems, pp. 594- 599.
[6] Eessaar, E. (2006) Relational and Object-Relational Database Management Systems as Platforms for Managing Software Engineering Artifacts. Ph.D. thesis, Tallinn University of Technology, 2006, 218 p.
[7] Melton, J. (2003) ISO/IEC 9075-2:2003 (E) Information technology — Database languages — SQL — Part 2: Foundation (SQL/Foundation), (available at http://www.wiscorp.com/SQLStandards.html)
[8] TPC BENCHMARK C Standard Specification Revision 5.9, (available at http://www.tpc.org/tpcc/)
[9] Fowler, M. (1997) Analysis Patterns: Reusable Object Models. Addison-Wesley, 1997, 384 p.
[10] Karanikolas, N.N., Nitsiou, M., Yannakoudakis, E.J, & Skourlas, C. (2007) CUDL language semantics, liven up the FDB data model. In Ionnadis, Y., Novikov, B., & Rachev, B. (eds), Local Proceedings of the 11th East-European Conference on Advances in Databases and Information Systems, pp. 1-16.
[11] Do, H.-H. & Rahm, E. (2004) Flexible Integration of Molecular-Biological Annotation Data: The GenMapper Approach. In Bertino, E., et Al. (eds) Proceedings of the 9th International Conference on Extending Database Technology, Berlin: Springer, (LNCS), pp. 811 – 822.
[12] Hageman, D., & Reeves, D.M. (2001) net-Trials ™ clinical trials information system. In Proceedings of 14th IEEE Symposium on Computer-Based Medical Systems, pp. 141-145.
[13] Marenco, L., Tosches, N., Crasto, C., Shepherd, G., Miller, P.L., & Nadkarni, P.M. (2003) Achieving evolvable web-database bioscience applications using the EAV/CR framework: recent advances, Journal of the American Medical Informatics Association, 10 (5): 444–453
[14] Li, J.-L., Li, M.-X., Deng, H.-Y., Duffy, P.E., & Deng, H.W. (2005) PhD: a web database application for phenotype data management, Bioinformatics, 21(16): 3443-3444
[15] Jäger, M., Kamm, L., Krushevskaja, D., Talvik, H.-A., Veldemann, J., Vilgota, A., & Vilo, J. (2008) Flexible Database Platform for Biomedical Research with Multiple User Interfaces and a Universal Query Engine. In Haav, H.-M., Kalja, A. (eds) Proceedings of the Eighth International Baltic Conference, Baltic Databases and Information Systems, pp. 279-287.
[16] Bernstein, P.A., Harry, B., Sanders, P., Shutt, D., & Zander, J. (1997) The Microsoft Repository. In Jarke, M., et Al. (eds) Proceedings of the 23rd International Conference on Very Large Data Bases, pp. 3-12.
[17] Habela, P. (2002) Metamodel for Object-Oriented Database Management Systems. Ph.D. Thesis, Polish Academy of Sciences, 2002, 138 p.
[18] Bednárek, D., Obdržálek, D., Yaghob, J., & Zavoral, F. (2005) Data Integration Using DataPile Structure. In Eder, J., et Al (eds) Communications of the Ninth East-European Conference on Advances in Databases and Information Systems, pp. 178-188.
[19] Boloix, G., & Robillard, P. N. (1995) A Software System Evaluation Framework, Computer, 28(12): 17-26
[20] Date, C. J. (2003) An Introduction to Database Systems. Addison Wesley, 2003, 8th ed., 1024 p.
[21] PostgreSQL 8.1.10 Documentation, (available at http://www.postgresql.org/docs/8.1/)
[22] Piattini, M., Calero, C., & Genero, M. (2001) Table Oriented Metrics for Relational Databases, Software Quality Journal, 9(2): 79–98
[23] Piattini, M., Calero, C., Sahraoui, H., & Lounis, H. (2001) Object-Relational Database Metrics, L'Object.
[24] Gulutzan, P. & Pelzer, T. (1999) SQL-99 Complete, Really. CMP Books, 1999, 1104 p.
[25] Ahnøj, J. (2003) Generic Design of Web-Based Clinical Databases, Journal of Medical Internet Research, 5(4)
[26] Piattini, M., & Martinez, A. (2000) Measuring for Database Programs Maintainability. In Ibrahim, M. T., Küng, J., & Revell, N. (eds) Proceedings of the 11th international Conference on Database and Expert Systems Applications, London: Springer-Verlag, (LNCS), pp. 65-78.
[27] Papastefanatos, G., Vassiliadis, P., Simitsis, A., Aggistalis, K., Pechlivani, F., & Vassiliou, Y. (2008) Language Extensions for the Automation of Database Schema Evolution. In Cordeiro, J., & Filipe, J. (eds) Proceedings of the 10th International Conference on Enterprise Information Systems, Vol. DISI, pp. 74-81.
[28] Tow, D. (2003) SQL Tuning. O'Reilly Media, Inc., 2003, 336 p.
[29] Latva-Koivisto, A. M. (2001) Finding a complexity measure for business process models, Research Report, (available at http://citeseerx.ist.psu.edu)
[30] Diaz, O., Piattini, M., & Calero, C. (2001) Measuring triggering-interaction complexity on active databases, Information Systems, 26(1): 15-34
[31] LocMetrics – Source Code Line Counting Tool, (available at http://www.locmetrics.com)

Databases and Information Systems V
H.-M. Haav and A. Kalja (Eds.)
IOS Press, 2009

doi:10.3233/978-1-58603-939-4-301

Flexible Database Platform for Biomedical Research with Multiple User Interfaces and a Universal Query Engine

Margus JÄGER[a,b], Liina KAMM[a,b], Darja KRUSHEVSKAJA[a,b], Harry-Anton TALVIK[b], Janno VELDEMANN[a,b], Andres VILGOTA[b] and Jaak VILO[a,b]
[a]*Institute of Computer Science, University of Tartu, Estonia*
[b]*Quretec Ltd, Tartu, Estonia*

Abstract. Biomedical research on human subjects often requires a large amount of data to be collected by personal interviews, Internet based questionnaires, lab measurements or by extracting data from paper or electronic health records. This data needs to be stored, analyzed and interpreted in a comprehensive manner. There is a great need for user-friendly software systems that allow to design and launch such data collection initiatives quickly, securely and reliably. We have designed a flexible software system that enables creating such data collection and management projects. Qure Data Management platform described in this paper contains tools for dynamic designing of data models and electronic questionnaires, multiple user interfaces for data entry and a universal query engine for filtered output. The platform enables to make database and questionnaire changes on the fly without any manual database table change. The data repository is based on the entity-attribute-value with classes and relationships (EAV/CR) approach which allows flexible storage and analysis of data from multiple studies. Although aimed at biomedical research, the software architecture is flexible and can be used for various different data collection and management projects.

Keywords. data management, questionnaires, entity-attribute-value, biomedical studies

Introduction

Data collection is essential for biomedical studies when gathering information in the form of questionnaires or clinical analysis results. Furthermore, it is important that analysis of the data collected can be performed. Hence, it is advisable to gather the data electronically. Usually studies last for a limited time and in practice they start rather abruptly therefore leaving little time to prepare the information system to back up the data collection.

New software systems are being developed even for individual research study projects [1]. In this paper a general system and architecture – the Qure Data Management™ platform – that allows many different research projects to benefit from the common research infrastructure is proposed. The developed system allows quick design of new surveys, hosting many simultaneous surveys on the same server hardware, and integration with statistical software using a user-friendly query and data export system that would work even on very large data models consisting of up to thousands of attributes. One key feature of the system is ability to work offline without needing continuous Internet access that most today's web-based applications need.

The development of Qure Data Management platform began from designing the software solutions for the needs of the Estonian Genome Project [2]. This large-scale data collection activity to establish a new large-scale biobank required a software system to enable country-wide data collection. While designing the software it became evident that the required system had to be flexible enough to support an ever-changing set of questionnaire requirements and also to support a large number of parallel on-going studies.

The system has evolved since then. Now, Qure Data Management platform consists of a study design application Qure Designer, data entry applications – the desktop based Qure Desktop and web-based Qure Browser, a central data repository and communication server Qure Server, and a query engine Qure DataView.

Qure Designer is a graphical application for study design. It allows the user to prepare, preview and upload the data gathering environment. Qure Desktop and its web-based counterpart Qure Browser allow the user to enter data into previously designed views. The key benefit is that different user interfaces operate in essence on the same central database server using the specially designed synchronization protocol exchanging encrypted XML messages from certified parties.

The underlying data repository in Qure Server is based on the entity-attribute-value model with classes and relationships (EAV/CR) [3, 4, 5, 6, 7]. This model provides the means for easily making changes to the structure of the study, thus making it simple to add new attributes or whole perspectives when new requirements arise, without changing the underlying database. The query engine Qure DataView allows the user to retrieve data for analysis from the hierarchical EAV/CR database.

Even though flexibility and dynamism through EAV/CR have their drawbacks – large overhead, inefficient data retrieval – this model has proved feasible in short term studies. Qure Data Management platform has successfully been used in clinical trials to track subject visits and make systematic monitoring reports with well defined data structure.

The Qure Data Management platform is used for the Estonian cohort data entry of the study "Concerted Action on SeroConversion to AIDS and Death in Europe" [8]. The structure of data in the study is based on the HIV Cohorts Data Exchange Protocol standards [9], but because of the flexibility of the platform, it was possible to add new data fields for local research without remarkable work effort. It is also used in the study of Colon and Breast Cancer Diagnostics (COBRED) [10] to capture both clinical and logistics data. The largest current survey being performed on the Qure Data Management platform has over 70 object types and almost a thousand attributes.

The system can with small variations be used for Computer-Aided Personal Interviewing (CAPI), Computer-Aided Self-Administered Interviewing (CASI), or Computer-Aided Telephone Interviewing (CATI).

1. Qure Data Management Platform

Qure Data Management platform is used for collection, handling, and analysis of well-structured data under the requirements for high quality, security and robustness. The platform incorporates tools for rapid designing of data models, user interface texts and entry form controls. End-user GUI is automatically created for an independent Windows client and web. The desktop clients and web interface can be used interchangeably, because they are built based on the same data model and views. The collected data is also shared and synchronized between clients. The user friendly Qure Desktop can even work off-line, fetching automatic updates and synchronizing data with the server as soon as the Internet connection becomes available. The description of the different parts of the platform and their relationships can be seen on Figure 1.

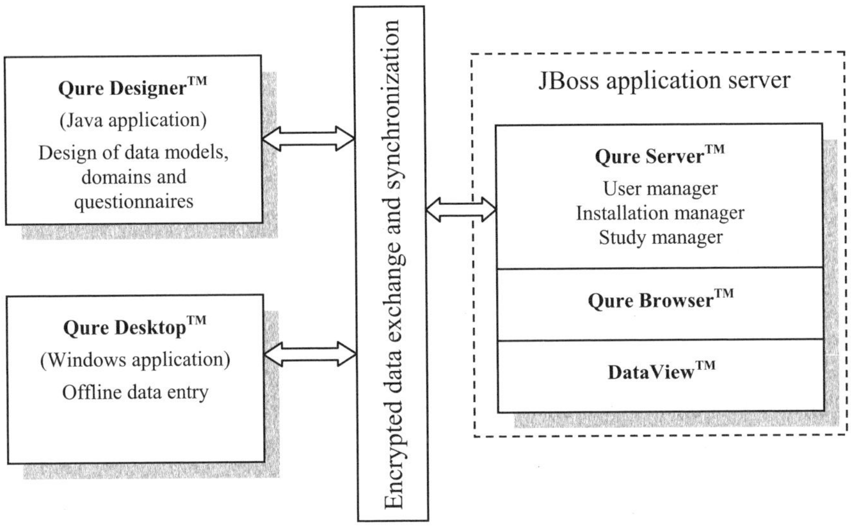

Figure 1. Qure Data Management platform

2. Central Data Repository

Qure Server consists of a central data storage engine and administration tools. Specialized web-based tools for data input, output, integration and queries are also integrated into to the server. The server implementation is based on J2EE technology and utilizes open source JBoss application server. The data storage technology is based on the EAV/CR architecture. An open source PostgreSQL database engine is used as a backend storage for the universal EAV/CR model (Figure 2).

The data is synchronized via an efficient synchronization protocol that propagates only the changes made to the entities, not the entities themselves. The synchronization messages are also compressed and encrypted to further minimize network utilization.

Security features of the server include certificate- and password-based authentication, single sign-on policy and role-based user management. The designer of the study can manage the roles, allowing differentiating the client access to study data. Restricting access to entities based on the entity creator is also possible.

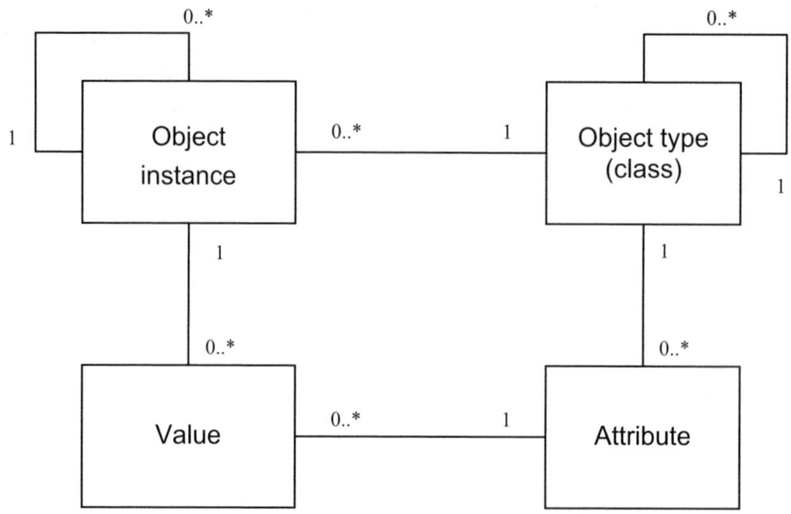

Figure 2. EAV/CR implementation

3. Data Model and User Interface Design

The data model is the backbone of a study. It is a hierarchical collection of object types and attributes definitions. In the context of the EAV/CR model, the term object type describes a class. Every object type contains attributes and may additionally contain other object types. Each attribute has a data type (eg. string, integer, date). Object types usually have one-to-many relationships, although if an entity has many different attributes, it becomes more difficult to find the necessary ones when for example trying to get output from the collected data. In that case the one-to-one relationship can be used for grouping purposes.

Domains are hierarchical classifiers or lists of items. Every item has a code and a label and may have sub items. Domains can be assigned to attributes and are usually used for one choice selection style data entry. Domains can also be assigned to object types – this possibility is mostly used for multiple value selections. The platform supports large hierarchical classification systems like ICD-10 [11] or standard geographical classifications.

User interface (view) is defined as a questionnaire. A questionnaire has multiple pages, every page contains question modules. Question modules are placed sequentially and every question module is connected to one attribute or object type. This connection defines where the data is stored. There can be multiple questionnaires based on the same data model covering different aspects for different users.

4. Pivoting Converter

Qure Server includes a tool for data integration with other systems. The data in entity-attribute-value storage model can be converted to the more conventional relational storage model. Introducing the pivoting converter allows us to harness the power of both models: internally we use EAV/CR model with metadata to support rapid model changes and synchronize data efficiently, but at the same time offer the query power and simplicity of relational databases to external clients [12].

In pivoting conversion every object type is transferred to a table in the relational database and attributes are transferred to table columns. In both cases the names from the object model are also converted respectively. As the object type names are unique in the data model scope and the attribute names are unique in the object type scope, there will be no naming conflicts. All tables in the relational database have primary key column "id" that contains the same object identifiers as in the entity-attribute-value storage. Relations with other objects are translated using the foreign key column naming convention (referred table name with the suffix "_fk").

The conversion process can be performed manually, but the server can be set up to convert incoming changes automatically, thus enabling us to make different reports and special applications customized according to user needs.

5. Designer Tool

The graphical tool Qure Designer can be used for designing object models, domains and questionnaires. It is a Java desktop application that stores all definition files in XML format.

The main purpose of the application is to give a more intuitive and usable interface to the user for designing study project files. As the study files are being validated in-place, the feedback is direct and the user can quickly fix the validation problems. The object model describes the object types and attributes that will later hold the data. Questionnaires define the graphical user interface for the object model – they present the attributes as questions and enable a more intuitive data entry environment. Questionnaire design is depicted on Figure 3. Qure designer also provides the user with a preview of the designed questionnaire.

The structure of a questionnaire can be changed quickly by dragging and dropping modules and the attributes can be modified by specific property fields. Questionnaires can be internationalized by translating question texts and domain item labels, thus, creating user interfaces in different languages.

The application provides the user with built-in searchable help system. With the help of Qure Designer the study files can be securely transferred to Qure Server.

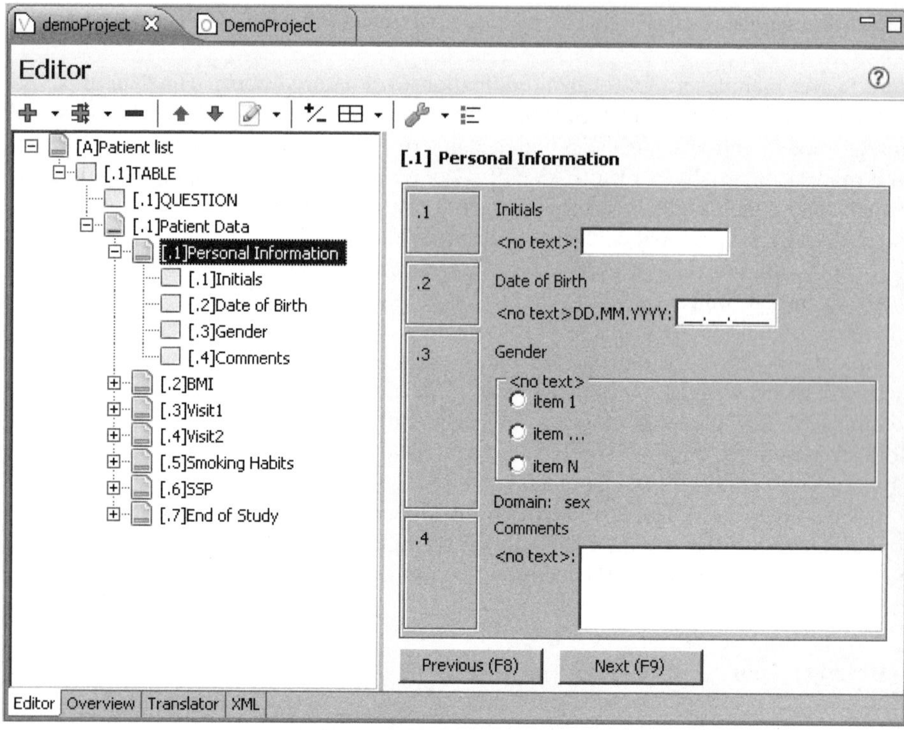

Figure 3. Questionnaire design

6. Online and Offline Data Entry

Qure Data Management platform has two user interfaces for data entry: Qure Browser for online usage and autonomous desktop client Qure Desktop for usage with low or no network connectivity. Qure Desktop (seen on Figure 4) requires Windows XP or Vista. Qure Browser (Figure 5) is integrated with Qure Server and is available to all web-enabled clients (tested with Firefox and Internet Explorer).

In clinical trials offline data entry support has been very important in conditions where Internet access is not always available [13]. For example CRA-s need to visit hospitals where Internet connection may not be available (for technical or security reasons). With offline support they can still access their study data in laptop computer and enter necessary information that can be synchronized later. In many cases Internet connection is just too slow or unstable that would make web-based or Internet dependent applications very hard and time consuming to use. In some cases computer-aided personal interviewing (CAPI) must be done, where an offline fat-client tool has a clear advantage in speed and stability.

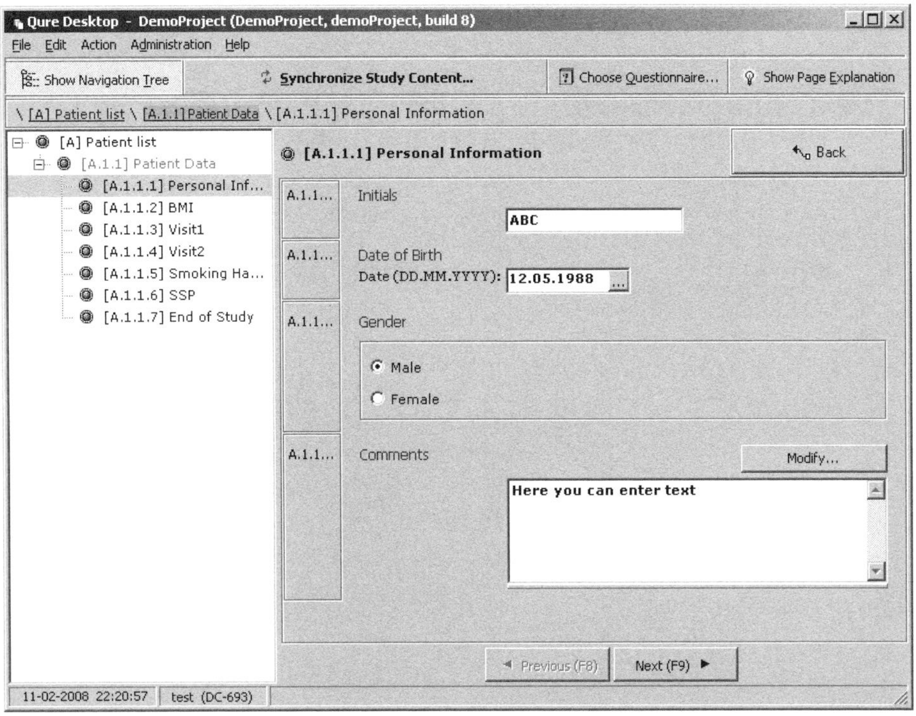

Figure 4. Qure Desktop user interface

Qure Desktop is an offline data entry tool that provides this possibility. In offline mode, the Qure Desktop caches the user changes in a local database and synchronizes the changes to the server when the Internet connection becomes available. While connected to the server, the user can also manually request data synchronization by one click of a button. The desktop client application is easily upgradeable to a next version via Software Update service.

The Qure Browser web tool is essentially an on-line version of Qure Desktop application, integrated to the server. The obvious benefit of Qure Browser is the ease of usage, the user does not have to download or install a specialized application. The user interface is generated from the same view definition and looks similar to Qure Desktop UI (Figure 5).

Data entry clients allow entering data to highly structurized model. The data quality and integrity can be improved by using various UI controls with pre-defined sets of answers, pattern-validated answers and even custom validation logic with dependencies to previous answers. For example, after asking persons age, a warning message can be displayed if a child's height does not fall within reasonable limits of persons age-group. Computed values can also be shown as default answers to questions.

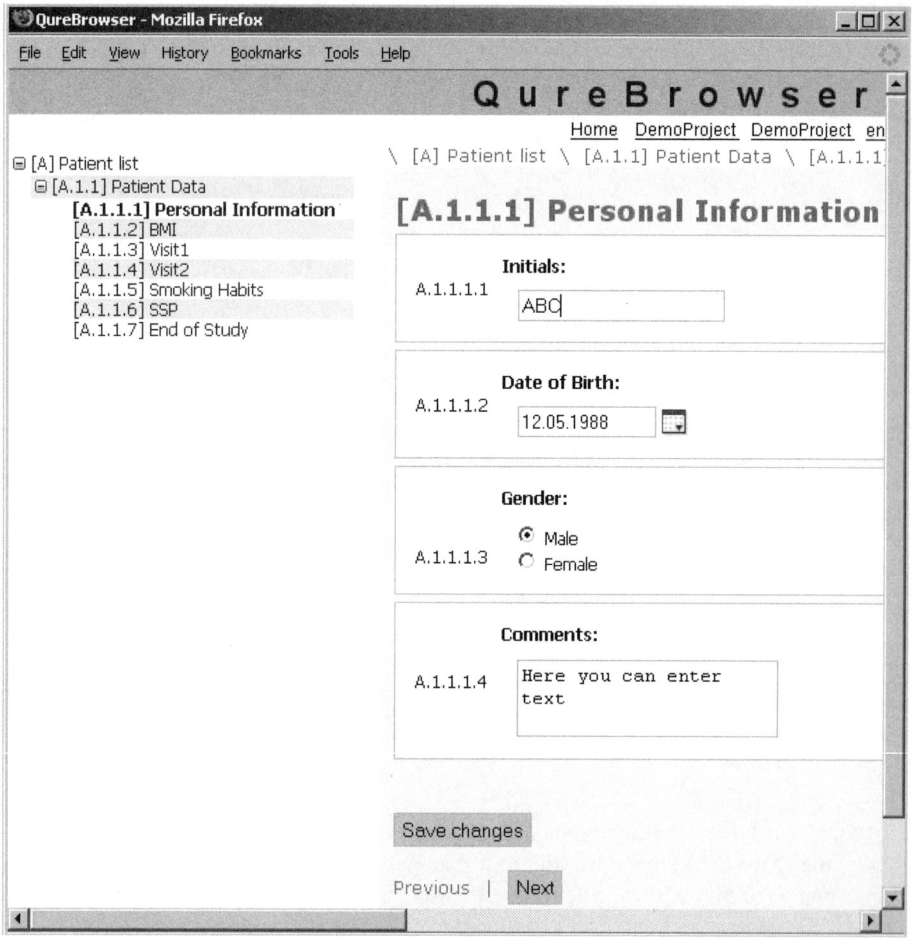

Figure 5. Qure Browser user interface

7. Universal Query Engine

Qure DataView is part of the web-based user interface of the central data repository. This tool enables the user to extract data from the Qure Server universal database fairly easy. The application takes the latest data from the database and transforms it into one flat dataset in the desired form (eg HTML, comma-separated values, XML), thus making it possible for the user to view the data or further analyze it in special data analysis tools. The main purpose of this tool is to extract data from the hierarchical database, and even though it is possible to carry out some basic filtering, aggregation and sorting, it is preferable to do the more complex analysis with tools that are specially designed for such a task.

As performance is a well-known problem [12, 14, 15] for systems with EAV data structure, a solution should be found for querying large amounts of data. To solve this problem, the inherent pivoting converter is put to use. If the data has been transferred to a relational database for one study, then, for that study, the queries are done on the relational database, using the power of the query engine of the database. That gives us a significant performance increase on large data sets.

The user can specify the needed query parameters in five easy steps. Firstly, it is necessary to choose the main object type from the data model of the study. This parameter determines which type of entity will be in each row of the resulting flat dataset. There is no need to define joins between objects manually because the hierarchical data structure already defines parent-child relations between objects and joins are done automatically.

Secondly it is possible to define certain basic filters for attributes of the entity so the output will hold only a necessary selection of entities. Thirdly the user can specify which attributes are needed in the output (Figure 6). The query engine is also capable of making some simple aggregations if necessary. Finally the user can determine the sorting parameters and the format of the output.

In addition, it is possible to save the specified query parameters at any time, so that the user can later rerun the queries on the most recent data.

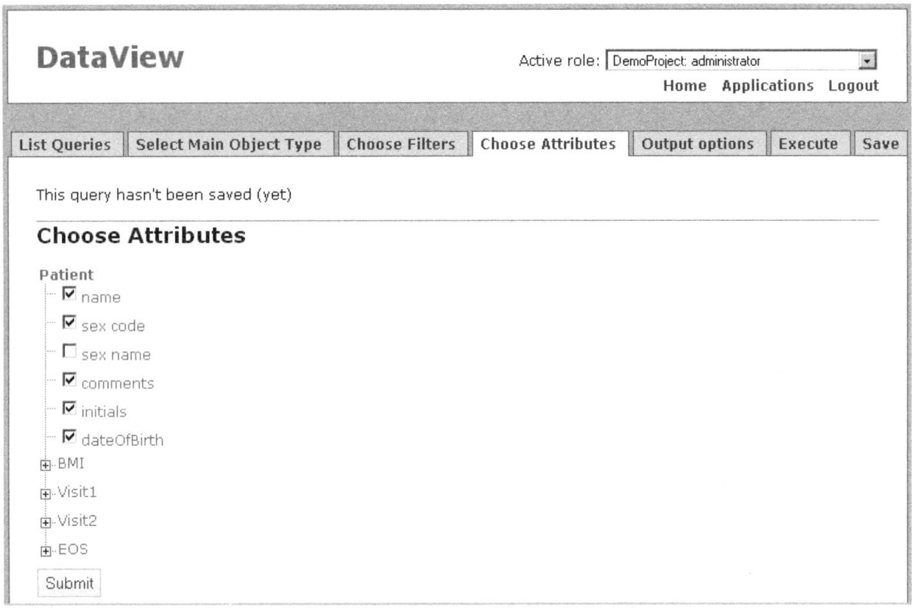

Figure 6. Selecting attributes in Qure DataView

8. Conclusion and Further Work

Qure Data Management platform is used for collection, handling and analysis of well-structured data under the requirements for high quality, security and robustness. The platform enables to make database and questionnaire changes on the fly without any database table structure changes that makes it suitable for biomedical studies where database changes are often a common requirement. Offline data entry support provided by the platform is an important feature where Internet connection is not always available or UI response speed and stability are needed. The system contains a query engine with a friendly web based user interface. Performance issues with EAV structure are solved using a pivoting conversion to a relational database, where queries can be performed more efficiently.

The platform, though already in use, is a work in progress. We are working on optimizing both the desktop client and the server. When this is finished, we plan to do further performance analysis on different parts of the platform. At present, we intend to write separate articles about the query engine and asynchronous user rights management on our hierarchical data model.

Acknowledgements

This work has been supported by Enterprise Estonia project EU21289.

References

[1] Edwards, RL., Edwards, SL., Bryner, J., Cunningham, K., Rogers, A., & Slattery, ML. (2008) A computer-assisted data collection system for use in a multicenter study of American Indians and Alaska Natives: SCAPES, Computer Methods and Programs in Biomedicine, 90(1): 38-55

[2] Metspalu, A., Köhler, F., Laschinski, G., Ganten, D., & Roots, I. (2004) The Estonian Genome Project in the context of European genome research, Dtsch Med Wochenschr, Apr 30; 129 Suppl 1:25-8

[3] Nadkarni, PM., Marencol, L., Chen, R., Skoufos, E., Shepherd, G., & P. Miller. (1999) Organization of heterogeneous scientific data using the EAV/CR representation, Journal of the American Medical Informatics Association, 6(6): 478-493

[4] Ganslandt, T., Mueller, M., & Krieglstein, F. (1999) A flexible repository for clinical trial data based on an entity-attribute-value model, Proceedings of the AMIA Symposium, 1999: 1064-1067

[5] Los, RK., van Ginneken, AM., de Wilde, M., & van der Lei, J. (2004) OpenSDE: row modeling applied to generic structured data entry, Journal of the American Medical Informatics Association, 11: 162–165

[6] Nadkarni, PM., Brandt, C., Frawley, S., Sayward, FG., Einbinder, R., Zelterman, D., Schacter, L., & Miller PL. (1998) Managing attribute-value clinical trials data using the ACT/DB client-server database system, Journal of the American Medical Informatics Association, 5(2): 139–51

[7] Nadkarni, PM., & Brandt, C. (1998) Data extraction and ad hoc query of an entity-attribute-value database, Journal of the American Medical Informatics Association, 5(6): 511–27

[8] CASCADE: Concerted Action on SeroConversion to AIDS and Death in Europe (available at http://www.ctu.mrc.ac.uk/cascade/)

[9] HICDEP: HIV Cohorts Data Exchange Protocol (available at http://www.cphiv.dk/Portals/_default/pdf_folder/HICDEP.pdf)

[10] COBRED: Colon and Breast Cancer Diagnostics (available at http://www.cobred.eu/)

[11] International Classification of Diseases (available at http://www.who.int/classifications/icd/en/)

[12] Beck, P., Truskaller, T., Rakovac, I., Cadonna, B., & Pieber, TR. (2006) On-the-fly form generation and on-line metadata configuration--a clinical data management Web infrastructure in Java, Studies in Health Technology and Informatics, 124: 271-276

[13] Fraser, HS., Jazayeri, D., Nevil, P., Karacaoglu, Y., Farmer, PE., Lyon, E., Fawzi, M.K., Leandre, F., Choi, SS., & Mukherjee JS. (2004) An information system and medical record to support HIV treatment in rural Haiti, British Medical Journal, 329(7475): 1142–1146

[14] Marenco, L., Tosches, N., Crasto, C., Shepherd, G., Miller, PL., & Nadkarni, PM. (2003) Achieving evolvable web-database bioscience applications using the EAV/CR framework: recent advances, Journal of the American Medical Informatics Association, 10(5): 444-453

[15] Chen, RS., Nadkarni, PM., Marenco, L., Levin, F., Erdos, J., & Miller, PL. (2000) Exploring performance issues for a clinical database organized using an entity-attribute-value representation, Journal of the American Medical Informatics Association, Sep–Oct; 7(5): 475–487

H.-M. Haav and A. Kalja (Eds.)
IOS Press, 2009

Author Index